C000197836

BOHN'S STANDARD LIBRARY.

TOUR IN IRELAND.

Vol. II.

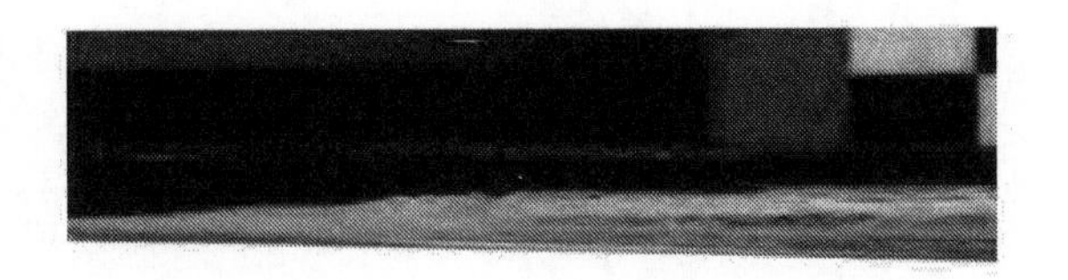

AN IRISH CABBIN.

Facsimile of a sketch made by Arthur Young in 1776.

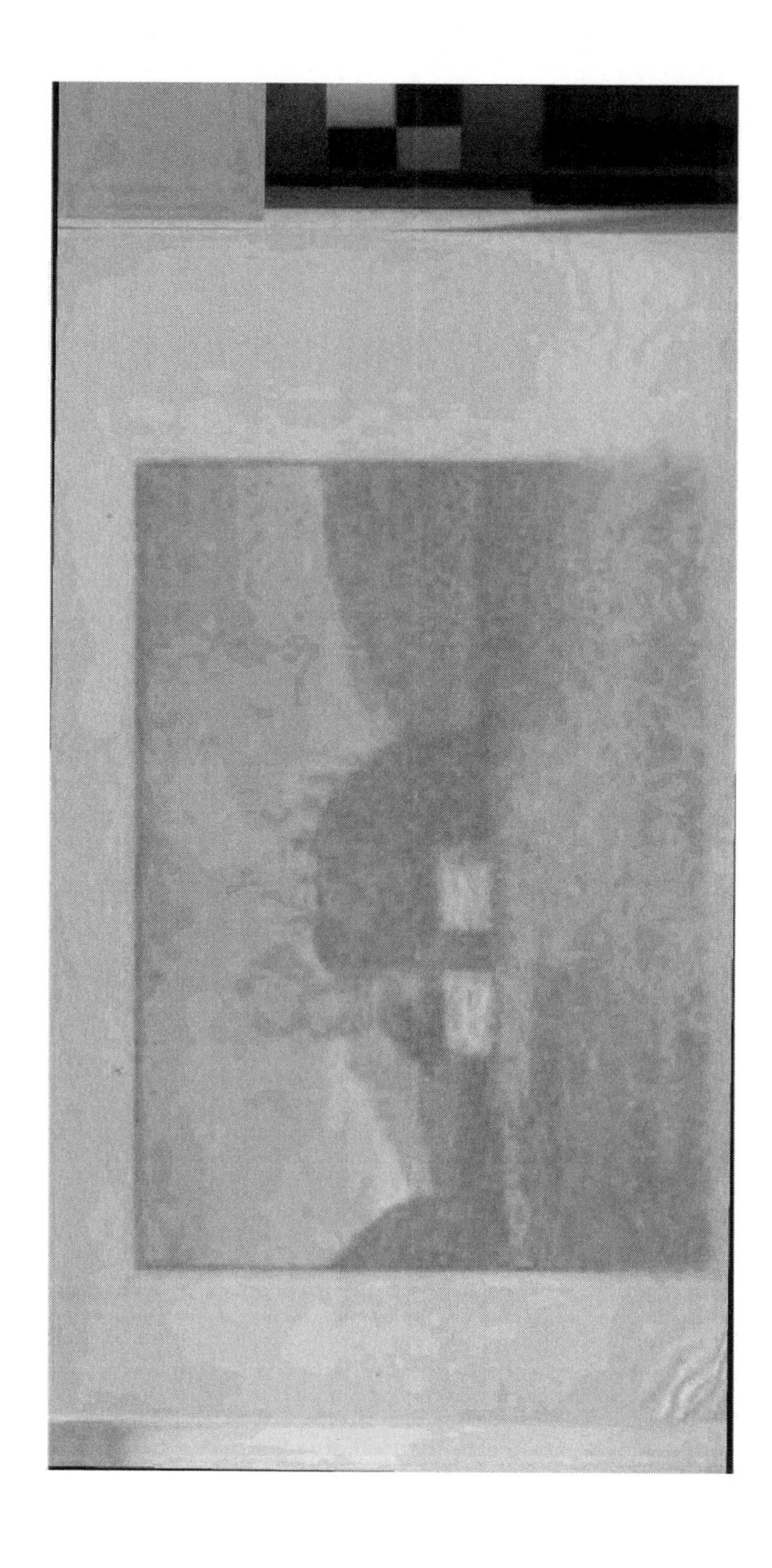

ARTHUR YOUNG'S TOUR IN IRELAND

(1776-1779)

EDITED WITH INTRODUCTION AND NOTES

BY

ARTHUR WOLLASTON HUTTON

WITH A BIBLIOGRAPHY BY

JOHN P. ANDERSON

Of the British Museum

VOL. II

CONTAINING PART II. OF THE TOUR, THE AUTHOR'S CONTRIBUTIONS ON IRELAND TO THE "ANNALS OF AGRICULTURE," BIBLIOGRAPHY, AND INDEX.

LONDON

GEORGE BELL & SONS, YORK ST., COVENT GARDEN

AND NEW YORK

1892

CONTENTS.

Vol. II.

APPENDIX.

ARTHUR YOUNG'S CONTRIBUTIONS ON IRELAND TO THE "ANNALS OF AGRICULTURE."

AUTHOR'S PREFATORY NOTE

TO PART II.

TO register the minutes received upon such a journey as this, and leave them simply to speak for themselves, would have its use; but it would leave to the inquisitive reader so much labour and trouble in collecting general facts, that not one in five hundred would attempt it. That it is a matter of importance to have accurate general ideas of a country, instead of erroneous ones, will hardly be disputed; no books of geography but speak generally of soil, climate, product, rental, population, &c. but they are too often mere guesses; or, if founded at all, the facts that support them of too old a date to yield the least truth at present in points subject to change. When one country is mentioned with another it is usually in general terms: and by comparison, *England has not so rich a soil as Ireland. Products in England larger than in France. Rents higher in Ireland than in Scotland.* A thousand instances might be produced, in which ideas of this sort are particularized, and in which general errors are often found the cause of political measures, even of the highest consequence. That my English "Tours" give *exact* information relative to England I cannot assert; but I may venture to say, that they are the only information extant, relative to the rental, produce, stock of that country, which are taken from an actual examination: I wish to offer equal information relative to our sister island; and I am encouraged to do it, not only from my own ideas, but the opinions of many persons with whom I have either corresponded or conversed from most parts of Europe, including some of the most respectable for abilities and rank.

A TOUR IN IRELAND.

SECTION I.

EXTENT OF IRELAND.

IN order to know the consequence and relative importance of any country, it is necessary to be acquainted with its extent; I have reason to believe that that of Ireland is not accurately known. I insert the following table of the acres of each county, plantation measure, because there are several observations to be made on it.

Province	County	Acres.
Ulster	Antrim	383,020
	Armagh	170,620
	Cavan	274,800
	Down	344,658
	Donegal	630,157
	Fermanagh	224,807
	Londonderry	251,510
	Monaghan	170,090
	Tyrone	387,175
Total		2,836,837
Leinster	Carlow	116,900
	Dublin	123,784
	Kildare	228,590
	Kilkenny	287,650
	King's County	257,510
	Longford	134,700
	Louth	111,180
	Meath	326,480
	Queen's County	238,415
	Westmeath	249,943
	Wexford	315,396
	Wicklow	252,410
Total		2,642,958
Munster	Clare	428,187
	Corke	991,010
	Kerry	636,905
	Limerick	375,320
	Tipperary	599,500
	Waterford	259,010
Total		3,289,932
Connaught	Galway	775,525
	Leitrim	206,830
	Mayo	724,640
	Roscommon	324,370
	Sligo	241,550
Total		2,272,915
In all Ireland		11,042,642

Gerard Malines makes the acres of Ireland eighteen millions: ("Lex Mercatoria," part 1, p. 49.) I suppose English measure, which is eleven millions Irish; these two accounts flow therefore from the same source. Templeman's measurement gives it 27,457 square miles, or 17,572,480 acres ("Survey of the Globe") English on a scale of 60 miles to a degree, but consequently it is professedly erroneous, as a degree is 69½; according to this measure therefore, the contents in real acres would be 20,354,789 English, and 12,721,743 Irish.[1] These accounts come so nearly together, that they are all drawn from similar data; that is, from old maps. Newer ones have many blunders; but as no late actual survey has been made of the kingdom, we must depend on the authority we find.

[1] The acreage of Ireland (English measure) is 20,819,928. Young's correction of Templeman's estimate thus comes nearest to the mark, though that is an under-statement by nearly half a million acres. The estimate, however, that gives to Ireland nearly twenty-one million acres, includes inland waters. The actual land surface is estimated at 20,150,612 acres. If Young intended to exclude inland waters, and apparently he did not, as he often reckons them in when calculating the extent of private estates, his estimate is excessive by 200,000 acres.

SECTION II.

SOIL, FACE OF THE COUNTRY AND CLIMATE.

TO judge of Ireland by the conversation one sometimes hears in England, it would be supposed that one half of it was covered with bogs, and the other with mountains filled with Irish ready to fly at the sight of a civilized being. There are people who will smile when they hear that in proportion, to the size of the two countries, Ireland is more cultivated than England, having much less waste land of all sorts. Of uncultivated mountains there are no such tracts as are found in our four northern counties, and the North Riding of Yorkshire, with the eastern line of Lancaster, nearly down to the Peak of Derby, which form an extent of above an hundred miles of waste. The most considerable of this sort in Ireland are in Kerry, Galway, and Mayo, and some in Sligo and Donnegal. But all these together will not make the quantity we have in the four northern counties; the vallies in the Irish mountains are also more inhabited, I think, than those of England, except where there are mines, and consequently some sort of cultivation creeping up the sides. Natural fertility, acre for acre, over the two kingdoms is certainly in favour of Ireland; of this I believe there can scarcely be a doubt entertained, when it is considered that some of the more beautiful, and even best cultivated counties in England, owe almost every thing to the capital, art and industry of the inhabitants.

The circumstance which strikes me as the greatest singularity of Ireland, is the rockyness of the soil, which should seem at first sight against that degree of fertility; but the contrary is the fact. Stone is so general, that I have great reason to believe the whole island is one vast rock of different strata and kinds rising out of the sea. I have rarely heard of any great depths being sunk without meeting with it. In general it appears on the surface in every part of the kingdom, the flattest and most fertile parts, as Limerick, Tipperary and Meath, have it at no great depth, almost as much as the more barren ones. May we not recognize in this the hand of bounteous Providence, which has given perhaps the most stoney soil in Europe to the moistest climate in it? If as much rain fell upon the clays of England (a soil very rarely met with in Ireland, and never without much stone) as falls upon the rocks of her sister island, those lands could not be cultivated. But the rocks here are cloathed with verdure;—those of lime stone, with only a thin covering of mould, have the softest and most beautiful turf imaginable.

Of the great advantages resulting from the general plenty of lime-stone, and lime-stone gravel, and the nature of the bogs, I shall have occasion to speak more particularly hereafter.

The rockyness of the soil in Ireland is so universal, that it predominates in every sort. One cannot use with propriety the terms clay, loam, sand, &c. it must be a *stoney* clay, a *stoney* loam, a *gravelly* sand. Clay, especially the yellow, is much talked of in Ireland, but it is for want of proper discrimination. I have once or twice seen almost a pure clay upon the surface, but it is extremely rare. The true yellow clay is usually found in a thin stratum under the surface mould, and over a rock; harsh, tenacious, stoney, strong loams, difficult to work, are not uncommon; but they are quite different from English clays.

Friable sandy loams dry, but fertile, are very common, and they form the best soils in the kingdom for tillage and sheep. Tipperary, and Roscommon abound particularly in them. The most fertile of all are the bullock pastures of Limerick, and the banks of the Shannon in Clare, called the *corcasses*. These are a mellow, putrid, friable loam.

Sand, which is so common in England, and yet more common through Spain, France, Germany, and Poland, quite from Gibraltar to Petersburgh, is no where met with in Ireland, except for narrow slips of hillocks, upon the sea coast. Nor did I ever meet with or hear of a chalky soil.[1]

The bogs of which foreigners have heard so much, are very extensive in Ireland; that of Allen extends 80 miles, and is computed to contain 300,000 acres. There are others also, very extensive, and smaller ones scattered over the whole kingdom; but these are not in general more than are wanted for fuel. When I come to speak of the improvement of waste lands, I shall describe them particularly.

Besides the great fertility of the soil, there are other circumstances, which come within my sphere to mention. Few countries can be better watered by large and beautiful rivers; and it is remarkable that by much the finest parts of the kingdom are on the banks of these rivers. Witness the Suer, Blackwater, the Liffy, the Boyne, the Nore, the Barrow, and part of the Shannon, they wash a scenery that can hardly be exceeded. From the rockyness of the country however, there are few of them that have not obstructions, which are great impediments to inland navigation.

The mountains of Ireland give to travelling that interesting variety, which a flat country can never abound with. And at the same time, they are not in such number as to confer the usual character of poverty, which attends them. I was either upon or very near the most considerable in the kingdom. Mangerton, and the Reeks, in Kerry; the Galties in Corke; those of Mourne in Down; Crow Patrick, and Nephin in Mayo; these are the principal in Ireland, and they are of a character, in height and sublimity, which should render them the objects of every traveller's attention.

Relative to the climate of Ireland, a short residence cannot enable a man to speak much from his own experience; the observations I have made myself confirm the idea of its being vastly wetter than England; from the 20th of June, to the 20th of October, I kept a register, and there were in 122 days, 75 of rain, and very many of them incessant and heavy. I have examined similar registers I kept in England, and can find no year that even approaches to

[1] There is, however, a little chalky soil in co. Antrim.

such a moisture as this. But there is the register of an accurate diary published, which compares London and Corke. The result is, that the quantity at the latter place was double to that at London.[1] See Smith's "Hist. of Corke."

From the information I received, I have reason to believe, that the rainy season sets in usually about the first of July, and continues very wet till September or October, when there is usually a dry fine season of a month or six weeks. I resided in the county of Corke, &c. from October till March, and found the winter much more soft and mild, than ever I experienced one in England. I was also a whole summer there (1778), and it is fair to mention, that it was as fine a one, as ever I knew in England, though by no means so hot. I think hardly so wet as very many I have known in England. The tops of the Galty Mountains exhibited the only snow we saw; and as to frosts, they were so slight and rare, that I believe myrtles, and yet tenderer plants, would have survived without any covering. But when I say that the winter was not remarkable for being wet, I do not mean that we had a dry atmosphere. The inches of rain which fell, in the winter I speak of, would not mark the moisture of the climate. As many inches will fall in a single tropical shower, as in a whole year in England. See Mitchel's "Present State of Great Britain, and North America." But if the clouds presently disperse, and a bright sun shines, the air may soon be dry. The worst circumstance of the climate of Ireland, is the constant moisture without rain. Wet a piece of leather, and lay it in a room, where there is neither sun nor fire, and it will not, in summer even, be dry in a month.[2] I have known gentlemen in Ireland deny their climate being

[1] The average annual rainfall in Ireland is about 40 inches; that in England is about 32 inches. But, oddly enough, a field of turnips—a crop which Young was always urging on the Irish farmers—sown by him near Mitchelstown, failed on account of the "continual drought." See below, section xi.

[2] I have had this happen myself with a pair of wet gloves.

The myriads of flies also which buz about one's ears, and are ready to go in shoals into one's mouth at every word—and those almost imperceptible flies called midges, which perfectly devour one in a wood, or near a river, prove the same thing.—[*Author's note.*]

moister than England;—but if they have eyes let them open them, and see the verdure that cloathes their rocks, and compare it with ours in England—where rocky soils are of a russet brown, however sweet the food for sheep. Does not their island lye more exposed to the great Atlantic, and does not the west wind blow three fourths of a year? If there was another island yet more to the westward, would not the climate of Ireland be improved? Such persons speak equally against fact, reason, and philosophy. That the moisture of a climate does not depend on the quantity of rain that falls, but on the powers of aerial evaporation, Dr. Dobson has clearly proved. "Phil. Trans," Vol. lxvii. part i. p. 244.

SECTION III.

RENTAL.

NO country can ever be held in a just estimation when the rental of it is unknown. It is not the only circumstance which a political arithmetician should attend to, but it is a most important one. The value of a country is rarely the subject of a conversation without guesses at its rental being made, and comparisons between different ones. I contend for nothing more through this and the ensuing tables, than the superiority of actual information on the spot, drawn into one point of view, over any guesses whatever. I shall therefore proceed at once to lay it before the reader,

Places.	Rent per Acre.	Rent at Irish Acre.	Rise.	Fall.	Year's purchase of land.	Leases, years or lives.
			s. d.	s. d.		
County of Dublin . . .					22	41 61 L
Celbridge	1 10 0				22	31 or L
Dollestown	1 1 0			5 0		
Summerhill	1 0 0				23	
Slaine Castle	1 5 0				22½	31 or L
Headfort	1 0 0				21.	
Druestown	1 6 0					
Fore	0 15 0					
Packenham Hall . . .	0 17 6			4 4	21	
Mullengar to Tullespace	1 0 0					
Charleville	0 16 0			4 0	20	
Shaen Castle, Queen's Co.	0 13 0			5 0	20	
Athy to Carlow . . .	0 18 0					
Kilfaine	0 15 6			2 0	21	21 31

Places.	Rent per Acre.	Rent at Irish Acre.	Rise.	Fall.	Year's purchase of land.	Leases, years or lives.
			s. d.	*s. d.*		
Ross to Taghmon . . .	0 15 0					
Bargie and Forth . . .	1 2 9		a little		23½	
Wexford to Wells. . .	0 11 0					
Wells to Gowry . . .	0 17 0					
Courtown	0 17 6		none		22½	31 L
New Town M. Kennedy	2 0 0		8 0		19½	31 L
Ditto Mountain . . .	0 8 0					
Kilrue	1 2 0					
Hampton	1 5 0				20	
Cullen	1 0 0					
Ravenadale	0 7 0					
Market-hill	0 11 6	14 9				
Armagh	0 10 0	13 0				
Armagh to Newry . .	0 10 0	13 0				
To Dungannon. . . .	0 11 0	14 0				
To Lurgan	0 10 0	13 0				
Mahon	0 13 6	17 4				
Down.	0 16 0	20 0				
To Belfast	0 16 0	20 0				
Castle Hill	0 15 0	9 0				
Ards	0 10 6	13 6				
Lecale	1 0 0					
Redemon to Saintfield .	0 10 6	13 6				
Belfast	0 13 0	17 0				
Belfast to Antrim . .	0 8 0	10 0				
Shanes Castle, co. Antrim	0 8 0	10 0			21	31 L
Lesly Hill	0 12 0	15 0	3 0		21	
Near Giant's Causway .	0 12 0	15 0				
Coleraine	0 10 6					
Newtown Limm . . .	0 10 0	13 0	1 6			
Clonleigh county . . .	0 17 6	21 6			25	L
Mount Charles	0 10 0				21½	
Castle Caldwell . . .	0 17 6		2 0		22	
Inniskilling	0 11 0					
Ditto	0 15 0					
Florence Court . . .	0 10 0					
Farnham	0 17 0		5 6		22	
Granard	1 1 0					
Longford	0 13 6		2 0		18½	
Strokestown	1 5 0					
Elphin	0 13 6					
Kingston	0 17 6					

Places.	Rent per Acre.	Rent at Irish Acre.	Rise.	Fall.	Year's purchase of land.	Leases, years or lives.
			s. d.	s. d.		
Mercra	0 15 0				20	31 L
Tyrera	0 14 6					
Ditto	0 18 0					
Tyrawley	0 17 0					
Foxford to Castlebar	0 12 0					
Castlebar	0 17 6					
Westport	0 8 0			1 0	21½	21 31 L
Holymount	0 13 6					
Moniva	0 14 0				21	
Wood Lawn	0 16 0					
Drumoland corcasses	1 0 0				20	
Limerick				8 0	20	
Annsgrove	0 15 0			2 6	20	31 L
Orrery	1 10 0					
Fermoy	0 13 0					
Duhallow	0 7 0					
Condons and Clangibbons	0 15 0					
Barrymore	0 7 0	11 0				
Barrets	0 4 0	6 0				
Mushery	0 4 0	6 0				
Kinclea	0 14 0	22 0				
Kerrycurrity	0 10 0	16 0				
Courcy's	0 10 0	16 0				
Mallow	0 12 0	19 0				31 L
Castle Martyr					25	
Imokilly	0 12 0	19 0				
Kilnatalton	0 8 0	12 0				
Coolmore	0 14 0	22 0				
Killarney	0 8 0					
Castle Island to Tralee	1 7 0					
Mahagree	0 14 6				17	
Tarbat	0 14 0					
Adair	1 0 0					
Castle Oliver	0 12 0			3 0		
100,000 acres in Limerick	1 10 0					
20 miles sheepland Tipperary	1 2 6			4 6	20	
Ballycavan	0 15 0				19½	
Furness	1 0 0					
Gloster	0 15 0			3 0	25	31 L
Johnstown	1 0 0				20	31 L
Derry	0 15 0					

Places.	Rent per Acre.	Rent at Irish Acre.	Rise.	Fall.	Year's purchase of land.	Leases, years or lives.
			s. d.	s. d.		
Cullen	1 10 0				20	31 L
Mitchels Town	0 2 6				20	21
Average		16 6			21	
Average per English acre		10 3				

The first column of rent is either plantation measure, Cunningham, or English; and the second reduces the two last to plantation.

The Cunningham acre is reduced to the plantation measure as seven to nine, and the English as five to eight, which, though not perfectly accurate, is near it.

The following table contains the information I received relative to the general average rental of whole counties; and as there are several with more than one account, the medium of those different accounts is given in a separate column.

Counties.	Different minutes.	Average.	Reduced to plantation.	Total rental of the County.
	£ s. d.	£ s. d.	£ s. d.	£
Dublin		1 11 6	1 11 6	194,959
Meath	1 0 0			
Ditto	1 5 0			
Ditto	0 18 6			
		1 1 2	1 1 2	345,524
Westmeath . . .		0 7 0	0 7 0	87,480
King's County . .	0 13 0			
Ditto	0 12 6			
		0 12 9	0 12 9	164,161
Carlow		0 15 0	0 15 0	87,675
			Carried forward	879,799

Counties.	Different minutes.	Average.	Reduced to plantation.	Total rental of the County.
	£ s. d.	£ s. d.	£ s. d.	£
		Brought forward		879,799
Wexford		0 0 15	0 15 0	236,547
Wicklow		0 0 15	0 15 0	189,307
Louth		1 1 0	1 1 0	116,739
Armagh	0 8 0			
Ditto	0 14 0			
		0 11 0	0 14 0	119,434
Down	0 10 0			
Ditto	0 10 0			
Ditto	0 10 0			
		0 10 0	0 12 10	221,154
Antrim	0 5 6			
Ditto	0 4 9			
		0 5 1½	0 6 6	124,481
Derry	0 4 6			
Ditto	0 4 0			
		0 4 3	0 5 6	69,164
Donegal	0 1 0			
Ditto	0 1 0			
Ditto	0 2 6			
		0 1 6	0 1 6	47,260
Fermanagh		0 8 5	0 8 5	94,603
Cavan	0 6 0			
Ditto	0 7 6			
		0 6 9	0 6 9	92,745
Longford		0 10 0	0 10 0	67,350
Leitrim	0 4 0			
Ditto	0 2 0			
Ditto	0 1 4			
		0 2 5	0 2 5	24,990
Roscommon	0 11 0			
Ditto	0 10 0			
		0 10 6	0 10 6	170,294
Sligo	0 12 6			
Ditto	0 12 10			
Ditto	0 10 10			
		0 12 0	0 12 0	144,930
Mayo		0 8 0	0 8 0	289,856
Galway		0 8 1	0 8 1	313,440
Clare		0 5 0	0 5 0	107,046
Corke	0 7 0			
Ditto	0 3 1			
			Carried forward	3,308,133

Counties.	Different minutes.	Average.	Reduced to plantation.	Total rental of the County.
	£ s. d.	£ s. d.	£ s. d.	£
			Brought forward	3,308,133
Corke	0 5 8			
Ditto	0 5 4			
Ditto	0 5 0			
		0 5 2	0 5 2	256,010
Kerry.	0 2 0			
Ditto	0 2 11			
Ditto	0 1 7			
Ditto	0 4 10			
		0 2 10	0 2 10	90,226
Limerick	1 0 0			
Ditto	1 0 0			
Ditto	0 10 6			
		0 16 10	0 16 10	315,893
Tipperary . . .	0 16 3			
Ditto	0 17 4			
Ditto	1 0 0			
Ditto	0 12 6			
		0 16 6	0 16 6	494,587
Waterford . . .	0 5 0			
Ditto	0 6 10			
		0 5 11	0 5 11	76,622
Kildare		0 14 6	0 14 6	165,727
Tyrone	0 4 0			
Ditto	0 7 0			
		0 5 6	0 5 6	106,472

Since the journey I have procured the information for the following:

Counties.	Different minutes.	Average.	Reduced to plantation.	Total rental of the County.
Kilkenny . . .		0 16 0	0 16 0	230,119
Monaghan . . .		0 11 0	0 11 0	93,549
Queen's		0 13 0	0 13 0	154,968
			Total . .	5,293,312[1]

11,042,642 plantation acres, giving the rent of £5,293,312 is at the rate of 9*s.* 7*d.* *per* acre. The average of all the minutes made it 16*s.* 6*d.* from hence there is reason to imagine, that the line travelled was better than the medium

[1] It may be interesting to compare with this the official return issued in 1876, which gave the total valuation of land in Ireland as £13,419,258.

of the kingdom; or, on the contrary, that the suppositions of the rents *per* county are *under* the truth, the real rent of the kingdom, if it could be ascertained, would probably be found rather to exceed than fall short of six millions. Especially as the rents, upon which these particulars are drawn, were not those paid by the occupying tenant, but a general average of all tenures; whereas the object one would ascertain is the sum paid by the occupyer, including consequently, not only the landlord rents, but the profit of the middle men.

But farther, as the computation that makes the total of 11,042,642 acres is professedly erroneous above a seventh, being drawn from geographic miles, there should be added above £700,000 to this rental on that account.

The difference of money and measure included 35*s*. Irish makes just 20*s*. English. Suppose therefore the rental of Ireland 9*s*. 7*d*. per acre, it makes 5*s*. 6*d*. English.

If Ireland is 10*s*. it would be 5*s*. 9*d*. English.

Suppose it 11*s*. or the total of six millions, it is per English acre 6*s*. 4*d*.

It is a curious disquisition to compare the rent of land in different countries, and to mark the various circumstances to which the superiority may be attributed. The rental of England has been pretty accurately ascertained to be 13*s*. an acre.[1] Poor-rates in the same 1*s*. 10½*d*. in the pound, or 1*s*. 2½*d*. per acre. The[2] information I received in Ireland concerning the amount of the money raised for presentments throughout the kingdom, made the total £140,000 or 3*d*. an acre.

	£	s.	d.
Landlord's rent of Ireland	£0	9	7
Roads	0	0	3
	0	9	10
Rent of England	0	13	0
Rates	0	1	2½
	0	14	2½
Irish acre and money makes	0	9	10
Which for an English acre and English money is	0	5	7

[1] "Eastern Tour through England," vol. iv. p. 229.—[*Author's note.*]

[2] The average of the Eastern and Northern Tours which make a total

Instead of which is 14*s*. 2½*d*.; consequently the proportion between the rent of land in England and Ireland is nearly as two to five: in other words, that space of land which in Ireland lets for 2*s*. would in England produce 5*s*.

In this comparison the value of land in England appears to be so much greater than it is in Ireland, that several circumstances should be considered. The idea I found common in Ireland upon that matter was, that rents there were *higher* than in England; but the extreme absurdity of the notion arose from the difference of measure and money, the exact par being as 20 to 35. As far as I can form a general idea of the soil of the two kingdoms, Ireland has much the advantage; and, if I am accurate in this, surely a stronger argument cannot be used, to shew the immense importance of CAPITAL, first in the hands of the landlords of a country, and then in that of the farmers. I have reason to believe that five pounds sterling per English acre, expended over all Ireland, which amounts to £88,341,136 would not more than build, fence, plant, drain, and improve that country to be upon a par in those respects with England. And farther, that if those 88 millions were so expended, it would take much above 20 millions more (or above 20*s*. an acre) in the hands of the farmers, in stock of husbandry, to put them on an equal footing with those of her sister kingdom; nor is this calculation so vague as it might at first sight appear, since the expences of improvements and stock are very easily estimated in both countries. This is the solution of that surprising inferiority in the rent of Ireland: the English farmer pays a rent for his land in the state he finds it, which includes, not only the natural fertility of the soil, but the immense expenditure

of £1,926,666. By the returns laid before Parliament it appeared to be actually £1,720,316 14*s*. 7*d*.; but that return was incomplete, for there are very many parishes named, from which, through neglect, no returns were made. I may remark that this fact is a strong confirmation of the truth of the data upon which I formed these calculations, the above sum coming vastly nearer to the truth afterwards ascertained by Parliament, than any other calculation or conjecture which ever found its way into print.

The roads of England are a very heavy article; I conjecture much heavier than in Ireland but I have no data whereby to ascertain the amount.—[*Author's note.*]

which national wealth has in the progress of time poured into it; but the Irishman finds nothing he can afford to pay a rent for, but what the bounty of God has given, unaided by either wealth or industry. The second point is of equal consequence—when the land is to be let, the rent it will bring must depend on the capability of the cultivators to make it productive. If they have but half the capital they ought to be possessed of, how is it possible they should be able to offer a rent proportioned to the rates of another country, in which a variety of causes have long directed a stream of abundant wealth into the purses of her farmers?

These facts call for one very obvious reflection, which will often recur in the progress of these papers: the consequences of it are felt in Ireland; but I am sorry to say, very ill understood in England: that portion of national wealth which is employed in the improvement of the lands of a State is the best employed for the general welfare of a country; while trade and manufactures, national funds, banking, &c. swallow up prodigious sums in England, but yield a profit of not above 5 to 10 per cent.; the lands of Ireland are unimproved, upon which money would pay 15 to 20 per cent. exclusive of a variety of advantages which must strike the most superficial reader.—Hence the vast importance to *England* of the improvement of her Irish territory. It is an old observation, that the wealth of Ireland will always center in England; and the fact is true, though not in the way commonly asserted: No employment of 100 millions, not upon the actual soil of Britain, can ever pay her a tenth of the advantage which would result from Ireland being in the above respects upon that par which I have described with England. The more attentively this matter is considered, I am apt to think the more clearly this will appear; and that, whenever old illiberal jealousies are worn out, which, thanks to the good sense of the age, are daily disappearing, we shall be fully convinced, that the benefit of Ireland is so intimately connected with the good of England, that we shall be as forward to give to that hitherto unhappy country, as she can be to receive, from the firm conviction, that whatever we thus sow will yield to us a most abundant harvest.

SECTION IV.

PRODUCTS.

THE products per acre were, in every place, an object of my enquiries. The following table will at one view shew what they are in most parts of the kingdom.

Places.	Wheat, Barrels.[1]	Barley, Barrels.	Oats, Barrels.	Bere, Barrels.
Dublin	8		16	
Celbridge	7		14	
Dollestown	7		13	13½
Summershill	6		10	
Slaine	7		16	
Headfort	7		12	
Packenham	7		10	15½
Tullamore	5½		12½	16
Shaens Castle	5½	13	11½	13
Near Athy	8	15	17½	
Athy to Carlow	5½			
Near Carlow		14	12	
Kilfaine	6	10	8	10
Bargie		9	9	
Ditto	8½	12		
Bargy and Forth	15	12½	11	
Wells		6	7½	
Courtown	8	9	9	
M. Kennedy	8		10	
Kilrue	11½	11½	14½	
Hampton	7	11	10	
Louth	6	15	15	
Mahon	5		6	
Ards	7			
Lecale	7	10	12	
Shaen Castle	6		8	

Places.	Wheat, Barrels.	Barley, Barrels.	Oats, Barrels.	Bere, Barrels.
Newtown Limm.		9		
Innishoen		8	7	
Clonleigh		10	8½	
Castle Caldwell		10	12	
Belleisle		12½	8	
Florence Court		8	12	
Farnham	7	9	10	
Longford		12	15	10
Strokestown	6	9	10	
Ballymoat	6½		10	
Mercra	6	14	10	
Tyrera		13½	10	
Ditto		15	10	
Westport			12	
Holymount	6		9	9
Moniva			8	
Woodlawn	8	12	12	
Drumoland	6½	12	12	
Annsgrove	7			
Mallow	8		12	12
Dunkettle	8½			
Adair	9		14	10
Castle Oliver	12		15	
Tipperary	12	15	14	27
Ballycanvan	8	14	12	
Furness	7		9	
Gloster	6	16	13	17
Johnstown	7		12	16
Derry	8		11½	15
Cullen	10	20	18	20
Mitchel's Town			11½	
Cunningham acre reduced.				
Mahon	6½		7¾	
Ards	9			
Shaens Castle	7¾		10	
English acre reduced.				
Mallow	12		19	19
Dunkettle	13			
Averages	7½	11½	11½	14

These quantities per English acre are:

	Qrs.	Bush.	Pecks.
Wheat	2	2	3
Barley	3	4	3
Oats	3	4	3
Bere	4	3	0

The averages of the "Farmer's Tour through the East of England" were:

	Qrs.	Bush.	Pecks.
Wheat	3	0	0
Barley	4	0	0
Oats	4	6	0

Of the "Six Months' Tour through the North of England":

	Qrs.	Bush.	Pecks.
Wheat	3	0	0
Barley	4	0	0
Oats	4	4	0

The products upon the whole are much inferior to those of England, though not more so than I should have expected; not from inferiority of soil, but the extreme inferiority of management. They are not to be considered as points whereon to found a full comparison of the two countries; since a small crop of wheat in England, gained after beans, clover, &c. would be of much more importance than a larger one in Ireland by a fallow: And this remark extends to other crops.

Tillage in Ireland is very little understood. In the greatest corn counties, such as Louth, Kildare, Carlow and Kilkenny, where are to be seen many very fine crops of wheat, all is under the old system, exploded by good farmers in England, of sowing wheat upon a fallow, and succeeding it with as many crops of spring corn as the soil will bear. Where they do best by their land, it is only two of barley or oats before the fallow returns again, which is something worse than the open field management in England, of 1. fallow; 2. wheat; 3. oats; to which, while the fields are open and common, the farmers are by cruel necessity tied down. The bounty on the inland carriage of corn to Dublin has increased tillage very considerably, but it has no where introduced any other system. And to this extreme bad management, of adopting the exploded practice of a century ago, instead of turneps and clover, it is owing that Ireland, with a soil, acre for acre, much better than England, has its products inferior.

But keeping cattle of every sort, is a business so much more adapted to the laziness of the farmer, that it is no wonder the tillage is so bad. It is every where left to the cottars, or to the very poorest of the farmers, who are all utterly unable to make those exertions, upon which alone a vigorous culture of the earth can be founded; and were it not for potatoes, which necessarily prepare for corn, there would not be half of what we see at present. While it is in such hands, no wonder tillage is reckoned so unprofitable; profit in all undertakings depends on capital; and is it any wonder that the profit should be small when the capital is nothing at all? Every man that has one gets into cattle, which will give him an idle, lazy superintendence, instead of an active attentive one.

That the *system* of tillage has improved very little, much as it has been extended in the last fourteen years, there is great reason to believe, from the very small increase in the import of clover seed, which would have doubled and trebled, had tillage got into the train it ought. This the following table proves.

Import of Clover seed.

	Cwt.
In the year 1764	2,990
1765	2,798
1766	3,654
1767	1,479
1768	4,476
1769	2,483
1770	5,563
Average of seven years	3,349
1771	4,083
1772	2,956
1773	2,820
1774	3,085

1775 . .	3,910
1776 . .	4,648
1777 . .	5,988
Average of seven years[1]	3,927

[1] Taken from the Records of imports and exports kept by order of the House of Commons. MS.—[*Author's note.*]

SECTION V.

OF THE TENANTRY OF IRELAND.

IT has been probably owing to the small value of land in Ireland, before, and even through a considerable part of, the present century, that landlords became so careless of the interests of posterity, as readily to grant their tenants leases for ever. It might also be partly owing to the unfortunate civil wars, and other intestine divisions, which for so long a space of time kept that unhappy country in a state rather of devastation than improvement. When a castle, or a fortified house, and a family strong enough for a garrison, were essentially necessary to the security of life and property among Protestants, no man could occupy land unless he had substance for defence as well as cultivation; short, or even determinable tenures were not encouragement enough for settling in such a situation of warfare. To increase the force of an estate, leases for ever were given of lands, which from their waste state were deemed of little value. The practice, once become common, continued long after the motives which originally gave rise to it, and has not yet ceased entirely in any part of the kingdom. Hence, therefore, tenants holding large tracts of land under a lease for ever, and which have been relet to a variety of undertenants, must in this enquiry be considered as landlords.

The obvious distinction to be applied is, that of the occupying and unoccupying tenantry: in other words, the real farmer, and the middle-man. The very idea, as well as the practice, of permitting a tenant to relet at a profit rent, seems confined to the distant and unimproved parts of every empire. In the highly cultivated counties of England the practice has no existence, but there are traces of it in the extremities; in Scotland it has been very common; and I am informed that the same observation is partly applicable to France. In proportion as any country becomes improved the practice necessarily wears out.

It is in Ireland a question greatly agitated, whether the system has or has not advantages, which may yet induce a landlord to continue in it. The friends to this mode of letting lands contend, that the extreme poverty of the lower classes renders them such an insecure tenantry, that no gentleman of fortune can depend on the least punctuality in the payment of rent from such people; and therefore to let a large farm to some intermediate person of substance, at a lower rent, in order that the profit may be his inducement and reward for becoming a collector from the immediate occupiers, and answerable for their punctuality, becomes necessary to any person who will not submit to the drudgery of such a minute attention. Also, that such a man will at least improve a spot around his own residence, whereas the mere cottar can do nothing. If the intermediate tenant is, or from the accumulation of several farms becomes, a man of property, the same argument is applicable to his reletting to another intermediate man, giving up a part of his profit to escape that trouble, which induced the landlord to begin this system; and at the same time accounts for the number of tenants, one under another, who have all a profit out of the rent of the occupying farmer. In the variety of conversations on this point, of which I have partook in Ireland, I never heard any other arguments that had the least foundation in the actual state of the country; for as to ingenious theories, which relate more to what might be, than to what is, little regard should be paid to them.

That a man of substance, whose rent is not only secure, but regularly paid, is in many respects a more eligible tenant than a poor cottar, or little farmer, cannot be disputed; if the landlord looks no farther than those circumstances, the question is at an end, for the argument must be allowed to have its full weight, even to victory. But there are many other considerations: I was particularly attentive to every class of tenants throughout the kingdom, and shall therefore describe these middle-men, from whence their merit may be the more easily decided. Sometimes they are resident on a part of the land, but very often they are not. Dublin, Bath, London, and the country towns of Ireland, contain great numbers of them; the merit of this class is surely ascertained in a moment; there cannot be a shadow of a pretence for the intervention of a man, whose single concern with an estate is to deduct a portion from the rent of it. They are however sometimes resident on a part of the land they hire, where it is natural to suppose they would work some improvements; it is however very rarely the case. I have in different parts of the kingdom seen farms just fallen in after leases of three lives, of the duration of fifty, sixty, and even seventy years, in which the residence of the principal tenant was not to be distinguished from the cottared fields surrounding it. I was at first much surprized at this; but after repeated observation, I found these men very generally were the masters of packs of wretched hounds, with which they wasted their time and money, and it is a notorious fact, that they are the hardest drinkers in Ireland. Indeed, the class of the small country gentlemen, chiefly consisting of these profit renters, seems at present to monopolize that drinking spirit, which was, not many years ago, the disgrace of the kingdom at large: this I conjecture to be the reason why those who might improve are so very far from doing it; but there are still greater objections to them.

Living upon the spot, surrounded by their little undertenants, they prove the most oppressive species of tyrant that ever lent assistance to the destruction of a country. They relet the land, at short tenures, to the occupiers of small farms; and often give no leases at all. Not satisfied with screwing up the rent to the uttermost farthing, they are rapacious and relentless in the collection of it. Many of them have defended themselves in conversation with me, upon the plea of taking their rents, partly in kind, when their undertenants are much distressed: "What," say they, "would the head landlord, suppose him a great noble-"man, do with a miserable cottar, who, disappointed in the "sale of a heifer, a few barrels of corn, or firkins of butter, "brings his five instead of his ten guineas? But we can "favour him by taking his commodities at a fair price, and "wait for reimbursement until the market rises. Can my lord do that?" A very common plea, but the most unfortunate that could be used to any one whoever remarked that portion of human nature which takes the garb of an Irish land-jobber! For upon what issue does this remark place the question? Does it not acknowledge that, calling for their rents, when they cannot be paid in cash, they take the substance of the debtor at the very moment when he cannot sell it to another? Can it be necessary to ask what the price is? It is at the option of the creditor; and the miserable culprit meets his oppression, perhaps his ruin, in the very action that is trumpeted as a favour to him. It may seem harsh to attribute a want of feeling to any class of men; but let not the reader misapprehend me; it is the *situation*, not the *man*, that I condemn. An injudicious system places a great number of persons, not of any liberal rank in life, in a state abounding with a variety of opportunities of oppression, every act of which is profitable to themselves. I am afraid it is human nature for men to fail in such posts; and I appeal to the experience of mankind, in other lines of life, whether it is ever found advantageous to a poor debtor to sell his products, or wares, to his richer creditor, at the moment of demand.

But farther; the dependance of the occupier on the resident middle-man goes to other circumstances, personal service of themselves, their cars and horses, is exacted for leading turf, hay, corn, gravel, &c. insomuch that the poor undertenants often lose their own crops and turf, from being obliged to obey these calls of their superiors. Nay, I have even heard these jobbers gravely assert, that without undertenants to furnish cars and teams at half or two thirds the common price of the country, they could carry on no improvements at all; yet taking a merit to themselves for works wrought out of the sweat and ruin of a pack of wretches, assigned to their plunder by the inhumanity of the landholders.

In a word, the case is reducible to a short compass; intermediate tenants work no improvements; if non-resident they *cannot*, and if resident they *do not;* but they oppress the occupiers, and render them as incapable as they are themselves unwilling. The kingdom is an aggregate proof of these facts; for if long leases at low rents, and profit incomes given, would have improved it, Ireland had long ago been a garden. It remains to enquire, whether the landlord's security is a full recompence for so much mischief.

But here it is proper to observe that, though the intermediate man is generally better security than the little occupier; yet it is not from thence to be concluded, as I have often heard it, that the latter is beyond all comparison beneath him in this respect: the contrary is often the case; and I have known the fact, that the landlord, disappointed of his rent, has *drove* (distrained) the undertenants for it at a time when they had actually paid it to the middle-man. If the profit rent is spent, as it very generally is, in claret and hounds, the notion of good security will prove visionary, as many a landlord in Ireland has found it: several very considerable ones have assured me, that the little occupiers were the *best* pay they had on their estates; and the intermediate *gentlemen* tenants by much the *worst*.

By the minutes of the journey it appears, that a very considerable part of the kingdom, and the most enlightened landlords in it, have discarded this injurious system, and let their farms to none but the occupying tenantry; their experience has proved that the apprehension of a want of security was merely idle, finding their rents much better paid than ever. At the last extremity, it is the occupier's stock which is the real security of the landlord. It is that he distrains, and finds abundantly more valuable than the laced hat, hounds and pistols of the gentleman jobber, from whom he is more likely in such a case to receive a *message*, than a remittance.

And here let me observe, that a defence of intermediate tenants has been founded upon the circumstance of lessening the remittance of absentee rents; the profit of the middle-man was spent in Ireland, whereas upon his dismission the whole is remitted to England. I admit this to be an evil, but it appears to be in no degree proportioned to the mischiefs I have dwelt on. It is always to be remembered, that in the arrangement of landed property, the *produce* is the great object; the system of letting, which encourages most the occupying tenant, will always be the most advantageous to the community. I think that I have proved that the middle-man oppresses the cottar incomparably more than the principal landlord; to the one he is usually tenant at will, or at least under short terms, but under the other has the most advantageous tenure. This single point, that the person most favoured is in one instance an idle burthen, and in the other the industrious occupier, sufficiently decides the superiority. To look therefore at the rent, after it is paid, is to put the question on a wrong issue; the payment of that rent, by means of ample products, arising from animated industry, is the only point deserving attention; and I had rather the whole of it should go to the antipodes than exact it in a manner that shall cramp that industry, and lessen those products.

When therefore it is considered, that no advantages to the estate can arise from a non-resident tenant, and that a resident intermediate one improves no more than the poor occupiers who are prevented by his oppressions, that the landlord often gains little or nothing in security from employing them, but that he suffers a prodigious deduction in his rental for mere expectations, which every hour's experience proves to be delusive. When these facts are duly weighed, it is presumed that the gentlemen in those parts of the kingdom, which yet groan under such a system of absurdity, folly and oppression, will follow the example set by such a variety of intelligent landlords, and be deaf to the deceitful asseverations with which their ears are assailed, to treat the anecdotes retailed of the cottar's poverty, with the contempt they deserve, when coming from the mouth of a jobber; when these bloodsuckers of the poor tenantry boast of their own improvements, to open their eyes and view the ruins which are dignified by such a term, and finally determine, as friends to themselves, to their posterity and their country, TO LET THEIR ESTATES TO NONE BUT THE OCCUPYING TENANTRY.

Having thus described the tenants that ought to be rejected, let me next mention the circumstances of the occupiers. The variety of these is very great in Ireland. In the North, where the linen manufacture has spread, the farms are so small, that ten acres in the occupation of one person is a large one, five or six will be found a good farm, and all the agriculture of the country so entirely subservient to the manufacture, that they no more deserve the name of farmers than the occupier of a mere cabbage garden. In Limerick, Tipperary, Clare, Meath and Waterford, there are to be found the greatest graziers and cowkeepers perhaps in the world, some who rent and occupy from £3,000 to £10,000 a year: these of course are men of property, and are the only occupiers in the kingdom who have any considerable substance. The effects are not so beneficial as might be expected. Rich graziers in England, who have a little tillage, usually manage it well, and are in other respects attentive to various improvements, though it must be confessed not in the same proportion with great arable farmers; but in Ireland these men are as arrant slovens as the most beggarly cottars. The rich lands of Limerick are, in respect of fences, drains, buildings, weeds, &c. in as waste a state as the mountains of Kerry; the fertility of nature is so little seconded, that few tracts yield less pleasure to the spectator. From what I observed, I attributed this to the idleness and dissipation so general in Ireland. These graziers are too apt to attend to their claret as much as to their bullocks, live expensively, and being enabled, from the nature of their business, to pass nine tenths of the year without any exertion of industry, contract such a habit of ease, that works of improvement would be mortifying to their sloth.

In the arable counties of Louth, part of Meath, Kildare, Kilkenny, Carlow, Queen's, and part of King's, and Tipperary, they are much more industrious. It is the nature of tillage, to raise a more regular and animated attention to business; but the farms are too small, and the tenants too poor, to exhibit any appearances that can strike an English traveller. They have a great deal of corn, and many fine wheat crops; but being gained at the expence and loss of a fallow, as in the open fields of England, they do not suggest the ideas of profit to the individual, or advantage to the state, which worse crops in a well appointed rotation would do. Their manuring is trivial, their tackle and implements wretched, their teams weak, their profit small, and their living little better than that of the cottars they employ. These circumstances are the necessary result of the smallness of their capitals, which even in these tillage counties do not usually amount to a third of what an English farmer would have to

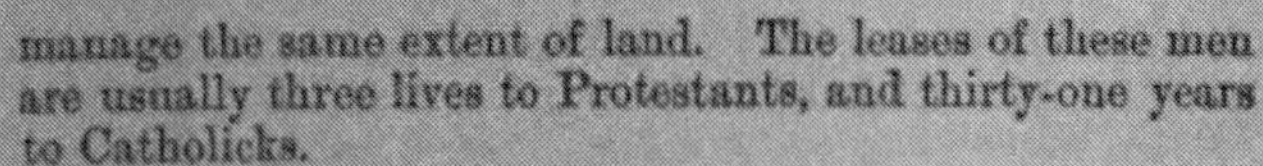

manage the same extent of land. The leases of these men are usually three lives to Protestants, and thirty-one years to Catholicks.

The tenantry in the more unimproved parts, such as Corke, Wicklow, Longford, and all the mountainous counties, where it is part tillage, and part pasturage, are generally in a very backward state. Their capitals are smaller than the class I just mentioned, and among them is chiefly found the practice of many poor cottars hiring large farms in partnership. They make their rents by a little butter, a little wool, a little corn, and a few young cattle and lambs. Their lands, at extreme low rents, are the most unimproved, (mountain and bog excepted,) in the kingdom. They have, however, more industry than capital; and with a very little management, might be brought greatly to improve their husbandry. I think they hold more generally from intermediate tenants than any other set; one reason why the land they occupy is in so waste a state. In the mountainous tracts, I saw instances of greater industry than in any other part of Ireland. Little occupiers, who can get leases of a mountain side, make exertions in improvement, which, though far enough from being complete, or accurate, yet prove clearly what great effects encouragement would have among them.

In the King's county, and also in some other parts, I saw many tracts of land, not large enough to be relet, which were occupied under leases for ever, very well planted and improved by men of substance and industry.

The poverty, common among the small occupying tenantry, may be pretty well ascertained from their general conduct in hiring a farm. They will manage to take one with a sum surprizingly small; they provide labour, which in England is so considerable an article, by assigning portions of land to cottars for their potatoe gardens, and keeping one or two cows for each of them. To lessen the live stock necessary, they will, whenever the neighbourhood enables them, take in the cattle at so much per month, or season, of any person that is deficient in pasturage at home, or of any labourers that have no land. Next, they will let out some old lay for grass potatoes to such labourers; and if they are in a county where corn-acres are known, they will do the same with some corn land. If there is any meadow on their farm, they will sell a part of it as the hay grows. By all these means the necessity of a full stock is very much lessened; and, by means of living themselves in the very poorest manner, and converting every pig, fowl, and even egg into cash, they will make up their rent, and get by very slow degrees into somewhat better circumstances. Where it is the custom to take in partnership, the difficulties are easier got over; for one man brings a few sheep, another a cow, a third a horse, a fourth a car and some seed potatoes, a fifth a few barrels of corn, and so on, until the farm among them is tolerably stocked, and hands upon it in plenty for the labour.

But it is from the whole evident, that they are uncommon masters of the art of overcoming difficulties by patience and contrivance. Travellers, who take a superficial view of them, are apt to think their poverty and wretchedness, viewed in the light of farmers, greater than they are. Perhaps there is an impropriety in considering a man merely as the occupier of such a quantity of land; and that, instead of the land, his capital should be the object of contemplation. Give the farmer of twenty acres in England no more capital than his brother in Ireland, and I will venture to say he will be much poorer, for he would be utterly unable to go on at all.

I shall conclude what I have to say upon this subject, with stating, in few words, what I think would prove a very advantageous conduct in landlords towards the poor tenantry of the kingdom; and I shall do this with the greater readiness, as I speak, not only as a passing traveller, but from a year's residence among several hundred tenants, whose circumstances and situation I had particular opportunities of observing.

Let me remark, that the power and influence of a resident landlord is so great in Ireland, that, whatever system he adopts, be it well or ill imagined, he is much more able to introduce and accomplish it than Englishmen can well have an idea of; consequently one may suppose him to determine more authoritatively than a person in a similar situation in this kingdom could do. The first object is a settled determination, never to be departed from, to let his farms only to the immediate occupier of the land, and, to avoid deceit, not to allow a cottar, herdsman, or steward, to have more than three or four acres on any of his farms. By no means to reject the little occupier of a few acres from being a tenant to himself, rather than annex his land to a larger spot. Having, by this previous step, eased these inferior tenantry of the burthen of the intermediate man, let him give out, and steadily adhere to it, that he shall insist on the regular and punctual payment of his rent, but shall take no personal service whatever. The meanest occupier to have a lease, and none shorter than twenty-one years, which I am inclined also to believe is long enough for his advantage. There will arise, in spite of his tenderness, a necessity of securing a regular payment of rent: I would advise him to distrain without favour or affection, at a certain period of deficiency. This will appear harsh only upon a superficial consideration. The object is to establish the system; but it will fall before it is on its legs, if founded on a landlord's forgiving arrears, or permitting them to encrease. He need not be apprehensive, since they who can, under disadvantages, pay the *jobber*, can certainly pay the *landlord* himself, when freed from those incumbrances. At all events, let him persist in this firmness, though it be the ruin of a few; for he must remember, that if he ruins five, he assuredly saves ten; he will, it is true, know the fall of a few, but many, with an intermediate tenant, might be destroyed without his knowing it. Such a steady regular conduct would infallibly have its effect, in animating all the tenantry of the estate to exert every nerve to be punctual; whereas favour shewn now and then would make every one, the least inclined to remissness, hope for its exertion towards himself, and every partial good would be attended with a diffusive evil; exceptions, however, to be made for very great and unavoidable misfortunes, clearly and undoubtedly proved. This stern administration on the one hand should be accompanied on the other with every species of encouragement to those who showed the least disposition to improve; premiums should be given, rewards adjudged, difficulties smoothed, and notice taken in the most flattering manner of those whose conduct merited it. I shall in another part of these papers point out in detail the advantageous systems; it is here only requisite to observe, that whatever novelties a landlord wishes to introduce, he should give seed gratis, and be at a part of the expence, promising to be at the whole loss if he is well satisfied it is really incurred. From various observations I am convinced that such a conduct would very rarely prove unsuccessful. The profit to a landlord would be immense; he would in the course of a lease find his tenantry paying a high rent, with greater ease to themselves, than they before yielded a low one.

A few considerable landlords, many years ago, made the experiment of fixing, at great expence, colonies of Palatines on their estates. Some of them I viewed, and made many enquiries. The scheme did not appear to me to answer. They had houses built for them; plots of land assigned to each at a rent of favour, assisted in stock, and all of them with leases for lives from the head landlord. The poor Irish are very rarely treated in this manner; when they are, they work much greater improvements than common among these Germans; witness Sir William Osborne's mountaineers![1] a few beneficial practices were introduced, but never travelled beyond their own farms; they were viewed with eyes too envious to allow them to be patterns, and it was human nature that it should be so: but encourage a few of your own poor, and if their practices thrive they will spread. I am convinced no country, whatever state it may be in, can be improved by colonies of foreigners; and whatever foreigner, as a superintendent of any great improvement, asks for colonies of his own countrymen to execute his ideas, manifests a mean genius and but little knowledge of the human heart; if he has talents he will find tools wherever he finds men, and make the natives of the country the means of encreasing their own happiness. Whatever he does then will live and take root; but if effected by foreign hands, it will prove a sickly and short-lived exotic; brilliant perhaps, for a time, in the eyes of the ignorant, but of no solid advantage to the country that employs him.

[1] See above, vol. i., p. 398 *sq.*

SECTION VI.

OF THE LABOURING POOR.

SUCH is the weight of the lower classes in the great scale of national importance, that a traveller can never give too much attention to every circumstance that concerns them; their welfare forms the broad basis of public prosperity; it is they that feed, cloath, enrich, and fight the battles of all the other ranks of a community; it is their being able to support these various burthens without oppression, which constitutes the general felicity; in proportion to their ease is the strength and wealth of nations, as public debility will be the certain attendant on their misery. Convinced that to be ignorant of their state and situation, in different countries, is to be deficient in the first rudiments of political knowledge, I have upon every occasion made the necessary enquiries, to get the best information circumstances will allow me. What passes daily, and even hourly, before our eyes, we are very apt entirely to overlook; hence the surprising inattention of various people to the food, cloathing, possessions and state of the poor, even in their own neighbourhood; many a question have I put to gentlemen upon these points, which were not answered without having recourse to the next cabbin; a source of information the more necessary, as I found upon various occasions that some gentlemen in Ireland are infected with the rage of adopting *systems* as well as those of England: with one party the poor are all starving, with the other they are deemed in a very tolerable situation, and a third, who look with an evil eye on the administration of the British Government, are fond of exclaiming at poverty and rags as proofs of the cruel treatment of Ireland. When truth is likely to be thus warped, a traveller must be very circumspect to *believe*, and very assiduous to *see*.

Places.	Rent of cabbin and garden.	Cow's grass rent.	Cows per family.
Dublin	1 8 0		
Celbridge	2 0 0		
Dollestown	2 0 0		
Summerhill			1 or 2
Slaine	2 0 0	2 0 0	
Packenham	1 10 0		
Tullamore	2 0 0		
Shaen Castle	1 5 0	1 5 0	
Ballynakill	1 0 0	1 10 0	
Kilfaine	3 3 0		1
Bargy and Forth	3 0 0		1
Mount Kennedy	2 10 0		1
Kilrue	1 10 0	1 10 0	
Hampton	2 10 0	1 10 0	2
Warrenstown	1 10 0	1 10 0	
Lecale	2 2 0		
Castle Caldwell	1 0 0	1 10 0	2
Longford	1 10 0	1 10 0	all
Strokestown	1 0 0	1 2 0	
Merera	1 0 0	1 10 0	
Moniva	1 10 0		
Woodlawn			3
Limerick	1 0 0		
Mallow	1 10 0	2 2 0	all
Dunkettle	1 12 6		
Coolmore	1 0 0		
Nedeen	1 2 9	2 0 0	
Adair	2 5 6		
Castle Oliver	2 0 0	2 2 6	
Tipperary	3 0 0	2 2 0	
Ballycanvan	1 10 0	1 7 0	
Gloster	1 10 0	1 5 0	
Johnstown	1 0 0	1 0 0	
Derry	1 10 0	1 10 0	
Mitchel's Town	1 10 0	1 10 0	
Average	1 13 10	1 11 3	

From the minutes of the journey it will be found, that there is no determinate quantity of land for the potatoe garden; it is usually an acre; sometimes half an acre, and -times one acre and an half; but according to the soil, quantity which is understood (right or wrong) to be necessary, is called the garden. The grass for a cow is for the green food only, the cottar himself finds or buys hay. From the blanks in the number of cows it is not to be implied that they have none, but that the information was not received.

But it is necessary here to explain the common cottar system of labour in Ireland, which much resembles that of Scotland until very lately; and which was probably the same all over Europe before arts and commerce changed the face of it. If there are cabbins on a farm they are the residence of the cottars; if there are none, the farmer marks out the potatoe gardens, and the labourers, who apply to him on his hiring the land, raise their own cabbins on such spots; in some places the farmer builds; in others he only assists them with the roof, &c., a verbal compact is then made, that the new cottar shall have his potatoe garden at such a rent, and one or two cows kept him at the price of the neighbourhood, he finding the cows. He then works with the farmer at the rate of the place, usually sixpence halfpenny a day, a tally being kept (half by each party) and a notch cut for every day's labour: at the end of six months, or a year, they reckon, and the balance is paid. The cottar works for himself as his potatoes require.

	£	s.	d.
The rates of . .	£1	13	10
And	1	11	3
Forming together .	3	5	1

for milk and potatoes appear to be very reasonable; if two cows are kept, it is only £4 16*s.* 4*d.*, from whence it is evident, as far merely as this charge goes, there is no oppression upon them which can ever amount to starving. In particular instances, where there is much inhumanity in the greater tenants, they are made to pay too high a rent for their gardens; and though the price at which their cows are supported may not appear high, yet they may be so poorly kept as to make it very unreasonable. I believe, from what I saw, that such instances are not uncommon.

Potatoes.

Places.	Expence per acre.			Product Barrels.	Price per Barrel.		Produce Value.			Prime cost.		Rent potatoe ground.		
	£	s.	d.		s.	d.	£	s.	d.	s.	d.	£	s.	d.
Dublin				65										
Celbridge				100	5	0						8	0	0
Dollestown	15	15	0	60			15	15	0	5	0	5	12	6
Summerhill				80								6	3	0
Slaine Castle	12	4	0	64	3	6	11	4	0	4	0	4	10	0
Headfort				85								4	10	0
Packenham	10	10	0	80						2	6	5	0	0
Mullengar to Tullespace				60										
Tullamore												6	0	0
General Walsh				176										
Near Athy	8	14	2	80	3	4	13	7	0	2	2			
Ballynakill	10	16	0	60	4	6				3	6			
Kilfaine	5	4	0	40										
Prospect				80	5	0								
Armagh				45										
Warrenstown				40										
Shaen Castle				87										
Lesly Hill	7	7	0	80	4	0	16	0	0	1	10			
North of ditto	8	5	6	75	4	0	15	0	0	2	0½			
Newtown Limavaddy							10	0	0					
Florence Court	7	7	5				12	16	0					
Farnham	13	0	4	60	7	6	22	10	0	4	4			
Longford				120	8	0								
Strokestown				50	8	0	20	0	0			5	5	0
Mercra	7	4	4				7	10	0			5	0	0
Westport	5	13	0				12	0	0					
Holymount												3	15	0
Moniva				50	4	0	10	0	0					
Woodlawn				60	4	0	12	0	0					
Drumoland				100										
Annsgrove												1	17	6
Mallow				42										
Dunkettle				50								4	15	0
Castle Martyr	6	4	0	70	3	0	10	10	0	1	9			
Coolmore				50										
Adair				60	8	0	24	0	0			6	16	6
Castle Oliver	15	3	2	150	4	0	30	0	0	2	0	4	10	0
Tipperary				90	5	0						6	0	0
Ballycanvan				60										
Furness	14	0	0	100	5	0	15	0	0	2	9			
Gloster	11	5	2	100	3	4	16	13	4	2	3	6	8	0

Places.	Expence per acre.			Product Barrels.	Price per Barrel.		Produce Value.			Prime cost.		Rent potatoe ground.		
	£	s.	d.		s.	d.	£	s.	d.	s.	d.	£	s.	d.
Johnstown	11	0	6	90	4	0	18	0	0	2	5	7	0	0
Derry				35								4	5	0
Callen	10	11	8	120	3	0	18	0	0	1	2½	6	0	0
Mitchelstown	6	0	7	60	4	4	13	0	0	2	0			
Cunningham Acre reduced.														
Armagh				58										
Warrenstown				51										
Shaen Castle				112										
Lesly Hill	9	9	0	103	4	0	20	11	0	1	10			
Ditto	10	12	0	96	4	0	19	5	0	2	0½			
English Acre reduced.														
Mallow				67										
Dunkettle				80								7	12	0
Castle Martyr	9	18	0	112	3	0	16	16	0	1	9			
Coolmore				80										
Averages	10	4	9	82	4	9	16	12	6	2	7½	5	10	2
Averages per English acre	6	7	6	52	4	9	10	7	0	2	7½	3	8	6

These tables together will enable the reader to have a pretty accurate idea of the expences at which the poor in Ireland are fed. The first column is the total expence of an acre of potatoes, the third is the price at which potatoes are bought and sold, for seed or food. The prime cost is the price formed by the first and second columns, being the rate at which they are eaten by those who raise them. The last column requires rather more explanation to those who were never in that country. There are a great many cabbins, usually by the roadside, or in the ditch, which have no potatoe gardens at all. Ireland being free from the curse of English poor-laws, the people move about the country and settle where they will. A wandering family will fix themselves under a dry bank, and with a few sticks, furze, fern, &c., make up a hovel much worse than an English pigstie, support themselves how they can, by work, begging and stealing; if the neighbourhood wants hands, or takes no notice of them, the hovel grows into a cabbin. In my rides about Mitchelstown, I have passed places in the road one day without any appearance of a habitation, and next morning found a hovel, filled with a man and woman, six or eight children, and a pig. These people are not kept by anybody as cottars, but are taken at busy seasons by the day or week, and paid in money; consequently, having no potatoe garden, they are necessitated every year to hire a spot from some neighbouring farmer; and, of the preceding table, the last column is the rent per acre paid for it. The cabbins in little towns are in the same situation.

I think £5 10*s.* 2*d.* for liberty to plant a crop so beneficial to the land as potatoes a very extravagant rent, and by no means upon a fair level with the other circumstances of the poor. The prime cost of two shillings and seven pence halpenny per barrel, generally of twenty stone, being equal to about eight pence the bushel of seventy pounds, is not a high price for the root, yet might it be much lower if they gave up their lazy bad method of culture, and adopted that of the plough, for the average produce of three hundred twenty-eight bushels, or eighty-two barrels per acre, compared with crops in England, is perfectly insignificant; yet, to gain this miserable produce, much old lay, and nineteen twentieths of all the dung in the kingdom is employed. A total alteration in this point is therefore much to be wished.

Relative to the cottar system, wherever it is found, it may be observed that the recompence for labour is *the means of living*. In England these are dispensed in money, but in Ireland in land or commodities. In the former country paying the poor with anything but money has been found so oppressive, that various and repeated statutes have been made to prohibit it. Is it to be considered in the same light in Ireland? this is a question which involves many considerations. First let me remark that the two modes of payment prohibited in England but common in Ireland, are not exactly the same, though upon similar principles.

In England it is the payment of manufacturing labourers in necessaries, as bread, candles, soap, &c. In Ireland it is a quantity of land for the support of a labourer a year. The former, it must strike every one, is more open to abuse, involving more complex accounts than the latter. The great question is, which system is most advantageous to the poor family, the payment to be in land for potatoes and milk, or in money, supposing the payment to be fairly made: here lies the discussion.

On one hand, the Irish labourer, in the very circumstance which gives him any appearance of plenty, the possession of cattle, is subjected to chances which must be heavy in proportion to his poverty; ill-fed cattle, we know from the experience of English commons, are very far from being so advantageous to a man as they at first seem; accidents happen without a resource to supply the loss, and leave the man much worse than him who, being paid in money, is independent of such events. But, to reverse the medal, there appear advantages, and very great ones, by being paid in land; he has plenty of articles of the utmost importance to the sustenance of a family, potatoes and milk. Generally speaking the Irish poor have a fair belly-full of potatoes, and they have milk the greatest part of the year. What I would particularly insist on here is the value of his labour being food not money; food not for himself only, but for his wife and children. An Irishman loves whisky as well as an Englisman does strong beer; but he cannot go on Saturday night to the whisky-house, and drink out the week's support of himself, his wife, and his children, not uncommon in the ale-house of the Englishman. It may indeed be said that we should not argue against a mode of payment because it may be abused, which is very true; but we certainly may reason against that which carries in its very principles the seed of abuse. That the Irishman's cow may be ill fed, is admitted; but, ill fed as it is, it is better than the no cow of the Englishman; the children of the Irish cabbin are nourished with milk, which, small as the quantity may be, is far preferable to the beer or vile tea which is the beverage of the English infant; for nowhere but in a town is milk to be bought. Farther, in a country where bread, cheese or meat, are the common food, it is consumed with great œconomy, and kept under lock and key, where the children can have no resort; but the case with potatoes is different, they are in greater plenty, the children help themselves; they are scarce ever seen about a cabbin without being in the act of eating them, it is their employment all day long. Another circumstance not to be forgotten, is the regularity of the supply. The crop of potatoes, and the milk of the cow is more regular in Ireland than the *price* at which the Englishman buys his food. In England complaints rise even to riots when the rates of provisions are high; but in Ireland the poor have nothing to do with prices; they depend not on prices, but crops of a vegetable very regular in its produce. Attend the English labourer when he is in sickness, he must then have resort to his savings; but those will be nought among nine tenths of the poor of a country that have a legal dependence on the parish; which therefore is best off, the Englishman supported by the parish, or the Irishman by his potato-bed and cow?

Money I am ready enough to grant has many advantages; but they depend almost entirely on the prudence with which it is expended. They know little of the human mind who suppose that the poor man with his seven or eight shillings on a Saturday night has not his temptations to be imprudent as well as his superior with as many hundreds or thousands a year. He has his alehouse, his brandy-shop, and skittle-ground, as much as the other his ball, opera, or masquerade. Examine the state of the English poor, and see if facts do not coincide here with theory; do we not see numbers of half-starved and half-cloathed families owing to the superfluities of ale and brandy, tea and sugar. An Irishman cannot do this in any degree; he can neither drink whisky from his potatoes, nor milk it from his cow.

But after all that can be said on this subject, the custom of both countries is consistent with their respective circumstances and situations. When great wealth from immense branches of industry has brought on a rapid circulation, and much of what is commonly called luxury, the more simple mode of paying labour with land can scarcely hold. It does not, however, follow that the poor are in that respect better off; other advantages of a different kind attend the evils of such a situation; among which, perhaps, the employment of the wife and all the children, are the greatest. In such a country, also, markets and shops will be established in every corner, where the poor may buy their necessaries without difficulty; but in Ireland there are neither one nor the other; the labourer there with his pay in his pocket would find nothing readily but whisky.

I have gone into this enquiry in order to satisfy the people of Ireland, that the mode there common of paying the labouring poor is consistent with the situation of the kingdom: whether it is good or bad, or better or worse than that of England, it is what will necessarily continue until a great increase of national wealth has introduced a more general circulation of money; they will then have the English mode with its defects as well as its advantages.

Food.

The food of the common Irish, potatoes and milk, have been produced more than once as an instance of the extreme poverty of the country; but this, I believe, is an opinion embraced with more alacrity than reflection. I have heard it stigmatized as being unhealthy, and not sufficiently nourishing for the support of hard labour; but this opinion is very amazing in a country, many of whose poor people are as athletic in their form, as robust, and as capable of enduring labour as any upon earth. The idleness seen among many, when working for those who oppress them, is a very contrast to the vigour and activity with which the same people work when themselves alone reap the benefit of their labour. To what country must we have recourse for a stronger instance than lime carried by little miserable mountaineers thirty miles on horse's back to the foot of their hills, and up the steeps on their own? When I see the people of a country, in spite of political oppression, with well-formed vigorous bodies, and their cottages swarming with children; when I see their men athletic, and their women beautiful, I know not how to believe them subsisting on an unwholesome food.

At the same time, however, that both reason and observation convince me of the justice of these remarks, I will candidly allow that I have seen such an excess in the laziness of great numbers, even when working for themselves, and such an apparent weakness in their exertions when encouraged to work, that I have had my doubts of the heartiness of their food. But here arise fresh difficulties; were their food ever so nourishing, I can easily conceive an habitual inactivity of exertion would give them an air of debility compared with a more industrious people. Though my residence in Ireland was not long enough to become a perfect master of the question, yet I have employed from twenty to fifty men for several months, and found their habitual laziness or weakness so great, whether working by measure or by day, that I am absolutely convinced 1*s.* 6*d.* and even 2*s.* a day in Suffolk or Hertfordshire much cheaper than sixpence halfpenny at Mitchelstown: It would not be fair to consider this as a representation of the kingdom, that place being remarkably backward in every species of industry and improvement; but I am afraid this observation would hold true in a less degree for the whole. But is this owing to habit or food? Granting their food to be the cause, it decides very little against potatoes, unless they were tried with good nourishing beer instead of their vile potations of whisky. When they are encouraged, or animate themselves to work hard, it is all by whisky, which, though it has a notable effect in giving a perpetual motion to their tongues, can have but little of that invigorating substance which is found in strong beer or porter; probably it has an effect as pernicious as the other is beneficial. One circumstance I should mention, which seems to confirm this; I have known the Irish reapers in Hertfordshire work as laboriously as any of our own men, and living upon potatoes which they procured from London, but drinking nothing but ale. If their bodies are weak I attribute it to whisky, not potatoes; but it is still a question with me whether their miserable working arises from any such weakness, or from an habitual laziness. A friend of mine always refused Irishmen work in Surrey, saying his bailiff could do nothing but settle their quarrels.

But of this food there is one circumstance which must ever recommend it, they have a bellyful; and that, let me add, is more than the superfluities of an Englishman leave to his family; let any person examine minutely into the receipt and expenditure of an English cottage, and he will find that tea, sugar, and strong liquors can come only from pinched bellies. I will not assert that potatoes are a better food than bread and cheese; but I have no doubt of a bellyfull of the one being much better than half a bellyfull of the other; still less have I that the milk of the Irishman is incomparably better than the small beer, gin, or tea of the Englishman; and this even for the father; how much better must it be for the poor infants! milk to them is nourishment, is health, is life.

If any one doubts the comparative plenty which attends the board of the poor natives of England and Ireland, let him attend to their meals; the sparingness with which our labourer eats his bread and cheese is well known; mark the Irishman's potatoe bowl placed on the floor, the whole family upon their hams around it, devouring a quantity almost incredible, the beggar seating himself to it with a hearty welcome, the pig taking his share as readily as the wife, the cocks, hens, turkies, geese, the cur, the cat, and perhaps the cow—and all partaking of the same dish. No man can often have been a witness of it without being convinced of the plenty, and I will add the chearfulness, that attends it.

Is it, or is it not a matter of consequence, for the great body of the people of a country to subsist upon that species of food which is produced in the greatest quantity by the smallest space of land? One need only to state, in order to answer the question. It certainly is an object of the highest consequence; what in this respect is the comparison between wheat or cheese, or meat and potatoes?

The minutes of the journey will enable us to shew this.

No. 1. At Shaen Castle, Queen's county, a barrel of potatoes lasts a family of six persons a week.

No 2. At Shaen Castle, Antrim, six people eat three bushels, and twenty pounds of oatmeal besides, in a week, twenty pounds of meal are equal to one bushel of potatoes; this therefore is a barrel also.

No. 3. Leslie Hill, a barrel of four bushels six persons a week.

No. 4. Near Giant's Causeway, a barrel six people eight days.

No. 5. Castle Caldwell, a barrel of eighteen stone six people a week.

No. 6. Gloster, a barrel five persons a week.

No. 7. Derry, five persons eat and waste two barrels a week.

No. 8. Cullen, two barrels six persons a week.

	Barrels.	Persons.	Days.
No. 1	1	6	7
2	1	6	7
3	1	6	7
4	1	6	8
5	1	6	7
6	1	5	7
7	2	5	7
8	2	6	7

A barrel is twenty stones, or two hundred and eighty pounds, which is the weight of four English bushels; the average of these accounts is nearly that quantity lasting a family of six people six days, which makes a year's food sixty barrels. Now the average produce of the whole kingdom being eighty-two barrels per acre, plantation measure, one acre does rather more than support eight persons the year through, which is five persons to the English acre. To feed on wheat those eight persons would require eight quarters, or two Irish acres, which at present, imply two more for fallow, or four in all.

When, however, I speak of potatoes and buttermilk being the food of the poor, the tables already inserted shew, that in some parts of the north that root forms their diet but for a part of the year, much oatmeal and some meat being consumed. I need not dwell on this, as there is nothing particular to attend to in it; whereas potatoes, as the staple dependence, is a peculiarity met with in no country but the other parts of Ireland.

Cloathing.

The common Irish are in general cloathed so very indifferently, that it impresses every stranger with a strong idea of universal poverty. Shoes and stockings are scarcely ever found on the feet of children of either sex; and great numbers of men and women are without them: a change however, in this respect, as in most others, is coming in; for there are many more of them with those articles of cloathing now than ten years ago.

An Irishman and his wife are much more solicitous to feed than to cloathe their children: whereas in England it is surprising to see the expence they put themselves to, to deck out children whose principal subsistence is tea. Very many of them in Ireland are so ragged that their nakedness is scarcely covered; yet are they in health and active. As to the want of shoes and stockings, I consider it as no evil, but a much more cleanly custom than the beastiality of stockings and feet that are washed no oftener than those of our own poor. Women are oftener without shoes than men; and by washing their cloathes no where but in rivers and streams, the cold, especially as they roast their legs in their cabbins till they are *fire* spotted, must swell them to a wonderful size, and horrid black and blue colour, always met with both in young and old. They stand in rivers and beat the linen against the great stones found there with a beetle.

I remarked generally, that they were not ill-dressed of Sundays and holidays, and that black or dark blue was almost the universal hue.

Habitations.

The cottages of the Irish, which are all called cabbins, are the most miserable looking hovels that can well be conceived: they generally consist of only one room: mud kneaded with straw is the common material of the walls; these are rarely above seven feet high, and not always above five or six; they are about two feet thick, and have only a door, which lets in light instead of a window, and should let the smoak out instead of a chimney, but they had rather keep it in: these two conveniences they hold so cheap, that I have seen them both stopped up in stone cottages, built by improving landlords; the smoak warms them, but certainly is as injurious to their eyes as it is to the complexions of the women, which in general in the cabbins of Ireland has a near resemblance to that of a smoaked ham. The number of the blind poor I think greater there than in England, which is probably owing to this cause.

The roofs of the cabbins are rafters, raised from the tops of the mud walls, and the covering varies; some are thatched with straw, potatoe stalks, or with heath, others only covered with sods of turf cut from a grass field; and I have seen several that were partly composed of all three; the bad repair these roofs are kept in, a hole in the thatch being often mended with turf, and weeds sprouting from every part, gives them the appearance of a weedy dunghill, especially when the cabbin is not built with regular walls, but supported on one, or perhaps on both sides by the banks of a broad dry ditch, the roof then seems a hillock, upon which perhaps the pig grazes. Some of these cabbins are much less and more miserable habitations than I have ever seen in England. I was told they were the worst in Connaught; but I found it an error; I saw many in Leinster to the full as bad; and in Wicklow, some worse than any in Connaught. When they are well roofed, and built, not of stones, ill put together, but of mud, they are much warmer, independently of smoak, than the clay, or lath and mortar cottages of England, the walls of which are so thin, that a rat hole lets in the wind, to the annoyance of the whole family. The furniture of the cabbins is as bad as the architecture; in very many consisting only of a pot for boiling their potatoes, a bit of a table, and one or two broken stools; beds are not found universally, the family lying on straw, equally partook of by cows, calves and pigs; though the luxury of sties is coming in in Ireland, which excludes the poor pigs from the warmth of the bodies of their master and mistress: I remarked little hovels of earth thrown up near the cabbins; and in some places they build their turf stacks hollow, in order to afford shelter to the hogs. This is a general description, but the exceptions are very numerous. I have been in a multitude of cabbins that had much useful furniture, and some even superfluous; chairs, tables, boxes, chests of drawers, earthen ware, and in short most of the articles found in a middling English cottage; but, upon enquiry, I very generally found that these acquisitions were all made within the last ten years; a sure sign of a rising national prosperity. I think the bad cabbins and furniture the greatest instances of Irish poverty; and this must flow from the mode of payment for labour, which makes cattle so valuable to the peasant, that every farthing they can spare is saved for their purchase; from hence also results another observation, which is, that the apparent poverty of it is greater than the real; for the house of a man that is master of four or five cows, will have scarce any thing but deficiencies; nay, I was in the cabbins of dairymen and farmers, not small ones, whose cabbins were not at all better, nor better furnished than those of the poorest labourer: before, therefore, we can attribute it to absolute poverty, we must take into the account the customs and inclinations of the people. In England a man's cottage will be filled with superfluities before he possesses a cow. I think the comparison much in favour of the Irishman; a hog is a much more valuable piece of goods than a set of tea things; and though his snout in a *crock*[1] of potatoes is an idea not so poetical as

——— Broken tea cups, wisely kept for shew,
Rang'd o'er the chimney, glistened in a row—

yet will the cottar and his family, at Christmas, find the solidity of it an ample recompence for the ornament of the other.

Live Stock.

In every part of the kingdom the common Irish have all sorts of live stock: the tables already inserted shew this in respect of cows. I should add here that pigs are yet more general; and poultry in many parts of the kingdom, especially Leinster, are in such quantities as amazed me, not only cocks and hens, but alse geese and turkies; this is owing probably to three circumstances; first, to the plenty of potatoes with which they are fed; secondly, to the warmth of the cabbins; and thirdly to the great quantity of spon-

[1] The iron pot of an Irish cabbin.

taneous white clover (*trifolium repens*) in almost all the fields, which much exceeds any thing we know in England; upon the seeds of this plant the young poultry rear themselves; much is sold, but a considerable portion eaten by the family, probably because they cannot find a market for the whole. Many of the cocks, hens, turkies and geese, have their legs tied together to prevent them from trespassing on the farmers' grounds. Indeed all the live stock of the poor man in Ireland is in this sort of thraldom; the horses are all hopping about, the pigs have a rope of straw from around their necks to their hind legs. In the county of Down they have an ingenious contrivance for a sheep just to feed down the grass of a ditch, a rope with a stake at each end, and the sheep tied to a ring, through which it passes; so that the animal can move from one end of the rope to the other, and eat whatever grows within two or three feet of it.

Price of Labour.

Places.	Hay and harvest.		Winter.		Year round.	Rise in Labour.
	s.	*d.*	*s.*	*d.*	*d.*	
Dublin					10	Twopence in 30 years.
Celbridge					8	
Kilcock	1	8	0	8		
Slaine	1	2			7½	Threepence in 10 years.
Headfort	0	9		7		
Packenham		10		6	7½	None.
Tullamore		8		4	5	None.
Shaen Castle, Queen's Co.		10		6	7	Very little.
Carlow	1	1		7½		One fifth in 20 years.
Kilfain		10½		6	7	One fourth in 20 years.
Taghmon	1	3	1	0		
Forth	1	0	0	9	6	A little in 20 years.
Prospect		10		5		Twopence in 20 years.
Mount Kennedy		10		8		One third in 20 years.
Ballybriggan					8½	One half in 20 years.
Market-hill		8[1]		8	8	Near double in 20 years.
Ardmagh						One fourth in 20 years.
Warrenstown		11		8	8	A little.
Portaferry		10		8	7	

[1] And board.

Places.	Hay and harvest.		Winter.	Year round.	Rise in Labour.
	s.	d.	d.	d.	
Shaen Castle, co. Antrim		9	8	8½	One third in 20 years.
Lesly Hill	1	2		9	Near double in 20 years.
Limmavady	1	0	8	9	
Innishoen		7	6	6½	None.
Clonleigh		10[1]		6	One third in 20 years.
Mount Charles		7	6		One penny in 20 years.
Castle Caldwell . . .		7	7	7	
Castle Cool		0[1]	7	7	
Belle Isle		0[1]	0[1]	6[1]	
Florence Court . . .		8	6	8	Twopence a day in 20 years.
Farnham	1	0	6	6	
Strokestown		6[1]	6	6	None.
Ballyna		6	4	5	One sixth in 20 years.
Mercra		8	6	6	
Fortland.		8		5½	
Killala		6	4½	5½	
Westport		6	4	5	One third in 20 years.
Moniva		6	5		One sixth in 20 years.
Drumoland		6	6	6	None.
Doneraile		8[1]	6½	6½	One third in 20 years.
Castle Martyr		8	6	6	One third in ditto.
Nedeen		6	6	6	One third in ditto.
Tarbat		6	6	6	One penny in ditto.
Adair		6	5		One third in ditto.
Castle Oliver		6	5	6	One penny a day in ditto.
Tipperary		6	5	6	
Curraghmore		6	5		
Waterford		6½	6½	6½	
Furness		8	7		One penny a day.
Gloster				6	One third in 20 years.
Johnstown		8	6½	5	Considerable.
Derry		6½	5		None.
Castle Lloyd				5½	One penny a day.
Mitchel's Town . . .		6½	6½	6½	1½d. a day in 5 years.
Average		8¾	6½	6½	1⅔d. in 20 years.

[1] And board.

The rise is very near a fourth in twenty years; and it is remarkable that, in my Eastern Tour through England (vol. 4, p. 338). I found the rise of labour one fourth in eighteen years; from which it appears, that the two kingdoms, in this respect, have been nearly on a par.

Places.	Carpenter.		Mason.		Thatcher.	
	s.	d.	s.	d.	s.	d.
Dublin	2	3	2	0		
Lutrell's Town	2	3	2	0		
Slaine	2	0	2	0	1	6
Packenham	1	8	1	10		
Shaens Castle, Queen's Co.	2	0	2	0		
Kilfain	1	3	1	3		
Forth	2	0	2	0	2	0
Prospect	2	0	2	0	1	0
Mount Kennedy	2	3	2	0		
Market Hill	2	2	1	10		
Armagh	2	2	2	0		
Shaen Castle	1	9	2	0	3	6
Limavaddy	2	0	2	0	2	0
Clonleigh	2	0	2	0	5	1
Mount Charles	2	2	2	2	1	6
Castle Caldwell	2	0	1	10	1	6
Florence Court	1	9	1	9	1	1
Farnham	2	2	2	2	1	6
Strokestown	2	0	2	0	1	0
Ballynogh	1	4	1	10	1	0
Mercra	1	6	1	7	1	7½
Fortland			1	6		
Kilalla	1	6	1	6	1	4
Westport	1	6	1	7	0	10
Moniva	1	7	1	7	1	4
Drumoland	1	6	1	6	1	0
Donneraile	1	6	1	6	1	0
Corke	1	6	1	6	1	6
Nedeen	1	4	1	4	1	0
Tarbat	1	6	1	6	1	0
Castle Oliver	1	6	1	6	1	0
Tipperary	1	6	1	6	1	6
Curraghmore	1	9	1	9	0	10
Waterford	2	0	2	0	0	6
Furness	2	0	2	0	1	6
Gloster	1	6	1	8		
Johnstown	1	7½	1	7½		
Derry	1	6	1	6		
Castle Lloyd	1	8	1	8	1	0
Mitchel's Town	1	6	1	6	1	0
Average	1	9	1	9	1	3

When it is considered that common labour in Ireland is but little more than a third of what it is in England, it may appear extraordinary that artizans are paid nearly, if not full, as high as in that kingdom.

Oppression.

Before I conclude this article of the common labouring poor in Ireland, I must observe, that their happiness depends not merely upon the payment of their labour, their cloaths, or their food; the subordination of the lower classes, degenerating into oppression, is not to be overlooked. The poor in all countries, and under all governments, are both paid and fed; yet is there an infinite difference between them in different ones. This enquiry will by no means turn out so favourable as the preceding articles. It must be very apparent to every traveller through that country, that the labouring poor are treated with harshness, and are in all respects so little considered, that their want of importance seems a perfect contrast to their situation in England, of which country, comparatively speaking, they reign the sovereigns. The age has improved so much in humanity, that even the poor Irish have experienced its influence, and are every day treated better and better; but still the remnant of the old manners, the abominable distinction of religion, united with the oppressive conduct of the little country gentlemen, or rather vermin of the kingdom, who never were out of it, altogether bear still very heavy on the poor people, and subject them to situations more mortifying than we ever behold in England. The landlord of an Irish estate, inhabited by Roman Catholicks, is a sort of despot who yields obedience, in whatever concerns the poor, to no law but that of his will. To discover what the liberty of a people is, we must live among them, and not look for it in the statutes of the realm: the language of written law may be that of liberty, but the situation of the poor may speak no language but that of slavery; there is too much of this contradiction in Ireland; a long series of oppressions, aided by many very ill-judged laws, have brought landlords into a habit of exerting a very lofty superiority, and their vassals into that of an almost unlimited submission: speaking a language that is despised, professing a religion that is abhorred, and being disarmed, the poor find themselves in many cases slaves even in the bosom of *written* liberty. Landlords that have resided much abroad, are usually humane in their ideas; but the habit of tyranny naturally contracts the mind, so that even in this polished age, there are instances of a severe carriage towards the poor, which is quite unknown in England.

A landlord in Ireland can scarcely invent an order which a servant labourer or cottar dares to refuse to execute. Nothing satisfies him but an unlimited submission. Disrespect or any thing tending towards sauciness he may punish with his cane or his horsewhip with the most perfect security; a poor man would have his bones broke if he offered to lift his hand in his own defence. Knocking down is spoken of in the country in a manner that makes an Englishman stare. Landlords of consequence have assured me that many of their cottars would think themselves honoured by having their wives and daughters sent for to the bed of their master; a mark of slavery that proves the oppression under which such people must live.[1] Nay, I have heard anecdotes of the lives of people being made free with, without any apprehension of the justice of a jury. But let it not be imagined that this is common; formerly it happened every day, but law gains ground. It must strike the most careless traveller to see whole strings of cars whipt into a ditch by a gentleman's footman, to make way for his carriage; if they are overturned or broken in pieces, no matter, it is taken in patience; were they to complain they would perhaps be horsewhipped. The execution of the laws lies very much in the hands of justices of the peace, many of whom are drawn from the most illiberal class in the kingdom. If a poor man lodges a complaint against a gentleman, or any animal that chuses

[1] This, however, is altogether incredible; for, whatever may have been the faults of the poor Irish in other respects, in the matter of domestic purity the testimony to their high standard is unanimous. Young must have been misled by the boastful language of some of these "landlords of consequence"; who, after all, state no positive facts, but only express their opinion as to what the people, whom they despised, would be ready to do under certain circumstances.

to call itself a gentleman, and the justice issues out a summons for his appearance, it is a fixed affront, and he will infallibly be *called out*. Where MANNERS are in conspiracy against LAW, to whom are the oppressed people to have recourse? It is a fact that a poor man having a contest with a gentleman must—but I am talking nonsense, they know their situation too well to think of it; they can have no defence but by means of protection from one gentleman against another, who probably protects his vassal as he would the sheep he intends to eat.

The colours of this picture are not charged. To assert that all these cases are common would be an exaggeration; but to say that an unfeeling landlord will do all this with impunity is to keep strictly to truth: and what is liberty but a farce and a jest if its blessings are received as the favour of kindness and humanity, instead of being the inheritance of RIGHT?

Consequences have flowed from these oppressions which ought long ago to have put a stop to them. In England we have heard much of Whiteboys, Steelboys, Oakboys, Peep-of-day-boys, &c. But these various insurgents are not to be confounded, for they are very different. The proper distinction in the discontents of the people is into Protestant and Catholick. All but the Whiteboys were among the manufacturing Protestants in the north: the Whiteboys Catholick labourers in the south. From the best intelligence I could gain, the riots of the manufacturers had no other foundation, but such variations in the manufacture as all fabrics experience, and which they had themselves known and submitted to before. The case, however, was different with the Whiteboys; who, being labouring Catholicks, met with all those oppressions I have described, and would probably have continued in full submission, had not very severe treatment in respect of tythes, united with a great speculative rise of rents about the same time, blown up the flame of resistance; the atrocious acts they were guilty of made them the object of general indignation. Acts were passed for their punishment which seemed calculated for the meridian of Barbary; this arose to such a height that by one they were to be hanged under certain circumstances without the common formalities of a trial, which, though repealed the following sessions, marks the spirit of punishment; while others remain yet the law of the land, that would, if executed, tend more to raise than quell an insurrection. From all which it is manifest that the gentlemen of Ireland never thought of a radical cure, from overlooking the real cause of the disease, which in fact lay in themselves, and not in the wretches they doomed to the gallows. Let them change their own conduct entirely, and the poor will not long riot. Treat them like men who ought to be as free as yourselves: put an end to that system of religious persecution which for seventy years has divided the kingdom against itself; in these two circumstances lies the cure of insurrection; perform them completely, and you will have an affectionate poor, instead of oppressed and discontented vassals.

A better treatment of the poor in Ireland is a very material point to the welfare of the whole British Empire. Events may happen which may convince us fatally of this truth—If not, oppression must have broken all the spirit and resentment of men. By what policy the Government of England can for so many years have permitted such an absurd system to be matured in Ireland, is beyond the power of plain sense to discover.

Emigrations.

Before the American war broke out, the Irish and Scotch emigrations were a constant subject of conversation in England, and occasioned much discourse even in Parliament. The common observation was, that if they were not stopped, those countries would be ruined; and they were generally attributed to a great rise of rents. Upon going over to Ireland I determined to omit no opportunities of discovering the cause and extent of this emigration; and my information, as may be seen in the minutes of the journey, was very regular. I have only a few general remarks to make on it here.

The spirit of emigrating in Ireland appeared to be confined to two circumstances, the Presbyterian religion, and the linen manufacture. I heard of very few emigrants except among manufacturers of that persuasion. The Catholicks never went; they seem not only tied to the country but almost to the parish in which their ancestors lived. As to the emigration in the north, it was an error in England to suppose it a novelty which arose with the increase in rents. The contrary was the fact; it had subsisted, perhaps, forty years; insomuch that at the ports of Belfast, Derry, &c., the *passenger trade* as they called it, had long been a regular branch of commerce, which employed several ships, and consisted in carrying people to America. The increasing population of the country made it an increasing trade; but when the linen trade was low, the *passenger trade* was always high. At the time of Lord Donegal's letting his estate in the north the linen business suffered a temporary decline, which sent great numbers to America, and gave rise to the error that it was occasioned by the increase of his rents: the fact, however, was otherwise; for great numbers of those who went from his lands actually sold those leases for considerable sums, the hardship of which was supposed to have driven them to America. Some emigration, therefore, always existed, and its increase depended on the fluctuations of linen; but as to the *effect* there was as much error in the conclusions drawn in England as before in the *cause*.

It is the misfortune of all manufactures worked for a foreign market to be upon an insecure footing; periods of declension will come, and when in consequence of them great numbers of people are out of employment, the best circumstance is their enlisting in the army or navy; and it is the common result; but unfortunately the manufacture in Ireland (of which I shall have occasion to speak more hereafter) is not confined, as it ought to be, to towns, but spreads into all the cabbins of the country. Being half farmers, half manufacturers, they have too much property in cattle, &c., to enlist when idle; if they convert it into cash it will enable them to pay their passage to America, an alternative always chosen in preference to the military life. The consequence is, that they must live without work till their substance is quite consumed before they will enlist. Men who are in such a situation that from various causes they cannot work and won't enlist, should emigrate; if they stay at home they must remain a burthen upon the community; emigration should not, therefore, be condemned in states so ill-governed as to possess many people willing to work, but without employment.

SECTION VII.

OF RELIGION.

THE history of the two religions in Ireland is too generally known to require any detail introductory to the subject. The conflict for two centuries occasioned a scene of devastation and bloodshed; till at last, by the arms of king William, the decision left the uncontrouled power in the hands of the Protestants. The landed property of the kingdom had been greatly changed in the period of the reigns of Elizabeth and James I. Still more under Cromwell, who parcelled out an immense proportion of the kingdom to the officers of his army, the ancestors of great numbers of the present possessors: the colonels of his regiments left estates which are now eight and ten thousand a year; and I know several gentlemen of two and three thousand pounds a year at present, which they inherited from captains in the same service. The last forfeitures were incurred in that war which stripped and banished James II. Upon the whole, nineteen twentieths of the kingdom changed hands from Catholic to Protestant. The lineal descendants of great families, once possessed of vast property, are now to be found all over the kingdom in the lowest situation, working as cottars for the great-great-grandsons of men, many of whom were of no greater account in England than these poor labourers are at present, on that property which was once their own. So entire an overthrow, and change of landed possession, is, within the period, to be found in scarce any country in the world. In such great revolutions of property the ruined proprietors have usually been extirpated or banished; but in Ireland the case was otherwise: families were so numerous and so united in clans, that the heir of an estate was always known; and it is a fact that in most parts of the kingdom the descendants of the old land-owners regularly transmit by testamentary deed the memorial of their right to those estates which once belonged to their families. From hence it results that the question of religion has always in Ireland been intimately connected with the right to and possession of the landed property of the kingdom; and has probably received from this source a degree of acrimony, not at all wanting to influence the superstitious prejudices of the human mind.

Flushed with success after the victory of the Boyne, and animated with the recollection of recent injuries, it would not have been surprizing if the triumphant party had exceeded the bounds of moderation towards the Catholick; but the amazing circumstance is that the great category of persecuting laws was not framed during the life of that monarch who wisely was a friend to toleration: if ever such a system as would crush the minds of a conquered people into a slavish submission was necessary, it must have been under that new, and in many respects weak establishment, when the late conflict might have been an apparent justification: but why such a system should be embraced six or seven years after the death of king William is not so easy to be accounted for.

By the laws of discovery, as they are called:

1. The whole body of Roman Catholicks are absolutely disarmed.

2. They are incapacitated from purchasing land.

3. The entails of their estates are broken, and they gavel among the children.

4. If one child abjures that religion he inherits the whole estate, though he is the youngest.

5. If the son abjures the religion, the father has no power over his estate, but becomes a pensioner on it in favour of such son.

6. No Catholick can take a lease for more than thirty-one years.

7. If the rent of any Catholick is less than two thirds of the full improved value, whoever discovers takes the benefit of the lease.

8. Priests who celebrate mass to be transported, and if they return to be hanged.

9. A Catholick having a horse in his possession above the value of five pound, to forfeit the same to the discoverer.

10. By a construction of Lord Hardwick's, they are incapacitated from lending money on mortgage.[1]

The preceding catalogue is very imperfect, but here is an exhibition of oppression fully sufficient. The great national objects in framing laws against the profession and practice of any religion, may be reduced to three heads. 1st. The

[1] For a fuller account of the oppression of the Irish Catholics the reader may be referred to Henry Parnell's "History of the Penal Laws" (1808); but a passage from Sydney Smith's Essay on Ireland ("Edinburgh Review," 1820) gives a more graphic summary. "The great misfortune of Ireland is that the mass of the people have been given up for a century to a handful of Protestants, by whom they have been treated as helots, and subjected to every species of persecution and disgrace. . . . During the reigns of George I. and George II. the Irish Roman Catholics were disabled from holding any civil or military office, from voting at elections, from admission into corporations, from practising law or physic. A younger brother by turning Protestant might deprive his elder brother of his birth-right; by the same process he might force his father, under the name of a liberal provision, to yield up to him a part of his landed property; and, if an eldest son, he might in the same way reduce his father's fee-simple to a life estate. A Papist was disabled from purchasing freehold lands, and even from holding long leases, and any person might take his Catholic neighbour's horse by paying £5 for it. If the child of a Catholic father turned Protestant, he was taken away from his father and put into the hands of a Protestant relation. No Papist could purchase a freehold, or a lease for more than thirty years, or inherit from an intestate Protestant, nor from an intestate Catholic, nor dwell in Limerick or Galway, nor hold an advowson, nor buy an annuity for life. £50 was given for discovering a Popish archbishop, £30 for a Popish clergyman, and 10s. for a schoolmaster. No one was allowed to be trustee for Catholics; no Catholic was allowed to take more than two apprentices; no Papist to be solicitor or sheriff, or to serve on Grand Juries. Horses of Papists might be seized for the militia; for which militia Papists were to pay double, and to find Protestant substitutes. Papists were prohibited from being present at vestries, or from being high or petty constables; and, when resident in towns, they were compelled to find Protestant watchmen. Barristers and solicitors marrying Catholics were exposed to the penalties of Catholics. Persons plundered by privateers during a war with any Popish prince were reimbursed by a levy on the Catholic inhabitants where they lived. All Popish priests celebrating marriages contrary to the George I. cap. 3, were to be hanged."

propagation of the dominant faith. 2nd. Internal security. 3rd. National prosperity. The fairest way to judge of the laws of Ireland will be to enquire how far they have answered any or all of these ends.

That it is a desirable object in some respects to have a people, if not all of one persuasion, at least in good friendship and brotherhood as to religion, is undeniable. Though I think there are reasons against wishing a whole kingdom to possess only one similar faith. It excludes a variety of disquisitions which exercise and animate the talents of mankind; it encourages the priests of the national religion to a relaxation of their studies, their activity, and even their morals; and tends to introduce a lazy, wretched, vicious, and ignorant clergy: it is opposition and contrast that sharpen the wits of men.

But waving these objections, and considering the question only in a political view, I admit that such a similarity of worship, as is followed by laws equal to the whole community, to be an advantage; let us therefore examine whether the Irish intolerant laws have had the effect or not.

That they have lessened the landed property in the hands of the Catholicks is certain; their violence could not have had any other effect; but not, however, to such a degree as might have been imagined. There are principles of honour, religion, and ties of blood, too powerful for tyrannic laws to overcome, and which have prevented their full effect. I am not convinced that the conversion of the land-owners, while all the rabble retained their religion, was an advantage to the kingdom. Great possessions gave those landlords an interest in the public welfare, which in emergencies of danger might induce them to use their influence to keep their dependants quiet; but when none are connected with them richer than themselves, and the whole party consisting of a poor and half-ruined peasantry, and priests almost as poor as themselves, what tie, or what call is there upon them to restrain the dictates of resentment and revenge? At this day the best subjects among the Catholicks, —and many there are very much to be depended on, notwithstanding all their oppressions,—are the men of landed property: how impolitick to wish to lessen the number!

to be desirous of cutting off two millions of peasantry from every possible connection that can influence their submission. The same observation is applicable to mortgages, and in short to all investments of money within the kingdom. Surely the obedience of a man who has property in the realm is much securer than if all he is worth is in the English or Dutch funds! While property lay exposed to the practices of power, the great body of the people, who had been stripped of their all, were more enraged than converted: they adhered to the persuasion of their forefathers with the steadiest and most determined zeal; while the priests, actuated by the spirit of a thousand inducements, made proselytes among the common Protestants in defiance of every danger. And the great glaring fact yet remains, and is even admitted by the warmest advocates for the laws of discovery, that the established religion has not gained upon the Catholick in point of numbers, but on the contrary, that the latter have been rather on the increase. Public lists have been returned in the several dioceses which confirm this fact; and the intelligence I received on my journey spoke the same language.

Now, as it is the great body of the common people that form the strength of a country when willing subjects, and its weakness when ill-affected, this fact is a decision of the question: after seventy years undisturbed operation, the system adopted in Queen Anne's reign has failed in this great end and aim, and meets at this day with a more numerous and equally determined body of Catholicks as it had to oppose when it was first promulgated. Has not the experience of every age and every nation proved that the effect is invariable and universal? Let a religion be what it may, and under whatever circumstances, no system of persecution ever yet had any other effect than to confirm its professors in their tenets, and spread their doctrines instead of restraining them. Thus the great plea of the Roman Catholick priests, and their merit with their congregations, are the dangers they hazard, and the persecutions they suffer for the sake of their faith; arguments that ever had and ever will have weight, while human nature continues formed of its present materials.

The question of internal security is decided almost as

soon as named: the submission of the Catholicks is yet felt to be so much constrained, that no idea has been formed that their being trusted with arms is consistent with the safety of the kingdom. Laws founded in the very spirit of persecution, and receiving an edge in their operation from the unlimited power assumed by the Protestant landlord, are strangely calculated to conciliate the affection, or secure the loyalty of a people. All the emotions of the heart of man revolt at such an idea. It was the opinion of a vast majority of the gentlemen I conversed with on the subject, that no people could be worse affected; all Ireland knows and agrees in the fact; nay, the arguments for a continuation of the laws of discovery are founded on the principle, that the lower classes of the Catholicks are not to be trusted. Is not this declaring that the disarmed, disgusted multitude, have not lost in their misfortunes the importance of their numbers? The fears of an invasion speak the strength of the oppressed, and the extent of the oppression.

The disturbances of the Whiteboys, which lasted ten years, in spite of every exertion of legal power, were in many circumstances very remarkable; and in none more so than the surprizing intelligence among the insurgents where ever found: it was universal, and almost instantaneous: the numerous bodies of them, at whatever distance from each other, seemed animated with one soul; and not an instance was known in that long course of time of a single individual betraying the cause; the severest threats, and the most splendid promises of reward, had no other effect but to draw closer the bands which connected a multitude, to all appearance so desultory. It was then evident that the iron rod of oppression had been far enough from securing the obedience, or crushing the spirit of the people. And all reflecting men, who consider the value of religious liberty, will wish it never may have that effect; will trust in the wisdom of Almighty God for teaching man to respect even those prejudices of his brethren that are imbibed as sacred rights from their earliest infancy, that by dear-bought experience of the futility and ruin of the attempt, the persecuting spirit may cease, and TOLERATION establish that harmony and security which fourscore years' experience has told us is not to be purchased at the expence of HUMANITY!

But if these exertions of a succession of ignorant legislatures have failed continually in propagating the religion of government, or in adding to the internal security of the kingdom, much more have they failed in the great object of national prosperity. The only considerable manufacture in Ireland, which carries in all its parts the appearance of industry, is the linen; and it ought never to be forgotten that this is solely confined to the Protestant parts of the kingdom; yet we may see from the example of France and other countries that there is nothing in the Roman Catholick religion itself that is incompatible with manufacturing industry. The poor Catholicks in the south of Ireland spin wool very generally, but the purchasers of their labour, and the whole worsted trade, is in the hands of the Quakers of Clonmell, Carrick, Bandon, &c. The fact is, the professors of that religion are under such discouragements that they cannot engage in any trade which requires both industry and capital. If they succeed and make a fortune, what are they to do with it? They can neither buy land, nor take a mortgage, nor even fine down the rent of a lease. Where is there a people in the world to be found industrious under such a circumstance? But it seems to be the meaning, wish, and intent of the discovery laws, that none of them should ever be rich. It is the principle of that system that wealthy subjects would be nuisances; and therefore every means is taken to reduce and keep them to a state of poverty. If this is not the intention of the laws, they are the most abominable heap of self-contradictions that ever were issued in the world. They are framed in such a manner that no Catholick shall have the inducement to become rich. But if, in spite of these laws, he should accidentally gain wealth, that the whole kingdom should not afford him a possibility of investing it. Take the laws and their execution into one view, and this state of the case is so true, that they actually do not seem to be so much levelled at the religion, as at the property that is found in it. By the law a priest is to be transported and hanged for reading mass; but the mass is very readily left to them with impunity. Let the same priest, however, make a fortune by his mass; and from that moment he is the object of persecution. The domineering aristocracy of five hundred thousand Protestants feel the sweets of having two millions of slaves; they have not the least objection to the tenets of that religion which keeps them by the law of the land in subjection; but property and slavery are too incompatible to live together. Hence the special care taken that no such thing should arise among them.

I must be free to own that when I have heard gentlemen who have favoured the laws as they now stand, urge the dangerous tenets of the Church of Rome, quote the cruelties which have disgraced that religion in Ireland, and led them into the common routine of declamation on that side the question (I cannot call it argument, for I never yet heard anything that deserved the name); when I have been a witness to such conversations, I could not but smile to see subscriptions handed about for building a mass-house, at the very time that the heaviest vengeance of the law fully executed fell on those who possessed a landed property, or ventured a mortgage upon it.

It is no superficial view I have taken of this matter in Ireland; and being at Dublin at the time a very trifling part of these laws was agitated in Parliament, I attended the debates, with my mind open to conviction, and auditor for the mere purpose of information: I have conversed on the subject with some of the most distinguished characters in the kingdom, and I cannot after all but declare that the scope, purport, and aim of the laws of discovery, as executed, are not against the Catholick religion, which increases under them, but against the industry, and property of whoever professes that religion. In vain has it been said that consequence and power follow property, and that the attack is made in order to wound the doctrine through its property. If such was the intention, I reply, that seventy years' experience prove the folly and futility of it. Those laws have crushed all the industry, and wrested most of the property from the Catholicks; but the religion triumphs; it is thought to encrease. Those who have * handed about calculations to prove a decrease, admit on the face of them that it will require FOUR THOUSAND YEARS to make converts of the whole, supposing that work to go on in future, as it has in the past time. But the whole pretence is an affront to common sense, for it implies that you will lessen a religion by persecuting it: all history and experience condemn such a proposition.

The system pursued in Ireland has had no other tendency but that of driving out of the kingdom all the personal wealth of the Catholicks, and prohibiting their industry within it. The face of the country, every object in short which presents itself to the eye of a traveller, tells him how effectually this has been done. I urge it not as an argument, the whole kingdom speaks it as a fact. We have seen that this conduct has not converted the people to the religion of government; and instead of adding to the internal security of the realm, it has endangered it; if therefore it does not add to the national prosperity, for what purpose but that of private tyranny could it have been embraced and persisted in? Mistaken ideas of private interest account for the actions of individuals; but what could haye influenced the British Government to permit a system which must inevitably prevent the island from ever becoming of the importance which nature intended?

Relative to the national welfare, it must appear extremely evident to the unprejudiced, that an aristocracy of five hundred thousand Protestants, crushing the industry of two millions of poor Catholicks, can never advance the public interest. Secure the industry of your people, and leave their religion to itself. It is their hands, not their faith, you want; but do not tie these behind them, and then ask why they are not better employed. How is agriculture to flourish, manufactures to be established, or commerce to extend, in a dependant country labouring under great disadvantages, if the united capitals, industry, activity and attention of the whole community be not employed for such purposes? When the territory of an island lies in such a wretched state, that, though blessed with a better soil, it yields on comparison with England as only two to five; when manufactures are of so sickly a growth as to be confined almost to one province; and when trade is known to exist only by the ships of other countries appearing in the harbours; while a kingdom is in such a situation, is it wisdom to persist in a system which has no other effect than to clog, defeat, or exterminate the capital and industry of four fifths of the inhabitants! Surely the gentlemen of that country, when they complain of restricted commerce, and the remittance of the rentals of the absentees to England, cannot be thought serious in lamenting the situation of their country, while they continue wedded to that internal ruin which is the work of their own hands, and the favourite child of their most active exertions. Complain not of restrictions while you yourselves inforce the most enormous restriction; and what are the body of absentees when compared with the absence of industry and wealth from the immense mass of two millions of subjects? I should be well founded in the assertion that both these evils, great and acknowledged as they are, are trifles when compared with the poverty and debility which results from the oppression of the Roman Catholicks. Encourage the industry of those two millions of idle people, and the wealth arising from it will make ample amends for most of the evils complained of in Ireland. This remedy is in your hands; you have no rivals to fear; no ministers to oppose you.

Think of the loss to Ireland of so many Catholicks of small property, resorting to the armies of France, Spain, Sardinia, and Austria, for employment. Can it be imagined, that they would be so ready to leave their own country, if they could stay in it with any prospect of promotion, successful industry, or even liberal protection? It is known they would not; and that under a different system, instead of adding strength to the enemies of this Empire, they would be among the foremost to enrich and defend it. Upon the whole it appears sufficiently clear that in these three great objects, of making the religion of government general, internal security, and national prosperity, the laws of discovery have totally failed; a long series of experience enables us to discuss the subject by a reference to facts, instead of a reliance on theory and argument; the language of those facts is so uniform, that private interest must unite with habitual prejudice, to permit it for a moment to be misunderstood.

Upon the general question it has been asserted by the friends of the law, that gentlemen in England are apt very much to mistake the point from being ignorant of Irish Popery, which, from the ignorance of the people, is more bigoted than anything known in the sister kingdom; also that the Papists in England are not claimants of all the landed property, which is the case in Ireland.

Both these observations are too shallow to bear the least examination; oppression has reduced the major part of the Irish Catholicks to a poor ignorant rabble; you have made them ignorant, and then it is cried, "Your ignorance is a reason for keeping you so; you shall live and die, and remain in ignorance, for you are too wretched to be enlightened." Take it as argument, or humanity, it is of a most precious kind. In all other parts of Europe the Catholick religion has grown mild and even tolerant; a softer humanity is seen diffused in those countries, once the most bigoted; Spain and Portugal are no longer what they were. Had property taken its natural course in Ireland, the religion of the Catholicks there would have improved with that of their neighbours. Ignorance is the child of poverty; and you cannot expect the modern improvements, which have resulted from disseminated industry and wealth, should spread among a sect, whose property you have detached, and whose industry you have crushed: to stigmatize them with ignorance and bigotry, therefore, is to reproach them with the evils which your own conduct has entailed; it is to bury them in darkness, and vilify them because they are not enlightened.

But they claim your estates; they do so, as steadily at this moment as they did fourscore years ago; your system therefore has utterly failed even in this respect. Has the rod of oppression obliterated the memory or tradition of better days? Has severity conciliated the forgiveness of past, perhaps necessary, injuries? Would protection, favour, and encouragement add fresh stings to their resentments? None can assert it. Ample experience ought to have convinced you, that the harshness of the law has not annihilated a single claim; if claims could have restored their estates, they would have regained them before now: but here, as I shewed before, the laws have weakened instead of strengthening the Protestant interest; had a milder system encouraged their industry and property, they would have had something to lose, and would, with an enemy in the land, have thought twice before they joined him; in such a case whatever they had got would be endangered, and the hope of being reinstated in antient possessions, being distant and hazardous, present advantage might have induced them not only to be quiet, but to have defended the government, under whose humanity they found protection and happiness. Compare such a situation with the present, and then determine whether the system you have persisted in has added a jot to the security of your possessions.

But, let me ask, if these Catholick claims on the landed property were not full as strong an argument in the reign of King William as they are at present? The moment of conflict was then but just decided; if ever rancour and danger could arise from them, that certainly was the season of apprehension: but it is curious to observe that that wise monarch would permit few Acts to pass to oppress the Catholicks. It was not until the reign of Anne that the great system of oppression was opened: if therefore these laws were not necessary from the Revolution to the death of King William,—and the experience of that reign tells us they were not,—most certainly they cannot be so at present.

The enlightened spirit of TOLERATION, so well understood and practised in the greatest part of Europe, is making progress every day, save in Ireland alone: while the Protestant religion enjoys peace and protection in Catholick countries, why should a nation, in all other respects so generous and liberal as the Irish, refuse at home what they receive and enjoy abroad?

As the absurdity of the present system can no longer be doubted, the question is, in what degree it should immediately be changed? Would it be prudent directly to arm, and put upon a level with the rest of the community, so large and necessarily so disgusted a body of the people? Great sudden changes are rarely prudent; old habits are not immediately laid aside; and the temper of men's minds, nursed in ignorance, should have time to open and expand, that they may clearly comprehend their true interests: for this reason the alteration of the laws should be gradual, rather than by one or two repealing clauses at once to overthrow the whole. But, all things considered, there ought not to be a single sessions without doing something in so necessary a work. For instance, in one sessions to give them a power of taking mortgages; in another of purchasing lands; in a third, to repeal the abominable premiums on the division of a family against itself, by restoring to parents their rights; in a fourth, mass to be rendered legal; in a fifth, a seminary to be established by law for the education of priests, and a bishop to be allowed, with those powers which are necessary for the exercise of the religion; by which means the foreign interest from a priesthood, entirely educated abroad, would be at once cut off. Thus far the most zealous friends to the Protestant religion could not object upon any well-founded principles. When once the operations of the new system had raised a spirit of industry and attendant wealth among the lower classes of them, no evil consequences would flow from permitting them the use of arms. Give them an interest in the kingdom, and they will use their arms, not to overturn, but to defend it. Upon first principles, it is a miserable government, which acknowledges itself incapable of retaining men to their obedience that have arms in their hands; and such an one as is to be found in Ireland alone. In like manner I should apprehend that it might be proper to give them a voice in the election of members of Parliament. There is great reason to believe that they will not be treated by gentlemen in the country in the manner they ought to be until this sort of importance is given them.

Let it in general be remembered, that no country in the world has felt any inconveniences from the most liberal spirit of toleration: that, on the contrary, those are universally acknowledged to be the most prosperous, and the most flourishing, which have governed their subjects on the most tolerating principles. That other countries, which have been actuated by the spirit of bigotry, have continued poor, weak, and helpless: these are circumstances which bear so immediately upon the question, that we may determine, without any hazard of extravagance, that Ireland will never prosper to any great degree until she profits by the example of her neighbours. Let her dismiss her illiberal fears and apprehensions; let her keep pace with the improvement of the age, and with the mild spirit of European manners; let her transfer her anxiety from the faith to the industry of her subjects; let her embrace, cherish, and protect the Catholicks as good subjects, and they will become such; let her, despising and detesting every species of religious persecution, consider all religions as brethren, employed in one great aim, the wealth, power, and happiness of the general community; let these be the maxims of her policy, and she will no longer complain of poverty and debility; she will be at home prosperous, and abroad formidable.

SECTION VIII.

PRICE OF PROVISIONS.

IN the speculations of modern politicians, so many conclusions have been drawn from the prices of provisions in different countries, and some of them with so much reason, that every one must readily admit a considerable degree of importance to be annexed to such information: with this view, I was as particular in these enquiries, as I had been before in my English journies. The following table shews the result.

Places.	Beef, per lb.	Mutton, per lb.	Veal, per lb.	Pork, per lb.	Butter, per lb.	Chick.		Turkey.		Goose.	
	d.	*d.*	*d.*	*d.*	*d.*	*s.*	*d.*	*s.*	*d.*	*s.*	*d.*
Dublin	3½	3½	5	3½	8	1	0	2	6	1	6
Lottrelstown	3½	3½	4	3	8						
Kilcock	2½	3¼	3¼	2½	6½	0	2½	1	0	0	8¾
Slane	3¼	3½	4	1¾	6	0	3	0	10	0	6
Packenham	2½	3½	4	3	6	0	3	1	0	0	8
Tullamore	2¾	2	3	2¼	2	0	2			0	8
Shaen Castle, Queen's Co.	2½	2½	3	2¼	5½	0	2½	1	1	0	7
Carlow	2½	2¾	3	3	6	0	2	1	0	0	8
Kilfaine	2½	2½		2	6½	0	2	0	8	0	6½
Taghmon	2	2½	2	2		0	2	0	8	0	7½
Forth	2	2½	2½	2	7						
Prospect	2½	2½			5	0	2	0	6	1	0
Mount Kennedy	3½	3½	5	3½	8						
Market Hill	3	3½	4	2½	6	0	2½	1	6	0	11
Armagh	2¾	3	3¼	3¼	5½	0	2½	1	4	1	1
Warrenstown	2¾	3	3	2½	5	0	2	1	3	1	0
Portaferry	2¾	2½	3	2	5	0	1¾	1	1	1	1
Shaen Castle, co. Antrim.	2½	2½	3¼	2½	5	0	1½			1	1
Belfast	2¾	3	2½	2½	5	0	2½	1	0	1	2

Places.	Beef, per lb.	Mutton, per lb.	Veal, per lb.	Pork, per lb.	Butter, per lb.	Chick.	Turkey,		Goose,	
	d.	d.	d.	d.	d.	d.	s.	d.	s.	d.
Lesly Hill	2	3	3½	2½	4½	2	1	0	1	0
Limavaddy	2¾	3¼	3¼	2	5¼	1½	1	0	1	0
Innishoen	2¼	2½	3	2½	4½	2				
Clonleigh	3	2½	3½	2½	5½	2	1	0	1	1
Mount Charles	2	2½	3½	2	4	1	1	0	0	6
Castle Caldwell	2¼	3	3¼	2	3½	2	0	10	0	5½
Belle Isle	2	2		1¾	5	1½	0	6	0	6
Florence Court	2½	3		2	4½	2	1	0	0	6
Farnham	2½	3	3¾	1¾	5	1¾	1	0	0	8
Ballynogh	2½	2¼		1½	4½	2	0	9	0	6
Strokestown	2	2¾	4	1½	4	2	0	7½	0	3½
Mercra	2¼	2	3½	1¾	5	2	0	8	0	8
Fortland	3	3	4	2		1½	0	8	0	6
Kilalla	2¼	2½		2	4¾	2	1	1	0	8
Westport	2¼	3		2	6	1¾	0	10	0	3¼
Moniva	3	3		2	6	2	0	10	0	9
Drumoland	2½	2½		2	7	1½	0	6	0	6
Limerick	2¾	2½		2¼	5	2½	0	5	0	6
Doneraile	2½	2½		2½	7	2¾	0	8	0	4½
Corke	3	3	3	2½	7½	2¾	0	10	0	6
Nedeen	1¾	2		1¾	6	2			0	6
Arbella	2¾	2½			4½	1½	0	10½	0	6
Tarbat	2½	2½		2½	5					
Castle Oliver	3	3		2½						
Tipperary	3	3		2½		2¾	1	0	1	0
Curraghmore	3	3	3¾	2¼	6					
Waterford	3	3	3½	2½	7	3	1	0	0	10
Furness	2¾	2¾	4¾	2¾	8	3	1	0	1	0
Gloster	2½	2¾	2¾	2	5½	2¾	1	0	1	0
Johnstown	3	3½	3	3	6	3	0	11	0	6
Derry	2½	3	6	3	5	2	0	10	1	0
Castle Lloyd	3	2¾	2½	2½	6	2	0	7½	0	3
Mitchel's Town	2½	2½	2½	2½	6	2½	0	8	0	8
Average	2½	2¾	3½	2¼	5¾	2½	0	10¾	0	8½

In order for a comparison, I shall add the prices of my English Tours.

	Butter.	Mutton.	Beef.	Veal.	Pork.
	d.	*d.*	*d.*	*d.*	*d.*
The Southern Tour, 1767 . . .	6½	4¼	4	3¾	
The Northern Tour, 1768. . .	6	3	3	3	3½
The Eastern Tour, 1770 . . .	6½	3½	3½	3½	3½
Average of the three	6¼	3½	3⅓	3¼	3½
Ireland in 1776	5¾	2¾	2½	3½	2¼

Average of the four meats in England . 3¼*d.*
Ditto in Ireland . . . . 2¾*d.*
Ireland to England as 11 to 14.

I should remark, that there has been very little variation in the prices of meat in England since the dates of those journies; the rates in Ireland are higher than I conceived them, and do not from cheapness afford any reason to conclude that country, as far as cattle extends, to be in a state of backwardness. The whole of these minutes, however, concerns the home consumption only; for, as to the immense trade in beef and pork, (of which hereafter) their rates are considerably under these, as may be supposed from the greatness of the scale; in like manner as the consumption prices in England are near double those of the Victualling Office.

Poultry being so extremely cheap is owing to several causes: First, The smallness of the demand; the towns are few, small, and poor; and all gentlemen's families raise a quantity for themselves. Second, The plenty of potatoes, upon which they are fed, being vastly greater, and dispensed with less œconomy than the corn in England, upon which poultry is there reared. Third, The extreme warmth of the cabbins, in which the young broods are nourished. Fourth, The natural produce of white clover, which is much greater than in England, and upon the seeds of which young turkies in particular are advantageously fed. I know a gentleman in England, who reared an amazing number of turkies and pea-chicks the year his lawn was sown with white clover, but, the soil being improper, it lasted but one year; and he neither before nor after had such success with those broods.

SECTION IX.

ROADS—CARS.

FOR a country so very far behind us as Ireland, to have got suddenly so much the start of us in the article of roads, is a spectacle that cannot fail to strike the English traveller exceedingly. But from this commendation the turnpikes in general must be excluded; they are as bad as the bye-roads are admirable. It is a common complaint that the tolls of the turnpikes are so many jobs, and the roads left in a state that disgraces the kingdom.

The following is the system on which the cross-roads are made. Any person wishing to make or mend a road has it measured by two persons, who swear to the measurement before a justice of the peace. It is described as leading from one market town to another (it matters not in what direction) that it will be a public good, and that it will require such a sum, per perch of twenty-one feet, to make or repair the same; a certificate to this purpose (of which printed forms are sold) with the blanks filled up, is signed by the measurers, and also by two persons called overseers, one of whom is usually the person applying for the road, the other the labourer he intends to employ as an overseer of the work, which overseer swears also before the justice the truth of the valuation. The certificate, thus prepared, is given by any person to some one of the Grand Jury, at either of the assizes, but usually in the spring. When all the common business of trials is over, the jury meets on that of roads; the chairman reads the certificates, and they are all put to the vote, whether to be granted or not. If rejected, they are torn in pieces and no farther notice taken, if granted, they are put on the file.

This vote of approbation, without any farther form, enables the person, who applied for the presentment, immediately to construct or repair the road in question, which he must do at his own expence; he must finish it by the following assizes, when he is to send a certificate of his having expended the money pursuant to the application; this certificate is signed by the foreman, who also signs an order on the treasurer of the county to pay him, which is done immediately. In like manner are bridges, houses of correction, gaols, &c. &c. built and repaired. If a bridge over a river, which parts two counties, half is done by one, and the other half by the other county.

The expence of these works is raised by a tax on the lands, paid by the tenant; in some counties it is acreable, but in others it is on the *plough land;* and, as no two plough lands are of the same size, is a very unequal tax. In the county of Meath it is acreable, and amounts to one shilling per acre, being the highest in Ireland; but in general it is from threepence to sixpence per acre, and amounts of late years, through the whole kingdom, to one hundred and forty thousand pounds a year.

The juries will very rarely grant a presentment for a road, which amounts to above fifty pounds, or for more than six or seven shillings a perch; so that if a person wants more to be made than such a sum will do, he divides it into two or three different measurements or presentments. By the Act of Parliament all presentment roads must be twenty-one feet wide at least from fence to fence, and fourteen feet of it formed with stone or gravel.

As the power of the Grand Jury extends in this manner to the cutting new roads, where none ever were before, as well as to the repairing and widening old ones, exclusive, however, of parks, gardens, &c. it was necessary to put a restriction against the wanton expence of it. Any presentment may be traversed that is opposed, by denying the allegations of the certificate; this is sure of delaying it until another assizes; and in the mean time persons are appointed to view the line of road demanded, and report on the necessity or hardship of the case. The payment of the money may also be traversed after the certificate of its being laid out; for, if any person views, and finds it a manifest imposition and job, he has that power to delay payment until the cause is cleared up and proved. But this traverse is not common. Any persons are eligible for asking presentments; but it is usually done only by resident gentlemen, agents, clergy, or respectable tenantry. It follows necessarily, that every person is desirous of making the roads leading to his own house, and that private interest alone is considered in it, which I have heard objected to the measure; but this I must own appears to me the great merit of it. Whenever individuals act for the public alone, the public is very badly served; but when the pursuit of their own interest is the way to benefit the public, then is the public good sure to be promoted; such is the case of presentment of roads; for a few years the good roads were all found leading from houses like rays from a center, with a surrounding space, without any communication; but every year brought the remedy, until in a short time, those rays, pointing from so many centers, met; and then the communication was complete. The original Act passed but seventeen years ago, and the effect of it in all parts of the kingdom is so great, that I found it perfectly practicable to travel upon wheels by a map. I will go here; I will go there; I could trace a route upon paper as wild as fancy could dictate, and everywhere I found beautiful roads without break or hindrance, to enable me to realize my design. What a figure would a person make in England, who should attempt to move in that manner; where the roads, as Dr. Burn has very well observed, are almost in as bad a state as in the time of Philip and Mary. In a few years there will not be a piece of bad road, except turnpikes, in all Ireland. The money raised for this first and most important of all national purposes, is expended among the people who pay it, employs themselves and their teams, encourages their agriculture, and facilitates so greatly the improvement of waste lands, that it ought always to be considered as the first step to any undertaking of that sort.

At first, roads, in common with bridges, were paid out of the general treasure of the county; but by a subsequent Act, the road tax is now on baronies; each barony pays for its own roads. By another Act, juries were enabled to grant presentments of narrow mountain roads, at two shillings and sixpence a perch. By another, they were empowered to grant presentments of footpaths, by the side of roads, to one shilling a perch. By a very late Act, they are also enabled to contract, at three halfpence per perch per annum, from the first making of a road, for keeping it in repair, which before could not be done without a fresh presentment. Arthur French, Esq., of Moniva, whose agriculture is described in the preceding minutes, and who at that time represented the county of Galway, was the worthy citizen who first brought this excellent measure into Parliament: Ireland, and every traveller that ever visits it, ought, to the latest time, to revere the memory of such a distinguished benefactor to the public. Before that time the roads, like those of England, remained impassable, under the miserable police of the six days labour. Similar good effects would here flow from adopting the measure, which would ease the kingdom of a great burthen, in its public effect absolutely contemptible; and the tax here, as in Ireland, ought to be so laid as to be borne by the tenant, whose business it is at present to repair.

Upon the imperfections of the Irish system I have only to remark, that juries should, in some cases, be more ready than they are to grant these presentments. In general they are extremely liberal, but sometimes they take silly freaks of giving none, or very few. Experience having proved from the general goodness of the roads that abuses cannot be very great, they should go on with spirit to perfect the great work throughout the kingdom; and, as a check upon those who lay out the money, it might perhaps be adviseable to print county maps of the presentment roads, with corresponding lists and tables of the names of all persons who have obtained presentments, the sums they received, and for what roads. These should be given freely by the jurymen to all their acquaintance, that every man might know to whose carelessness or jobbing the public was indebted for bad roads, when they had paid for good ones. Such a practice would certainly deter many.

At 11,042,642 acres in the kingdom, one hundred and forty thousand pounds a year amounts to just threepence an acre for the whole territory, a very trifling tax for such an improvement, and which almost ranks in public ease and benefit with that of the post-office.

It is not to this system singly, that Ireland is indebted for the goodness of her roads; another circumstance calls materially for observation, which is the vehicle of carriage: all land-carriage in that kingdom is performed with one-horse cars or carts. Those of the poor people are wretched things, formed with a view to cheapness alone; and the loads they carry on them, when working by the day, are such as an Englishman would be ashamed to take in a wheelbarrow; yet they suffer their horses to walk so slow with these burthens, that I am confident, work of this sort, done by hire, is five hundred per cent. dearer than in England. Even when they work for themselves, their loads are contemptible, and not equal to what their *garrens*, miserable as they are, would draw. Cars, however, which work regularly for mills in carrying flour to Dublin, do better; the common load is from six to ten hundred weight, which, considering the horses, is very well; eighteen hundred weight has been often carried thither from Slane mills. The lowness of the wheels suits a mountainous country; but, if there is truth in the mechanic powers, is in general a great disadvantage to the animal. Great numbers of these cars consist only of a flat bottom over the axletree, on which a few sacks, logs, or stones, may be laid, or a little heap of gravel in the center. Others have side-boards, and some baskets fixed. But such an imperfect and miserable machine deserves not a moment's attention; the object of importance arising only from one horse for draught.

Some gentlemen have carts very well made in respect of strength, but so heavy as to be almost as faulty as the common car. Others have larger and heavier two-horse carts; and a few have been absurd enough to introduce English waggons. The well-made roads preserving themselves for so many years, is owing to this practice of using one-horse carriages, which is worthy of universal imitation. Notwithstanding the expence bestowed on the turnpikes in England, great numbers of them are in a most wretched state, which will continue while the legislature permits so many horses to be harnessed in one carriage. A proof how little one-horse carriages wear roads, is the method used in Ireland to construct them; they throw up a foundation of earth in the middle of the space from the outsides, on that they immediately form a layer of limestone, broken to the size of a turkey's egg; on this a thin scattering of earth to bind the stones together, and over that a coat of gravel, where it is to be had. Their carriages considered, no fault is to be found with this mode, for the road is beautiful and durable; but, being all finished at once, with very little or no time for settling, an English waggon would presently cut through the whole, and demolish the road as soon as made, yet it is perfectly durable under cars and coaches.

I have weighed common cars in Ireland, and find the lightest weigh 2 cwt. 2 qrs. 14 lb. good carts for one horse at Mr. O'Neil's, 4 cwt. 2 qrs. 21 lb. and Lord Kingsborough had larger carts from Dublin, with five-feet wheels, which weighed 7 cwt. but these are much too heavy; in the lightness of the machine consists a great part of the merit. A common English waggon with nine-inch wheels from 55 cwt. to three tons. I built a narrow-wheeled one in Suffolk for four horses, the weight of which was 25 cwt.

	Cwt.	*qrs.*	*lb.*
Every horse in the Irish car draws, weight of carriage	2	2	14
In Mr. O'Neil's carts	4	2	21
In Lord Kingsborough's	7	0	0
In a broad wheeled waggon	7	1	0
In a narrow ditto	6	1	0

The extreme lightness of the common car is not to be taken into the question, as it is inapplicable to a profitable load of anything, except a single block, or sacks. It is absolutely necessary a cart should be capacious enough for a very light but bulky load, such as malt dust, bran, dry ashes, &c. as well as for hay and straw. The Suffolk waggon for four horses is twelve feet long, four broad, and two deep in the sides and ends; consequently, the body of it contains just 96 cubical feet; the end ladders extended for hay or straw four feet more, and there was a fixed side one, which added two feet to the breadth, consequently the surface on which hay was built, extended just ninety-six square feet. In a great variety of uses, to which I applied that waggon, I found four middling horses, worth about twelve pounds each, would draw a full load of everything in it; viz. from fifty to sixty hundred weight of hay, twelve quarters of wheat, or fifty-five hundred weight, and the sullage of Bury streets, by computation, judging by the labour of the horses, to a much greater weight, perhaps above three tons. I have more than once taken these measures as a guide for a one-horse cart. To give one horse an exact proportion of what four did in that waggon, the dimensions of the cart must be as follow: the body of it must be just four feet long, three feet broad, and two feet deep; the end ladders each one foot, and the side ones six inches. This will be upon a par with the waggon; but I gave the carts the advantage, by end ladders being each eighteen inches, and the side ones twelve, which made the whole surface thirty-five square feet, four times which is one hundred and forty instead of ninety-six. The weight of these carts complete were from four to five hundred; the wheels five feet high, and the axle-tree iron, which is essential to a light draft; such carts cost in England, complete and painted, from nine pounds to ten guineas. Whoever tries them will find a horse will draw in them far more than the fourth of the load of a four-horse team, or than the eighth of an eight-horse one; for he will, in a tolerably level country, draw a ton.

I have often conversed with the drivers of carriers' waggons, as well as with intelligent carters in the service of farmers, and their accounts have united with my own observation, to prove that one horse in eight, and to the amount of half a horse in four, are always absolutely idle, moving on without drawing any weight; a most unremitting attention is necessary even for a partial remedy of this; but with careless drivers the evil is greater; hence, the superiority of horses drawing single, in which mode they cannot fail of performing their share of the work. The expence, trouble and disappointment of an accident, are in proportion to the size of the team; with a broad-wheeled waggon and eight horses, they are very great; but with eight carts they are very trifling; if one breaks down, the load and cart are easily distributed among the other seven, and little time lost. When business is carried on by means of single-horse carts, every horse in a stable is employed; but with waggons, he who keeps one, two, or three horses, must stand still; and what is to be done with five, six, or seven? It is only four or eight horses that form an exact team; but the great object is the preservation of the roads; to save these the legislature has prescribed wheels, even sixteen inches broad; but all such machines are so enormously heavy, that they are ruinous to those who use them; besides, they form such exact paths for the following teams to walk in, that the hardest road is presently cut into ruts, the most solid materials ground into dust, and every exertion in repairing baffled as fast as tried. Roads, which are made annually at a vast expence, are found almost impassable from the weights carried in waggons. It may be asserted, without exaggeration, that if there were nothing but one-horse carriages in England, half the present highway expence might be saved, and the roads at the same time incomparably better.

It must be admitted that the expence of drivers would at first be greater, for a man would not drive above three of them; a man and two boys would do for nine: but why they should not be as well managed here as in Ireland I cannot see; a man there will often drive five, six, or even eight cars. I have myself seen a single girl drive six. Even in this respect there is an advantage which does not attend waggons,—a boy could anywhere manage one or two, but twenty boys would not be trusted to drive a waggon. Granting, however, that the expence under this head was something greater, still is it vastly more than counterbalanced by the superior advantages stated above, which render it an equal object to individuals and the public.

SECTION X.

TIMBER—PLANTING.

THROUGH every part of Ireland, in which I have been, one hundred contiguous acres are not to be found without evident signs that they were once wood, or at least very well wooded. Trees, and the roots of trees of the largest size, are dug up in all the bogs; and, in the cultivated countries, the stumps of trees destroyed shew that the destruction has not been of any antient date. A vast number of the Irish names for hills, mountains, vallies and plains, have forests, woods, groves, or trees for the signification; Lord Kingsborough has an hundred thousand acres about Mitchelstown, in which you must take a breathing gallop to find a stick large enough to beat a dog; yet is there not an enclosure without the remnants of trees, many of them large; nor is it a peculiarity to that estate: in a word, the greatest part of the kingdom exhibits a naked, bleak, dreary view for want of wood, which has been destroyed for a century past, with the most thoughtless prodigality, and still continues to be cut and wasted, as if it was not worth the preservation. The Baltic fir supplies all the uses of the kingdom, even those for which nothing is proper but oak; and the distance of all the ports of Ireland from that sea, makes the supply much dearer than it is in England.

In conversation with gentlemen, I found they very generally laid the destruction of timber to the common people, who, they say, have an aversion to a tree; at the earliest age they steal it for a walking-stick; afterwards for a spade handle; later for a car shaft; and later still for a cabin rafter. That the poor do steal it is certain, but I am clear the gentlemen of the country may thank themselves. Is it the consumption of sticks and handles that has destroyed millions of acres? Absurdity! The profligate, prodigal, worthless landowner cuts down his acres, and leaves them unfenced against cattle, and then he has the impudence to charge the scarcity of trees to the walking-sticks of the poor, goes into the House of Commons and votes for an Act, which lays a penalty of forty shillings on any poor man having a twig in his possession which he cannot account for. This Act, and twenty more in the same spirit, stands at present a monument of their self-condemnation and oppression. They have made wood so scarce, that the wretched cottars cannot procure enough for their necessary consumption; and then they pass penal laws on their stealing, or even possessing, what it is impossible for them to buy. If by another Act you would hang up all the landlords who cut woods without fencing, and destroy trees without planting, you would lay your axe to the root of the evil, and rid the kingdom of some of the greatest pests in it; but, in the name of humanity and common sense, let the poor alone, for whose stealing in this, as in most other cases, nobody ought to be answerable but yourselves. I was an eye-witness, in various parts of the kingdom, of woods cut down and not copsed. The honestest poor upon earth, if in the same situation as the Irish, would be stealers of wood; for they must either steal or go without what is an absolute necessary of life. Instead of being the destroyers of trees, I am confident they may be made preservers of them; recollect Sir William Osborne's mountaineers, to whom he gave a few Lombardy poplars; they cherished them with as much care as his own gardener could have done. At Mitchelstown I had opportunities of making observations which convinced me of the same thing; I saw in every respect, indeed all over Ireland, the greatest readiness to do whatever would recommend them to their landlord's favour. I had three plans relative to wood, which I have reason to believe would answer in any part of the kingdom: *First*, To give premiums to the cottars who planted and *preserved trees*; and not to let it depend on the premium alone, but to keep a list of those who appeared as candidates, and upon every other occasion to let them be objects of favour. *Second*, To force all the tenantry to plant under the following clause in their leases:

"*And also, that the said A. B. his heirs and assigns, shall*
"*and will, every year, during the continuance of this demise,*
"*well and truly plant, and thoroughly secure until the end*
"*of the said term, from all injury or damage by cattle, or*
"*otherwise, one timber tree for every*   *acres that are*
"*contained in the herein demised premises, provided that*
"*such trees shall be supplied gratis, on demand, by the said*
"*C. D. his heirs and assigns; and in case any trees shall*
"*die or fail, that in such case the said A. B. shall and will*
"*plant in the year next after such death or failure, an equal*
"*number of timber trees in the said demised premises, in the*
"*place or stead of such tree or trees so dying or failing as*
"*aforesaid; and in case, at the expiration of the said*
"*demise, the proper number of trees, of a due age, according*
"*to the meaning and intent of these premises, be not left*
"*growing and standing upon the said demised premises, or*
"*some part thereof, that then the said A. B. his heirs or*
"*assigns, shall forfeit and pay unto the said C. D. his heirs*
"*and assigns, the sum of five shillings for every tree so*
"*deficient by death, failure, injury, or negligence.*"

The proportion of acres per tree to be according to circumstances. It should always be remembered, that the clauses of a lease rarely execute themselves; it is the landlord's, or his agent's attention that must make them efficient. A tenantry everywhere is very much dependent, unless leases for lives are given; but I suppose them for twenty-one years. In Ireland their poverty makes this dependance still greater. They ask time for the payment of their rent; they run in arrears; they are threatened or driven; if they pay well, still they have some favour to ask, or expect; in a word, they are in such a situation, that *attention* would secure the most entire compliance with such a clause. If once, or twice, upon an estate, a man was drove for his rent, who neglected the trees, while another in the same circumstances had time given him, because he preserved them, the effect would presently be seen. *Third*, To have a magazine of sticks, spade handles, pieces for cars, and cabbins, etc. laid in at the cheapest rate, and kept for selling at prime cost to whoever would buy them. These would want to be purchased but for a few years; as small plantations of the timber willow would in four years furnish an ample supply.

That these three circumstances united, would presently plant a country, I am convinced; I saw a willingness among Lord Kingsborough's little tenants to do it; some even who made a beginning the very first year; and hundreds assured me of their most assiduous compliance. Such a plan most certainly should not preclude large annual plantations on the land which a gentleman keeps in hand; but the beauty of the country depends on trees, scattered over the whole face of it. What a figure would Ireland make on a comparison with its present state, if one tree now stood by each cabbin! but it is the spirit of the Irish nation to attempt everything by laws, and then leave those laws to execute themselves; which indeed with many of them is not at all amiss. It is by no means clear, whether the Act which gives to the tenant a property in the trees he plants, to be ascertained by a jury at the end of the lease, and paid by the landlord, has any great tendency to increase the quantity of wood. It has unfortunately raised an undecided question of law, whether the Act goes to trees, which were originally furnished from the landlord's nursery, or planted in consequence of a clause in a lease. If it should so interfere with such plantations, it would be highly mischievous: Also, for a man to be forced either to buy or to sell his property, at the price fixed by a jury, is a harsh circumstance. To this cause it is probably owing, that the plantations made in consequence of that Act, are perfectly insignificant.

I have made many very minute calculations of the expence, growth, and value of plantations in Ireland, and am convinced from them that there is no application of the best land in that kingdom will equal the profit of planting the worst in it. A regard for the interest of posterity calls for the oak and other trees which require more than an age to come to maturity; but with other views the quick growing ones are for profit much superior;

these come to perfection so speedily that three fourths of the landlords of the kingdom might expect to cut where they planted, and reap those great profits, which most certainly attend it. There are timber willows (sallies as they are called in Ireland) which rise with incredible rapidity. I have measured them at Mr. Bolton's, near Waterford, twenty-one feet high in the third year from the planting, and as straight as a larch. With this willow, woods would arise as it were by enchantment, and all sorts of farm offices and cabbins might be built of it in seven years from planting. Is it not inexcusable to complain of a want of wood, when it is to be had with so much ease? Larch and beech thrive wonderfully wherever I have seen them planted; and the Lombardy poplar makes the same luxuriant shoots for which it is famous in England; and, though a soft wood, yet it is applicable to such a multiplicity of purposes, and so easily propagated, that it deserves the greatest attention.

As to oak, they are always planted in Ireland from a nursery. I have seen very handsome trees as old as fifteen years, some perhaps older; but even at that age they run incomparably more into head than plants in England which have never been transplanted. It is a great misfortune that a century at least is necessary to prove the mischief of the practice: We know by most ample experience that the noble oaks in England, applicable to the use of the large ships of war, were all *sown* where they remained. That tree pushes its tap root so powerfully that I have the greatest reason to believe the future growth suffers essentially from its being injured, and I defy the most skilful nurseryman to take them up upon a large scale without breaking; if it is broke in the part where it is an almost imperceptible thread, it is just the same as cutting it off in a larger part, the steady perpendicular power is lost, and the surface roots must feed the plant; these may do for a certain growth and to a certain period; but the tree will never become the sovereign of the forest, or the waves. I know several plantations of sown oak in England from twelve to thirty, and some forty years growth, which are truly beautiful, and infinitely beyond anything I have seen in Ireland.

The woods yet remaining in that kingdom are what in England would be called copses. They are cut down at various growths, some being permitted to stand forty years. Attentive landlords fence when they cut, to preserve the future shoots; others do not. But this is by no means the system with a view to which I recommend planting, timber of any kind cut as such will pay double and treble what the shoots from any stubs in the world will do. They may come to a tolerable size, and yield a large value; but the profit is not to be compared with. To explain this, permit me one or two remarks.

If willow, poplars, ash, etc. are planted for timber, to be cut at whatever age, ten, twenty or thirty years; when cut, the stools will throw out many shoots; but let it not be imagined that these shoots will ever again become timber; they will never be any thing but copse wood, and attended in future with no more than the copse profit, which is not half that of timber; in such a case the land should be new planted, and the old stools either grubbed up for fewel, or else the growth from them cut very often for faggots, till the new timber gets up enough to drip on and destroy it. The common practice in Ireland is cutting young trees down when they do not shoot well; this is converting timber to copse wood; attention to cutting off all the shoots but one will train up a stem, but I question whether it will ever make a capital tree: if the other shoots are not annually cut, it will never be any tree at all; and yet it is certainly a fact that the new shoot is much finer than the old one, which perhaps would have come to nothing; but better remove it entirely than depend on new shoots for making timber. The gentlemen in that kingdom are much too apt to think they have got timber, when in fact they have nothing but fine large copse wood. A strong proof of this is the great double ditches made thirty or forty years ago, and planted with double rows of trees, generally ash; these for two reasons are usually (for the age) not half so good as trees of the same growth in England; one is, many of them were cut when young, and arose from stools; the other is their growing out of a high dry bank, full of the roots of four rows of white thorn or apple quick, besides those of the trees themselves. It is a fact that I never saw a single capital tree growing on these banks: all hedge trees are difficult to preserve, and therefore must have been cut when young. Ash in England, growing from a level, are generally worth in forty years from forty shillings to three pounds. And I know many trees of fifty to sixty years growth that would fell readily at from four to eight pounds; yet the price in Ireland is higher. Another practice, which is common in that kingdom, is pruning timber trees, and even oaks. I was petrified at seeing oaks of ten and fifteen feet high with all the side shoots cut off. There are treatises upon planting which recommend this practice, as well as cutting down young trees to make the better *timber*. There are no follies which are not countenanced, and even prescribed in some book or other; but unhappy is it for a kingdom when they are listened to. Burn your books, and attend to nature; come to England, and view our oak, our ash, and our beech, all self-sown, and never cursed with the exertions of art. Shew me such trees from the hands of nurserymen and pruners before you waste your breath with shallow reasoning to prove that the most common of the operations of nature must be assisted by the axe or pruning hook.

One reason why both fences and trees in Ireland, which have once been made, are now neglected and in ruin, is owing to the first planting being all that is thought of; the hedges are suffered to grow for thirty or forty years without cutting; the consequence of which is their being ragged, and open at bottom, and full of gaps whole perches long. But all fences should be cut periodically, for the same reason that trees ought never to be touched, *viz.*, their pushing out many shoots for every one that is taken off; this should be repeated every fifteen years; a proper portion of the thorns should be plashed down to form an impenetrable live hedge, and the rest cut off, and made into faggots. But in the Irish way the fences yield no fewel at all. To permit a hedge to grow too long without cutting, not only ruins it for a fence, but spoils the trees that are planted with it.

Lastly let me observe, that the amazing neglect in not

planting osier grounds for making baskets and small hoops, is unpardonable throughout the kingdom; they no where thrive better; a small one I planted in the county of Corke grew six feet the first year; yet at that port there is a considerable importation of them from Portugal.

SECTION XI.

MANURES—WASTE LANDS—BOGS.

THE manure commonly used in Ireland is lime; inexhaustible quarries of the finest limestone are found in most parts of that island, with either turf, or culm at a moderate price to burn it. To do the gentlemen of that country justice, they understand this branch of husbandry very well, and practice it with uncommon spirit. Their kilns are the best I have anywhere seen, and great numbers are kept burning the whole year through, without a thought of stopping on account of the winter. Their draw-kilns burn up to forty barrels a day; and what they call French kilns, which burn the stone without breaking, have been made even to five thousand barrels in a kiln. Mr. Leslie laying ten thousand barrels on his land in one year, and Mr. Aldworth as much, are instances which I never heard equalled. The following table will show the general practice.

	Barrels per acre.	Price per Barrel.
		s. d.
Mr. M'Farlan	160	0 7
Slaine	120	0 7
Headfort	80	
Packenham		0 6
Mr. Marley	160	1 0
Kilfaine	80	
Mr. Kennedy	40	2 6
Hampton	125	0 7
Ld. Ch. Baron Forster	160	0 9

	Barrels per acre.	Price per Barrel.
		s. d.
Market Hill	30	1 6
Warrenstown	140	1 1
Lecale	115	0 11
Mr. Leslie	160	
Newtown Limavatly	100	1 0
Castle Caldwel		0 6
Inniskilling	80	0 8
Florence Court	60	0 8
Farnham	150	
Mr. Mahon		0 5
Mr. Brown		0 3
Mr. French		0 4
Woodlawn		0 4
Annagrove	100	0 8
Mr. Aldworth	160	0 6
Lord Donneraile	80	0 5½
Mallow	100	1 1
Mr. Gordon	50	0 7½
Coolmore	40	0 9
Nedeen		1 0
Mucrus	70	0 7
Mr. Blennerhasset	100	0 6
Mr. Bateman	50	0 6
Tarbat	40	1 0
Lord Tyrone	200	1 0
Average	100	9

These quantities are upon the whole considerable. The price shews the plenty of this manure in Ireland. To find any place where it can be burnt for three pence and four pence is truly wonderful, but can only be from the union of turf and limestone at the same place.

I no where heard of any land that had been over limed, or on which the repetition of it had proved so disadvantageous as it has sometimes been found in England.[1]

Limestone gravel is a manure peculiar to Ireland and is most excellent. It is a blue gravel, mixed with stones

[1] See a Letter from the late Earl of Holderness to me, inserted in the second edition of the "Northern Tour."—[*Author's Note.*]

as large as a man's fist, and sometimes with a clay loam; but the whole mass has a very strong effervescence with acid. On uncultivated lands it has the same wonderful effect as lime, and on clay arable, a much greater; but it is beneficial to all soils. In the isle of Anglesea, a country which very much resembles Ireland, there is a gravel much like it, which has also some effervescence; but I never met with it in any other part of England.

Marle in Ireland is not so common as these manures. That which is oftenest found is white, and remarkably light; it lies generally under bogs. Shell marle is dredged up in the Shannon, and in the harbour of Waterford.

In the catalogue of manures, I wish I could add the composts formed in well-littered farm yards; but there is not any part of husbandry in the kingdom more neglected than this; indeed I have scarce anywhere seen the least vestige of such a convenience as a yard surrounded with offices for the winter shelter and feeding of cattle. All sorts of animals range about the field in winter, by which means the quantity of dung raised is contemptible. To dwell upon a point of such acknowledged importance is needless. Time it is to be hoped will introduce a better system.

WASTE LANDS.

Although the proportion of waste territory is not, I apprehend, so great in Ireland as it is in England, certainly owing to the rights of commonage in the latter country, which fortunately have no existence in Ireland; yet are the tracts of desart mountains and bogs very considerable. Upon these lands is to be practised the most profitable husbandry in the King's dominions; for so I am persuaded the improvement of mountain land to be. By that expression is not to be understood only very high lands; all waste in Ireland that is not bog they call *mountain;* so that you hear of land under that denomination where even a hillock is not to be seen. The largest tracts, however, are adjoining to real mountains, especially where they slope off, to a large extent gradually to the south. Of this sort Lord Kingsborough has a very extensive and most unprofitable range. In examining it, with many other mountains, and in about five months experience of the beginning only of an improvement under my direction there, I had an opportunity of ascertaining a few points which made me better acquainted with the practicability of those improvements than if I had only passed as a traveller through the kingdom. By stating a few of the circumstances of this attempt, others who have mountains under similar circumstances may judge of the propriety of undertaking their improvement. The land has a very gentle declivity from the Galty mountains towards the south, and to a new road Lord Kingsborough made, leading from Mitchelstown towards Cahir, which road he very wisely judged was the first step to the improvement of the waste parts of his estate, as well as a great publick benefit. On the south side of this road limestone is found, and on the north side the improvement was begun, in a spot that included some tolerable good land, some exceeding rough and stoney, and a wet bottom where there was a bog two, three, or four feet deep; the land yielded no other profit than being a commonage to the adjoining farm, in which way it might pay the rent possibly of a shilling an acre: Twenty thousand acres by estimation joined it in the same situation, which did not yield the fourth of that rent. In June I built a lime-kiln which burnt twenty barrels a day, and cut, led, and stacked turf enough to keep it burning a whole twelvemonth, sketched the fences of four inclosures, making thirty-four acres, and finished the first work of them, leaving the rest and planting till winter.[1] I cleared two inclosures of stones; pared and burnt them; burnt eight hundred barrels of lime; limed one inclosure, and sowed one third with wheat, a third with rye, and the other with bere, as an experiment; the other field with turneps, which,

[1] Where fences must be done by the day and not the perch, which will generally be the case in the beginning of an improvement in a very wild country, from the labourers being totally ignorant of taking work by measure; all that is possible should be executed in summer, especially in so wet a climate as Ireland, and where no more is paid for a day in July than in December. Some of my banks fell with the autumn rains, owing to two causes; first, the men, instead of knowing how to make a ditch, were mountaineers, who scarcely know the right end of a spade; and secondly, it proved the dryest season that ever was known in Ireland.—[*Author's Note.*]

from the continual drought, failed. Two cabbins were built. And the whole expence in five months, including the price of all ploughing, and carriage, (the latter from the miserable cars and *garrens* at a most extravagant rate) buying timber, steward's wages, etc., amounted to one hundred and fifty pounds. The moment the neighbours understood the works were at an end, some of them offered me ten shillings an acre for the land to take it as it was, which is just eleven per cent. for the money; but I could have got more. The following were the only data gained: lime burnt for fivepence a barrel; paring with the graffan in stony land, 30*s.* to 40*s.* an acre, and done by the plough at eight shillings much better; burning and spreading the ashes depends on weather; one piece cost above twenty shillings an acre, the other not five; but on an average I should calculate it at ten shillings. The whole operation may be very well done with the plough at twenty shillings. Clearing from stones and carting away, various; I found a very stoney piece could be cleared at twelve shillings an acre. A single ditch, seven feet broad, and from three to five deep, the bank nine feet high from the bottom of the ditch, cost one shilling and sixpence; but this expence would have lessened when they were more accustomed to it: consequently, a double fence with a space between left for planting, three shillings.

My design was to purchase a stock of mountain sheep in the following spring, and keep them through the summer in the mountains, but folding them every night in the improvement, in which work I could have instructed the people; and, when once they had seen the benefit, I do not think the practice would ever have been lost. To have provided plenty of turneps for their winter support, and improved the breed by giving them some better tups, but to have done this gradually in proportion as their food improved. Turneps to be for some years the only crop, except small pieces by way of trial. To have laid down the land to grass after a proper course of turneps in the manner and with the seeds I practised in Hertfordshire, which would have shewn what that operation is. There is not a complete meadow in the whole country. To have proportioned the sheep to the turneps at the rate of from twenty to thirty an acre according to the goodness of the crop: there is a power in such waste tracts of keeping any number in summer; the common people keep them all the year round on the mountains. The annual product of the improved land is in this system very easily ascertained. Suppose only twenty sheep[1] per acre, and no more than fifteen lambs from them, worth two shillings and sixpence each, it is thirty seven shillings and sixpence, and the twenty fleeces at one shilling make fifty-seven shillings and sixpence: about three pound therefore may be reckoned the lowest value of an acre of turneps at first; but as successive crops on the same land improve greatly, they would winter more than twenty, and both lambs and wool be more valuable; so that from a variety of circumstances I have attended to in that country, I am clear the common value of the turneps might be carried to four pounds, and in the course of a few years perhaps to five pounds an acre. And to state the expence of such an improvement completely finished at ten pounds an acre, including every article whatever; three crops of turneps amply repay the whole, and the future produce or rent of the land, neat profit. This would be twenty shillings an acre; twenty-five shillings are commonly paid for much worse land. The real fact of such improvements is a landlord's accepting an estate gratis, or at least paying nothing but trouble for it. Nearly such conclusions must be drawn from Lord Altamont's mountain works, of which an account is given in the minutes. I should remark that the people I employed, though as ignorant as any in the kingdom, and had never seen a turnep-hoe, hoed the turneps, when I shewed them the manner, very readily, and, though not skilfully, well enough to prove their docility would not be wanting; it was the same with the paring mattock, and the Norfolk turnep-sower. They very readily execute orders, and seem to give their inclination to it.

There are several reasons which make these improvements more profitable and easy in Ireland than they are in

[1] It is to be noted that stock-sheep are only *baited*, and that chiefly in bad weather. The winters in Ireland are much milder than in England. —[*Author's Note.*]

England. There are no common rights to encounter, which are the curse of our moors. Buildings, which in England form one of the heaviest articles, are but a trifling expence; make the land good, and you will let it readily without any at all; or at least with an allowance of a roof towards a cabbin; and lastly, the proportionate value of improved land compared with that of unimproved is much higher than it is with us, owing to the want of capital, rendering all improvements so rare, and to the common people so difficult. Three hundred pounds a year, steadily employed in such an undertaking, would in a few years create an estate sufficient for the greatest undertakings: but success depends on a regular unbroken exertion, a point I found very few persons in Ireland thoroughly understood, owing to their not being accustomed to large flocks of sheep regularly depending on turneps. At the same time that this work was carrying on, his Lordship, by my advice, encouraged the peasantry to take in small parts of these mountains themselves. The adjoining farms being out of lease, he had a power of doing what he pleased; I marked a road, and assigned portions of the waste on each side to such as were willing to form the fences in the manner prescribed, to cultivate and inhabit the land, allowing each a guinea towards his cabbin, and promising the best land rent free for three years, and the worst for five; the eagerness with which the poor people came into this scheme, convinced me that they wanted nothing but a little encouragement to enter with all their might and spirit into the great work of improvement. They trusted to my assurance enough to go to work upon the ditches, and actually made a considerable progress. In all undertakings of this sort in Ireland it is the poor cottars, and the very little farmers, who are the best tools to employ, and the best tenants to let the land to; but this circumstance raises many enemies to the work; the better sort, who have been used to tread upon and oppress, are ill pleased to see any importance or independancy given to them: and the whole race of jobbing gentlemen, whose conversation for ever takes the turn of ridiculing the poverty of the cottar tenants, will always be ready with an equal cargo of falsehood and ignorance to decry and depreciate any undertaking which is not to conduce to their own benefit: if a landlord does not steadily resolve to laugh at all this trash, he had better never think of improvements.

BOGS.

Trifling as they have been on the Irish mountains yet are the bogs still more neglected. The minutes of the journey shew that a few gentlemen have executed very meritorious works even in these; but as they, unfortunately for the publick, do not live upon any of the very extensive bogs, the inhabitants near the latter deny the application of their remarks. Bogs are of two sorts, black and red. The black bog is generally very good, it is solid almost to the surface, yields many ashes in burning, and generally admitted to be improveable, though at a heavy expence. The red sort has usually a reddish substance five or six feet deep from the surface, which holds water like a spunge, yields no ashes in burning, and is supposed to be utterly irreclaimable.

In the variety of theories which have been started to account for the formation of bogs, difficulties occur which are not easily solved: yet are there many circumstances which assist in tracing the cause. Various sorts of trees, some of them of a great size, are very generally found in them, and usually at the bottom, oak, fir, and yew the most common; the roots of these trees are fast in the earth; some of the trees seem broken off, others appear to be cut, but more with the marks of fire on them. Under some bogs of a considerable depth there are yet to be seen the furrows of land once ploughed. The black bog is a solid weighty mass, which cuts almost like butter, and upon examination appears to resemble rotten wood. Under the red bogs there is always a stratum, if not equally solid with the black bog, nearly so, and makes as good fuel. There is upon the black as well as the red ones a surface of that spungy vegetable mass which is cleared away to get at the bog for fuel; but it is shallow on these. Sound trees are found equally in both sorts. Both differ extremely from the bogs I have seen in England, in the inequality of the surface; the Irish ones are rarely level, but rise into hills. I have seen one in Donegal which is a perfect scenery of hill and dale. The spontaneous growth most common is heath, with some bog-myrtle, rushes and a little sedgy grass. As far as I can judge by roads, laying gravel of any sort, clay, earth, etc., improves the bog, and brings good grass. The depth of them is various; they have been fathomed to that of fifty feet, and some are said to be still deeper.

From these circumstances it appears, that a forest, cut, burnt, or broken down, is probably the origin of a bog. In all countries where wood is so common as to be a weed, it is destroyed by burning; it is so around the Baltick, and in America at present. The native Irish might cut and burn their woods enough for the tree to fall, and in the interim between such an operation, and successive culture, wars and other intestine divisions might prevent it in those spots, which so neglected afterwards became bogs. Trees lying very thick on the ground would become an impediment to all streams and currents; and, gathering in their branches whatever rubbish such waters brought with them, form a mass of a substance which time might putrify, and give that acid quality to, which would preserve some of the trunks, though not the branches of the trees. The circumstance of red bogs being black and solid at the bottom, would seem to indicate that a black bog has received less accession from the growth and putrefaction of vegetables after the formation than the red ones, which from some circumstances of soil or water might yield a more luxuriant surface vegetation, till it produced that mass of spunge which is now found on the surface. That this supposition is quite satisfactory I cannot assert; but the effect appears to be at least possible, and accounts for the distinction between the two kinds. That they receive their form and increase from a constant vegetation appear from their rising into hills; if they did not vegetate the quantity of water they contain would keep them on a level. The places where the traces of ploughing are found, I should suppose were once fields adjoining to the woods, and when the bog rose to a certain height it flowed gradually over the surrounding land.

But the means of improving them is the most important consideration at present. Various methods have been prescribed, and some small improvements have been effected by a few gentlemen, but at so large an expence that it is a question how far their operations answered. Here, therefore, one must call in theory to our aid from a deficiency of practice. Fortunately for a bog-improver, drains are cut at so small an expence in them, that that necessary work is done at a very moderate cost. But in spungy ones it must be repeated annually, according to the substance of the bog; and no other work attended to but sinking the drains lower and lower, by no means till you come to the bottom, (the necessity of which is a vulgar error) but till the spaces between them will bear an ox in boots. Then the surface should be levelled and burnt; and I would advise nothing to be done for a year or two, but rollers, as heavy as might be, kept repeatedly going over it, in order to press and consolidate the surface. Before anything else was attempted I would see the effect of this; probably the draining and rolling would bring up a fresh surface of vegetables not seen before; in that case I should have very few doubts of finishing the work with the feeding, treading, and fold of sheep, which would encourage the white clover and grasses to vegetate strongly; fortunately for any operation with sheep, they can be kept safely, as they never rot in a drained bog. A very ingenious friend of mine thinks the whole might be done with sheep, with little or no draining, but from viewing the bogs I am clear that is impossible. During the time of rolling and sheep-feeding, the drains I would have kept clean and open, the labour of which would regularly be less and less. When the surface was so hard as to bear cars, marle, clay, gravel, or earth, might be carried on according to distance, which with the sheep feeding would convert it into good meadow. But as carting in a large improvement would probably be too expensive, I should think it worth while to try the experiment whether it would not be practicable to sink a shaft through the bog into the gravel or earth beneath it, boarding or walling, and plastering with terrass or cement, in order to be able to draw up the under stratum, as all the chalk in Hertfordshire is raised, that is, wound up in buckets; chalk is so raised and wheeled on to the land for the price of eight-pence the load of twenty bushels, and is found a cheap improvement at that price; yet the chalk drawers, as they call themselves, earn two shillings and two and sixpence each day. Whatever the means used, certain it is that no meadows are equal to those gained by improving a bog; they are of a value which scarcely any other lands rise to: in Ireland I should suppose it would not fall short of forty shillings an acre, and rise in many cases to three pounds.

SECTION XII.

CATTLE—WOOL—WINTER FOOD.

THE cattle in Ireland are much better than the tillage; in the management of the arable ground the Irish are five centuries behind the best cultivated of the English counties; but the moisture of the climate, and the richness of the soil, have reared, assisted with importations from England, a breed of cattle and sheep, though not equal to ours, yet not so many degrees below them as might be expected from other circumstances. The following table will shew the prices and profit on fattening bullocks and cows.

Fat Bullocks and Cows.

Places.	Price Bull.	Profit.	Price Cow.	Profit.
	£ s. d.	£ s. d.	£ s. d.	£ s. d.
Gibbstown	10 0 0	4 0 0	5 10 0	1 15 0
Lord Bective			4 2 6	1 17 6
Packenham			4 0 0	2 0 0
Tullamore			3 7 6	2 0 0
Shaen Castle			4 10 0	1 16 0
Ballynakill	5 10 0	2 5 0		
Mr. Butler	5 0 0	3 0 0	3 5 0	2 0 0
Belle Isle			3 15 0	1 11 6
Longford			4 0 0	1 15 0
Mercra	4 10 0	2 10 0	3 10 0	1 10 0
Holymount			2 16 0	1 10 0
Drumoland			3 10 0	2 0 0
Clare	6 0 0	4 0 0	3 10 0	2 0 0
Castle Oliver	5 0 0	3 8 3		
Tipperary		4 5 0		
Cullen	6 0 0	3 10 0	4 10 0	2 0 0
Average	6 0 0	3 7 6	3 16 0	1 16 6

The system pursued in fatting these beasts is explained fully in the minutes of the journey. I think the profit remarkably small. The exportation of beef, and its prices, will be given under the article *Trade*, as it forms a principal branch of the commerce of Ireland.

Sheep.

Places.	Fleece.		Profit.	
	lb.	*qrs.*	*s.*	*d.*
Slaine	4	2		
Tullamore	6	0		
Shaen Castle	4	0		
Mr. Vicars	6	2		
Mr. Brown			10	0
Kilfain	5	3		
Prospect	5	3		
Mr. Pepper	8	0		
Florence Court	3	0		
Strokestown	5	0	17	0
Ditto			10	0
Elphin	5	0	10	0
Mercra	4	0		
Mr. Brown	4	0		
Westport	5	0		
Moniva	4	2		
Drumoland	5	3		
Annsgrove	4	0		
Lord Donneraile	8	0		
Adair	7	0		
Tipperary	5	3	10	0
Mr. Moore	7	0		
Furness	5	3		
Gloster	5	3		
Johnstown	5	3		
Mr. Head			10	0
Cullen	5	3	9	0
Mitchell's Town	3	0		
Averages	5	0	11	0
Averages of the Tour through the North of England	5	0	10	0
Ditto East of England	5	2	11	8
Average of England	5	1	10	10
Average of Ireland	5	0	11	0

From hence the remark I often made in Ireland is confirmed, that their sheep are on an average better than those in England; the weight of the fleece is nearly equal to it, and profit rather higher, notwithstanding mutton is dearer in England; this is owing to the price of wool being so much higher in Ireland than it is with us. The following table will shew the price of it for fourteen years in both kingdoms.

Wool in the Fleece, Ireland.

	Per stone 16 lb.	
	s.	*d.*
In the year 1764 ...	11	0
1765 ...	10	0
1766 ...	11	0
1767 ...	13	0
1768 ...	13	6
1769 ...	13	6
1770 ...	14	0
1771 ...	14	0
1772[1] ...	0	0
1773[1] ...	0	0
1774 ...	14	0
1775 ...	16	0
1776 ...	16	6
1777[2] ...	17	6
1778 ...	0	0
1779 ...	0	0
Average	13	8

Wool in the Fleece, Lincolnshire.

	Tod reduced to stone of 16 lb.	
	s.	*d.*
In the year 1764 ...	11	4
1765 ...	11	4
1766 ...	12	0
1767 ...	10	8
1768 ...	8	0
1769 ...	8	0
1770 ...	8	3
1771 ...	8	0
1772 ...	8	3
1773 ...	8	4
1774 ...	9	0
1775 ...	9	6
1776 ...	10	0
1777 ...	9	9
1778 ...	8	0
1779[3] ...	6	9
Average	9	3

47 per cent. higher in Ireland than in England.

From hence it appears, that wool has been amazingly higher in Ireland, which accounts for the superiority in the profit of sheep. There are several reasons for their height of price, but the principal are a decrease in the quantity produced, and at the same time an increase in the consumption. The bounty on the inland carriage of corn,

[1] Unsettled but very high.

[2] Communicated by Mr. Joshua Pine in the woollen trade, Dublin.

[3] Communicated by Mr. James Oaks in the woollen trade, Bury, Suffolk.

as I shall shew hereafter, has occasioned the ploughing up great tracts of sheep-walk; and at the same time the poor people have improved in their cloathing very much: these reasons are fully sufficient to account for that rise in the price of wool, which has brought it to be higher than the English rate. There is, however, another very powerful reason, which has had a constant operation, and which is the cheapness of spinning; in Ireland this is twopence halfpenny and threepence, but in England fivepence and sixpence. Great quantities are therefore spun into yarn in Ireland, and in that state exported to England; for the price of the labour is so low, that a yarn manufacturer can afford to give a much higher price for wool than an English one, and yet sell the yarn itself, after the expence of freight is added, as cheap as English yarn. The quantities of yarn, etc. exported, will be seen hereafter.

Many gentlemen have made very spirited attempts in improving the cattle and sheep in Ireland, so that the mixture of the English breed of cattle has spread all over the kingdom; English sheep are also extending. The minutes of the journey shew that the size of the bullocks is much increased in the last twenty years.

But, profitable as sheep are in Ireland, they are not near so as they might be, if turneps were properly attended to; and the reason why oxen and cows yield still less is the same deficiency. The mildness of the climate enables the stock-master to do with but little winter food; and this natural advantage proves an artificial evil, for it prevents those exertions, which the farmers in other countries are obliged to make, in order to support their flocks and herds. Mild as the Irish climate is, the graziers in Tipperary, that is in the south of the kingdom, find nothing more profitable than turneps, though hoeing them is quite unknown; and by means of that root, so very imperfectly managed, supply Dublin with mutton in the spring, to their very great emolument. But the want of winter food is more apparent in black cattle, which, upon such very rich land, ought to rise to a size which is scarce ever met with in Ireland, the usual weight being from four to eight hundred; but from four hundred and a half to five and six hundred weight, the common size on the rich grounds of Limerick;

such land in England is covered with herds that weigh from ten to fifteen hundred weight each; this vast difference is owing to their being reared the two first winters with such a deficiency of food, that their growth is stinted, so that when they come upon the fine bullock-land, they are of a size which can never be fattened to the weight of English oxen. The deficiency in turneps, etc. renders hay very valuable in Ireland, which occasions its being given sparingly to cattle; but if they had while young as many turneps as they would eat, in addition to their present quantity of hay, and were protected in warm yards against the wind and rain, they would rise to a size unknown at present in that kingdom. Upon this and a variety of other accounts, there is scarcely any object in its agriculture of so much importance as the introduction of that plant under the right cultivation.

SECTION XIII.

TYTHES—CHURCH LANDS.

OUR sister kingdom labours under this heavy burthen as well as her neighbours, to which is very much owing the uncultivated state of so great a part of her territory. The following are the minutes of the journey:

Places.	Wheat.		Barley.		Oats.		Bere.		Potatoes.		Mowing.		Sheep.	
	s.	d.	s.	d.	s.	d.	s.	d.	s.	d.	s.	d.	s.	d.
Celbridge	7	0			5	0	5	0			5	0		
Dollestown	5	0			3	0	5	0			3	0		
Slaine	7	0	5	0	3	6					3	6		
Packenham	7	0	7	0	5	0	7	0			2	0	0	3
Tullamore	5	0	3	0	3	0	5	0			5	0	0	$0\frac{1}{4}$
Shaen Castle	7	0	5	0	3	6	6	0			3	0		
Brownshill	5	0	3	0	2	6	4	0			3	0		
Kilfaine	8	0	7	0	4	0	7	0			4	0		
Mount Kennedy	10	0	4	0	4	0								
Hampton	8	6	8	0	5	0					4	6		
Armagh			5	0	3	0								
Lecale	2	2 an acre for the whole crop.												
Shaen Castle					2	0								
Clonleigh			7	0	5	0			5	0	5	0		
Strokestown	8	0	8	0	3	0	8	0						
Mercra	8	0	6	0	4	0					3	0		
Drumoland	5	0	3	0	2	0			10	0			0	$2\frac{1}{2}$
Annagrove	8	0	6	0			6	0	6	0	2	0	0	3
Adair	6	0	5	0	4	0			9	0	2	0	0	2
Ballycanvan	5	6	5	6	5	6			5	6			0	6
Johnstown	6	0	3	0	3	0	6	0	6	0				
Derry	5	0	5	0	2	6	5	0	5	0	2	0		
Colleen	8	0	7	0	4	6	7	0	11	0	2	8		
Averages	6	9	5	4	3	8	5	11	7	2	3	3	0	$2\frac{3}{4}$

	Wheat.	Barley.	Oats.	Hay.
	s. d.	s. d.	s. d.	s. d.
Average of the Tour through the North of England . . .	5 2	3 11	3 4	1 10
Eastern ditto	4 8	4 0	2 8	
Average	4 11	3 11½	3 0	1 10
Ireland, per English acre . . .	4 2½	3 4	2 3½	2 0

This table does not contain any proof that tythes in Ireland are unreasonably rated; but that there are abuses in the modes of levying them is undoubted: the greatest that I heard of were the notes and bonds taken in some parts of that kingdom by the proctors for the payment of tithes, which bear interest, and which are sometimes continued for several years, principal and interest being consolidated, until the sum becomes too great for the poor man to pay, when great extortions are complained of, and formed the grievance which seemed most to raise the resentment of the rioters, called Whiteboys. The great power of the Protestant gentlemen render their compositions very light, while the poor Catholic is made in too many cases to pay severely for the deficiencies of his betters. This is a great abuse, but not to be remedied till the whole kingdom is animated with a different spirit.

The House of Commons some years ago passed a vote, declaring every lawyer an enemy to his country, who in any way whatever was concerned in any case of tythe for fat bullocks and cows; and, without its becoming a law, was so completely obeyed, that it has regulated the business ever since; it was certainly a reproach to that Parliament, that potatoes and turf were not the objects; for if anything called for so violent an exemption, it was certainly the potatoe garden and fuel of the poor cottar.

No object in both the kingdoms can well be of greater importance than a fixed composition for tythe. It is a mode of payment so disagreeable in every respect to the clergy, and so ruinous to the laity, that a general public improvement would follow such a measure. In Ireland there can be no doubt but the recompence should be land, were it for no other reason but having in every parish a glebe sufficient for the ample and agreeable residence of a rector. Force, by the most express penalties by statute law, the residence of the clergy; after which, extend that most excellent law, which enables any Bishop to expend, in a palace, offices, or domain wall, two years' revenues of the see, with a power of charging, by his last will, his successor with the payment of the whole of the sum to whatever uses he leaves it, who in like manner is enabled to charge his successor with three fourths, and so on. This law should be extended to parsonage houses, with this assistance, that wherever the rector or vicar proved the expenditure of two years' revenue in a house, he should receive a permit from the Grand Jury, for expending half as much more for offices, walling, etc. and, when in like manner he brought his certificate of so doing, the money to be paid him by the county treasurer, in like manner as the presentment roads are done at present, not however to leave it at the option of the Jury. A resident clergy, spending in the parish the whole of their receipts, would in all respects be so advantageous and desirable, that it is fair the county should assist in enabling them to do it in a liberal manner. The expence would be gradual, and never amount very high, if churches, when greatly wanted, were built at the same time. If the expence was for a time considerable, still it would be laid out in a manner amply to repay it. Decent edifices rising in all parts of the kingdom, would alone, in the great business of civilization, be advantageous; it would ornament the country, as well as humanize minds, accustomed to nothing better than cabbins of mud; and securing one resident gentleman of some learning and ideas in every parish of the kingdom, living on a property in which he had an interest for life, could scarcely fail of introducing improvements in agriculture and planting; the whole country would profit by such circumstances, and ought to assist in the expence. I must observe, however, that such plans should depend entirely on the clergy accepting a perpetual recompence in lieu of tythes; for, as to a public expence, to introduce resident rectors, whose business, when fixed, would be an extension and severity in that tax, and prove a premium on taking them in kind, to the ruin of agriculture, common sense would certainly dictate a very different expenditure of the public money. So burthensome is this mode of payment, that, where their residence is followed by tythes being paid in kind, the clergyman, who ought to be an object beloved and revered, lives really upon the ruin of all his parishioners; so that, instead of giving public money to bring him into a parish, no application of those funds would be more beneficial in such a case, than to purchase his absence. If ever such plans came in agitation, it would certainly be right to establish a provision for parish clerks, to teach the children of all religions to read and write.

The revenues of the clergy in Ireland are very considerable. Here is a list of the bishopricks with the annual value, which I have had corrected so often in the neighbourhood of each, that I believe it will be found nearly exact.

	£		£
The Primacy per annum	8,000	Brought over	45,500
Dublin	5,000	Clonfert	2,400
Tuam	4,000	Clogher	4,000
Cashel	4,000	Kilmore	2,600
Derry	7,000	Elphin	3,700
Limerick	3,500	Killala	2,900
Corke	2,700	Kildare	2,600
Cloyne	2,500	Raphoe	2,600
Ossory	2,000	Meath	3,400
Waterford	2,500	Kilalloo	2,300
Down	2,300	Leighlin and Ferns	2,200
Dromore	2,000		
Carried over	£45,500		£74,200

This total does not, however, mark the extent or value of the land which yields it. I was informed in conversation that the lands of the Primacy would, if lett as a private estate, be worth near one hundred thousand a year. Those of Derry half as much, and those of Cashel near thirty thousand a year. These circumstances taken into the ac-

count will shew that seventy-four thousand pounds a year include no inconsiderable portion of the kingdom. I have been also informed, but not on any certain authority, that these sees have the patronage of an ecclesiastical revenue of above one hundred and fifty thousand pounds a year more.

SECTION XIV.

ABSENTEES.[1]

THERE are very few countries in the world that do not experience the disadvantage of remitting a part of their rents to landlords who reside elsewhere; and it must ever be so while there is any liberty left to mankind of living where they please. In Ireland the amount proportioned to the territory is greater probably than in most other instances; and, not having a free trade with the kingdom in which such absentees spend their fortunes, it is cut off from that return which Scotland experiences for the loss of her rents.

Some years ago Mr. Morris published a list of the Irish absentees, and their rentals; but, as every day makes considerable alterations, it is of course grown obsolete; this induced me to form a new one, which I got corrected by a variety of persons living in the neighbourhood of many of the respective estates: in such a detail, however, of private property there must necessarily be many mistakes.

Lord Donnegal	£31,000	Earl of Milton	£18,000
Lord Courtenay	30,000	Earl of Shelburne	18,000
Duke of Devonshire	18,000	Lady Shelburne	15,000

[1] Prior's List of the Absentees of Ireland (2nd edition, Dublin, 1729), estimates the total sum remitted yearly out of Ireland at about £627,800. A later list, taken in January, 1769, by including a variety of other out-goings, raises this sum to over a million and a half, the proportion assigned to absentee landlords and pensioners being £645,575. Young's total (£732,200) is thus shown to be not exaggerated, allowing for the increase in the value of the land, which was greater between 1769 and 1779 than during the preceding forty years. Both these lists were reprinted in Vol. II. of "A Collection of Tracts and Treatises illustrative of the Natural History, Antiquities, and the Political and Social State of Ireland," Dublin (Thom), 1861.

Lord Hertford	£14,000
Marquiss of Rockingham	14,000
Lord Barrymore	10,000
Lord Montrath	10,000
Lord Besborough	10,000
Lord Egremont	10,000
Lord Middleton	10,000
Lord Hisborough	10,000
Mr. Stackpoole	10,000
Lord Darnley	9,000
Lord Abercorn	8,000
Mr. Dutton	8,000
Mr. Barnard	8,000
London Society	8,000
Lord Conyngham	8,000
Lord Cahir	8,000
Earl of Antrim	8,000
Mr. Bagnall	7,000
Mr. Longfield	7,000
Lord Kenmare	7,000
Lord Nugent	7,000
Lord Kingston	7,000
Lord Valentia	7,000
Lord Grandisson	7,000
Lord Clifford	6,000
Mr. Sloane	6,000
Lord Egmont	6,000
Lord Upper Ossory	6,000
Mr. Silver Oliver	6,000
Mr. Dunbar	6,000
Mr. Henry OBrien	6,000
Mr. Mathew	6,000
Lord Irnham	6,000
Lord Sandwich	6,000
Lord Vane	6,000
Lord Dartry	6,000
Lord Fane	5,000
Lord Claremont	5,000
Lord Carbury	5,000
Lord Clanrickard	5,000
Lord Farnham	5,000
Lord Dillon	5,000
Sir W. Rowley	4,000
Mr. Palmer	4,000
Lord Clanbrassil	4,000
Lord Massareen	4,000
Lord Corke	4,000
Lord Portemouth	4,000
Lord Ashbrook	4,000
Lord Villiers	4,000
Lord Bellew	4,000
Sir Laurance Dundass	£4,000
Allen family	4,000
Mr. O'Callagan	4,000
General Montagu	4,000
Mr. Fitzmaurice	4,000
Mr. Needham	4,000
Mr. Cook	4,000
Mr. Annesley	4,000
Lord Kerry	4,000
Lord Fitzwilliam	4,000
Viscount Fitzwilliam	4,000
English Corporation	3,500
Lord Bingly	3,500
Lord Dacre	3,000
Mr. Murray of Broughton	3,000
Lord Ludlow	3,000
Lord Weymouth	3,000
Lord Digby	3,000
Lord Fortescue	3,000
Lord Derby	3,000
Lord Fingall	3,000
Blunden heiresses	3,000
Lady Charleville	3,000
Mr. Warren	3,000
Mr. St. George	3,000
Mr. John Barry	3,000
Mr. Edwards	3,000
Mr. Freeman	3,000
Lord Newhaven	3,000
Mr. Welsh (Kerry)	3,000
Lord Palmerstown	2,500
Lord Beaulieu	2,500
Lord Verney	2,500
Mr. Bunbury	2,500
Sir George Saville	2,000
Mrs. Newman	2,000
Col. Shirley	2,000
Mr. Campbell	2,000
Mr. Minchin	2,000
Mr. Burton	2,000
Duke of Dorset	2,000
Lord Powis	2,000
Mr. Whitshead	2,000
Sir Eyre Coote	2,000
Mr. Upton	2,000
Mr. John Baker Holroyd	2,000
Sir N. Bayley	2,000
Duke of Chandois	2,000
Mr. S. Campbell	2,000
Mr. Ashroby	2,000
Mr. Damer	2,000

Mr. Whitehead	£2,000
Mr. Welbore Ellis	2,000
Mr. Folliot	2,000
Mr. Donellan	2,000
Mrs. Wilson	2,000
Mr. Forward	2,000
Lord Middlesex	2,000
Mr. Supple	2,000
Mr. Nagles	2,000
Lady Raneleigh	2,000
Mr. Addair	2,000
Lord Sefton	2,000
Lord Tyrawley	2,000
Mr. Woodcock	2,000
Sir John Millar	2,000
Mr. Baldwyn	2,000
Dr. Moreton	1,800
Dr. Delany	1,800
Sir William Yorke	1,700
Mr. Arthur Barry	1,600
Lord Dysart	1,600
Lord Clive	1,600
Mr. Bridges	1,500
Mr. Cavanagh	1,500
Mr. Cuperden	1,500
Lady Cunnigby	1,500
Mr. Annesley	1,500
Mr. Hauren	1,500
Mr. Long	1,500
Mr. Oliver Tilson	1,500
Mr. Plumtree	1,400
Mr. Pen	1,400
Mr. Ratheormue	1,200
Mr. Worthington	1,200
Mr. Rice	1,200
Mr. Ponsonby	1,200
General Sandford	1,200
Mr. Basil	1,200
Mr. Dodwell	1,200
Mr. Lock	1,200
Mr. Cramer	1,200
Mr. W. Long	1,200
Mr. Rowley	1,200
Miss Mac Artney	1,200
Mr. Sabine	£1,100
Mr. Carr	1,000
Mr. Howard	1,000
Sir F. and Lady Lum	1,000
Lord Albemarle	1,000
Mr. Butler	1,000
Mr. J. Pleydell	1,000
Mrs. Clayton	1,000
Mr. Obins	1,000
Lord M'Cartney	1,000
Mr. Chichester	1,000
Mr. Shepherd	1,000
Sir P. Dennis	1,000
Lady Dean	1,000
Lord Lisburne	1,000
Mr. Ralph Smith	1,000
Mr. Ormsby	1,000
Lord Stanhope	1,000
Lord Tilney	1,000
Lord Vere	1,000
Mr. Hoar	1,000
Mrs. Grevill	1,000
Mr. Nappier	1,000
Mr. Echlin	800
Mr. Taaf	800
Mr. Alexander	800
Mr. Hamilton	800
Mr. Hamilton (Longford)	800
Mr. William Barnard	800
Sir P. Leicester	800
Mr. Moreland	800
Mr. Cam	700
Mr. Jonathan Lovett	700
Mr. Hull	700
Mr. Staunton	700
Mr. Richard Barry	700
Colonel Barrè	600
Mr. Ashon	600
Lady St. Leger	600
Sir John Hort	500
Mr. Edmund Burke	500
Mr. Ambrose	500
Total	£732,200

This total, though not equal to what has been reported, is certainly an amazing drain upon a kingdom cut off from the re-action of a free trade; and such an one as must have a very considerable effect in preventing the natural course of its prosperity. It is not the simple amount of the rental being remitted into another country, but the damp on all sorts of improvements, and the total want of countenance and encouragement which the lower tenantry labour under. The landlord at such a great distance is out of the way of all complaints, or, which is the same thing, of examining into, or remedying evils; miseries of which he can see nothing, and probably hear as little of, can make no impression. All that is required of the agent is to be punctual in his remittances; and, as to the people who pay him, they are too often, welcome to go to the devil, provided their rents could be paid from his territories. This is the general picture. God forbid it should be universally true! there are absentees who expend large sums upon their estates in Ireland; the earl of Shelburne has made great exertions for the introduction of English agriculture. Mr. Fitzmaurice has taken every means to establish a manufacture. The bridge at Lismore is an instance of liberal magnificence in the Duke of Devonshire. The church and other buildings at Belfast do honour to Lord Donnegall. The church and town of Hilsborough, are striking monuments of what that nobleman performs. Lord Conyngham's expenditure, in his absence, in building and planting, merits the highest praise; nor are many other instances wanting, equally to the advantage of the kingdom, and the honour of the individuals.

It will not be improper here to add that the amount of the pension list of Ireland, the 29th of September 1779, amounted to £84,591 per annum; probably therefore absentees, pensions, offices, and interest of money, amount to above A MILLION.

SECTION XV.

POPULATION.

IT is very astonishing that this subject should be so little understood in most countries; even in England, which has given birth to so many treatises on the state, causes and consequences of it, so little is known, that those who have the best means of information, confess their ignorance in the variety of their opinions. Those political principles which should long, ere this time, have been fixed and acknowledged, are disputed; erroneous theories started, and even the evidence of facts denied. But these mischievous errors usually proceed from the rage of condemnation, and the croaking jaundiced spirit, which determines to deduce publick ruin from something; if not from a king, a minister, a war, a debt, or a pestilence, from depopulation. In short, if it was not to be attributed to any thing, many a calculator would be in Bedlam with disappointment. We have seen these absurdities carried to such a length, as to see grave treatises published, and with respectable names to them, which have declared the depopulation of England itself to take place, even in the most productive period of her industry and her wealth. This is not surprising, for there are no follies too ridiculous for wise men sometimes to patronize; but the amazing circumstance is that such tracts are believed, and that harmless politicians sigh in the very hey day of propagation, lest another age should see a fertile land without people to eat the fruits of it. Let population alone, and there is no fear of its taking care of itself; but when such fooleries are made a pretence of recommending laws for the regulation of landed property, which has been the case, such speculations should be treated with contempt and detestation; while merely speculative they are perfectly harmless; but let them become active in Parliament, and common sense should exert her power to kick the absurdity out of doors. To do justice to the Irish, I found none of this folly in that kingdom; many a violent opposer of Government is to be found in that country, ready enough to confess that population increases greatly; the general tenour of the information in the minutes declare the same thing.

There are several circumstances in Ireland extremely favourable to population, to which must be attributed that country being so much more populous than the state of manufacturing industry would seem to imply. There are five causes, which may be particularized among others of less consequence. First, There being no Poor Laws. Second, The habitations. Third, The generality of marriage. Fourth, Children not being burthensome. Fifth, Potatoes the food.

The laws of settlement in England, which confine the poor people to what is called their legal settlements, one would think framed with no other view than to be a check upon the national industry; it was, however, a branch of, and arose from those monuments of barbarity and mischief, our poor rates; for, when once the poor were made, what they ought never to be considered, a burthen, it was incumbent on every parish to lessen as much as possible their numbers; these laws were therefore framed in the very spirit of depopulation, and most certainly have for near two centuries proved a bar to the kingdom's becoming as populous as it would otherwise have done. Fortunately for Ireland, it has hitherto kept free from these evils; and from thence results a great degree of her present population. Whole families in that country will move from one place to another with freedom, fixing according to the demand for their labour, and the encouragement they receive to settle. The liberty of doing this is certainly a premium on their industry, and consequently to their increase.

The cabbins of the poor Irish, being such apparently miserable habitations, is another very evident encouragement to population. In England, where the poor are in many respects in such a superior state, a couple will not marry unless they can get a house, to build which, take the kingdom through, will cost from twenty-five to sixty pounds; half the life, and all the vigour and youth of a man and woman are passed, before they can save such a sum; and when they have got it, so burthensome are poor to a parish, that it is twenty to one if they get permission to erect their cottage. But in Ireland the cabbin is not an object of a moment's consideration; to possess a cow and a pig is an earlier aim; the cabbin begins with a hovel, that is erected with two days' labour; and the young couple pass not their youth in celibacy for want of a nest to produce their young in. If it comes to a matter of calculation, it will then be but as four pounds to thirty.

Marriage is certainly more general in Ireland than in England: I scarce ever found an unmarried farmer or cottar; but it is seen more in other classes, which with us do not marry at all; such as servants; the generality of footmen and maids, in gentlemen's families, are married, a circumstance we very rarely see in England.

Another point of importance is their children not being burthensome. In all the enquiries I made into the state of the poor, I found their happiness and ease generally relative to the number of their children, and nothing considered as such a misfortune as having none: whenever this is the fact, or the general idea, it must necessarily have a considerable effect in promoting early marriages, and consequently population.

The food of the people being potatoes is a point not of less importance: for when the common food of the poor is so dear as to be an object of attentive œconomy, the children will want that plenty which is essential to rearing them; the article of milk, so general in the Irish cabbins, is a matter of the first consequence in rearing infants. The Irish poor in the Catholick parts of that country are subsisted entirely upon land; whereas the poor in England have so little to do with it, that they subsist almost entirely from shops, by a purchase of their necessaries; in the former case it must be a matter of prodigious consequence, that the product should be yielded by as small a space of land as possible; this is the case with potatoes more than with any other crop whatever.

As to the number of people in Ireland, I do not pretend to compute them, because there are no satisfactory data whereon to found any computation. I have seen several formed on the hearth-tax, but all computations by taxes must be erroneous; they may be below, but they cannot be above the truth. This is the case of calculating the number in England from the house and window-tax. In Ireland it is still more so, from the greater carelessness and abuses in collecting taxes. There is, however, another reason, the exemptions from the hearth-money, which in the words of the Act are as follow: "Those who live upon alms and are not able to get their livelihood by work, and widows, who shall procure a certificate of two justices of the peace in writing yearly, that the house which they inhabit is not of greater value than eight shillings by the year, and that they do not occupy lands of the value of eight shillings by the year, and that they have not goods or chattels to the value of four pounds."[1] It must be very manifest from hence, that this tax can be no rule whereby to judge of the population of the kingdom. Captain South's account is drawn from this source in the last century, which made the people 1,034,102 in the year 1695[2]; the number was computed by Sir W. Petty, in the year 1657 to 850,000; in 1688 at 1,200,000; and in 1767 the houses taxed were 424,046. If the number of houses in a kingdom were known, we should be very far from knowing that of the people, for the computation of four or five per house, drawn from only a thousandth part of the total, and perhaps deduced from that of a family rather than a house, can never speak the real fact. I cannot conclude this subject, without earnestly recommending to the Legislature of Ireland to order an actual enumeration of the whole people, for which purpose I should apprehend a vote of the House of Commons would be sufficient. Such a measure would be attended with a variety of beneficial effects, would prevent the rise of those errors which have been mischievous in England, and would place the great importance of Ireland

[1] A Treatise of the Exchequer and Revenue of Ireland. By G. E. Howard, Esq; Vol. i. p. 90.

[2] Abridgement of Phil. Trans. Vol. iii. p. 665.

to the British Empire, in that truly conspicuous light in which it ought ever to be viewed, and in which it could not fail to be considered, while we have theorists, who insist that the people of England do not amount to five millions.

The common idea is, that there are something under three millions in Ireland.

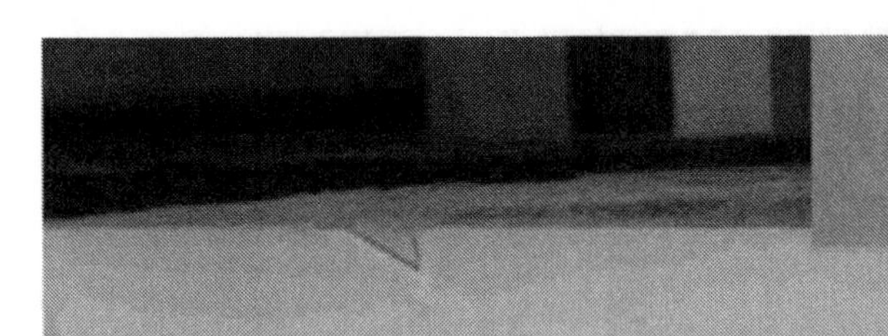

SECTION XVI.

PUBLICK WORKS—COALS—THE DUBLIN SOCIETY.

ABOUT twenty years ago, Ireland, instead of being burthened with a national debt, had at the end of every sessions of Parliament from fifty to sixty thousand pounds surplus revenue in the Exchequer, at the disposition of Parliament: this money was voted for public works. The members of the House of Commons, at the conclusion of the sessions, met for the purpose of voting the uses to which this money should be applied; the greater part of it was among themselves, their friends, or dependants; and though some work, of apparent use to the public at large, was always the plea, yet under that sanction, there were a great number of very scandalous private jobs, which by degrees brought such a discredit on this mode of applying public money, that the conclusion of it, from the increase of the real expences of the publick, was not much regretted. It must, however, be acknowledged, that during this period, there were some excellent works of acknowledged utility executed, such as harbours, piers, churches, schools, bridges, etc. built and executed by some gentlemen, if not with œconomy, at least without any dishonourable misapplication; and, as the whole was spent within the kingdom, it certainly was far from being any great national evil.

But of all publick works, none have been so much favoured as inland navigations; a Navigation Board was established many years ago for directing the expenditure of the sums, granted by Parliament for those purposes, and even regular funds fixed for their support. Under the administration of this Board, which consists of many of the most considerable persons in the kingdom, very great attempts have been made, but I am sorry to observe, very little completed. In order to examine this matter the more regularly, it will be proper to lay before the reader

the sums which have, from time to time, been granted for these objects.

An account of money, granted for public works by Parliament, or the Navigation Board, from 1753 to 1767, inclusive.[1]

Newry river	£9,000
Dromglass colliery and navigation	112,218
Dromreagh	3,000
Lagan River	40,304
Shannon River	31,500
Grand Canal	73,646
Blackwater River	11,000
River Lee	2,000
River Barrow	10,500
River Sure and Waterford	4,500
River Nore	25,250
River Boyne	36,998
Pier at Skerries	3,500
Pier at Envir	1,870
Pier at Dunleary	18,500
Pier at Balbriggen	5,252
Pier at Bangor	500
Pier at Killyleagh	1,200
Pier at Sligo	1,300
Antrim River	1,359
Ballast-office Wall	43,000
Widening Dublin streets	41,986
Trinity College	31,000
Baal's Bridge Limerick quays	7,773
Corke Channel Harbour	6,500
Corke Workhouse	1,500
Derry Quay	2,900
Shandon Street, Corke	1,500
Wicklow Harbour	6,850
St. Patrick's Hospital	6,000
Publick Records	£5,000
Aqueduct Dungarvon	1,300
Soldiers' Children's Hospital	7,000
Lying-in Hospital	19,300
Mercer's Hospital	500
Shannon bridge	2,000
Kilkenny ditto	9,130
Corke bridges	4,000
Kildare bridges	600
St. Mark's church	2,000
St. Thomas's church	5,440
St. Catherine's church	3,990
St. John's church	2,000
Building churches	12,000
Athlone church	476
Cashel church	800
Wexford church	
Quay at Dingle	1,000
Minsterkenry collieries	2,000
Marine nursery	1,000
Road round Dublin	1,500
Dundalk	2,000
Whale-fishery	1,000
Dry dock	2,000
Mills at Naul	3,498
Balty-castle	3,000
Lord Longford	3,000
	£717,944
Or per annum	47,863

This period of fifteen years, I believe was that of the surplus of the revenue, during which the objects were as various as the inclinations of those individuals who had any interest in Parliament. It appears from the list, that the article of navigation swallows up the greatest proportion of it.

[1] Commons' Journal, Vol. xiv. p. 485.

Sums paid out of the revenues at large for certain public works, pursuant to the several bills of supply, from 1703 to 1771, inclusive.

Navigations, collieries, docks, &c.	£379,388
To build churches	17,706
Parliament House	16,270
Dublin Workhouse, South Wall passages, New Road and Marshalsea	140,372
Hospitals	44,251
Trinity College	45,000

Also, for the following purposes during the same period.

Rewards and bounties to manufacturers	29,829
Linen manufacture	180,546
Cambrick ditto	4,000
Whale fishery	1,500
Incorporated Society	96,000
Dublin Society	64,000
	£1,018,862

It is to be noted, however, that this account includes the disbursements neither of the Navigation, nor the Linen Board, for it is upon record, that the Grand Canal alone has cost above three hundred thousand pounds; by some accounts, half a million.

Granted by the Navigation Board only, from 1768 to 1771.

	1768.	1769.	1770.	1771.	Total.
	£	£	£	£	£
Newry Canal	2,216	130	—	88	2,434
Drumglass Navigation	1,971	244	2,151	1,200	5,566
Barrow Navigation	—	—	3,000	100	3,100
Shannon Navigation	4,162	162	3,336	—	7,660
Grand Canal	550	1,280	755	2,000	4,585
Boyne Navigation	2,143	2,860	2,000	2,504	9,507
Fergus Navigation	500	—	350	—	850
	11,542	4,676	11,592	5,892	33,702

Incomplete as these data are, we find from them that great sums of money have been granted for inland navigations, and are to this day given for the same purpose; let us therefore enquire how this money has been expended, and what has been the effect of it.

I made some enquiries, and travelled many miles to view some of the navigations; and the only one which appeared to me really completed is the canal from the town of Newry to the sea, on which I saw a brig of eighty or one hundred tons burthen. The same canal is extended farther than that town, but stops short of the great object for which it was begun and made, viz. the Drumglass and Dungannon collieries; this may therefore be classed as incomplete relative to the object; but, as Newry is a place of considerable trade, finishing it so far has merit. The great design was to furnish Dublin with Irish coals, which was probably feasible, for the seams of coals in those collieries are asserted to be of such a thickness, and goodness, as proved them more than equal to the consumption of half a dozen such cities as Dublin; but two great difficulties were to be overcome: first, to make the navigation, so that all land carriage might be saved, which was properly a publick work; and secondly, to work the collieries, which was properly private business; but from the utter deficiency of capital in the hands of the individuals concerned, could never have been done without public assistance. To get over these difficulties Parliament went very eagerly into the business; they granted so liberally to the canal, that I think it has been finished to within two or three miles of the collieries; at the same time a private company was formed for working the mines, to whom considerable grants were made to enable them to proceed. The property in the works changed hands several times; among others, the late Archbishop of Tuam (Ryder) was deeply concerned in them, entering with great spirit into the design; but, what with the impositions of the people employed, the loss of some that were able and honest, the ignorance of others, and the jobbing spirit of some proprietors, Parliament, after granting enormous sums, both to the canal and collieries, had the mortification, instead of seeing coals come to Dublin, nothing but gold sent from Dublin, to do that which fate seemed determined should never be done, and so in despair abandoned the design to the Navigation Board, to see if their lesser exertions would effect what the mightier ones failed in. A Mr. Dularte, an Italian engineer, and very ingenious architect, has had for a few years the superintendance of the work; but the temper of the nation has been so soured by disappointments, that he has not the support which he thinks necessary to do any thing effectual.

COALS.

The following Table of the Import of Coal to Ireland, will shew the importance of the object.

		Tons.			Tons.
In the year	1764 ...	161,970	In the year	1771 ...	182,973
,,	1765 ...	185,927	,,	1772 ...	211,438
,,	1766 ...	186,612	,,	1773 ...	186,057
,,	1767 ...	172,276	,,	1774 ...	189,237
,,	1768 ...	185,554	,,	1775 ...	203,403
,,	1769 ...	171,323	,,	1776 ...	217,938
,,	1770 ...	197,135	,,	1777 ...	240,893
Average of seven years		180,113	Average of seven years		204,566

From this table it appears, that not only the quantity itself is great, but that it is a very rising import, owing to the increase of Dublin, which has arose with the increasing prosperity of the kingdom.

The little effect of all attempts to supply Dublin with Irish coals will be seen by the following table of the bounties paid for that purpose.

In the year	1761 .	£107	15	6	In the year	1770 .	169	11	4
,,	1762 .	220	3	10	,,	1771 .	105	4	10
,,	1763 .	125	14	9	,,	1772 .	113	11	0
,,	1764 .	218	19	3	,,	1773 .	209	11	8
,,	1765 .	135	13	3	,,	1774 .	204	7	2
,,	1766 .	81	13	0	,,	1775 .	213	14	4
,,	1767 .	75	4	0	,,	1776 .	86	0	0
,,	1768 .	150	18	4	,,	1777 .	88	0	0
,,	1769 .	164	15	4					

Before I entirely dismiss this undertaking, I cannot but remark, that nothing can more clearly prove the amazing want of capital in Ireland than the present state of these works. The navigation is complete except two or three miles; I will venture to assert, that Parliament would grant the money for finishing it without hesitation, provided men of undoubted substance engaged for working the collieries at their own expence: we may therefore assert, there is water carriage from some of the finest seams of coal in the world, and at a very slight depth, directly into the heart of the second market in the British dominions, with the advantage of a Parliamentary bounty per chaldron on their import into Dublin. Yet, with all these advantages, nobody has capital enough to undertake the work. This fact seems to call also for another observation. I remember in the English House of Commons, in the session 1777-8, when the friends of the Irish trade bills urged, that the want of capital in Ireland was such that she could never rival the manufactures of Great Britain: it was replied, that English capitals would go over to do it for them; but what I just recited proves that this remark is perfectly unfounded. If capitals were so readily moved from one country to another, the Drumglass colleries would have attracted them, especially as an interest for ever is to be purchased in them; but the fact is that removeable capitals are in the hands of men who have been educated, and perhaps have made them *locally* in some trade or undertaking which they will not venture to remove. Prejudice and habit govern mankind as much even as their interest; so that no apprehension can be so little founded as that of a country losing the capital she has made, by transferring it into another for greater seeming advantages in trade. But this point I shall have occasion hereafter to dwell more particularly on.

The Grand Canal, as it has been ridiculously termed, was another inland navigation which has cost the publick still greater sums. The design, as the maps of Ireland shew, was to form a communication by water between Dublin and the Shannon by this cut, most of the way through the immense bog of Allen. The former plan of bringing coals to Dublin was a very wise one, but this of the Grand Canal had scarcely any object that seemed to call for such an exertion. If the country is examined, through which the intended canal was to pass, and also that through which the Shannon runs, it will be found, considering its extent, to be the least productive for the Dublin market, perhaps of the whole kingdom. Examine Leitrim, Roscommon, Longford, Galway, Clare, Limerick, and those parts of West Meath and Kings, which the line of the canal and the Shannon lead through, there are scarcely any commodities in them for Dublin. Nay, the present bounty on the inland carriage of corn to Dublin proves to a demonstration that the quantity of corn raised in all these counties for the market is contemptible. What other products are there? Raw wool takes another direction, it goes at present from Roscommon to Corke. Manufactures in that line are very insignificant; there are some in Galway; but the ports of Limerick and Galway are perfectly sufficient for the small exportation of them. There remains nothing but turf; and who at Dublin would burn that, while Whitehaven coals are at the present price?

Most of the inland navigations in England have been executed with private funds; the interest paid by the tolls. One strong reason for this mode is the prevention of unnecessary and idle schemes; the manufactures must be wrought, or the products raised, and feel the clog of an expensive carriage, before private persons will subscribe their money towards a cheaper conveyance; in which case, the very application to Parliament is generally proof sufficient that a canal ought to be cut. Have something to carry, before you seek the means of carriage. I will venture to say that if the Grand Canal was entirely complete, the navigation of it, including whatever the country towns took from Dublin, would prove of such a beggarly account, that it would then remain a greater monument of folly, if possible, than at present. Some gentlemen I have talked with on this subject, have replied *it is a job; 'twas meant as as a job; you are not to consider it as a canal of trade, but as a canal for publick money*; but even this, though advanced in Ireland, is not upon principle. I answer that something has been done; fourteen miles with innumerable locks, quays, bridges, &c. are absolutely finished, though only for the benefit of eels and skating: Why throw this money away? Half what these fourteen miles have cost would have finished the Newry canal, and perfected the Dungannon collieries. Admit your argument of the job;

I feel its weight; I see its force; but that does not account for the sums actually expended. Might not the same persons have plundered the public to the same amount, in executing some work of real utility; from which something else might have resulted than disgrace and ignominy to the nation?

As to the other navigations, there is in general this objection to be made to them all,—however necessary they might be, they are useless for want of being completed: three fourths are only begun. The gentlemen in the neighbourhood of them have had interest enough in the Navigation Board to get a part only voted; and, from the variety of undertakings going on at the same time, and all for the the same reason incomplete, the public utility has been more trifling from all than from a single one finished. Sorry I am to say that a history of public works in Ireland would be a history of jobs, which has and will prove of much worse consequence than may be at first apparent: it has given a considerable check to permitting grants of money. Administration, seeing the uses to which it has been applied, have viewed these misapplications, as they term them, of the public money with a very jealous eye. They have curtailed much: until another very questionable measure, the bounty on the inland carriage of corn to Dublin, demanded so much as to leave nothing for jobs of another sort; that measure may be repealed, and the money applied to it will be at the disposal of Parliament, either for the common purpose of government, or applicable to some national improvement of a more decisive nature; the latter may, after so many instances, be rejected for fear of jobs: how melancholy a consideration is it, that in a kingdom which from various causes had been so fortunate as to see a great portion of public treasure annually voted for public purposes, so abominably misapplied, and pocketed by individuals, as to bring a ridicule and reproach upon the very idea of such grants. There is such a want of public spirit, of candour and of care for the interests of posterity in such a conduct, that it cannot be branded with an expression too harsh, or a condemnation too pointed: nor less deserving of severity is it, if flowing from political and secret motives of burthening the *publick* revenues to make *private* factions the more important.

THE DUBLIN SOCIETY.

Great honour is due to Ireland for having given birth to the DUBLIN SOCIETY, which has the undisputed merit of being the father of all the similar societies now existing in Europe. It was established in 1731, and owed its origin to one of the most patriotic individuals which any country has produced, DR. SAMUEL MADAN.[1] For some years it was supported only by the voluntary subscriptions of the members, forming a fund much under a thousand pounds a year; yet was there such a liberality of sentiment in their conduct, and so pure a love of the public interest apparent in all their transactions, as enabled them with that small sum to effect much greater things than they have done in later times since Parliament has granted them regularly ten thousand pounds a sessions. A well written history of their transactions would be a work extremely useful to Ireland; for it would explain much better than any reasoning could do, the proper objects for the patronage both of the Society and Parliament. I shall confine myself to a few general observations. It was instituted, as their charter expresses, for the improvement of agriculture; and for many years that material object possessed by far the greatest amount of their attention; but, when their funds by the aid of Parliament grew more considerable, they deviated so far into manufactures, (in which branch they have been continually increasing their efforts), that at present agriculture seems to be but a secondary object with them. During the life-time of that ingenious but unfortunate man, *Mr. John Wynn Baker*, his support drew so many friends of agriculture to their meetings, that the premiums in its favour were very numerous; since his death, the nobility and gentry, not having the same inducement to attend the transactions of the Society, they

[1] Dr. Samuel Madden, born in Dublin, 1686, died 1765, was familiarly known as "Premium Madden" on account of a system of quarterly premiums which he promoted at Trinity College about the year 1738, when he also published his "Reflections and Resolutions proper for the Gentlemen of Ireland." He gave out of his private purse at first £130 and later £300 per annum in premiums for the encouragement of arts and manufactures. Dr. Johnson said his name was one "which Ireland ought to honour."

were chiefly directed by some gentlemen of Dublin, who understand fabrics much better than lands; and, being more interested in them, they are attended to, perhaps, in too exclusive a manner. It would be tedious to enter into an examination of many of their measures; there are some, however, which demand a few remarks.

In order to encourage the manufacture of Irish woollen cloths and Irish silks, the Society have two warehouses,[1] in one of which silk is sold on their account, wholesale and retail, and in the other cloth; both are sent to them by the weaver, whose name is written on the piece, and the price per yard on it; nothing but ready money is taken; the stock of silks generally amounts to the value of twelve or thirteen thousand pounds in hand; and of woollens to ten or eleven thousand more; and the expences in rent and salaries of these warehouses amount to five hundred pounds a year each. Call the stock twenty-five thousand pounds at six per cent., the total expence of this measure is just two thousand five hundred pounds a year; or four times over the whole revenue of the Society for the Encouragement of Arts, Manufactures and Commerce at London. I have examined their sales from the weekly returns published, and find that from June 23, 1777, to February 7, 1778, their average weekly receipt was

	Silk	...	£150
	Wool	...	339
Or per annum,	Silk	...	7,800
	Wool	...	17,628

As the Society give a premium of £3 per cent. on *all the Irish wrought silk bought in the kingdom by wholesale for the purpose of retailing, that is above four shillings a yard*, it will help us to form an idea of the silk manufacture. From the first of June, 1776, to the first of June, 1777, the amount was £34,023 8*s*. 2*d*., including Corke, Limerick, Belfast, &c., and they paid six hundred and fifty pounds premium on it; from hence we find that their own silk sales must be a large proportion of the wholesale in Dublin. This has been the greatest exertion of the Dublin Society of late years.

[1] The woollen warehouse was opened May 29, 1773; that for silk Feb. 18, 1765.

The intention of the measure is evidently to take the weavers, both of silk and wool, out of the hands of the mercers and drapers, and let their manufactures come to market without any intermediate profit on them. There is one effect certain to result from this, which is, taking a great part of the ready money custom from the draper and mercer, which, being the most beneficial part of their trade, is to all intents and purposes laying a heavy tax on them: now, upon every principle of common sense as well as commerce, it will appear a strange mode of encouraging a manufacture to lay taxes upon the master-manufacturers. But all taxes laid upon a tradesman in consequence of his trade, must be drawn back in the sale of his commodities; and this tax must be so as well as others; whatever he does sell must be so much the dearer, or he can carry on no trade at all; here therefore is a fresh tax, that of enhancing the prices paid by all who do not buy with ready money, a very great majority of the whole: the dearer a commodity is, the less is consumed of it; so the consumption on credit is undoubtedly lessened, in order that those who have ready money in their hands may be served something the cheaper: here is a manifest and self-evident mischief, in order to attain a very doubtful and questionable benefit.

Is there under the sun an instance of a manufacture made to flourish by such measures? Master-manufacturers, with that vigour, attention, skill and invention, which are the result of a profitable business, are, in all parts of the world, the very soul of prosperous fabricks. It is their profit which animates them to those spirited exertions, upon which the advance of manufactures depends. If the Dublin Society's conduct is right in part, it is right in the whole, which would be attracting *all* the demand to their own warehouses; in which case there would not be a mercer or draper left in Dublin. Their committees, and gentlemen, and weavers, may choose and pay clerks, and discharge their rent; but where are the directors of finer fabricks to come from? Where the men of taste who are to invent? Where the quickness and sagacity to mark and follow the caprice of fashion? Are these to come from weavers? Absurd the idea! It is the active and intelligent master that is to do all this. Go to the weavers in Spitalfields, and see them mere tools directed by their masters. Go to any other fabrick upon earth, and see what would become of it, if the heads were considered as useless, and rivalled in their profits with publick money. If the manufacture is of such a sickly growth that it will not support the master as well as the man, it is not worth a country's notice. What is it that induces individuals to embark in a fabrick their capital and industry? Profit. The greater this is, the greater the capital that will be attracted; but, establish a system that shall rival, lessen, and destroy this profit, who will bring their capital to such a trade? And can any people be so senseless as to imagine that a manufacture is to be encouraged by banishing capital from it?

There is another effect, which I should suppose must flow from this extraordinary idea, which is, that of raising great heart-burnings and jealousies among the trade; the drapers and mercers are not probably at all pleased with the weavers who work for the Society's warehouses; this must be very detrimental to the business at large. I may also observe that master-manufacturers have more ways of encouraging skilful and industrious workmen than the mere buying their goods and employing them; there are a thousand little points of favour in their power, which the Society cannot practice; but how can they be inclined to such things while steps are taken to deprive them of every workman that can do without their assistance?

Fortunately for the kingdom, it is at Dublin as in other cities, the ready-money trade is by no means equal to that of credit; consequently the pernicious tendency of this measure cannot fully be seen. The drapers and mercers do and will support their trade, in spite of this formidable rival, backed with a premium of two thousand five hundred pounds a year, appropriated to their ruin, in order to encourage their trade! The tendency of the measure is evidently the destruction of both the manufactures.

This is a fact which appears so obvious, that I should apprehend it must have done mischief in direct proportion to the amount of the operation. It is extremely difficult to discover facts that can prove this from the nature of the case; no wonder if the import of foreign silk and woollens should have encreased from such a measure. Let us examine this point.

Account of Silk Imported into Ireland in Twenty-six Years.[1]

Years.	Manufactured.	Raw.	Ribband.
	lb.	*lb.*	*lb.*
1752	14,654	53,705	160
1753	13,360	60,155	184
1754	15,441	42,665	361
1755	9,874	43,947	265
1756	13,715	32,948	140
1757	7,709	41,354	17
1758	17,292	51,303	271
1759	13,836	44,493	118
1760	21,878	55,905	366
1761	14,815	51,348	180
1762	21,054	70,292	306
1763	17,741	41,021	469
1764	23,511	36,581	746
1765	21,582	54,655	1,543
1766	17,260	54,418	1,724
1767	19,104	46,067	1,527
1768	23,446	52,062	1,646
1769	17,522	57,001	1,401
1770	20,581	44,273	1,183
1771	14,095	38,107	650
1772	15,804	33,611	644
1773	17,379	53,662	378
1774	14,665	38,811	553
1775	13,658	29,578	355
1776	17,326	41,594	717
1777	24,187	54,043	1,574
Average .	16,980	47,061	671

Considering the extent of the period, I will not assert that this table is very decisive; whatever conclusions, however, that are to be drawn from it, are, as far as they go, *against* the late measures that respect the Irish silk manufacture; for the imported fabricks have *encreased*, while the raw material, worked up in Ireland, has *decreased*;

[1] MS. Communicated by Mr. Forster.

a proof that the manufacture has not been of any very healthy growth.

An Account of the Import of Woollen Goods for Fourteen Years.[1]

Years.	New Drapery.	Old Drapery.
	Yards.	*Yards.*
1764	248,062	220,828
1765	239,365	176,161
1766	313,216	197,316
1767	325,585	189,882
1768	337,558	198,664
1769	394,553	207,117
1770	462,499	249,666
1771	362,096	217,395
1772	314,703	153,566
1773	387,143	210,065
1774	461,407	282,317
1775	465,611	281,379
1776	676,485	290,215
1777	731,819	381,330
Average . . .	408,578	232,564
Last 7 years . .	485,609	259,466
Former ditto . .	331,548	205,662
Increase . . .	154,061	53,804

The increase is so great that it might justify conclusions against all the late measures, none of which are near so much to be condemned as the establishment of the Society's warehouse.

Import of Linen, Cotton, and Silk, British Manufacture.

		Value.			Value.
In the year 1764	...	£18,858	In the year 1771	...	£20,282
1765	...	18,037	1772	...	14,081
1766	...	15,557	1773	...	20,472
1767	...	12,710	1774	...	21,611
1768	...	16,021	1775	...	24,234

[1] Parl. Rec. of Exp. and Imp. MS.

		Value.			Value.
In the year 1769	...	£13,402	In the year 1776	...	£30,371
1770	...	20,907	1777	...	45,411
Average of seven years		£16,784	Average of seven years		£25,208

When it is considered that the undoubted mischief of this system is not submitted to as an unavoidable evil, but purchased with great expence, attention, and anxiety; and that the two thousand five hundred a year thus bestowed, as the price of so much harm might be expended in objects of great consequence to the publick, it will surely seem unpardonable in Parliament to appear so little solicitous for the welfare of their manufactures as to give ten thousand pounds a session, at large, and not limit the application of such a liberal grant to purposes of certain advantage. And it surely behoves the Society itself to recommit this matter; to extend their views; to consider the principles upon which all the manufactures in the world are carried on, supported, and increased; and, if they see no vestige of such a policy as they patronize and practice in any country that has pushed her fabricks to a great height, at least to be dubious of this favourite measure, and not persist in forcing it at such a considerable expence.

Another measure of the Society, which I hinted at before, is to give three per cent. to the wholesale purchasers of Irish silks for retailing; and this costs them above six hundred pounds a year. Upon what sound principles this is done I cannot discover; if the mercers have not a demand for these Irish silks, five times the Society's premiums will not make them purchasers; on the contrary, if they have a demand for them, they most undoubtedly will buy them without any premium for so doing. It appears therefore to me, that the only end which such a measure could answer, was to discover the absolute insignificance of the whole Irish silk manufacture, which is proved through the whole kingdom to be to the amount only of thirty-four thousand pounds a year, of four shillings a yard and upwards; but the repetition of the premium shews that this was not the design. Of all other fabricks this is the most improper for Ireland, and for any dependant country; it is an absolute manufacture of taste, fancy, and fashion; the seat of empire will always command these, and if Dublin made superior silks, they would be despised on comparison with those of London; we feel something of this in England from France being the source of most of the fashions in Europe. To force a silk manufacture in Ireland is therefore to strive against whim, caprice, fashion, and all the prejudices of mankind; instead of which, it is these that become a solid support of fabricks when wisely set on foot. There are no linens fashionable in England, but the Irish people will not wear any other; and yet gulic hollands are asserted to be much stronger. Should not the Irish, therefore, bend their force to drive the nail that will go, instead of plaguing themselves with one which never will. This is a general observation; but the particular measure of the Society, supposing the object valuable, is perfectly insignificant; it is throwing away six hundred pounds a year to answer no one purpose whatever.

The Society offers a great number of other premiums for manufactures, many of which are very exceptionable; but it would take up too much room to be particular in an examination of them. In agriculture they have a great number offered to *poor* renters separately.

Upon the general spirit of these I have to remark, that the design of encouraging poor renters is very meritorious, and does honour to the humanity of the Society; but, from a great variety of instances which were pointed out to me, as I travelled through the kingdom, I have too much reason to believe that abuses and deceptions are numerous; that the Society has actually paid premiums per acre to great numbers of claimants, who have, as soon as they received the money, let the land run waste again, so that no person could distinguish it from the adjoining bog or moor. There are two reasons why these premiums must very much fail of their wished-for success; the extreme difficulty, not to say impossibility, of ascertaining the merit of the candidates, or the facts alleged; and the utter impossibility that such very poor fellows should work any improvements worthy the Society's patronage. The London Society have found, by repeated experience, their utter incapacity of doing anything by weight of money, in bounties per acre for any object; I am convinced the same fact will hold true with that of Dublin; the funds even of the latter are much too inconsiderable for this mode. The object ought to be to inspire those men who have the necessary capital to employ it in the way the Society thinks for the publick good: the premiums should be honorary but considerable, with that degree of variety and novelty that should attract the attention of men of fortune.

But nothing was ever better imagined than the plan of fixing an English farmer in the kingdom, so much at the Society's expence as to give them a power over a part of his management. This was the case with Mr. Baker; and it was also a very wise measure to enable him to establish a manufactory of husbandry implements. The only errors in the execution of this scheme were: First, Not supporting him much more liberally, when it was found that his private fortune was too inconsiderable to support himself and family; had he been easy in his private circumstances, his husbandry would have been perfect. Second, The not directing him in the choice of his farm, which was not a proper one for an example to the kingdom, it should have been in some mountainous track, where there was bog, and tolerable soil. Third, In permitting him to make and publish small and trifling experiments, objects of curiosity to a private speculatist, but quite unworthy of the Dublin Society; besides, such a person should be brought to establish what a previous experience has convinced him is right, not to gain his own knowledge at the Society's expence.

The scheme, had it, in the case of Mr. Baker, been executed in this manner, or was such an one now to be adopted, would tend more to spreading a true practical knowledge of agriculture than any other that could be executed; and the union of a manufactory of implements unites with it perfectly. To inform a backward country of right systems has its use, but it is very weak compared with the actual practice and exhibition of it before their eyes; such an object, in full perfection of management, with an annual publication of the result, simply related, would tend more to the improvement of the national husbandry than any other system. The farm should not be less than five hundred acres, it should have a tract of bog and another of mountain; one thousand pounds should be applied in the necessary buildings; five hundred pounds immediately in fences; one thousand pounds a year for five years in stocking it; one thousand pounds for establishing a manufactory of implements, not to be sold but given away by the Society as premiums; five hundred pounds a year allowed to the superintendant for his private emolument, that no distresses of his own might interfere with the publick views; and, in addition, to animate his attention, ten per cent. upon the gross product of the farm. The Society to delegate their power over it to a select committee, and no member to be eligible to that committee, who had not in his own occupation one hundred acres of land, or more. The first expence would be seven thousand five hundred pounds, and the annual charge five hundred pounds; this would be an effective establishment that could not fail, if the manager was properly chosen. He should be an active, spirited man, not so low as to have no reputation to lose, but at the same time more a practical than a speculative farmer, and who could teach the common Irish with his own hands the operations he wished them to perform. The annual charge of only one of the Society's warehouses is equal to this, and the capital appropriated to it near twice as large; how much more beneficial would this application of the money be!

Relative to the premiums for the encouragement of agriculture, I shall venture to hint some which I apprehend would be of great advantage; and by throwing them into the words common in offering premiums, my meaning will be better explained.

1. Turnep Husbandry, 1779. To the person who shall cultivate the most land, not less than twenty acres, in the following course of crops during four years, viz. 1. Turneps. 2. Barley or oats. 3. Clover. 4. Wheat. The turneps to be twice thoroughly hand-hoed, and eaten where they grow by sheep, and to make a full report of the cultivation, expences, produce, and effect of the turneps on the sheep fed,

a piece of plate of the value of one hundred pounds, with a suitable inscription. Accounts to be delivered in the year 1784.

2. For the next greatest quantity of land, not less than ten acres so cultivated, a piece of plate of the value of fifty pounds, with a suitable inscription.

3. To the person who shall in the year 1780, have the most acres of turneps, not less than twenty, twice thoroughly hand-hoed; to report the effect, a piece of plate of the value of one hundred pounds, with a suitable inscription.

4. For the next greatest quantity, not less than ten acres, a piece of plate of the value of fifty pounds, with a suitable inscription.

5. Bean Husbandry, 1779. To the person who shall cultivate the most land, not less than twenty acres, in the following course of crops during four years, viz. 1. Beans. 2. Wheat. 3. Beans. 4. Wheat. The beans to be in rows, eighteen inches as under, and three times thoroughly hoed, and to report the effect to the Society. A piece of plate of the value of one hundred pounds, with an inscription. Accounts to be laid in in the year 1784.

6. For the next greatest quantity, not less than ten acres, a piece of plate of the value of fifty pounds, with an inscription.

7. To the person who shall cultivate the greatest quantity of land, not less than twenty acres, in the following course of crops during the four years, viz. 1. Beans. 2. Barley or oats. 3. Clover. 4. Wheat. The beans as before, and to report the effect. A piece of plate of the value of one hundred pounds, with an inscription.

8. Next greatest quantity, not less than ten acres. The value of £50 with an inscription.

9. Flax Husbandry, 1779. To the person who shall cultivate the most land, not less than twenty acres, in the following course of crops during four years, viz. 1. Turneps. 2. Flax. 3. Clover. 4. Wheat. The turneps to be twice hand-hoed, and the flax to be seeded, stacked and threshed like corn, and then watered and dressed; and to report the effect to the Society. A piece of plate of the value of one hundred and fifty pounds, with a suitable inscription.

10. For the next greatest quantity, not less than ten acres. The plate eighty pounds. Accounts to be delivered in in 1784.

11. MOUNTAIN IMPROVEMENT, 1779. To the person who shall improve the largest tract of mountain land, not less than one hundred acres, at present waste, and not let at one shilling an acre, and make a full report of the cultivation, expences and produce to the Society in the year 1787. A piece of plate of the value of five hundred pounds, with a suitable inscription. *Conditions.*

The improvement at the time of the certificates being signed to be completely inclosed; to be divided into fields of not more than ten acres each; the fences to be either walls in mortar, or double ditches well planted with white-thorns and timber, the gates, piers, &c. to be perfect. The land to have had four crops in the following course: 1. Turneps. 2. Oats, bere or rye. 3. Turneps. 4. Oats. The turneps twice hand-hoed, and eaten when green by sheep; and one half of the improvement to be in grass laid down with the last crop of oats. Not less than one hundred barrels of lime per acre to have been spread on the whole. An orchard of two acres to be well planted; and a sally garden of as much. One good farm house, with a barn, stable, cowhouse, &c. and four cabbins to be built and inhabited, the whole of stone or mortar, and covered with slate. And the tract to be actually let on lease to one or more tenants, not occupying any other land, and residing on the premises. Whoever intend to be claimants to give notice to the Society that they may appoint inspectors.

12. To the next greatest quantity, not less than sixty acres, on the like conditions, the plate three hundred pounds.

13. BOG IMPROVEMENT, 1779. To the person who shall drain and improve into rich meadow the greatest quantity of bog, not less than 50 acres, being part of a bog not less than 100 acres, and make a full report to the Society of the mode, expences, and produce in the year 1788, a piece of plate of the value of £400 with an honorary inscription. The Society leaves to the claimant to pursue whatever mode he pleases; but the land must have a good house, cowhouse, and necessary offices, with two cabbins

built all of stone or slate, and the improvement let to resident tenants occupying no other land.

14. For the next greatest quantity, not less than thirty acres, the plate two hundred pounds.

15. PLANTING. To the person who shall inclose with a wet wall, not less than six feet high, and plant the greatest quantity of land, not less than fifty acres, in the year 1780, a piece of plate of the value of four hundred pounds, with a suitable inscription. The trees to be ash, elm, poplar, beech, larch, Scotch spruce, or silver fir, to be not more than four years old, nor more than four feet asunder; and in the centre of every such space, acorns to be sown and covered.

16. For the next greatest quantity, not less than thirty acres, the plate two hundred pounds.

17. To the person who shall in the year 1780, plant and fence, so as to be completely secured from cattle, the greatest quantity of land with the common basket sallow in beds six feet broad, and four rows on each bed, not less than thirty acres, a piece of plate of the value of one hundred pounds, with a suitable inscription.

18. For the next greatest quantity, not less than fifteen acres, the plate fifty pounds. All to be continued by previous notice, every year when once they came into turn.

I have to observe upon them, that the courses of crops here recommended can only have fair justice done them, in the infancy of the husbandry, by gentlemen, or men of considerable capital; consequently, it is the wisest to offer a premium that shall attract their notice, and not vary it for lesser tenants, who at first would be incapable of executing the conditions. The mountain and bog improvement are great objects, and therefore well deserve ample encouragement; I have added the condition of *being let*, by way of satisfactory proof that the improvement is completely finished; for, if it was kept in hand, it would be a matter of opinion and valuation, which is never satisfactory. The planting premiums would in all probability have many claimants. The stone wall is essential; planting without preservation is trifling.

As to the nature of the premiums I recommend, viz. pieces of plate, I think they would have a greater effect than anything else; money would be out of sight and forgotten; a medal, that has been prostituted to all sorts of trifles, would be a contemptible reward for such exertions; but a handsome cup, vase, tray, table, etc. would be always in sight, and on every occasion a subject for conversation, to animate others to gain the same. The experience of a few years would prove whether the quantities of land required were too high or not. An inspector to view all proceedings would be absolutely necessary, whose reward should be devised in such a manner as to secure his integrity; unless some gentlemen of considerable consequence in the neighbourhood took that office voluntarily upon them.

Some premiums upon these principles, united with such a plan as I have stated for the establishment of a farm, would be attended with all the advantage to the national agriculture in the power of any Society to effect. The expence would not be so large as not to leave a considerable portion of the Society's funds for trade and manufactures; and consequently to please those who wished such objects not to be neglected.

SECTION XVII.

MANNERS AND CUSTOMS.

Quid leges, sine moribus,
Vanæ proficiunt?

IT is but an illiberal business for a traveller, who designs to publish remarks upon a country, to sit down coolly in his closet and write a satire on the inhabitants. Severity of that sort must be enlivened with an uncommon share of wit and ridicule to please. Where very gross absurdities are found, it is fair and manly to note them; but to enter into character and disposition is generally uncandid, since there are no people but might be better than they are found, and none but have virtues which deserve attention, at least as much as their failings; for these reasons this section would not have found a place in my observations, had not some persons, of much more flippancy than wisdom, given very gross misrepresentations of the Irish nation. It is with pleasure, therefore, that I take up the pen on the present occasion; as a much longer residence there enables me to exhibit a very different picture; in doing this I shall be free to remark wherein I think the conduct of certain classes may have given rise to general and consequently injurious condemnation.

There are three races of people in Ireland, so distinct as to strike the least attentive traveller: these are the Spanish which are found in Kerry and a part of Limerick and Corke, tall and thin, but well made, a long visage, dark eyes, and long, black, lank hair. The time is not remote when the Spaniards had a kind of settlement on the coast of Kerry, which seemed to be overlooked by Government. There were many of them in Queen Elizabeth's reign, nor were they entirely driven out till the time of Cromwell. There is an island of Valentia on that coast, with various other names, certainly Spanish. The Scotch race is in the north, where are to be found the features which are supposed to mark that people, their accent, and many of their customs. In a district near Dublin, but more particularly in the baronies of Bargie and Forth in the county of Wexford, the Saxon tongue is spoken without any mixture of the Irish, and the people have a variety of customs mentioned in the minutes, which distinguish them from their neighbours. The rest of the kingdom is made up of mongrels. The Milesian race of Irish, which may be called *native*, are scattered over the kingdom, but chiefly found in Connaught and Munster; a few considerable families, whose genealogy is undoubted, remain; but none of them with considerable possessions, except the O'Briens and Mr. O'Neil; the former have near twenty thousand pounds a year in the family; the latter half as much, the remnant of a property once his ancestors', which now forms six or seven of the greatest estates in the kingdom. O'Hara and M'Dermot are great names in Connaught, and O'Donoghue a considerable one in Kerry; but I heard of a family of O'Drischal's in Corke, who claim an origin prior in Ireland to any of the Milesian race.

The only divisions which a traveller, who passed through the kingdom without making any residence, could make, would be into people of considerable fortune, and mob. The intermediate division of the scale, so numerous and respectable in England, would hardly attract the least notice in Ireland. A residence in the kingdom convinces one, however, that there is another class in general of small fortune,—country gentlemen and renters of land. The manners, habits, and customs of people of considerable fortune, are much the same everywhere; at least, there is very little difference between England and Ireland; it is among the common people one must look for those traits by which we discriminate a national character. The circumstances which struck me most in the common Irish were vivacity and a great and eloquent volubility of speech; one would think they could take snuff and talk without tiring till doomsday. They are infinitely more chearful and lively than anything we commonly see in England, having nothing of that incivility of sullen silence, with which so many enlightened Englishmen seem to wrap themselves up, as if retiring within their own importance. Lazy to an extent at *work*, but so spiritedly active at *play*, that at *hurling*, which is the cricket of savages, they shew the greatest feats of agility. Their love of society is as remarkable as their curiosity is insatiable; and their hospitality to all comers, be their own poverty ever so pinching, has too much merit to be forgotten. Pleased to enjoyment with a joke, or witty repartee, they will repeat it with such expression, that the laugh will be universal. Warm friends and revengeful enemies, they are inviolable in their secrecy, and inevitable in their resentment; with such a notion of honour, that neither threat nor reward would induce them to betray the secret or person of a man, though an oppressor whose property they would plunder without ceremony. Hard drinkers and quarrelsome; great liars, but civil, submissive, and obedient. Dancing is so universal among them that there are everywhere itinerant dancing-masters, to whom the cottars pay sixpence a quarter for teaching their families. Besides the Irish jig, which they can dance with a most *luxuriant* expression, minuets and country dances are taught; and I even heard some talk of cotilions coming in.

Some degree of education is also general, hedge-schools, as they are called (they might as well be termed *ditch* ones, for I have seen many a ditch full of scholars) are everywhere to be met with, where reading and writing are taught; schools are also common for men; I have seen a dozen great fellows at school, and was told they were educating with an intention of being priests. Many strokes in their character are evidently to be ascribed to the extreme oppression under which they live. If they are as great thieves and liars as they are reported, it is certainly owing to this cause.

If from the lowest class we rise to the highest, all there is gaiety, pleasure, luxury, and extravagance; the town life at Dublin is formed on the model of that of London. Every night in the winter there is a ball or a party, where the polite circle meet, not to enjoy but to sweat each other; a great crowd crammed into twenty feet square gives a zest to the *agréments* of small talk and whist. There are four or five houses large enough to receive a company commodiously, but the rest are so small as to make parties detestable. There is, however, an agreeable society in Dublin, in which a man of large fortune will not find his time heavy. The stile of living may be guessed from the fortunes of the resident nobility and great commoners; there are about thirty that possess incomes from seven to twenty thousand pounds a year. The Court has nothing remarkable or splendid in it, but varies very much, according to the private fortune or liberality of disposition in the Lord Lieutenant.

In the country their life has some circumstances which are not commonly seen in England. Large tracts of land are kept in hand by everybody, to supply the deficiencies of markets; this gives such a plenty that, united with the lowness of taxes and prices, one would suppose it difficult for them to spend their incomes, if Dublin in the winter did not lend assistance. Let it be considered that the prices of meat are much lower than in England; poultry only a fourth of the price; wild fowl and fish in vastly greater plenty; rum and brandy not half the price; coffee, tea, and wines far cheaper; labour not above a third; servants' wages upon an average thirty per cent. cheaper. That taxes are inconsiderable; for there is no land tax, no poor rates, no window tax, no candle or soap tax, only half a wheel tax, no servants' tax, and a variety of other articles heavily burthened in England, but not in Ireland. Considering all this, one would think they could not spend their incomes; they do contrive it, however. In this business they are assisted by two customs that have an admirable tendency to it, great numbers of horses and servants. The excess in the latter are in the lower sort; owing, not only to the general laziness, but also to the number of attendants every one of a higher class will have; this is common in great families in England, but in Ireland a man of five hundred pounds a year feels it. As to horses, the number is carried quite to a folly; in order to explain this point, I shall insert a table of the demesnes of many of the nobility and gentry, which will shew not only the number of horses, but of other cattle, the quantity of land they keep, and other circumstances explanatory of their country life.

Demesnes.

Names.	Acres.	Wood.	Corn.	Turn. and Cabb.	Rent.	Labourers.	Horses.	Plough Oxen.	Sheep.
Mr. Clements . . .	240	—	14	—	£420	20	22	6	163
Col. Marley	200	—	31	1½	300	—	8	4	40
Mr. Rowley	700	100	—	3	700	—	90	—	250
Lord Conyngham . .	447	120	32	3	—	—	37	—	44
Lord Bective . . .	1600	—	84	—	2000	140	100	20	500
Mr. Gerard	1200	—	64	—	1300	—	12	—	1300
Lord Longford . . .	320	—	32	5	300	20	26	12	100
Mr. Johnson . . .	410	110	10	5	320	9	8	4	200
Dean Coote	500	—	35	8	350	30	35	8	200
General Walsh . . .	700	—	71	5	—	50	—	—	150
Mr. Brown	300	—	—	—	460	—	8	—	800
Mr. Bushe	170	30	50	2	330	—	15	8	70
Lord Courtown . . .	300	—	30	7	315	30	21	12	70
General Cuninghame.	150	—	34	—	375	20	16	5	70
Lord Gosfort. . . .	300	—	25	3	450	30	43	4	46
Mr. Close	100	—	23	—	135	9	10	—	40
Mr. Lesly	350	100	32	—	350	30	37	20	150
Mr. Savage	190	—	35	2	250	—	32	—	40
Mr. O'Neil	733	—	57	17	549	40	68	24	500
Mr. Leslie	1026	60	101	—	790	50	46	24	80
Sir J. Caldwell . . .	700	300	41	11	900	—	—	—	—
Mr. Corry	1000	—	68	—	900	120	—	—	500
Lord Ross	950	125	—	—	—	30	30	—	120
Lord Farnham . . .	1000	200	55	10	800	100	108	22	285
Mr. Newcomen . .	400	—	40	—	—	—	—	18	—
Mr. Mahon	1100	100	60	—	840	20	30	—	500
Mr. Cooper	1000	300	22	8	—	60	25	12	130
Mr. Brown	370	—	18	—	—	10	30	—	300
Mr. Gore	3300	—	160	—	2310	120	170	—	5000
Lord Altamont . .	1500	—	120	6	1000	100	70	20	200
Mr. French	1790	252	55	—	—	100	20	14	424
Mr. Trench	1046	100	13	—	600	80	45	10	980
Sir Lucius O'Brien .	399	30	47	—	560	60	26	11	138
Mr. Fitzgerald . . .	3000	—	—	—	2000	26	54	18	1800
Mr. Aldworth . . .	1270	600	550	12	1010	—	33	16	500
Lord Donneraile . .	1200	200	200	5	1500	60	54	40	400
Colonel Jepson . . .	300	—	35	—	900	—	24	—	120
Mr. Gordon	915	—	114	—	700	45	13	15	187

Names.	Acres.	Wood.	Corn.	Turn. and Cabb.	Rent.	Labourers.	Horses.	Plough Oxen.	Sheep.
Mr. Jeffries	304	—	20	—	£300	—	32	—	200
Mr. Trent	238	24	21	—	—	—	13	5	200
Lord Shannon . . .	1600	268	81	—	1500	132	11	36	470
Mr. Longfield . . .	1100	—	78	—	800	20	65	14	200
Rev. Archd. Oliver .	900	—	136	16	650	50	25	21	100
Mr. Herbert	1300	780	—	—	400	—	18	30	300
Mr. Bateman . . .	250	—	5	—	250	—	30	—	60
Lord Glendour . . .	1000	100	55	—	1000	—	50	—	200
Mr. Fitzgerald . . .	200	—	23	3	200	—	21	8	60
Mr. Leslie	250	50	27	—	230	—	24	6	60
Mr. Oliver	500	100	24	10	500	50	30	10	125
Mr. Ryves	300	—	25	—	450	6	20	—	300
Lord Clanwilliam . .	640	—	34	8	600	30	40	—	600
Mr. Macartney . . .	9000	—	—	—	10000	170	180	80	8000
Lord de Montalt . .	1300	300	—	—	—	75	40	40	1500
Mr. Moore	600	—	17	—	1155	—	—	—	1000
Lord Tyrone . . .	2100	1500	64	—	1200	200	36	48	400
Mr. Bolton	200	—	28	—	300	40	25	6	70
Mr. Nevill	220	24	—	—	350	—	22	—	100
Mr. Lloyd	200	—	—	—	150	—	12	—	182
Mr. Holmes	540	49	25	15	540	40	30	14	590
Mr. Head	450	16	27	—	675	20	—	—	400
Lord Kingsborough .	600	100	30	5	400	100	40	—	200

The intelligent reader will collect something more than mere curiosity from this table; it will necessarily strike him, that a country residence in Ireland demands a much larger quantity of land in hand than in England; from which might be deduced, if not from any thing else, how much backwarder the former is than the latter; where markets are wanting, every thing must be had at home, a case stronger still in America. In England such extensive demenses would be parks around the seats, for beauty as much as use, but it is not so in Ireland; the words *deer-park* and *demesne* are to be distinguished; there are great demesnes without any parks, but a want of taste, too common in Ireland, is having a deer-park at a distance from the house; the residence surrounded by walls, or hedges, or cabbins; and the lawn enclosure scattered with animals of various sorts, perhaps three miles off. The small quantity of corn proportioned to the total acres, shews how little tillage is attended to, even by those who are the best able to carry it on; and the column of turneps proves in the clearest manner, what the progress of improvement is in that kingdom. The number of horses may almost be esteemed a satire upon common sense; were they well fed enough to be useful, they would not be so numerous, but I have found a good hack for a common ride scarce in a house where there were a hundred. Upon an average, the horses in gentlemen's stables, throughout the kingdom, are not fed half so well as they are in England by men of equal fortune; yet the number makes the expence of them very heavy.

Another circumstance to be remarked in the country life is the miserableness of many of their houses; there are men of five thousand a year in Ireland, who live in habitations that a man of seven hundred a year in England would disdain; an air of neatness, order, dress, and *proprete*, is wanting to a surprizing degree around the mansion; even new and excellent houses have often nothing of this about them. But the badness of the houses is remedying every hour throughout the whole kingdom, for the number of new ones just built, or building, is prodigiously great. I should suppose there were not ten dwellings in the kingdom thirty years ago that were fit for an English pig to live in. Gardens were equally bad; but now they are running into the contrary extreme, and wall in five, six, ten, and even twenty Irish acres for a garden, but generally double or treble what is necessary.

The tables of people of fortune are very plentifully spread; many elegantly; differing in nothing from those of England. I think I remarked that venison wants the flavour it has with us, probably for the same reason, that the produce of rich parks is never equal to to that of poor ones; the moisture of the climate and the richness of the soil give fat but not flavour. Another reason is the smallness of the parks; a man who has three or four thousand acres in his hands has not, perhaps, above three or four hundred in his deer park; and range is a great point for good venison. Nor do I think that garden vegetables have the flavour found in those of England, certainly owing to the climate; green peas I found every where perfectly insipid, and lettuce, &c. not good. Claret is the common wine of all tables, and so much inferior to what is drank in England, that it does not appear to be the same wine; but their port is incomparable, so much better than the English as to prove, if proof was wanting, the abominable adulterations it must undergo with us. Drinking and duelling are two charges which have long been alledged against the gentlemen of Ireland, but the change of manners which has taken place in that kingdom is not generally known in England. Drunkenness ought no longer to be a reproach; for at every table I was at in Ireland I saw a perfect freedom reign; every person drank just as little as they pleased, nor have I ever been asked to drink a single glass more than I had an inclination for; I may go farther and assert that hard drinking is very rare among people of fortune; yet it is certain that they sit much longer at table than in England. I was much surprized at first going over to find no summons to coffee, the company often sitting till eight, nine, or ten o'clock before they went to the ladies. If a gentleman likes tea or coffee, he retires without saying any thing; a stranger of rank may propose it to the master of the house, who from custom, contrary to that of England, will not stir till he receives such a hint, as they think it would imply a desire to save their wine. If the gentlemen were generally desirous of tea, I take it for granted they would have it; but their slighting is one inconvenience to such as desire it; not knowing when it is provided, conversation may carry them beyond the time; and then, if they do *trifle* over the coffee it will certainly be *cold*. There is a want of attention in this, which the ladies should remedy; if they will not break the old custom and send to the gentlemen, which is what they ought to do, they certainly should have a salver fresh. I must however remark that at the politest tables, which are those of people who have resided much out of Ireland, this point is conducted exactly as it is in England.

Duelling was once carried to an excess, which was a real reproach and scandal to the kingdom; it of course proceeded from excessive drinking; as the cause has disappeared, the effect has nearly followed: not, however, entirely; for it is yet far more common among people of fashion than in England. Of all practices a man, who felt for the honour of his country, would wish soonest to banish this; for there is not one favourable conclusion to be drawn from it: as to courage, nobody can question that of a polite and enlightened nation, entitled to a share of the reputation of the age; but it implies uncivilized manners, an ignorance of those forms which govern polite societies, or else a brutal drunkenness; the latter is no longer the cause or the pretence. As to the former, they would place the national character so backward, would take from it so much of its pretence to civilization, elegance and politeness of manners, that no true Irishman would be pleased with the imputation. Certain it is, that none are so captious as those who think themselves neglected or despised; and none are so ready to believe themselves either one or the other, as persons unused to good company. Captious people, therefore, who are ready to take an affront, must inevitably have been accustomed to ill company, unless there should be something uncommonly crooked in their natural dispositions, which is not to be supposed. Let every man that fights his one, two, three, or half a dozen duels, receive it as a maxim, that every one he adds to the number is but an additional proof of his being ill educated, and having vitiated his manners by the contagion of bad company; who is it that can reckon the most numerous rencontres? who but the bucks, bloods, land-jobbers, and little drunken country gentlemen? Ought not people of fashion to blush at a practice which will very soon be the distinction only of the most contemptible of the people? the point of honour will and must remain for the decision of certain affronts; but it will rarely be had recourse to in polite, sensible, and well bred company. The practice among *real* gentlemen in Ireland every day declining is a strong proof, that a knowledge of the world corrects the old manners; and, consequently, its having ever been prevalent was owing to the causes to which I have attributed it.

There is another point of manners somewhat connected with the present subject, which partly induced me to place a motto at the head of this section. It is the conduct of juries. The criminal law of Ireland is the same as that of England; but in the execution it is so different, as scarcely to be known. I believe it is a fact, at least I have been assured so, that no man was ever hanged in Ireland for killing another in a duel: the security is such that nobody ever thought of removing out of the way of justice; yet there have been deaths of that sort, which had no more to do with *honour* than stabbing in the dark. I believe Ireland is the only country in Europe, I am sure it is the only part of the British dominions, where associations among men of fortune are necessary for apprehending ravishers. It is scarcely credible how many young women, have even of late years been ravished, and carried off, in order (as they generally have fortunes) to gain to appearance a voluntary marriage. These actions it is true are not committed by the class I am considering at present; but they are tried by them, and ACQUITTED. I think there has been only one man executed for that crime, which is so common as to occasion the associations I mentioned; it is to this supine execution of the law that such enormities are owing. Another circumstance, which has the effect of screening all sorts of offenders, is men of fortune protecting them, and making interest for their acquittal, which is attended with a variety of evil consequences. I heard it boasted in the county of Fermanagh, that there had not been a man hanged in it for two and twenty years; all I concluded from this was, that there had been many a jury who deserved it richly.

Let me, however, conclude what I have to observe on the conduct of the principal people residing in Ireland; that there are great numbers among them who are as liberal in all their ideas as any people in Europe; that they have seen the errors which have given an ill character to the manners of their country, and done every thing that example could effect to produce a change: that that happy change has been partly effected, and is effecting every hour; insomuch that a man may go into a vast variety of families, which he will find actuated by no other principles than those of the most cultivated politeness, and the most liberal urbanity.

But I must now come to another class of people, to whose conduct it is almost entirely owing that the character of the nation has not that lustre abroad, which, I dare assert, it will soon very generally merit: this is the class of little country gentlemen;[1] tenants, who drink their claret by means of profit rents; jobbers in farms; bucks; your fellows with round hats, edged with gold, who hunt in the day, get drunk in the evening, and fight the next morning. I shall not dwell on a subject so perfectly disagreeable; but remark that these are the men among whom drinking, wrangling, quarrelling, fighting, ravishing, &c. &c. &c. are found as in their native soil; once to a degree that made them the pest of society; they are growing better, but even now, one or two of them, got by accident (where they have no business) into better company, are sufficient very much to *derange* the pleasures that result from a liberal conversation. A new spirit, new fashions, new modes of politeness, exhibited by the higher ranks, are imitated by the lower; which will, it is to be hoped, put an end to this race of beings; and either drive their sons and cousins into the army or navy, or sink them into plain farmers, like those we have in England, where it is common to see men, with much greater property, without pretending to be gentlemen. I repeat it from the intelligence I received, that even this class are very different from what they were twenty years ago, and improve so fast, that the time will soon come when the national character will not be degraded by any set.

That character is upon the whole respectable: it would be unfair to attribute to the nation at large the vices and follies of only one class of individuals. Those persons from whom it is candid to take a general estimate do credit to their country. That they are a people learned, lively and ingenious, the admirable authors they have produced will be an eternal monument; witness their Swift, Sterne,

[1] This expression is not to be taken in a general sense. God forbid I should give this character of all country gentlemen of small fortunes in Ireland: I have myself been acquainted with exceptions.—I mean only that in general they are not the most liberal people in the kingdom. —[*Author's note.*]

Congreve, Boyle, Berkeley, Steele, Farquhar, Southerne, and Goldsmith. Their talent for eloquence is felt and acknowledged in the Parliaments of both the kingdoms. Our own service both by sea and land, as well as that (unfortunately for us) of the principal monarchies of Europe, speak their steady and determined courage. Every unprejudiced traveller who visits them will be as much pleased with their chearfulness, as obliged by their hospitality: and will find them a brave, polite, and liberal people.

SECTION XVIII.

CORN TRADE OF IRELAND.—BOUNTY ON INLAND CARRIAGE.

THE police of corn in Ireland is almost confined to one of the most singular measures that have any where been adopted; which is, giving a bounty on the inland carriage of corn from all parts of the kingdom to the capital. Before it is fully explained, it will be necessary to state the motives that were the inducement to it.

Dublin, it was asserted, from the peculiarity of its situation on the eastern extremity, without any inland navigations leading to it, was found to be, in point of consumption, more an English than an Irish city, in corn almost as much as in coals. The import of corn and flour drained the kingdom of great sums, at the same time that the supply was uncertain and precarious. It was farther asserted that tillage was exceedingly neglected in Ireland, to the impoverishment of the kingdom, and the misery of the poor. That if some measure could be struck out, at once to remedy those two evils, it would be of singular advantage to the community.

This reasoning furnished the hint to a gentleman of very considerable abilities, now high in office, there to plan the measure I am speaking of. It has been perfected by repeated Acts giving a bounty on

5 Cwt.	or	40 stone	Flour	three-pence per mile.
ditto	—	ditto	Malt	two-pence halfp. ditto.
ditto	—	ditto	Wheat	three-halfpence ditto.
ditto	—	ditto	Oats	one penny ditto.
ditto	—	ditto	Bere	three-halfpence ditto.
ditto	—	ditto	Barley	three-halfpence ditto.

Oatmeal the same as oats; the ten first miles from

Dublin deducted, it amounts, as has been found by experience, to nearly twenty per cent. more for flour than the real expence of carriage, and one and a half per cent. more for wheat. In consequence of this Act many of the finest mills for grinding corn that are to be found in the world were erected, some of which have been built upon such a scale, as to have cost near £20,000. The effect has been considerable in extending tillage, and great quantities of the produce are carried to Dublin. Before I offer any observations on this system, it will be necessary to insert such tables as are necessary to explain the extent, effect, and expence of the measure, which took place in 1762, and, in 1766 and 7, arose to above £60,000. In order to see what the import was before that period, and also what it was before the bounty was in full play, as well as since, the following table will have its use.

Import of Corn and Flour.

Year.	Barley and malt. Qrs.	Wheat. Qrs.	Flour. Cwt.
1744	2,450	329	20,977
1745	11,305	6,342	24,708
1746	138,934	129,190	110,832
1747	85,316	28,973	37,190
1748	29,015	3,402	—
1749	39,121	8,720	30,502
Average	51,023	29,492	37,368
Value	£51,023	£44,238	£18,684
1750	44,836	16,275	50,637
1751	47,581	20,317	60,985
1752	69,861	30,425	78,282
1753	61,927	18,195	63,527
1754	109,539	39,635	91,583
1755	99,386	57,699	89,015
1756	78,061	20,412	71,343
Average	73,027	28,994	72,196
Value	£73,027	£43,491	£36,098

Import of Corn and Flour (continued).

Year.	Barley and Malt.		Wheat.		Flour.	
	Quantity.	Value.	Quantity.	Value.	Quantity.	Value.
	qrs.	£	qrs.	£	C.	£
1757	59,354	59,354	31,711	47,567	55,975	27,978
1758	38,123	38,123	27,850	41,775	72,490	36,245
1759	6,071	6,071	4,718	7,078	27,258	13,629
1760	34,678	34,678	3,697	5,546	30,093	15,046
1761	30,208	30,208	2,427	3,641	30,982	15,491
1762	37,500	37,500	17,129	25,694	51,522	25,761
1763	44,264	44,264	22,655	33,982	57,048	28,524
Average	35,742	35,743	15,741	23,612	46,481	23,382
1764	31,587	31,587	25,763	38,645	108,209	54,104
1765	48,854	48,854	10,529	15,794	67,409	33,704
1766	40,356	40,356	14,130	21,196	81,371	40,685
1767	30,681	30,681	39,456	59,184	58,182	29,091
1768	5,684	5,684	11,802	17,704	22,600	11,300
1769	4,759	5,948	2,199	3,299	15,447	7,723
1770	35,514	44,392	43,532	87,065	86,776	52,065
Average	28,205	29,643	21,059	34,698	62,856	32,667
1771	55,620	69,525	53,448	106,897	125,321	75,193
1772	22,372	27,965	12,163	24,327	47,754	28,652
1773	6,970	8,712	2,861	5,722	10,306	6,183
1774	189	236	4,104	8,893	23,465	14,079
1775	656	820	3,235	7,009	28,902	17,341
1776	7,857	8,643	7,547	16,353	26,292	15,775
1777	43,101	47,411	3,457	7,490	69,838	41,903
Average	19,538	23,330	12,402	25,242	47,697	[1]28,446

Barley and Malt.

Average import of the	Qrs.	Value. £
First period	51,023	51,023
Second ditto	73,027	73,027
Third ditto	35,742	35,743
Fourth ditto	28,205	29,643
Fifth ditto	19,538	23,330

Wheat.

Average of the	Qrs.	Value. £
First period	29,492	44,238
Second ditto	28,994	43,491
Third ditto	15,741	32,612
Fourth ditto	21,059	34,698
Fifth ditto	12,402	25,242

[1] MS. communicated by the Right Hon. John Beresford, First Commissioner of the Revenue in Ireland.

Flour.

Average of the	Cwt.	Value. £
First period	... 37,368	... 18,684
Second ditto	... 72,196	... 36,098
Third ditto	.. 46,481	... 23,382
Fourth ditto	... 62,856	... 32,667
Fifth ditto	... 47,697	... 28,446

	£
Average value of the three commodities in the three first periods	116,436
Ditto of the two last	71,013
The import in the last fourteen years is less than in the preceding twenty by .	45,423
Import of the fourth period	97,008
Ditto of the fifth, being the period in which the bounty hath taken full effect	77,018
Difference	19,990

These authentic comparisons differ most surprizingly from the assertions that have been made to me in conversation. I was led to believe that Dublin was no longer fed with English corn and flour, and that the difference of the import since the bounty took effect was not less than £200,000 a year. What those assertions could mean is to me perfectly ænigmatical. Have the gentlemen who are fast friends to this measure never taken the trouble to examine these papers? Has the business been so often before Parliament, and committees of Parliament, without having been particularly sifted? We here find that the import into Ireland of foreign barley and malt, wheat and flour, have lessened in the last seven years, compared with the preceding seven years, no more than to the amount of about £20,000. I read with attention the report of Mr. Forster's committee in 1774, the purport of which was to establish the principles whereon this bounty was given; but, as the whole of that performance turns on a comparison of fifteen years before 1758, and fifteen years after, though itself contains a declaration (page 7) that the great effect of the measure then concerned only the three last years, very little information of consequence is to be drawn from it, since it assigns a merit to the measure, while it admits none could flow from it; nor does the whole report contain one syllable of the decrease in the export of pasturage, which ought to have been minutely examined. But in order that we may have the whole corn-trade before us, let me insert the import of other sorts of corn.

Wheat Meal.		Oatmeal.		Beans and Pease.		Oats.	
Quantity.	Value.	Quantity.	Value.	Quantity.	Value.	Quantity.	Value.
Barrels.	£	Barrels.	£	Qrs.	£	Qrs.	£
		4,677	1,559	425	382		
		4,038	1,346	647	582	5,985	3,591
		10	3	269	242	59	35
9	11			410	369	72	43
				285	256	56	33
95	119	1,181	393	497	447	9	5
23	29	7,912	2,637	366	329		
18	22	2,545	848	414	373	883	529
1,136	1,420	55	18	543	489	139	83
46	57			868	781		
417	521	520	173	579	521	744	446
9,659	12,074	740	246	689	620	2,854	1,712
5,351	6,689			389	350	950	570
1,023	1,278			453	453	115	74
1,854	2,781	104	36	752	752	44	28
2,355	3,546	202	67	610	566	692	416
3,686	5,529	14,625	5,119	2,356	2,356	1,820	1,274
2,904	4,356	13,599	4,759	836	836	351	246
782	1,173	1,495	523	428	428	56	39
759	1,138	430	150	481	602	333	250
1,600	2,400	1,171	410	1,110	1,388	4	3
682	1,023			781	976	24	18
36	48	1,558	545	6,305	7,882	387	290
1,492	2,238	4,695	1,644	1,757	2,067	425	303[1]

lue of the import per annum of these articles in the
ast seven years £6,252
to in the preceding seven years 4,595

Increase . . . £1,657

Here therefore we find that, instead of a decrease in the port, the contrary has taken place.

[1] MS. communicated by the Right Hon. Isaac Barré.

Recapitulation of the total Value of Corn, Flour, &c. imported:—

In the year 1757	... £136,860		In the year 1764	... £126,346
1758	... 121,662		1765	... 99,190
1759	... 27,058		1766	... 103,898
1760	... 55,694		1767	... 133,608
1761	... 49,629		1768	... 42,297
1762	... 89,919		1769	... 18,776
1763	... 109,765		1770	... [1] 187,119
Average of seven years	£84,369		Average of seven years	£101,604

In the year 1771	... £265,897		In the year 1776	... £42,788
1772	... 91,141		1777	... 105,559
1773	... 22,780			
1774	... 25,348		Average of seven years	£84,697
1775	... 29,371			

Second period	£101,604
Last seven years	84,697
Decrease	£16,907

Here is the result of the whole import account; the balance of which in favour of the nation is no more than this trifling sum of sixteen thousand pounds. The account however must be farther examined; we must take the export side of the question, for there has been an export, notwithstanding this great import. We see something of this in the register of our English corn trade, where is a considerable speculative commerce in corn; but, as no such thing exists in Ireland, where the corn trade is a simple import of a necessary of life, it is a little surprizing if any great export appears. Let us however examine the account.

[1] The Dublin Society were not very accurate, when in their petition to Parliament they set forth, that in two years preceding 1771 the import amounted to *upwards of* £600,000.

	Corn.								Flour and Meal.				Totals.
	Barley.	Beans	Malt.	Meslin.	Oats.	Pease.	Rye	Wheat.	Flour.	Groat.	Oat.	Wheat.	
	£	£	£	£	£	£	£	£	£	£	£	£	£
Year 1757	44	75	3		5,369	5		4		9	6,576	20	12,105
1758	6,537	128	10		3,120	20		1,037		12	2,231	9	13,104
1759	2,076	312	422		12,281	38	13	3,521		378	12,536	65	31,642
1760	3,701	535	780		1,233	71	143	2,317		92	4,410	257	13,539
1761	2,942	853	1,210		686	53	310	1		30	5,816	26	11,927
1762	1,814	886	665		1,680	70	46	16		573	3,738	54	9,542
1763	2,734	105	70		4,314	13		154		4	4,988	21	12,403
Average .	2,835	413	451		4,097	38	73	1,007		156	5,756	64	14,894
Year 1764	1,785	318	376	64	6,684	78	6	44		158	9,189	166	18,868
1765	874	911	1,058		13,512	67	128	495		35	11,042	27	28,149
1766	8,712	840	1,032		8,365	237	68	351		222	15,701	29	35,557
1767					238	12				2	180	15	447
1768	8,205	108	13		9,300	433	5	3,627	2,867		17,897	15	42,470
1769	8,485	677	6,127		29,408	148	33	14,422	10,627	20	29,386	7	99,340
1770	1,066	60	1,234		12,924	20		103	12	3	13,840		29,268
Average .	4,161	416	1,405	9	11,490	142	34	2,720	1,929	62	13,890	37	36,299
Year 1771	168	3	390		3,217	18			29	6	495		4,326
1772	1,109	56	176		14,079	33	13	1,694	197	11	20,248		37,616
1773	5,784	428	155		10,250	55	54	4,374	115	25	10,040		31,280
1774	12,405	643	674		37,330	164	137	1,825	1,144	20	41,706		96,048
1775	13,327	13	375		23,347	121	140	8,268	3,524	30	18,749		65,894
1776	7,874	775	2		45,668	268	59	30,705	9,024	75	19,714	133	114,297
1777	859	2,217			47,911	348		26,158	18,405	170	8,574		104,642
Average .	5,932	590	253		25,971	143	57	10,432	4,634	48	17,075	19	64,871[1]

[1] Drawn from the totals of the export tables in the MS. communicated by Colonel Barré.

Exported in the last seven years per annum . . .	£64,871
Ditto in the seven preceding	36,299
Increase	£28,572

But as the preceding table includes the export from all the ports in the kingdom, I have inserted it as an object of general information, not as immediately necessary to the enquiry before us, which concerns the port of Dublin only. A measure which draws the corn to that capital from all the ports in the kingdom, can never promote an export from them, but must operate in a contrary manner: for this reason I have drawn the export of the port of Dublin from the general tables for twenty-one years, and find the averages of the three periods, each of seven years, to be in value as follows: the table itself is too voluminous to insert.

	£	s.	d.
Exported in the first seven years, per annum	2,692	5	0
——— second ditto	3,978	2	0
——— last ditto	7,550	9	0
The last period greater than that preceding by	3,572	7	0

Which sum is the profit to be carried to the account of the inland carriage bounty.

I must here observe, that there was a bounty given on exportation, which took place the 24th of June, 1774, viz. 3*s*. 2*d*. on the quarter of wheat, ground wheat, meal, or wheat flour. 2*s*. 4*d*. on the quarter of rye, pease or beans ground or unground. 1*s*. 3*d*. on the quarter of oats, which Act declares the half quarter of wheat, rye, pease, beans, meal, &c. shall be 224 lb. barley and malt were left out, to ensure the Acts passing in England.

The following sessions an additional duty on the import was laid of 2*s*. a barrel on all wheat, and 1*s*. per hundred weight on all flour, meal, bread, and biscuit, except of the produce of or manufacture of Great Britain, to be levied when the middle price of wheat at the port where imported shall exceed 23*s*. English, the barrel of 280 lb. The old duty on wheat was 2*d*. per barrel; on flour 1*s*. from all ports, Great Britain included.

Decrease in the import of the last seven years	£16,907
Increase in the export from Dublin	3,572

Total gain per annum according to this account in the last seven years £20,479

The reader is not to imagine from hence, that the corn trade of Ireland yields a balance of profit; the advantage to be attributed to the bounty from this account is only a *lessening* of loss, as will appear from the following state of export and import over the whole kingdom.

Import and Export compared in value.

	Import.	Export.	Balance profit.	Balance loss.
	£	£	£	£
Year 1757	136,860	12,105		124,755
1758	121,662	13,104		108,558
1759	27,058	31,642	4,584	
1760	55,694	13,539		42,155
1761	49,629	11,927		37,702
1762	89,919	9,542		80,377
1763	109,762	12,403		97,359
Average . .	84,369	14,894	654	70,129
Year 1764	126,346	18,868		107,478
1765	99,190	28,149		71,041
1766	103,898	35,557		68,341
1767	133,608	447		133,161
1768	42,297	42,470	173	
1769	18,776	99,340	80,564	
1770	187,119	29,268		157,851
Average . .	101,604	36,299	11,533	76,838
Year 1771	265,897	4,326		261,571
1772	91,141	37,616		53,525
1773	22,788	31,280	8,493	
1774	25,348	96,048	70,700	
1775	29,371	65,894	36,523	
1776	42,788	114,297	71,509	
1777	105,559	104,642		917
Average . .	83,270	64,871	26,746	45,144

Loss per annum in the middle seven years . . . £76,838
Gain ditto 11,533

Neat loss per annum £65,305

Loss per annum in the last seven years	£45,144
Gain ditto	26,746
Neat loss per annum	18,398

It is a reduction of the loss of £65,000 down to £18,000.

Having thus discovered the advantage of the measure, let us in the next place examine, at what expence this benefit has been obtained. The following table shews the payments of the bounty to each county; the totals; the stones of corn, and the cwts. of flour brought.

An Account of the Sums paid as Bounties on the Inland Carriage of Corn to Dublin. From the beginning to 1777.

	1762.	1763.	1764.	1765.	1766.	1767.	1768.	1769.
	£	£	£	£	£	£	£	£
Antrim								21
Armagh				1				
Carlow	160	161	228	94	151	59	197	849
Cavan				15			5	
Clare					1			31
Cork					83	133	587	907
Donegal								25
Dublin		4						133
Fermanagh								
Galway	50	12	107	327	345	18	178	303
Kildare	748	614	518	387	446	318	518	2,304
Kilkenny	2,079	2,507	2,647	2,719	4,506	3,172	5,712	9,294
Kings	447	327	461	524	380	133	669	1,207
Leitrim			5				8	41
Limerick				686	1,383	772	644	790
Longford	8		12	47	36	16	304	5,341
Louth				3	2	620	78	42
Mayo			3	7	11		6	61
Meath	506	422	396	303	267	461	1,314	2,567
Monaghan								
Queen's	651	707	756	596	597	48	1,065	2,308
Roscommon	12	6	105	312	159		346	653
Sligo			9	14	8	119	93	226
Tipperary	191	220	70	232	339	172	338	806
Waterford								
Westmeath	33	25	62	313	325	15	622	874
Wexford	33	30	61	45	143	3	910	1,106
Wicklow	21	55	35	25	22		53	124
Totals	4,940	5,096	5,483	6,660	9,212	6,074	13,675	25,225
	1,720,869 st.	1,592,418 st.	1,622,933 st.	1,409,726 st.	1,464,296 st.[1]	945,289 st.[1]	2,148,805 st.[1]	2,608,910 st. 107,986 Ct.

[1] Flour included.

An Account of the Sums paid as Bounties on the Inland Carriage of Corn to Dublin. (Continued.)

	1770.	1771.	1772.	1773.	1774.	1775.	1776.	1777.
	£	£	£	£	£	£	£	£
Antrim	267	133	7	27				
Armagh	3	4						
Carlow	800	423	1,025	2,676	2,813	2,425	1,994	2,479
Cavan	2			6		8	24	18
Clare	34	4	116	179	119	131	133	
Corke	979	1,399	1,360	1,491	1,902	783	4,200	2,350
Donegall								
Dublin	300	289	400	488	576	460	469	517
Fermanagh				2	5			
Galway	70	13	461	623	812	1,570	1,873	1,200
Kildare	1,910	2,187	2,939	3,372	2,922	2,603	3,199	3,485
Kilkenny	8,104	9,752	18,215	16,279	14,996	14,690	16,326	20,816
King's	624	678	2,243	2,021	2,647	1,750	3,138	3,161
Leitrim	3	1	20	20	3	8	45	17
Limerick	79	463	714	1,134	2,604	2,066	2,773	607
Longford	143	15	217	277	170	341	339	311
Louth	36	27	168	131	66	27	150	212
Mayo	4	5	85	214	208	339	201	157
Meath	2,158	1,351	2,333	2,455	2,733	2,739	3,633	4,504
Monaghan		3	4				13	66
Queen's	1,479	1,781	3,512	3,564	3,511	3,558	4,056	3,161
Roscommon	198	18	598	958	1,135	1,012	1,892	1,740
Sligo	202	14	391	433	388	198	320	192
Tipperary	381	103	2,997	4,963	8,070	10,426	10,577	9,862
Waterford				110	129	188	46	
Westmeath	350	292	877	1,467	1,912	1,415	2,045	1,562
Wexford	495	293	820	1,437	1,745	2,306	3,172	4,952
Wicklow	81	28	63	125	204	124	116	318
Totals	18,706	19,290	39,560	44,465	49,674	58,889	60,745	61,796
	1,920,973 st. 79,350 Ct.	1,641,867 st. 87,965 Ct.	3,146,960 st. 153,139 Ct.	3,263,199 st. 175,177 Ct.	3,553,996 st. 190,346 Ct.	3,211,214 st. 213,885 Ct.	3,622,076 st. 256,256 Ct.	3,240,692 st. 317,753 Ct.[1]

[1] Taken from the Journals of the House of Commons. In 1778 the total payment was £71,533, and in 1779, £67,904, besides £2,[illegible] for it coastways, a new bounty.

Total payment in 1764	.	£5,483
1765	.	6,660
1766	.	9,212
1767	.	6,074
1768	.	13,675
1769	.	25,225
1770	.	18,706
Paid in seven years	.	£85,038
Which is, per annum		£12,148

Total payment in 1771	.	£19,290
1772	.	39,560
1773	.	44,465
1774	.	49,674
1775	.	53,889
1776	.	60,745
1777	.	61,786
Paid in seven years	.	£329,413
Which is, per annum		£47,059

If therefore the account was to be closed here, it appears that forty-seven thousand pounds per annum have been given of the publick money for a gain in the export and import account of corn of twenty thousand pounds a year. Surely this is paying very dear for it!—but the account does not end here.

From this table the reader finds that the bounty has been continually rising, until it has exceeded sixty thousand pounds a year. It also appears that the encrease of tillage has been chiefly in the counties of Kilkenny, Tipperary, Carlow, Meath, Kildare, King's, Wexford, Queen's, and Limerick, as will appear by contrasting the first and the last years of those counties.

Counties.	1762.	1777
Kilkenny	£2,079	£20,816
Tipperary	191	9,862
Carlow	160	2,479
Meath	506	4,594
Kildare	748	3,485
King's	447	3,161
Wexford	33	4,952
Queen's	651	3,161
Roscommon	12	1,740

And Limerick arose from nothing at all to £2,773 in the year 1776; from hence one fact clearly appears, that the increase of tillage has by no means been in the poor counties, by breaking up uncultivated lands; on the contrary, it has been entirely in the richest counties in the kingdom; which confirms the intelligence I received on the journey, that it was good sheep land that had principally been tilled. The bounty to Tipperary, Carlow and Roscommon, once the greatest sheep counties in Ireland, was insignificant at the beginning of the measure, but has at last become very great.

This circumstance, so essential in the subject, renders it absolutely necessary to enlarge our enquiry, that we may examine, as well as our materials will permit, whether any national loss, as well as profit, has resulted from converting so much rich pasture land into tillage; and, in order to do this, it will be necessary to lay before the reader the exports of the produce of pasturage from Ireland during these two periods of seven years each, which serve us for a comparison.

An Account of the Export of the Produce of Pasturage, from 1753 to 1777.[1]

Year.	Barrels of Beef.	Ct. Butter.	Ct. Candles.	No. Hides.	Ct. Tallow.	Cows, bull. and horses.	Ct. Cheese
1753	180,877	200,060		160,656	29,128		
1754	149,558	107,998		128,739	20,156		
1755	180,980	223,294		154,184	26,029		
1756	142,686	203,876		113,523	21,217		
1757	147,804	181,134		158,822	18,006		
1758	195,789	181,454		161,197	17,960		
1759	136,356	237,169		117,113	22,331		
Average	162,034	203,569		142,033	22,118		
1764	218,220	257,976	8,895	163,812	50,501	1,089	[illegible]
1765	199,999	301,109	5,564	106,335	52,706	1,767	[illegible]
1766	190,409	271,946	3,293	121,854	46,543	2,135	[illegible]
1767	173,484	257,047	2,862	111,895	51,071	1,880	3,541
1768	209,847	304,623	4,222	124,149	51,662	3,505	4,113
1769	205,368	315,153	3,428	113,056	49,089	2,626	[illegible]
1770	208,269	262,717	1,730	131,130	48,260	1,887	[illegible]
Average	200,799	201,510	4,284	124,604	49,976	2,127	3,341
1771	201,010	238,801	2,170	139,759	46,842	1,298	[illegible]
1772	200,829	288,457	2,430	155,966	44,981	1,057	[illegible]
1773	215,191	272,399	2,183	119,978	39,920	1,476	2,101
1774	187,494	270,096	2,024	108,282	41,350	3,359	[illegible]
1775	192,452	264,140	2,234	136,782	42,295	7,418	[illegible]
1776	203,685	272,411	3,155	108,574	50,549	8,035	[illegible]
1777	168,578[2]	264,181	1,764	84,391	48,502	5,640	[illegible]
Average	195,605	267,212	2,280	121,963	44,919	4,040	[illegible]

[1] The first seven years from the Commons Journals, the last fourteen from the Parliamentary Records of Import and Export. MS.

[2] Since the preceding sheets were finished at press, I have obtained

The prices of all these commodities must be ascertained, in order to discover the increase or decrease of value.

The custom-house price of beef is £1 6*s.* 8*d.* per barrel; but I find that the average price at Waterford, from 1764 to 1776, was 16*s.* per cwt. or £1 12*s.* the barrel. The custom-house rate of butter is £2 per cwt. but by the same authority, I find the real price on the average of the last fourteen years to be £2 5*s.* 6*d.* Candles at the custom house £1 15*s.* per cwt. the real price £2 10*s.* Tallow at the custom-house £2 the true price £2 4*s.* 6*d.*

Average price of four and a half hundred beef per cwt.

	s.	*d.*		*s.*	*d.*		*s.*	*d.*
Year 1756 ...	12	3	Year 1763 ...	13	0	Year 1770 ...	16	0
1757 ...	11	6	1764 ...	13	6	1771 ...	16	6
1758 ...	12	0	1765 ...	14	0	1772 ...	16	0
1759 ...	11	6	1766 ...	16	0	1773 ...	16	6
1760 ...	12	6	1767 ...	17	0	1774 ...	18	0
1761 ...	12	6	1768 ...	13	0	1775 ...	18	0
1762 ...	12	0	1769 ...	15	0	1776 ...	20	0

Average of the last 13 years ... 16*s.*

---

one very important piece of information. My conjecture was right: the export for the troops was not included in the tables for the years, 1777, 1778, and 1779; the following is the addition to be made on this account.

	Beef.	Pork.	Butter.
	Barrels.	Barrels.	Cwt.
In the year 1777	13,206	49,296	8,701
1778	13,206	49,296	8,701
1779 to 25th April. .	14,801	52,260	9,974
1779 to 25th Oct. . .	11,572	41,164	8,572

The sum total of these years is therefore as follow:

	Barrels.	Barrels.	Cwt.
In the year 1777	181,784	122,227	272,882
1778	203,901	126,908	265,245

From hence it appears that, so far has the export of Ireland, in these greatest articles of her provision trade, been from falling off, that the increase is prodigious, and proves in the most satisfactory manner that the tide of her prosperity flows strongly. These were the articles, that, while I was ignorant of the fact, seemed most to speak of a decline; but they prove the contrary too clearly to be doubted.

In addition to this, let me add: I am just informed, that the Irish linen trade is at present in London in a very rising state, the prices high, and the import great.—[*Author's note.*]

Shipping prices of Butter, Tallow, Candles, and Pork, in Waterford, from the Year 1764 to 1777, both inclusive.[1]

	Butter per Cwt.	Tallow per Cwt.	Candles per Cwt.	Pork per barrel.
	s. *s.* *d.*	*s.* *s.* *d.*	*s.* *s.* *d.*	*s.* *s.* *d.*
In the year 1764	43 to 36 0	31 to 30 0	41 to 40 0	40 to 39 0
1765	36 — 38 0	39 — 40 0	40 — 41 0	38 — 40 0
1766	38 — 36 0	42 — 41 0	47 — 48 0	38 — 39 0
1767	47 — 38 0	43 — 44 0	49 — 50 0	43 — 45 0
1768	38 — 42 6	44 — 43 0	51 — 52 0	45 — 48 6
1769	42 — 53 0	44 — 45 0	54 — 53 0	42 — 38 0
1770	45 — 48 6	42 — 40 0	54 — 53 0	41 — 45 0
1771	57 — 48 0	44 — 45 0	53 — 54 0	44 — 46 0
1772	54 — 48 0	46 — 42 0	54 — 56 0	53 — 54 0
1773	56 — 44 0	44 — 42 0	51 — 52 0	58 — 60 0
1774	50 — 40 0	40 — 43 0	54 — 55 0	42 — 45 0
1775	53 — 44 0	40 — 41 0	50 — 51 0	45 — 42 0
1776	53 — 43 0	41 — 40 0	50 — 51 0	47 — 49 0
1777	58 — 55 0	41 — 43 0	51 — 52 0	66 — 70 0
Average . . .	45 6	44 6	50 0	46 6

Those are the prices as they appeared at the beginning and at the end of the year.

Prices of Ox-hides of 112 lbs. from the Year 1756 to 1776, both inclusive.

Year	£	*s.*	*d.*	Year	£	*s.*	*d.*	Year	£	*s.*	*d.*
Year 1756 .	1	7	0	Year 1763 .	0	19	6	Year 1770 .	1	8	0
1757 .	1	7	0	1764 .	0	18	6	1771 .	1	4	0
1758 .	1	2	6	1765 .	1	4	0	1772 .	1	1	0
1759 .	1	1	0	1766 .	1	5	0	1773 .	1	2	6
1760 .	1	0	6	1767 .	1	6	0	1774 .	1	10	0
1761 .	1	2	6	1768 .	1	8	6	1775 .	1	13	0
1762 .	1	2	0	1769 .	1	11	0	1776 .	1	14	0

The real price of hides I was disappointed in at Corke; must therefore take that of the Custom-house, which is, £1 13*s.* 4*d.* tanned, and £1 5*s.* untanned; as more of the latter, I shall suppose £1 8*s.* on an average. Of the cows, bullocks, and horses, I am quite igrorant; shall therefore

[1] MS. Communicated by Cornelius Bolton, Esq., member for that city.

guess them at £5 on an average. Cheese at the Custom-house £1 per cwt.

Total Exports of Pasturage.

First Period.	Per annum.
Export of beef from 1753 to 1759, 162,034 barrels, at £1 12*s.* per	£259,254
Ditto butter, 203,569 cwt. at £2 5*s.* 6*d.* per	463,119
Ditto hides, 142,033, at £1 8*s.* per	198,845
Ditto tallow, 22,118 cwt. at £2 4*s.* 6*d.* per	49,211
Average export of the first seven years	£970,429
Second Period.	
Beef from 1764 to 1770, 200,799 barrels, at £1 12*s.* per	£321,277
Butter, 281,510 cwt. at £2 5*s.* 6d. per	640,434
Candles, 4,284 cwt. at £2 10*s.* per	10,710
Hides, 124,604, at £1 8*s.* per	174,445
Tallow, 49,976 cwt. at £2 4*s.* 6*d.* per	111,196
Live stock, 2,127, at £5 per	10,635
Cheese, 3,341 cwt. at £1 per	3,341
Average export of the second seven years	£1,272,038
Third Period.	
Beef from 1771 to 1777, 195,605 barrels, at £1 12*s.* per	£312,967
Butter, 267,212 cwt. at £2 5*s.* 6*d.* per	607,907
Candles, 2,280 cwt. at £2 10*s.* per	5,016
Hides, 121,963, at £1 8*s.* per	170,747
Tallow, 44,919 cwt. at £2 4*s.* 6*d.* per	99,943
Live stock, 4,040, at £5 per	20,200
Cheese, 2,122 cwt. at £1 per	2,122
Average export of the last seven years	£1,218,902
Second period greater than the first by	£301,609
Second period greater than the last by	53,136

The second period being greater than the first by near three hundred thousand pounds, and Ireland having been throughout all three periods on the advance in prosperity, it follows that the increase should have continued, had not some other reason interfered, and occasioned, instead of a similar increase of three hundred thousand pounds, a falling off of above fifty thousand. I cannot suppose that the increase of tillage did all this; I should suppose that impossible. Most of these commodities are certainly consumed at home, which perhaps may account for there bein[g] no increase; but the increase of tillage must inevitabl[y] have had its share, and it is assigning a very moderate on[e] to it, to suppose the amount no more than this decrease o[f] fifty thousand pounds a year. We come next to sheep, an[d] the exports which depend on them. The following tabl[e] shews the whole at one view.

	Wool.	Value at 14*s.*	Woollen yarn.	Value at 17*s.* 6*d.*	Worsted yarn.	Value at 40*s.*	Total stones.	Total value.
	Stones.	£	Stones.	£	Stones.	£		£
Year 1764	10,128	7,089	9,991	8,742	139,412	278,824	159,531	294,655
1765	17,316	12,121	13,450	11,768	149,915	299,830	180,681	323,719
1766	21,722	15,205	7,980	6,982	152,122	304,244	181,824	326,431
1767	48,733	34,113	7,553	6,603	151,940	303,880	208,226	344,596
1768	28,521	19,964	11,387	9,963	157,721	315,442	197,629	345,369
1769	3,840	2,688	5,012	4,385	131,364	262,728	138,216	269,801
1770	2,578	1,804	3,833	3,353	117,753	235,506	124,164	240,663
Average. .	18,976	13,283	8,458	7,399	142,889	285,779	170,038	306,462
Year 1771	218	152	4,468	3,909	139,378	278,756	144,064	282,817
1772	2,045	1,431	5,947	5,203	115,904	231,808	123,896	238,442
1773	1,839	1,287			94,098	188,196	95,937	189,483
1774	1,007	704			63,920	127,840	64,927	128,544
1775	2,007	1,404			78,896	157,792	80,903	159,196
1776	1,059	741			86,527	173,054	87,586	173,795
1777	1,734	1,213			114,703	229,406	116,437	230,619
Average. .	1,415	990	1,459	1,301	99,060	198,121	101,964	200,413[1]

[1] The quantities taken from the Parliament Records of Import and Export, MS. and the value added.

In the last century the quantity of wool, &c., was much larger, indeed it was so great, as will appear from the following table, as to form a considerable proportion of the kingdom's exports.

	Wool.	Yarn.		Wool	Yarn.
	Stones.	Stones.		Stones.	Stones.
Year 1687	256,592	3,668	Year 1703	360,862	36,873
1697	217,678	13,480	1711	310,136	55,273
1700	336,292	26,617	1712	263,946	60,108
1701	302,812	23,390	1713	171,871	68,548
1702	315,473	43,148	1714	147,153	58,147

Relative to the prices I have charged, the following table is the authority:—

Market Prices of Wool in the Fleece, per stone of sixteen pounds; and of Bay-yarn, per Pack, containing fourteen great stones, of eighteen pounds each.

	Wool. per st.		Bay-yarn. per pack.				Wool. per st.		Bay-yarn. per pack.		
	s.	*d.*	£	*s.*	*d.*		*s.*	*d.*	£	*s.*	*d.*
Year 1764	11	0	26	5	0	Year 1772	[1]0	0	28	7	0
1765	10	0	24	13	6	1773	[1]0	0	27	6	0
1766	11	0	25	4	0	1774	14	0	25	4	0
1767	13	0	27	6	0	1775	16	0	29	8	0
1768	13	6	26	5	0	1776	16	6	30	9	0
1769	13	6	26	15	6	1777	17	6	30	9	0
1770	14	0	26	15	6						
1771	14	0	26	15	6	Average is nearly	14	0	27	4	5

Wool is here rated at the market price for combing-wool rough in the fleece; but no estimate can be formed from this upon what has been exported, the small quantities whereof have been for the most part wool upon skins,

[1] Unsettled but very high.—The pack of bay-yarn is taken to contain 2,100 skains.

or coarse fells, which must have come much lower than the prices herein mentioned.

Woollen yarn for export has not been an article for sale in Ireland; what has been sent out was directly from the manufacturer, I presume in very small quantities, and from the port of Corke only.

Worsted, or bay-yarn, is sent principally to Norwich and Manchester; it sells by the skain in Ireland, but in the preceding table it is rated by the pack; the cost at market is only noticed; the necessary charges on shipping amount to full two per cent. exclusive of commission, which is two per cent. more.

Wool, woollen, and bay-yarn, are exported by the great stone, containing eighteen pounds weight. A licence for exporting must be procured from the Lord Lieutenant, the cost of which is nearly fourpence halfpenny per stone.[1] From comparing the prices at different periods, exported woollen yarn may pretty safely be rated at seventeen shillings and sixpence per stone, of which five shillings a stone is labour.

Exported value in the first period . .	£306,462
Ditto in the last	300,413
Decrease	£106,049

Whoever recurs to the minutes of the journey, in the counties of Carlow, Tipperary, and Roscommon, the great sheep-walks of Ireland, will have no reason to be surprized at this loss of one hundred thousand pounds a year. There are yet other subjects so connected with the present enquiry, that, in order to have a clear and distinct idea of it, we must include them in the account. I think it fair to give tillage credit for any increase there may be in pork, bacon, lard, hogs, and bread; it is true they do not entirely belong to it, for dairies yield much; but, to obviate objections, I will suppose them totally connected with tillage. The following table includes all these articles.

[1] Communicated by Mr. Joshua Pine, in the yarn trade. The custom-house price of wool is 15*s.* woollen yarn 17*s.* and worsted yarn £1 13*s.* 4*d.*

Exports of Pork, &c.

Year.	Pork, barrels.	Flitches of Bacon.	Lard, Cwt.	Bread, Cwt.	Hogs.
1753	23,682				
1754	23,684				
1755	20,930				
1756	51,345				
1757	25,071				
1758	28,746				
1759	40,336				
Average .	30,542[1]				
1764	35,066	226	1,852	8,783	60
1765	44,361	3,592	3,940	7,417	140
1766	50,155	9,640	1,783	8,228	481
1767	34,995	5,778	1,055	6,876	0
1768	43,041	21,275	1,496	6,791	22
1769	40,039	8,156	1,549	6,792	444
1770	43,947	6,500	1,913	5,597	416
Average .	41,649	7,881	1,869	7,197	223
1771	42,519	5,773	1,841	8,006	76
1772	44,713	14,142	2,235	4,575	90
1773	51,112	19,256	2,156	5,827	135
1774	52,328	26,100	2,379	5,090	882
1775	50,367	32,644	1,686	4,012	680
1776	72,714	24,502	3,216	13,302	1,148
1777	72,931	11,462	2,981	29,627	1,358
Average .	55,240	19,125	2,356	10,062	624[2]

Export of pork per annum, from 1764 to 1770, 41,649 barrels, at £2 6s. 6d. per barrel[3]	£96,833
Bacon, 788 cwt. at 15s. per cwt.[4]	5,910
Lard, 1869 cwt. at £1 per cwt.[4]	1,869
Bread, 7197 cwt. at 10s. per cwt.[4]	3,598
Hogs, 223, at 15s. a piece[5]	166
Average export of seven years	108,376

[1] Journals of the House of Commons.
[2] Parliament Record of Export and Import, MS.
[3] Waterford price. [4] Custom House price.
[5] Supposed at that rate for want of authority.

Export of pork per annum, from 1771 to 1777, 55,240 barrels, at £2 6*s*. 6*d*. per barrel	£128,433
Bacon, 19,125 at 15*s*.	14,343
Lard, 2356 cwt. at £1 per cwt.	2,356
Bread, 10,062 cwt. at 10*s*. per cwt.	5,031
Hogs, 624, at 15*s*. a piece	468
Average exports of the last seven years . . .	£150,631
Increase in the last seven years	£42,253

The data are now very completely before the reader, from which the merit of this extraordinary measure may be estimated. I will not assert that any custom-house accounts are absolutely authentic; I know the common objections to them, and that there is a foundation for those objections; but the point of consequence in the present enquiry does not depend on their *absolute*, but comparative accuracy; that is to say, if the errors objected to them exist, they will be found as great in one period as in another; consequently their authority is perfectly competent for the comparison of different ones. Whoever will examine the entries with a minute attention, and compare them with a variety of other circumstances, will generally be able to distinguish the suspicious articles. In the present enquiry I will venture to assert that they speak truth, for they correspond exactly (as I shall by and by shew) with many other causes which could hardly have failed without a miracle of producing the effects they display. I should further add, that on the greatest number of the articles inserted in the preceding tables there are duties paid on the export which exempt them from the common objection to the entries. But to reason against the accuracy of such accounts is perfectly useless, while ministers, in defence of their measures, and patriots in opposition to them, found their arguments on them alone. Whoever attends either the English or Irish House of Commons will presently see this in a multiplicity of instances. All who come to the bar of those Houses, depend on these accounts; Committees of Parliament relie on them, and the best political writers of every period, from Child and Davenant to Campbell and Whitworth, have agreed in the same conduct, knowing the errors to which they are liable, but knowing also that there is no better authority, and that they are perfectly competent to comparisons.

Having thus closed my authorities, I shall now draw them into one view, by stating the account of the inland carriage bounty, Debtor and Creditor.

Dr. *Bounty on the Inland Carriage of Corn.* *Cr.*

Dr.	£	Cr.	£
To payments of public money on the average of the last 7 years	£47,059	By decrease in the import of corn, &c.	£16,907
To decrease in the export of beef, butter, &c.	53,136	By increase in the export of corn, &c. .	3,570
To decrease in the export of wool and yarn	106,049	By increase in the export of pork, hogs, bread, &c. . . .	42,255
			62,734
		Balance against the bounty . . .	143,510
	£206,244		£206,244

Thus far I have laid before the reader a connected chain of such facts as the records of the measure and the Parliamentary accounts would permit: it appears as clearly as the testimony of figures can speak, that it has had very ill effects upon the general national account. Had the effect we have seen taken place of itself without any artificial means to assist it, the friends of the publick would perhaps have been well employed to remedy the evil: how absurd therefore must it appear to find that it has been brought about with the utmost care and assiduity, and at an expence of near fifty thousand pounds a year of the publick money!

It is the intention and effect of this bounty to turn every local advantage and natural supply topsy turvy. We have had for several years in England, an importation of foreign corn more than proportioned (the kingdoms compared) to anything the Irish knew.[1] If any one, to remedy this, proposed a bounty on bringing corn by land from Devonshire and Northumberland, so as to give it a preference in the London market to that of Kent and Essex, with what contempt would the proposer and proposition be treated!

[1] In 1774 we imported to the value of £1,023,000; and in 1775 to that of £1,265,562.

The corn counties of Louth and Kildare in the vicinity of Dublin are not to supply that market, but it is to eat its bread from Corke and Wexford!

It must also be brought by land carriage! the absurdity and folly with which such an idea is pregnant, in a country blessed with such ports, and such a vast extent of coast, are so glaring, that it is amazing that sophistry could blind the Legislature to such a degree as to permit a second thought of it. Why not carry the corn in ships, as well as tear up all the roads leading to Dublin by cars? Why not increase your sailors instead of horses? Are they not as profitable an animal? If you must have an inland bounty, why not to the nearest port from which it could be carried with the most ease and at the least expence to Dublin? This would have answered the same end. The pretence for the measure was the great import of foreign corn at Dublin; this is granting that there was a great demand at Dublin; and can any one suppose that if the corn was forced to Corke or Wexford, it would not find the way to such a demand as easily as from the east of England, which is the only part of that kingdom which abounds with corn for exportation? But the very pretence was a falsehood; for with what regard to truth could it be asserted that Dublin was fed with English corn before this measure took effect, when it appears by the preceding accounts, that the import of the whole kingdom from 1757 to 1763 was only £84,000 a year, and from 1764 to 1770 no more than £101,604? This import account does not distinguish, like the export one, the ports at which the foreign corn was received; if it did I should in all probability find but a moderate part of this total belonging to Dublin, as it is very well known that in the north there is always a considerable import of oatmeal. Granting however the evil, still the plan of remedying it by a land carriage of 130 miles was absurd to the last degree. But suppose so considerable a city as Dublin did import foreign corn to a large amount, is it wise to think this so great a national evil, that all the principles of common policy are to be wounded in order to remedy it? Where is the country to be found that is free from considerable importations even of the product of land? Has not Ireland a prodigious export of her soil's produce in the effects of pasturage, for which her climate is singularly adapted? And while she has that, of what little account is a trifling import of corn to feed her capital city? We have seen the undoubted loss that has accrued to the nation from a violent endeavour to counteract this import; yet the measure has only lessened it to an inconsiderable degree.

I was at a mill on Corke harbour, above 120 miles from Dublin, and saw cars loading for that market on the bounty, with a ship laying at the mill-quay bound for Dublin, and waiting for a loading; could invention suggest any scheme more preposterous than thus to confound at the publick expence all the ideas of common practice and common sense! By means of this measure I have been assured it has happened that the flour of Slaine mills has found its way to Carlow, and that of Laughlin Bridge to Drogheda: that is to say, Mr. Jebb eats his bread of Captain Mercer's flour, and the latter makes his pudding with Mr. Jebb's assistance; they live 100 miles asunder, and the publick pays the piper while the flour dances the hay in this manner.

The vast difference between the expence of land and water carriage should ever induce the Legislature, though sailors were not in question, to encourage the latter rather than the former. From Corke there is paid bounty 5*s.* 6½*d.* yet the freight at 10*s.* a ton is only 6*d.* The bounty from Laughlin Bridge is 2*s.* 3½*d.* yet Captain Mercer pays in summer but 1*s.* 4*d.* and in winter no more than 1*s.* 6*d.* Mr. Moore at Marlefield receives 4*s.* bounty, but his carriage cost him only 2*s.* 6*d.* in summer, and 3*s.* in winter; hence therefore we find that the bounty more than pays the expence, and that the profit is in proportion to the distance, i.e. the absurdity.

In the year ending September 1777, there were 34,598 barrels of malt brought from Wexford to Dublin by land, receiving £7,077 4*s.* 11*d.* bounty.

34,598 barrels are 51,897 Cwt. which at 6 Cwt. per horse would take for one day	8,649 horses.
From Wexford to Dublin and back takes seven days, or	60,546 horses.
One man to two horses	30,273 men.

	£	s.	d.
The horses at 16*d*. a day	4,306	8	1
Men at 9*d*. a day	1,135	4	9
Seven days men and horses	5,171	12	9
The freight of which to Dublin at 8*s*. a ton should be	1,037	12	0
Saving by sea[1]	4,134	0	9

It is therefore *a loss* of about 80 per cent. *purchased* by the bounty.

In proportion as sailors are lessened, horses are increased. Suppose common coasting vessels navigated at the rate of one man to twenty tons, it requires sixty-six horses to draw that burthen, and thirty-three men: so that for every sailor lost there are above threescore of this worst of all stock kept; which is of itself an enormous national loss. If the number of horses kept at actual work by this bounty, with the mares, colts, &c. to supply them were known, it might probably be found so large as to lessen a little of the veneration with which this measure is considered in Ireland.

I find that in the sessions of 1769 and 1771, there was a bounty paid on the carriage of corn coastways to Dublin. It amounted in the first to £3,278,[2] and in the latter to £4,973;[3] the Act lasted only those four years. It was an experiment which surely ought to have been continued; for, if corn is to be forced to Dublin, this most certainly is the only rational way of doing it.

By the following table the amount of this coasting trade will be seen, with and without that bounty.

[1] MS. communicated by — Nevill, Esq., member for Wexford.

[2] June 1, 1768. 7th George III. Chap. 24.

4*d*. per Cwt. corn of Irish growth by water coastways to Dublin, southward between Wicklow and the Tuskar; north, between Drogheda or Carrickfergus.

5*d*. per Cwt. if southward of Tuskar or North Carrickfergus.

4*d*. per Cwt. southward of Cooley Point to Newry, Belfast or Londonderry.

Continued to 24th June 1771.

[3] MS. account of publick premiums communicated by the Right Hon. John Forster, member for the county of Louth.

Corn and Flour brought Coastways to Dublin from 1758 to 1777 :—

In the year	Wheat and wheat meal.	Bere and barley.	Malt.	Flour.	Oats and oatmeal.	Totals.
	Barrels.	Barrels.	Barrels.	Barrels.	Barrels.	Barrels.
1758	1,424	61,794	2,991	40	22,178	88,427
1759	527	69,326	5,106	37	10,963	85,959
1760	37	75,846	3,812	48	9,273	89,016
1761	43	64,589	3,272	40	9,792	77,736
1762	118	63,980	3,347	52	10,484	77,981
1763	902	66,150	3,505	124	10,762	81,443
1764	1,542	79,710	3,812	161	10,663	95,888
1765	1,611	64,705	3,427	142	10,053	79,938
1766	11,000	39,398	6,610	282	14,276	71,566
1767	8,006	61,346	6,266	1,150	12,006	88,774
					Total.	836,728
1768	2,430	76,684	15,507	39	15,858	110,518
1769	5,669	81,749	14,479	753	21,723	124,373
1770	6,062	68,378	18,522	381	9,130	102,473
1771	5,425	60,530	8,558	232	16,157	90,902
1772	8,130	49,658	18,455	743	14,468	91,454
1773	3,525	48,836	17,106	269	12,117	81,853
1774	4,755	46,724	27,659	76	17,181	96,395
1775	832	49,213	25,165	290	5,615	81,115
1776	1,182	51,778	21,790		6,591	81,341
1777	712	37,511	17,467	630	10,733	67,053[1]
					Total.	927,477
Average last 7 years.	3,508	49,178	19,457	320	11,837	84,301

With the the assistance of these particulars, united with the quantities on which the inland bounty is paid, given at page 167 and 168, we shall be able to see the principal part of the consumption of the city of Dublin.

[1] MS. communicated by — Nevill, Esq., member for Wexford.

Brought by Land-carriage Bounty.

	Stones.	Cwt.		Stones.	Cwt.
Year 1762	1,730,869		Year 1771	1,641,867	87,965
1763	1,592,418		1772	3,146,960	153,139
1764	1,622,933		1773	3,263,199	175,177
1765	1,409,726		1774	3,553,996	190,346
1766	1,464,296		1775	3,211,214	213,885
1767	945,289		1776	3,622,076	255,256
1768	2,148,805		1777	3,240,692	317,753
1769	2,608,910	107,986			
1770	1,920,978	79,350	Average of last 7 years .	3,097,143	199,074

By these accounts, Dublin on an average of the last seven years has consumed

3,097,143 Stones of corn,
199,074 Cwt. of Flour,
84,301 Barrels of both coastways.

If the average weight of the corn is 14 stone per barrel, the first of these articles

Will make in barrels	221,224
The 199,074 Cwt. of flour may be called in barrels of wheat	180,000
Add the above barrels coastways	84,301
Total	485,525

To this should be added the import of foreign corn, which is known to be considerably more than the export, and it will appear that, if there are 150,000 inhabitants in Dublin, they must consume above three barrels each of all sorts of corn in a year; which, considering that the mass of the people live very much upon potatoes, is a great allowance, and suggests the idea either that the people are more numerous, or that more money is paid in bounties than there ought to be by the Acts, which is probable.

I come now to consider one of the principal arguments used in favour of this measure. It is the increase of tillage being so beneficial to the kingdom. Taken as a general position there may, or may not, be truth in the assertion: I am apt to think rather more stress is laid on it than there ought to be; and some reasons for that opinion may be seen in "Political Arithmetic," p. 363, &c. But, not to enter into the general question at present, I have to observe two circumstances upon the state of Ireland; first, the moisture of the climate, and secondly, the sort of tillage introduced.

That the climate is far moister than that of England I have already given various reasons to conclude; but the amazing tendency of the soil to grass would prove it, if any proof was wanting. Let General Cunningham and Mr. Silver Oliver recollect the instances they shewed me of turnep land and stubble left without ploughing, and yielding the succeeding summer a full crop of hay. These are such facts as we have not an idea of in England. Nature therefore points out in the clearest manner the application of the soil in Ireland most suitable to the climate. But this moisture, which is so advantageous to grass, is pernicious to corn. The finest corn in Europe and the world is uniformly found in the driest countries; it is the weight of wheat which points out its goodness; which lessens per measure gradually from Barbary to Poland. The wheat of Ireland has no weight compared with that of dry countries; and I have on another occasion observed that there is not a sample of a good colour in the whole kingdom. The crops are full of grass and weeds, even in the best management; and the harvests are so wet and tedious as greatly to damage the produce; but at the same time, and for the same reason, cattle of all sorts look well, never failing of a full bite of excellent grass: the very driest summers do not affect the verdure as in England.

I do not make these observations in order to conclude that tillage will not do in Ireland. I know it may be made to do; but I would leave the vibrations from corn to pasturage, and from pasturage to corn, to the cultivators of the land, to guide themselves as prices and other circumstances direct; but by no means force an extended tillage at the expence of bounties.

But what is the tillage gained by this measure? It is that system which formed the agriculture of England two hundred years ago, and forms it yet in the worst of our common fields, but which all our exertions of enclosing and improving are bent to extirpate. 1. Fallow. 2. Wheat; and then spring-corn until the soil is exhausted: or else, 1. Fallow. 2. Wheat. 3. Spring-corn; and then fallow again. In this course the spring-corn goes to horses, &c. the fallow is a dead loss, and the whole national gain the crop of wheat; one year in three yields nothing, and one a trifle; whereas the grass yields a full crop every year. Let it not be imagined that waste and desart tracts, that wanted cultivation, are only turned to this tillage. Nine tenths of the change is in the rich sheep walks of Roscommon, Tipperary, Carlow and Kilkenny. I have already proved this fact; the question therefore is reduced to this: Ought you to turn some of the finest pastures in the world, and which in Ireland yielded twenty shillings an acre, into the most execrable tillage that is to be found on the face of the globe? The comparison is not between good grass and good tillage; it is *good* grass against *bad* tillage. The tables I inserted prove that Ireland has lost fifty-three thousand pounds a year for seven years in the produce of cows and bullocks, and one hundred and six thousand pounds in that of sheep; this is a prodigious loss, but it is not the whole; there is the loss of labour on above fifty thousand stones of woollen yarn annually, which is a great drawback from the superior population supposed, perhaps falsely, to flow from tillage. When these circumstances are therefore well considered, the nation will not, I apprehend, be thought to have gained by having converted her rich sheep walks, which yielded so amply in wool, and in the labour which is annexed to wool, into so execrable a tillage as is universally introduced.

Another circumstance of this measure is, that of sacrificing all the ports of the kingdom to Dublin; the natural trade, which ought to take a variety of different little channels, proportioned to vicinity, was by this system violently drawn away to the capital; a very ill-situated capital, the increase of which, at the expence of the out-ports, was by no means a national advantage.

A question naturally arises from the premises before us; should the bounty be repealed? Absurd as it is, I am free to declare, I think not at once. Upon the credit of the measure great sums have been laid out in raising mills, most in situations which render them dependant on this forced trade for work. Great loss would accrue in this to individuals, and the public faith rather injured. The following tables will show that this is not a slight consideration.

The principal mills of Ireland, from June 1773 to June 1774.

		Cwt.
Marlefield	Stephen Moore, Esq.	15,382
Slane	D. Jebb, Esq., and Co.	11,070
Anner	Mr. J. Grub	10,395
Rathnally	J. Nicholson, Esq.	9,870
Lodge	Richard Mercer, Esq.	9,826
Kilkarn	Wade and Williams	9,496
Carrick	D. Tighie, Esq.	6,996
Archer's Grove.	Mr. W. Ratican	5,503
Lock	Mr. H. Bready	5,446
Ballykilcavan	Doyle and Hoskins	5,396
Tyrone	H. O'Brien, Esq.	4,967
Newtown Barry	Hon. B. Barry	4,574

The most distant mill from Dublin is that of Barnahely, Corke, one hundred and thirty miles. A prodigious number of men and horses would be thrown at once out of employment, which would have bad effects; and a sudden diversion of that supply, which has now flowed to Dublin for so many years, would certainly have very ill consequences. The policy therefore to be embraced is this; lower the present bounty to the simple expence of the carriage, and no more; and counteract it by raising the bounty on the carriage of corn coastwise, until it rivalled and gradually put down the land carriage. Perhaps it might be necessary to accompany this measure with a land carriage bounty from the mill to the nearest exporting port; the Dublin bounty would therefore stand in order to prevent the evil of a sudden change; but when the other bounties had got so far into effect, as to lessen the old one considerably, then it should be totally discontinued; and it would then certainly be proper for the other bounties (having performed their office) to be discontinued also. The present system is so undoubtedly absurd, that the rival bounties should be raised higher and higher until they had turned the commerce into the natural channel; an expression I am sensible implies an apparent absurdity, for a natural channel of commerce does not want such bounties; but a bad proceeding has made it so exceedingly crooked, that a mere repeal, leaving the trade to itself, most certainly would not do. You must undo by art the mischief which art has done; and the commercial capital in Ireland is too small to bear any violence.

United with the conduct I have ventured to recommend, in case the tillage system was persisted in, it would be very well worth the attention of Parliament, to annex such conditions to the payment of any new bounties, as might have the effect of securing a good tillage instead of a bad one. If it was found practicable, which I should think it might be, no publick money should ever be given for barley, bere, or oats, that did not succeed turneps; nor for wheat, or rye, that did not follow beans, clover, or potatoes; by this means the nation would have the satisfaction of knowing that, if the plough was introduced in valuable pasture land, it would at least be in a good system.

Before I conclude this subject, it may be proper to observe a circumstance, which, however ill it may be received in England, has, and ought to have this weight in Ireland. The revenue of that kingdom is under some disadvantages which England is free from; the hereditary revenue is claimed *in property* by the Crown; a great pension list is charged on it, and much of the amount paid out of the kingdom; there is no free trade to compensate this; a large part of the military establishment is taken out of the kingdom, and of late years the nation has run very much in debt: in such a situation of affairs, it is thought wise and prudent to secure the payment of such a sum as fifty or sixty thousand pounds a year towards the internal improvement of the kingdom. Nobody can deny there being much good sense in this reasoning; but the argument is applicable to a well founded measure, as strongly as it is to an absurd one; and I should farther observe that, if this or any bounty is the means of running the nation so much in debt, that new taxes are necessarily the consequence, this idea is then visionary; the people do not secure an advantage but a burthen. I cannot here avoid a comparison of expending so large a sum annually

the depredations of rats and mice. I have been assured that very great abuses are found in the claims; if these are obviated, the measure seems not objectable in a country where little is done without some publick encouragement. The following are the payments in consequence of this bounty.

	£		£
In the year 1766 . . .	891	In the year 1772 . . .	5,487
1767 . . .	891	1773 . . .	5,487
1768 . . .	3,442	1774 . . .	6,565
1769 . . .	3,442	1775 . . .	6,565
1770 . . .	4,266	1776 . . .	6,866
1771 . . .	4,266	1777 . . .	6,866[1]

It would be a proper condition to annex to this bounty, that it be given only to corn preserved as required, and threshed on boarded floors; the samples of Irish wheat are exceedingly damaged by clay floors; an English miller knows, the moment he takes a sample in his hand, if it came off a clay floor, and it is a deduction in the value. The floors should be of deal plank two inches thick, and laid on joists two or three feet from the ground, for a free current of air to preserve them from rotting.

[1] The reason of the sums being the same for two years throughout, is their being returned every second year to Parliament.

SECTION XIX.

MANUFACTURES.

THE only manufacture of considerable importance in Ireland is that of linen, which the Irish have for near a century considered as the great staple of the kingdom. The history of it in its earlier periods is very little known; a committee of the House of Commons, of which Sir Lucius O'Brien was chairman, examined the national records with great attention, in order to discover how long they had been in it; all they discovered was that by an Act passed in 1542, the 33rd of Henry VIII., linen and woollen yarn were enumerated among the most considerable branches of trade possessed by the natives of Ireland, in an Act made against grey merchants forestalling. In the 11th of Queen Elizabeth the same Act was revived, and a further law made against watering hemp or flax, &c. in rivers. In the 13th of Elizabeth all persons were prohibited from exporting wool, flax, linen and woollen yarn, except merchants residing in cities and boroughs; and by a further Act the same year a penalty of 12*d*. a pound was imposed on all flax or linen yarn exported, and 8*d*. more for the use of the town exported from. In this last Act it is recited that the merchants of Ireland had been exporters of those articles in trade upwards of one hundred years preceding that period: and by many subsequent Acts and proclamations during the reigns of Charles I. and II. those manufactures were particularly attended to; from whence it evidently appeared that the kingdom possessed an export trade in these commodities at those early periods. The Earl of Strafford, Lord Lieutenant in the reign of Charles I., passed several laws and took various measures to encourage this manufacture, insomuch that he has by some authors been said to have established it originally. At the end of the last century, in King William's reign, it arose to be an object of consequence, but not singly so, for it appears from a variety of records, in both kingdoms, that the Irish had then a considerable woollen manufacture for exportation, which raised the jealousy of the English manufacturers in that commodity so much that they presented so many petitions to both Lords and Commons, as to induce those bodies to enter fully into their jealousies and illiberal views; which occasioned the famous compact between the two nations, brought on in the following manner.

Die Jovis 9°. Iunij. 1698.

The Earl of *Stamford* reported from the Lords' Committees (appointed to draw an address to be presented to his Majesty, relating to the woollen manufacture in *Ireland*) the following address. (*viz.*)

"WE the Lords spiritual and temporal in Parliament "assembled. Do humbly represent unto your Majesty, "that the growing manufacture of cloth in *Ireland*, both "by the cheapness of all sorts of necessaries for life, and "goodness of materials for making of all manner of cloth, "doth invite your subjects of England, with their families "and servants, to leave their habitations to settle there, "to the increase of the woollen manufacture in Ireland, "which makes your loyal subjects in this kingdom very "apprehensive that the further growth of it may greatly "prejudice the said manufacture here; by which the trade "of this nation and the value of lands will very much "decrease, and the numbers of your people be much "lessened here; wherefore, we do most humbly beseech "your most sacred Majesty, that your Majesty would be "pleased, in the most publick and effectual way, that may "be, to declare to all your subjects of Ireland, that the "growth and increase of the woollen manufacture there, "hath long, and will ever be looked upon with great "jealousie, by all your subjects of this kingdom: And, if "not timely remedied, may occasion very strict laws, totally "to prohibit and suppress the same, and on the other hand, "if they turn their industry and skill, to the settling and "improving the linen manufacture, for which generally the "lands of that kingdom are very proper, they shall receive, "all countenance, favour and protection from your royal "influence, for the incouragement and promoting of the "said linen manufacture, to all the advantage and profit, "that kingdom can be capable of.

To which the House agreed.

It is ordered, by the Lords spiritual and temporal in Parliament assembled, That the Lords with white staves doe humbly attend his Majesty with the address of this House, concerning the woollen manufacture in Ireland.

Die Veneris 10° *Iunij* 1698°.

"The Lord Steward reported his Majesty's answere to the address, to this effect. (*viz.*)

THAT his Majesty will take care to do what their Lordships have desired.

ASHLEY COWPER.

Clerk Parliamentor."

Die Jovis 30 *Junij* 1698.

"*Most Gracious Sovereign,*

"WE your Majesty's most dutiful and loyal subjects, "the Commons in Parliament assembled, being very "sensible that the wealth and power of this kingdom do, in "a great measure, depend on the preserving the woollen "manufacture, as much as possible entire to this realm, "think it becomes us, like our ancestors, to be jealous of the "establishment and increase thereof elsewhere; and to use "our utmost endeavours to prevent it.

"And therefore, we cannot without trouble observe, that "Ireland, is dependant on, and protected by England, in "the enjoyment of all they have; and which is so proper "for the linen manufacture, the establishment and growth "of which there, would be so enriching to themselves, and "so profitable to England; should, of late, apply itself to "the woollen manufacture, to the great prejudice of the "trade of this kingdom; and so unwillingly promote the "linen trade, which would benefit both them and us.

"The consequence whereof, will necessitate your Parlia-"ment of England, to interpose to prevent the mischief "that threatens us, unless your Majesty, by your authority, "and great wisdom, shall find means to secure the trade of "England, by making your subjects of Ireland, to pursue "the joint interest of both kingdoms.

"And we do most humbly implore your Majesty's pro-"tection and favour in this matter; and that you will make "it your royal care, and enjoin all those you imploy in "Ireland, to make it their care, and use their utmost "diligence, to hinder the exportation of wool from Ireland, "except to be imported hither, and for the discouraging "the woollen manufactures, and encouraging the linen "manufactures in Ireland, to which we shall always be "ready to give our utmost assistance.

Resolved, That the said address be presented to his Majesty by the whole House.

Sabbati. 2. die Julii.

HIS MAJESTY'S ANSWER.

"Gentlemen,

"I shall do all that in me lies to discourage the woollen "manufacture in Ireland, and to encourage the linen manu-"facture there; and to promote the trade of England."

Thursday 27th September, 1698.

Part of the Lords Justices' Speech.

"AMONGST these bills there is one for the encourage-"ment of the linen and hempen manufactures, at our first "meeting, we recommended to you that matter, and we "have now endeavoured to render that bill practicable and "useful for that effect, and as such we now recommend it "to you. The settlement of this manufacture will contri-

"bute much to people the country, and will be found much "more advantageous to this kingdom, than the woollen "manufacture, which, being the settled staple trade of "England, from whence all foreign markets are supplied, "can never be encouraged here for that purpose, whereas "the linen and hempen manufactures will not only be "encouraged, as consistent with the trade of England, but "will render the trade of this kingdom both useful and "necessary to England."

The Commons of IRELAND returned the following Answer to the Speech from the Throne.

"WE pray leave to assure your Excellencies that we "shall heartily endeavour to establish a linen and hempen "manufacture here, and to render the same useful to "England, as well as advantageous to this kingdom; and "that we hope to find such a temperament in respect to the "woollen trade here, that the same may not be injurious "to England."—And they passed a law that session commencing 25th of March, 1699, laying 4*s*. additional duty on every 20*s*. value of broad-cloth exported out of Ireland, and 2*s*. on every 20*s*. value of serges, baize, kerseys, stuffs, or any other sort of new drapery made of wool or mixed with wool (frizes only excepted), which was in effect a prohibition. And in the same session a law was passed in England, restraining Ireland from exporting those woollen manufactures, including frize to any other parts except to England and Wales.

The Addresses of the two Houses to the King carry the clearest evidence of their source, the jealousy of merchants and manufacturers; I might add their *ignorance* too; they are dictated upon the narrow idea that the prosperity of the woollen fabrics of Ireland was inconsistent with the welfare of those of England; it would at present be fortunate for both kingdoms if these errors had been confined to the last century. There is an equal mixture also of falsehood in the representations; for they assert that the cheapness of necessaries in Ireland drew from England the woollen manufacturers; but they forgot the cheapness of labour in Ireland, to which no workman in the world ever yet emigrated. The Irish were engaged in various slight fabricks not made in England; but had they been employed on broad cloth for exportation, the English manufacture would well have borne it; they did at that time and afterwards bear a rapid increase of the French fabricks, and yet flourished themselves. We have had so long an experience of markets increasing with industry and inventions, that the time ought to have come long ago for viewing competitors without the eye of jealousy.

The memoirs of the time, as well as the expression in the above transaction, evidently prove that it was understood by both kingdoms to be a sort of compact; that if Ireland gave up her woollen manufacture, that of linen should be left to her under every encouragement. I have however myself heard it in the British Parliament *denied* to have been any compact; but simply a promise of encouragement, not precluding a like or greater encouragement to the British linens. This is certainly an error; for, so understood, what is the meaning of the *ample encouragements promised* by the British Parliament? They could not mean internal encouragement or regulation, for they had nothing to do with either: it could simply mean, as the purport of the words evidently shews, that they would enter into no measures which should set up a linen manufacture to rival the Irish. That woollens should be considered and encouraged as the staple of England, and linens as that of Ireland: It must mean this, or it meant nothing. That the Irish understood it so cannot be doubted for a moment; for what did they in consequence? they were in possession of a flourishing woollen manufacture, which they actually put down and crippled by prohibiting exportation. Let me ask those who assert there was no compact, why they did this? it was their own act. Did they cut their own throats without either reward, or promise of reward? common sense tells us they did this under a perfect conviction that they should receive ample encouragement from England in their linen trade: but what moonshine would such encouragement prove, if England, departing from the letter and spirit of that compact, had encouraged her own linen manufacture to rival the Irish, after the Irish had destroyed their woollen fabricks to encourage those of England? Yet we did this in direct breach of the whole transaction, for the 23rd of George II. laid a tax on sail-cloth made of Irish hemp. Bounties also have been given in England, without extending fully to Irish linens. Checked, striped, printed, painted, stained or dyed linens of Irish manufacture are not allowed to be imported into Britain. In which, and in other articles, we have done every thing possible to extend and increase our own linen manufacture, to rival that of Ireland.

I admit readily that the apprehensions of the Irish at the progress of British linens are in the spirit of commercial jealousy, as well as our violence in relation to their woollens. But with this great difference; we forced them to put down a manufacture they were actually in possession of; and we, being the controuling power, do not leave them that freedom of market which we possess ourselves; points which necessarily place the two nations in this respect upon very different footings. Give them, as they ought to have, a free woollen trade, and they will then have no objection to any measures for the encouragement of our linens, which do not absolutely exclude theirs.

The following table will shew the progress of their linen manufacture through the present century.

An Account of the Export of Linen-Cloth, and Linen-Yarn, from Ireland.

In the year	Linen Cloth.	Yarn.	Value cloth at 1s. 3d. per yard.	Value yarn at £6 per 120 lb.	Total value.
	Yards	Cwt.	£	£	£
1700			14,112		
1710	1,688,574	7,975	105,537	47,853	153,389
1711	1,254,815	7,321	78,425	43,928	122,354
1712	1,376,122	7,916	86,007	47,496	133,504
1713	1,819,816	11,802	113,738	70,815	184,554
1714	2,188,272	15,078	155,002	158,326	313,329
1715	2,153,120	13,931	107,650	146,283	253,939
1716	2,188,105	10,747	109,405	112,847	222,252
1717	2,437,265	18,052	132,018	189,555	321,574
1718	2,247,375	14,050	121,732	147,527	269,260
1719	2,359,352	15,070	127,798	158,239	286,038

An Account of the Export of Linen-Cloth, and Linen-Yarn, from Ireland. (Continued).

In the year	Linen Cloth.	Yarn.	Value cloth at 1s. 3*d*. per yard.	Value yarn at £6 per 120 lb.	Total value.
	Yards.	Cwt.	£	£	£
1720	2,437,984	15,722	121,899	94,334	216,233
1721	2,520,701	14,696	126,035	88,178	214,213
1722	3,419,994	14,754	170,995	88,524	259,519
1723	4,378,545	15,672	218,927	94,637	312,964
1724	3,879,170	14,594	193,958	87,564	281,522
1725	3,864,987	13,701	193,249	82,207	275,457
1726	4,368,395	17,507	218,419	105,042	323,462
1727	4,768,889	17,287	238,444	103,720	342,171
1728	4,692,764	11,450	234,638	62,975	297,613
1729	3,927,918	11,855	196,395	65,206	261,602
1730	4,136,203	10,088	206,810	55,485	262,295
1731	3,775,830	13,746	220,256	84,194	304,451
1732	3,792,551	15,343	237,034	92,061	309,096
17·3	4,777,076	13,357	298,567	82,372	380,939
1734	5,451,758	18,122	340,734	108,733	449,468
1735	6,761,151	15,900	422,571	94,405	517,977
1736	6,508,151	14,743	406,759	88,463	495,222
1737	6,138,785	14,695	409,252	18,173	497,325
1738	5,175,744	15,945	345,049	95,674	440,724
1739	5,962,316	18,200	397,487	129,202	506,690
1740	6,627,771	18,542	441,851	111,256	553,108
1741	7,207,741	21,656	480,516	129,941	610,457
1742	7,074,168	16,330	471,611	97,984	569,595
1743	6,058,041	14,169	403,869	85,016	488,885
1744	6,124,892	18,011	459,366	108,066	567,432
1745	7,171,963	22,066	537,897	132,398	670,295
1746	6,820,786	27,741	511,588	166,451	678,010
1747	9,633,884	28,910	722,541	173,464	896,005
1748	8,692,671	19,418	543,291	116,508	659,800
1749	9,504,338	21,694	594,021	130,164	724,185
1750	11,200,460	22,373	653,360	134,238	787,598
1751	12,891,318	23,743	751,993	142,459	894,452
1752	10,656,003	23,407	621,600	140,442	762,042
1753	10,411,787	23,238	694,119	139,428	839,018
1754	12,090,903	22,594	806,060	135,567	941,732
1755	13,379,733	27,948	891,982	167,692	1,059,675
1756	11,944,328	26,997	796,288	161,982	1,046,841
Average in seven years	11,796,361	24,328	745,057	145,972	904,479

An Account of the Export of Linen-Cloth, and Linen-Yarn, from Ireland. (Continued.)

In the year	Linen Cloth.	Yarn.	Value cloth at 1s. 3d. per yard.	Value yarn at £6 per 120 lb.	Total value.
	Yards.	Cwt.	£	£	£
1757	15,508,709	31,078	1,033,913	186,473	1,220,387
1758	14,982,557	31,995	998,837	191,970	1,190,807
1759	14,093,431	27,571	939,562	165,426	1,104,988
1760	13,375,456	31,042	891,697	186,254	1,077,951
1761	12,048,881	39,699	803,251	238,198	1,041,457
1762	15,559,676	35,950	1,037,311	215,702	1,253,014
1763	16,013,105	34,468	1,067,540	206,808	1,274,348
Average .	14,511,973	33,114	967,445	198,690	1,166,136
1764	15,201,081	31,715	1,006,738	190,292	1,197,031
1765	14,355,205	26,127	957,013	156,762	1,233,492
1766	17,892,102	35,018	1,192,806	210,109	1,552,017
1767	20,148,170	30,274	1,343,211	181,648	1,692,761
1768	18,490.019	32,590	1,232,667	195,542	1,382,294
1769	17,790,705	37,037	1,186,047	222,223	1,556,328
1770	20,560,754	33,417	1,370,716	200,502	1,742,558
Average .	17,776,862	32,311	1,184,171	193,868	1,379,312
1771	25,376,808	34,166	1,691,787	204,996	2,108,257
1772	20,599,178	32,441	1,544,938	194,650	1,739,588
1773	18,450,700	28.078	1,383,802	168,473	1,552,276
1774	16.916,674	29,194	1,127,777	174,804	1,302,641
1775	20,205,087	30,598	1,346,985	183,588	1,530,573
1776	20,502,587	36,152	1,366,838	216,912	1,583,750
1777	19,714,638	29,698	1,314,308	178,188	1,492,496
Average .	20,252,239	31,475	1,390,919	188,810	1,615,654
	Average of 30 years since 1748 . . .				1,228,148
	Average of 30 years before				417,000

Mr. Henry Archdall, in the year 1771, asserted before a committee of the House of Commons, that Ireland manufactured for

Exportation	£1,541,200
And for home consumption	658,906
	£2,200,106 [1]

The latter article must be a mere guess; the first we find contradicted in the preceding table, unless he meant cloth only.

This ample table calls for several observations. It first appears that the manufacture has gone on in a regular increase, until it has arrived in the last seven years to be an object of prodigious consequence. The averages of each period of seven years are of particular importance; as there is one political lesson to be deduced from them which may be of great use hereafter: they prove in the clearest manner that no judgment is ever to be formed of the state of the manufacture from one or two years, but on the contrary from seven years alone. In 1774 it appears that the export was lower than it had been for nine years before, and we very well recollect the noise which this fall made in England. I was repeatedly in the gallery of the English House of Commons when they sat in a committee for months together upon the state of the linen trade; and from the evidence I heard at the bar I thought Ireland was sinking to nothing, and that all her fabricks were tumbling to pieces: the assertion of the linen fabricks declining *a third* was repeated violently, and it was very true. But they drew this comparison from 1771, when we find from the preceding table that it was at its zenith; to appearance a very unnatural one; for it rose at once five millions of yards, which was unparalleled. It was ridiculous to draw a sudden start into precedent; for what manufacture in the world but experiences moments of uncommon prosperity, the continuance of which is never to be expected; this fall of a third therefore, though true *in fact*, was utterly false *in argument*. In truth, the fall was exceedingly trivial; for the only comparison that ought to have been made was with the average of the preceding seven years; the decline then would have appeared only seven or eight hundred thousand yards, that is, not a *twentieth*, instead of a *third*.

[1] Journals of the Commons, vol. 16, page 368.

But, because the trade had run to a most extraordinary height in 1771, the manufacturers and merchants felt the fall the more, and were outrageously clamorous because every year was not a jubilee one. If such were to be the consequences of an unusual demand, ministers and legislatures would have reason to curse any extraordinary prosperity, and to prevent it if they could, under the conviction that the grasping avarice of commercial folly would be growling and dunning them with complaints when the trade returned to its usual and natural course. In the year 1773 and 4, all Ireland was undone; the linen manufacture was to be at an end; but lo! at the end of the period of seven years, upon examining the average, it is found to be in as great a state of increase as ever known before; for the four periods have all the same rise one above another of three millions of yards each: consequently I say, upon the evidence of the clearest facts, that there has been no *declension*, but an INCREASE. And I shall draw this manifest conclusion from it to disbelieve commercial complaints as long as I exist, and put no credit in that sort of proof which is carried to Parliament in support of such complaints. Falsehood and imposition I am confident find their way to the bar of a House; and I do not think it much for the credit of those who supported the Irish complaints at the period above mentioned, that I should find, in copying at Dublin part of this table from the parliamentary record of imports and exports, the export of the year 1775 erased; the only considerable erasure there is in those volumes, the total of particulars makes 19,447,250 yards, but it now stands written over that erasure 20,205,087. It is easily accounted for; if the trade had been known to have experienced so immediate a revival, half their arguments would have had no weight; it might therefore be convenient to sink the truth. If it was merely accidental in the clerk, I can only say it was at a most unfortunate *time* and *subject*.[1]

The following table will shew that England is the market for eighteen twentieths of the total Irish exportation.

[1] In the woollen manufacture of England the same spirit of complaint and falsehood has at different times pestered both Parliament and the publick. See this point discussed in my "Political Arithmetic," page 152.

Quantities of Irish Linens imported into England from Christmas 1756, *to Christmas* 1773.[1]

	Yards.	
In the year 1757 . .	11,925,290	
1758 . .	14,383,248	
1759 . .	12,793,412	
1760 . .	13,311,674	
1761 . .	13,354,448	
	65,768,072	or per annum 13,153,614.

	Yards.	
In the year 1762 . .	13,476,366	
1763 . .	13,110,858	
1764 . .	13,187,109	
1765 . .	14,757,353	
1766 . .	17,941,229	
	72,472,915	or per annum 14,494,583.

	Yards.	
In the year 1767 . .	16,500,755	
1768 . .	15,249,248	
1769 . .	16,496,271	
1770 . .	18,195,087	
1771 . .	20,622,217	
	87,063,578	or per annum 17,612,715.

	Yards.
In the year 1772 . .	19,171,771
1773 . .	17,896,994

The following table will shew the importation of the raw material for this fabrick.

[1] Substance of Mr. Glover's evidence before the House of Commons 1774, page 60.

Import of Flax, Hemp, and Flax-Seed, into Ireland.

	Hogsheads of flax-seed.[1]	Value.	Undressed flax.[2]	Value.	Undressed hemp.[3]	Value.	Total value.
		£	Cwt.	£	Cwt.	£	£
Year 1764	32,168	112,588	53,870	129,284	13,195	21,111	262,983
1765	27,769	97,191	12,871	30,870	23,951	38,321	166,382
1766	31,040	108,640	8,047	19,312	14,140	22,624	150,576
1767	43,076	150,766	7,397	17,752	7,780	12,448	180,966
1768	19,161	67,063	9,908	23,779	14,531	23,249	114,091
1769	50,022	175,077	7,690	18,456	12,263	19,620	213,153
1770	19,432	68,012	9,276	22,262	27,842	44,547	134,821
Average .	31,809	111,333	15,608	37,387	16,243	25,988	174,710
Year 1771	45,089	157,811	6,318	15,163	9,131	14,609	187,583
1772	24,230	84,203	6,054	14,529	13,685	21,895	121,229
1773	39,750	139,125	10,551	25,322	9,670	15,472	179,919
1774	25,375	88,812	8,677	20,824	22,361	35,777	145,413
1775	40,218	140,763	10,153	24,367	14,264	22,822	187,952
1776	24,077 [4]	84,269	5,295	12,708	13,602	21,763	118,740
1777	32,613 [5]	114,145	18,212	43,708	19,419	31,069	188,922
Average .	33,050	115,675	9,322	22,374	14,590	23,343	161,394

[1] At £3 10s. a hogshead from 28s. to £6.
[2] At 32s. from £24 to £40 per ton, average £32.
[3] At 48s. from £45 to £52 per ton.
[4] From the plantations of this 12,441.
[5] Ditto, 4,512.

This account is favourable to the state of the manufacture; for the increased import of flax-seed in the second period implies that the country supplied herself with more flax of her own producing, which accounts for the falling off in the import of undressed flax: the persons who hav studied the manufacture in all its branches with the most attention, agree that there is no greater improvement to be wished for than the raising the flax instead of importing foreign. It is much to be lamented that the flax-husbandry has not made a greater progress in the kingdom; for the profit of it is very great. The minutes of the tour furnish the following particulars:

Places.	Expences.			Stones scutched.	At per stone.		Value.		
	£	s.	d.		s.	d.	£	s.	d.
Armagh	6	6	4	30	4	2	6	5	0
Near ditto				48	8	0	19	4	0
Mahon	4	13	4	25	8	0	10	0	0
Warrenstown	13	3	10	40	7	6	15	0	0
Lisburne to Belfast	9	4	2	56	9	4	26	2	8
Ards	9	0	0						
Shaen Castle	8	4	6	54	7	10	21	3	0
Lesley Hill	8	2	4	16					
Newtown Limavaddy	9	3	0	28	5	4	7	9	4
Innishoen	5	14	0						
Clonleigh				30					
Florence Court	9	7	4				18	1	2
Ballymoat	12	7	0						
Merera				40					
Averages	8	13	2	36	7	2	15	8	1

From hence we find, that the profit is near seven pounds an acre, clear, after paying large expences; and that on the Cunningham acre.

There is a notion common in the north of Ireland, which I should suppose must be very prejudicial to the quality as well as the quantity of flax produced; it is, that rich land will not do for it, and that the soil should be pretty much exhausted by repeated crops of oats, in order to reduce it to the proper state for flax. The consequence of this is, as I every where saw, full crops of weeds, and of poor half-starved flax. The idea is absurd; there is no land in the north of Ireland, that I saw, too rich for it. A very rich soil sown thin produces a branching harsh flax; but if very clear of weeds, and sown thick for the stems to draw each other up, the crop will be in goodness and quantity proportioned to the richness of the land. A poor exhausted soil cannot produce a flax of a strong good staple; it is the nourishment it receives from the fertility of the land which fills the plant with oil; and bleachers very well know that the *oil* is the *strength* of the staple; and unfortunately it is, that bleaching cannot be performed without an exhalation of this oil, and consequent weakness. But, though it is necessary for colour to exhale a portion of the oil, flax that never had but little, from the poverty of the soil it grew in, is of little worth, and will not bear the operation of bleaching like the other. Potatoes kept very clean under the plough are an excellent preparation for flax; and turneps, well hoed, the same.

The following are the Earnings of the Manufacturers in Linen Fabricks.

Places.	Weavers.				Women.
	Fine linen.		Coarse lin.		Spin.
	s.	*d.*	*s.*	*d.*	*d.*
Market Hill	1	6	1	2	3
Armagh			1	2	
Mahon			1	0	3½
Lurgan	1	4	1	0	3
Warrenstown	1	6	1	1	3
Innishoen					4
Mount Charles					2½
Castle Caldwell					2½
Inniskilling					4
Belleisle			1	3	4
Florence Court				10	3
Farnham					4
Strokestown					3½
Ballymoat					3½
Mercra					2½
Fortland					3
Westport			1	0	3
Annsgrove					2
Averages	1	5	1	0½	3¼

These earnings are from double to near treble those of husbandry labour throughout the kingdom; and yet complaints of poverty are infinitely more common among these people than in those parts of the kingdom that have no share of the manufacture. It is so in all countries; and ought to prevent too assiduous an attention to such complaints. Those who for the sake of great earnings will become weavers, must do it under the knowledge that they embrace or continue in a life not of the same regular tenour with the lowest species of labourers. If they will not be more prudent and saving, they ought not to clamour and expect the publick to turn things topsy turvy to feed them, who, with any degree of attention, might have supported themselves much better than another class that never complains at all.

Having thus endeavoured to shew the rise, progress, and present amount of this manufacture, it will be necessary to lay before the reader some account of the sums of publick money which have, according to the fashion of Ireland, been expended in its encouragement. This is not easy to do fully and accurately as I could wish, but the following papers are the best authorities I could find.

An Account of the Net Produce of the Duties appropriated to the use of the Hempen and Linen Manufactures from their Commencement, and also the Bounties from Parliament.

	Nett duties.	Bounties		Nett duties.	Bounties
	£	£		£	£
In the year 1721		2,500	In the year 1737	8,676	8,000
1723		5,500	1738	10,623	
1725		4,000	1739	10,087	8,000
1727		4,000	1740	7,894	
1729		4,000	1741	13,180	8,540
			1742	12,561	
1731	5,637	4,000	1743	13,770	8,000
1733	6,328	8,000	1744	14,844	
1734	5,314		1745	18,066	8,000
1735	6,748	8,000	1746	15,046	
1736	9,181		1747	17,922	8,000

An Account of the Net Produce of the Duties appropriated to the use of the Hempen and Linen Manufactures from their Commencement, and also the Bounties from Parliament. (*Continued.*)

	Nett duties.	Bounties		Nett duties.	Bounties
	£	£		£	£
In the year 1748	12,657		In the year 1770	1,635	
1749	18,335	8,000	1771	861	8,000
1750	17,813		1772	1,348	
1751	12,477	8,000	1773	1,700	8,000
1752	17,175		1774	580	
1753	12,231	8,000	1775	1,387	8,000
1754	12,884				
1755	14,292	8,000	Totals. . . .	453,204	184,540
1756	12,239	4,000[1]	Nett tea duties for 7 years ending 1775 .	72,500	184,540
1757	1,722	8,000			
1758	9,772				
1759	8,933	8,000			
1760	6,581			710,244	
1761	11,841	8,000			
1762	14,014		Average of the last 7 years duties . .		
1763	15,064	8,000			
1764	14,998			1,385	
1765	15,820	8,000	Ditto of tea duties . . .		
1766	18,634			10,357	
1767	12,717	8,000			
1768	10,414		Together . . .	11,742	
1769	2,181[2]	8,000			

The tea duties were granted for the use of this manufacture.

But that this account is not complete appears by another[3] to the following effect.

[1] By King's Letter.

[2] Here the tea duties were separated, and produced in ½ year to L. D. £12,500, and £10,000 a year each year after.

[3] Commons Journals, vol. 17, p. 263.

An Account of the several Sums of Money for which the Vice-Treasurers have claimed Credit, as being paid by them for the use of the Hempen and Linen Manufactures, from the 25th of March 1700, to the 25th of March 1775, distinguishing each year; returned to the hon. House of Commons pursuant to their Order, November 25, 1775.

In the year		In the year		In the year	
	£		£		£
1700	100	1728	5,154	1754	17,402
1701	372	1729	11,340	1755	16,886
1702	213	1730	10,824	1756	12,762
1703	430	1731	13,711	1757	15,762
1705	3,384	1732	5,149	1758	13,792
1706	1,783	1733	7,422	1759	7,298
1707	1,498	1734	5,670	1760	16,247
1708	1,475	1735	13,103	1761	9,154
1709	1,180	1736	14,785	1762	32,865
1710	1,180	1737	12,927	1763	19,463
1711	1,770	1738	14,931	1764	22,041
1712	2,023	1739	13,085	1765	21,041
1713	1,596	1740	16,973	1766	16,824
1714	789	1741	15,484	1767	15,474
1715	1,597	1742	20,085	1768	17,061
1716	1,641	1743	17,917	1769	16,216
1717	3,981	1744	23,587	1770	19,030
1718	3,337	1745	18,948	1771	15,030
1719	4,784	1746	9,154	1772	12,546
1720	3,369	1747	11,216	1773	12,206
1721	4,421	1748	15,371	1774	16,030
1722	5,173	1749	20,979	1775	15,459
1723	3,439	1750	31,109	1776	14,751
1724	5,678	1751	16,680	1777	15,102
1725	6,290	1752	22,556		
1726	7,779	1753	16,886	Total .	847,504
1727	6,701				
		Average of the last 7 years . .			14,446

The expenditure of this money is under the direction of the Linen Board, upon a similar plan as the Navigation

Board explained above. Their mode of applying it will be seen by the following account.

Disbursements of the Linen Trustees, from 1757 to 1772.

Spinning-schools	£3,634
Flax shops	2,197
Flax dressers	4,145
Bleachers	14,323
Contractors	5,720
Yarn inspectors	654
Manufacturers	55,013
Utensils	69,445
Raising flax	5,101
Flax-seed mixed with potatoes	2,818
Fraudulent lapped linens	748
Buildings and repairs	25,936
Clerks, &c. at Linen Office	11,728
Ditto, Linen and Yarn Halls	7,642
Inspectors, itinerant men, and reed makers	7,723
Incidental charges	11,773
In sixteen years	225,606
Or per annum	14,100 [1]

Subsequent to 1698 Ireland, at *an enormous expence* to the publick, made a progress in the linen manufacture, &c.[2]

The Trustees of the Linen Board expended near half a million of money to extend and promote the linen manufacture before the year 1750.[3]

But these accounts do not yet show the full amount of publick money which has been granted for the use of this great manufacture; to have this complete we must take in the bounties on the import of seed, and on the export of canvas and sail-cloth, which have been as follow:

[1] Journal of the House of Commons, vol. xv. p. 373.
[2] Report of Sir Lucius O'Brien's Committee, Journals, vol. xv. p. 396.
[3] Ibid. p. 400.

Years, ending Lady-day.	Import hemp and flax-seed.	Export canvas and sail-cloth.	Years, ending Lady-day.	Import hemp and flax-seed.	Export canvas and sail-cloth.
	£	£		£	£
1731	1,211	1,446	1755	10,500	731[1]
1733	2,120	1,207	1757	9,873	
1735	2,658	1,301	1759	11,058	
1737	5,004	1,492	1761	11,273	
1739	6,792	3,664	1763	9,187	
1741	6,112	3,517	1765	11,464	
1743	5,911	1,540	1767	15,894	
1745	7,536	1,367	1769	16,810	
1747	4,482	2,283	1771	16,062	
1749	7,939	3,416	1773	16,279	
1751	8,027	4,802	1775	14,674	
1753	11,481	1,909	1777	14,479	
Totals				226,834	28,682[2]
Average of the last seven years				15,094	

By one of these accounts the annual net produce of those duties appropriated to this manufacture, on an average of the last seven years is	£11,742
But by the other, the Treasury charges the manufacture on the same average with	14,446
Difference	£2,704

The fact however is, that the larger of these sums is paid to this purpose, and the account of the Linen Board's disbursement amounts to £14,100.

The total annual sums at present applied appear to be these:

Produce of duties appropriated to the purpose	£14,446
Parliamentary bounty	4,000
Bounty on the import of flax-seed	15,094
Total per annum	£33,540

And that the total sums thus applied since the year 1700 have been:

[1] This year this bounty ceased.

[2] Extracted from an Account of National Premiums; MS., communicated by the Right Hon. John Forster.

Paid by the Vice Treasurers	£847,504
Parliamentary bounty	192,540
Bounty on flax import	226,834
Ditto on export of canvas	28,682
Total	£1,295,560

The most careless observer cannot help remarking the great amount of this total; and must think that an annual grant of £33,000 a year, in support of a manufacture which works to the annual amount of two millions sterling, an extraordinary measure. I must be free to own that I cannot, upon any principles, see the propriety of it. They cannot have done any considerable mischief, I grant; but, if they do no good, there is a great evil in the misapplication of so much money. That a manufacture in its very cradle, if it happens to be of a sickly growth, may be benefited by bounties and premiums, is certain; but that, even in such a case, it is wise to give them, I doubt very much; for fabricks being sickly in their growth is a reason against encouraging them. The truly valuable manufactures, such as linen in Ireland, wool and hardware in England, and silk in France, want no help but a demand for their produce. Ireland has always hitherto had a demand for her linens, and having, so much longer than the beginning of this century, been in the trade, would naturally increase it in proportion to the demand; and she would have done that though no Linen Board nor bounties had existed. It is contrary to all the principles of commerce to suppose, that such an increasing manufacture as this has been would want flax or flax-seed without bounties on the import; or that manufacturers in it would not earn their bread without a present of £33,000. The only instance in which these bounties would certainly have a considerable effect is, the case of expensive machines; the first introduction of which is difficult to individuals in a poor country. But this article, in its fullest extent, would have demanded but a small sum in the linen trade; for it by no means goes to common spinning-wheels, the construction of which is generally known. But, if there is any reason to suppose linen would, throughout the century, have stood upon its own legs, how much more is there for its doing so at present! I will venture to assert that there is not one yard of linen more made on account of the thirty-three thousand pounds a year now expended. It is to such a great manufacture a drop of water in the ocean.—An object too contemptible to have any effects attributed to it. It is idle and visionary to suppose, that a fabrick which has employed a fourth part of the kingdom for 70 years, and exports to the amount of a million and a half annually, wants Boards, and bounties, and premiums, and impertinence to support it. I have heard it said more than once in Ireland, that a seat at the Linen Board might easily be worth £300 a year; it is very well if the whole becomes a job; for it might just as well as be applied to inspectors, itinerant men, builders and salaries.

I before calculated the extent of waste land the bounty on the inland carriage of corn would have improved at £10 an acre; let me do the same with the 1,300,000 expended on linen. It would have improved 130,000 acres, which would now be yielding £520,000 a year, or a fourth part of the whole amount of all the linen manufacture of Ireland; so infinitely more productive is money bestowed on the land than on the fabricks of a state.

I do not mean to find fault with the establishment of this manufacture; it has grown to a great degree of national importance; but from some unfortunate circumstances in the police of it (if I may use the expression) that importance is not nearly equal to what it ought to be, from the extent of country it absolutely fills. It will be at least a curious enquiry to examine this point. From the best information I can assert that the linen and yarn made in Connaught, and part of Leinster, vastly exceed in value all the exports of Ulster, exclusive of those two commodities, which makes linen the whole exportable produce of that province, or £1,600,000 a year. Ulster contains 2,836,837 plantation acres; suppose that vast tract under sheep, and feeding no more than two to an acre, their fleeces only at five shillings each would amount raw to £1,418,418 and spun into bay yarn, without receiving any farther manufacture, the value would be £2,127,622 reckoning the labour half the value of the wool; that is to say, the amount would be more than the whole value of the linen manufacture both exported and consumed at home.

How exceeding different are the manufactures of England! That of the single city of Norwich amounts to near as much as the whole linen export of Ireland; but very far is that from being the whole exported produce of a province! It is not that of a single county; for Norfolk, besides feeding that city, Yarmouth and Lynn, two of the greatest ports in England, and a variety of other towns, exports, I believe, more corn than any other county in the kingdom; and whoever is acquainted with the supply of the London markets, knows that there are thousands of black cattle fattened every year on Norfolk turneps, and sent to Smithfield. What a spectacle is this! The agriculture in the world the most productive of wealth by exportation, around one of the greatest manufactures in Europe. It is thus that manufactures become the best friends to agriculture; that they animate the farmer's industry by giving him ready markets; until he is able, not only to supply them fully, but pushes his exertions with such effect that he finds a surplus in his hands to convert into gold in the national balance, by rendering foreigners tributary for their bread. Examine all the others fabricks in the kingdom, you see them prodigious markets for the surrounding lands; you see those lands doubling, trebling, quadrupling their rents, while the farmers of them increase daily in wealth; thus you see manufactures rearing up agriculture, and agriculture supporting manufactures; you see a reaction which gives a reciprocal animation to human industry; great national prosperity is the effect; wealth pours in from the fabricks, which, spreading like a fertile stream over all the surrounding lands, renders them, comparatively speaking, so many gardens, the most pleasing spectacles of successful industry.

Change the scene, and view the North of Ireland; you there behold a whole province peopled by weavers; it is they who cultivate, or rather beggar the soil, as well as work the looms; agriculture is there in ruins; it is cut up by the root; extirpated, annihilated; the whole region is the disgrace of the kingdom; all the crops you see are contemptible, are nothing but filth and weeds. No other part of Ireland can exhibit the soil in such a state of poverty and desolation. A farming traveller, who goes through that country with attention, will be shocked at seeing wretchedness in the shape of a few beggarly oats on a variety of most fertile soils, which, were they in Norfolk, would soon rival the best lands in that county.

But the cause of all these evils, which are absolute exceptions to every thing else on the face of the globe, is easily found. A most prosperous manufacture, so contrived as to be the destruction of agriculture, is certainly a spectacle for which we must go to Ireland. It is owing to the fabrick spreading over all the country, instead of being confined to towns. This in a certain degree is found in some manufactures in England, but never to the exclusion of farmers; there, literally speaking, is not a farmer in a hundred miles of the linen country in Ireland. The lands are infinitely subdivided; no weaver thinks of supporting himself by his loom; he has always a piece of potatoes, a piece of oats, a patch of flax, and grass or weeds for a cow; thus his time is divided between his farm and his loom. Ten acres are an uncommon quantity to be in one man's occupation; four, five, or six, the common extent. They sow their land with successive crops of oats until it does not produce the seed again; and they leave it to become grass as it may, in which state it is under weeds and rubbish for four or five years. Such a wretched management is constant destruction to the land; none of it becomes improved unless from a state of nature; all the rest is destroyed, and does not produce a tenth of what it would if cultivated by farmers, who had nothing to do but mind their business. As land thus managed will not yield rent, they depend for that on their web; if linen sells indifferently, they pay their rents indifferently, and if it sells badly, they do not pay them at all. Rents in general, at their value, being worse paid there than in any other part of Ireland.

Where agriculture is in such a state of ruin, the land cannot attain its true value; and in fact the linen counties, proportioned to their soil, are lower let than any others in Ireland. There has been a great rise on many estates, and so there has all over the kingdom, but not at all owing to the manufacture; and I am confident, from having gone over the whole with attention, that any given tract of land in the linen country, if it could be moved to some other part of the kingdom where there are no weavers, would let twenty per cent. higher than it does at present; and I am so convinced of this, that if I had an estate in the South of Ireland, I would as soon introduce pestilence and famine as the linen manufacture upon it, *carried on as it is at present in the North of that kingdom.* Particular spots may be, and are high let in the North; but I speak of the average of any large tract.

But if, instead of the manufacture having so diffused itself as absolutely to banish farmers, it had been confined to towns, which it might very easily have been, the very contrary effect would have taken place; and all those vast advantages to agriculture would have flowed, which flourishing manufactures in other countries occasion. The towns would have been large and numerous, and would have proved such ample markets to all the adjacent country, that it could not have failed becoming well cultivated, and letting probably at double the present rent. The manufacturers would have been confined to their own business, and the farmers to theirs; that both trades would have flourished the better for this, the minutes of the journey very generally shew; a weaver who works at a fine cloth, can never take the plough or the spade in hand without injury to his web.

I never heard but two objections to this: first, That the weavers would be unhealthy in towns: and second, That the country would be less populous.

To the first I reply, that ill health is the consequence of a sedentary life and a bended posture; whether the man has his farm or not, it is not a little work now and then that will remedy this evil, if he supports himself by the loom. I was in several of the linen markets, and never saw more pallid pictures of disease; I defy any town to shew worse. Robust, healthy, vigorous bodies are not to be found at looms; if the health of the people is your object, you must give up manufactures, and betake yourselves to agriculture altogether; but this in the present state of the world is visionary. If the weavers were confined to towns, as I propose, there would be a much greater aggregate of health than at present; for the country would be as healthy as it always is in the hands of farmers and labourers, but at present *all* is unhealthy as *all* are manufacturers.

The second objection I totally deny; for it is against all

the principles of population to assert that a measure, which is beneficial to both agriculture and manufactures, can be prejudicial to the increase of people; more food would be raised from well than from ill cultivated ground; a whole race of farmers and labourers would be employed in feeding the towns; to think that population could be injured by such an arrangement is an absurdity too gross to deserve attention.

That the circumstances of the Irish manufacture are lamentable, when the extent of country is considered, no man of reflection can doubt; for the value of it, taken in that light, (important as it is in its total amount) appears to be comparatively trivial. Fortunately the evil is not without a remedy; the landlords of the country might, with no great difficulty, effect the change. Let them steadily refuse to let an acre of land to any man that has a loom; the business would and ought to be gradual; but farms should be thrown by degrees into the hands of real farmers, and weavers driven into towns, where a cabbage garden should be the utmost space of their land; and those gentlemen, who are introducing the manufacture in other parts of the kingdom, should build the cabbins contiguous, and let the inhabitants on no account have any land. All encouragement, all attention, all bounty, all premium, all reward, should go to those alone who lived by, and attended to their looms alone, not in a separated cabbin, but in a street. The more a person attends to the abominable state of land in the North of Ireland, the more he will be convinced of the propriety, and even necessity of this measure; and if, contrary to common sense, a paltry Board is permitted to exist, by way of promoting a fabrick of two millions a year, let them have this object, and this only as their business. Let them devise the means of inducing landlords to drive their weavers into towns, and they will in a few years do more good to their country than all their inspectors, itinerant men, and spinning-wheels, will do in a century.

Relative to the other manufactures of Ireland, I am sorry to say they are too insignificant to merit a particular attention; upon the subject of that of wool I must however remark, that the policy of England, which has always hitherto been hostile to every appearance of an Irish woollen manufacture, has been founded upon the mean contractions of illiberal jealousy; it is a conduct that has been founded upon the ignorance and prejudices of mercantile people, who, knowing as they are in the science which teaches that two and two make four, are lost in a labyrinth the moment they leave their counting-houses and become statesmen; they are too apt to think of governing kingdoms upon the same principles they conduct their private business on, those of monopoly; which, though the soul of private interest, is the bane of publick commerce. It has been the mistaken policy of this country to suppose that all Ireland gained by a woollen manufacture would be so much loss to England; this is the true monopolizing ignorance. We did not think proper to draw these bands of commercial tyranny so tight as to interdict their linens; we gave them a free trade; nay we import an immense quantity of Russian and German linen; and yet, between this double fire of the Irish and foreigners, has our own linen manufacture flourished and increased; it is the spirit and effect of every species of monopoly to counteract the designs which dictate that mean policy. The rivalship of the Irish (if a rivalship was to ensue) would be beneficial to our woollen trade; as a fast friend to the interest of my native country, I wish success to those branches of the Irish woollens which would rival our own; a thousand beneficial consequences would flow from it; it would inspirit our manufacturers; it would awaken them from their lethargy, and give rise to the spirit of invention and enterprize. How long did our old broad-cloth trade sleep in the west without one sign of life strong enough to animate a new pursuit; but a different spirit breaking out in Yorkshire and Scotland, new fabricks were invented, and new trades opened. A free Irish woollen trade would put our manufacturers to their mettle, and would do more for the woollen trade of England than any other measure whatever. Our merchants think such a rivalship would ruin them; but do they think the French would not have reason for such fears also? Have we not lost the Levant and Turkey trade through the obstinacy of our monopolists? And why should not Ireland have a chance for such a branch as well as Languedoc? But such has been our narrow policy, with respect to that kingdom, that we have for a century sat down more contented with the successful rivalship of France, than with the chance of an Irish competitor.

Whenever any question, relative to commercial indulgence to Ireland, has come into the British Parliament, its friends have always urged the *distressed state of Ireland* as a motive. This is taking the ground of duplicity, perhaps of falsehood; they ought to be more liberal, and avow that their principle is, not to relax the present laws as a matter of humanity to Ireland, but of right and policy to themselves; to demand a free trade to Ireland as the best friends to Britain; to demand that France may be rivalled by the subjects of the British Empire, if those of one kingdom cannot, or will not do it, that those of another may.

One would have reason to suppose, from the spirit of commercial jealousy among our woollen towns, that whatever Ireland got was lost to England: I shall in a succeeding section insert a table, which will shew that, in exact proportion to the wealth of Ireland, is the balance of the Irish trade in favour of England. That kingdom is one of the greatest customers we have upon the globe; is it good policy to wish that our best customer may be poor? Do not the maxims of commercial life tell us that the richer he is the better? Can any one suppose that the immense wealth of Holland is not of vast advantage to our manufactures; and, though the Russia trade, upon the balance, is much against us, who can suppose that the increasing wealth of that vast empire, owing to the unparalleled wisdom of its present Empress, the first and most able sovereign in the world,[1] is not an increasing fund in favour of British industry?

The tabinets and poplins of Ireland (a fabrick partly of

[1] Catherine II., the German princess, Voltairian and debauchée, who as Empress of Russia 1762-96, witnessed and had the chief hand in the three partitions of Poland, and survived the last only a few months, doubtless deserved by her ability some of the praise Young here bestows upon her; but it would have been expressed less warmly had she not appreciated the need of developing Russian agriculture, and ordered, to that end, Young's "Six Weeks' Tour through the Southern Counties of England and Wales" to be translated into Russian. See "Annals of Agriculture," vol. ii. p. 232.

woollen, partly of silk) did that island possess a greater freedom in the woollen trade, would find their way to a successful market throughout all the South of Europe. A friend of mine travelled France and Spain with a suit of that pleasing fabrick among others; and it was more admired and envied than any thing he carried with him. This is a manufacture of which we have not a vestige in England.

Under another head I inserted the export of wool and yarn, and also the import of woollen goods from England; the following slight minute on the proportionate value of the labour to the material will conclude what I have to say on a manufacture, which, working only for home consumption, can never thrive.

Bay-yarn. A woman, on an average, spins three skains a day, which weigh a quarter of a pound; the value spun is from ten pence to a shilling, medium ten pence three farthings.

	d.
Combing it, not quite	1
Spinning	2½
	3½
Value of the wool	7¼
	10¾

The balls are a pound and an half each of twelve skains; the woman spins a ball in four days, being paid ten pence; in Leinster it is ten pence halfpenny, and in Munster it is nine pence; average nine pence three farthings. Combing a ball is about three pence, which, with spinning nine pence three farthings, makes twelve pence three farthings labour on a ball; and the price of a ball, both wool and labour, in the year 1778, was three shillings and six pence. In a war the price of wool generally falls in Ireland. The last French war did not sink prices in Ireland, but the Spanish one did. The silk manufacture of Ireland has been already discussed in Section 16, and is a fabrick that merits neither the encouragement of the natives, nor the attention of others.

SECTION XX.

REVENUE—TAXES.

THE rise, progress, and present state of the revenue of Ireland is very little understood in England, though an object of considerable importance to that kingdom. The variations of this revenue are useful marks among many others of the prosperity or declension of the island; and every thing which enables us to judge of the real state of a country with which we are so intimately connected well deserves our attention.

The publick revenue in that kingdom stands upon a very different footing from ours in England, owing to the operations of the Revolution relative to this object not having extended to Ireland. Before that epoch the two kingdoms were in this respect similar; but the old subsidies and other duties which formed the hereditary revenue of the Stuarts in England were purchased of the Crown at the Revolution with the civil list revenue of £700,000; no similar bargain took place in Ireland; consequently the old hereditary revenue in that kingdom is at present under the same circumstances as the like funds were in England before 1688. It is upon this old revenue that the pensions on the Irish establishment are granted; the Crown claims a right to apply the whole of it at its pleasure, but arguments have been urged against that claim.

The following tables will set the progress of late years, and present receipt of the revenue, in a clear light.

In the year	Customs in.	Customs out.	Import excise.	Inland excise.	Additional duty on ale, beer, and strong waters.	Hearth money.
	£	£	£	£	£	£
1730	97,821	27,012	78,248	64,360	50,909	42,301
1731	78,671	24,030	66,808	71,410	56,439	42,963
1732	76,880	25,807	74,259	76,473	60,374	42,810
1733	87,395	24,174	76,257	74,835	59,284	43,550
1734	84,542	25,780	75,974	76,076	60,501	43,926
1735	88,321	25,624	77,241	66,851	53,071	44,201
1736	104,580	24,124	84,875	63,636	50,542	44,112
1737	96,218	24,705	74,160	65,653	52,194	43,921
1738	98,086	26,131	87,302	70,787	56,114	44,035
1739	95,428	24,414	79,203	71,731	56,895	44,244
1740	84,912	25,388	73,336	69,675	55,375	45,045
1741	93,381	21,064	79,360	66,956	53,151	44,965
1742	97,630	21,093	72,104	67,156	53,419	41,828
1743	95,893	22,086	76,910	79,785	63,720	41,165
1744	88,451	27,647	69,759	88,874	70,939	41,823
1745	86,531	23,824	72,001	84,398	67,562	42,911
1746	89,685	22,836	63,710	74,626	59,564	41,410
1747	89,824	29,627	64,164	73,347	58,803	40,327
1748	95,819	26,486	84,916	84,282	67,895	40,960
1749	109,840	31,329	88,463	88,817	71,648	42,180
1750	151,279	29,698	123,858	92,294	74,404	43,039
1751	147,366	27,484	110,219	91,596	73,892	44,794
1752	137,731	30,726	105,492	94,802	76,389	51,924
1753	159,813	29,990	108,764	90,556	73,192	52,946
1754	186,990	26,770	131,906	88,694	71,566	53,405
1755	156,764	30,485	119,765	83,311	67,155	53,789
1756	147,469	26,884	98,262	80,728	65,042	54,283
1757	124,428	28,569	84,049	73,296	58,716	54,133
1758	137,570	32,135	95,086	67,622	54,416	52,859
1759	161,578	30,018	111,018	69,301	54,742	53,482
1760	148,445	33,673	116,831	77,411	61,533	54,570
1761	150,997	39,419	103,225	86,504	69,119	55,027
1762	190,553	39,988	132,540	93,543	76,349	55,970
1763	177,834	31,893	122,679	92,842	75,911	56,611
1764	209,999	38,805	144,585	92,745	75,878	56,878
1765	213,128	35,943	152,367	87,754	72,109	57,237
1766	214,985	37,788	173,313	85,752	70,250	57,523
1767	204,864	34,259	147,411	80,094	64,788	57,406
1768	212,743	39,754	155,258	79,765	65,536	57,930
1769	211,049	40,045	157,241	83,557	69,147	58,302
1770	210,490	37,390	152,996	79,631	63,328	58,820
Average	211,036	37,712	154,753	84,185	68,718	57,736

In the year	Customs in.	Customs out.	Import excise.	Inland excise.	Additional duty on ale, beer, and strong waters.	Hearth money.
	£	£	£	£	£	£
1771	200,270	35,712	146,329	70,743	49,160	58,970
1772	199,368	38,850	146,461	70,319	48,971	58,439
1773	232,767	37,397	151,662	74,991	53,274	59,938
1774	229,609	37,169	144,796	77,679	55,419	59,383
1775	203,008	38,010	130,104	77,251	54,894	60,900
1776	248,491	42,488	152,238	79,411	57,353	60,966
1777	251,055	35,883	153,727	80,461	57,750	60,580
Average of last 7 years .	223,709	37,929	146,473	75,839	53,831	59,868
1778	198,550	36,027	131,284	81,761	58,612	61,646
1779	165,802	31,717	106,070	76,335	54,934	60,617

A very slight examination of these columns will shew a great increase in all (except the inland excise, and customs outward) about the year 1748. The conclusion of the Peace of Aix la Chapelle seems, from this table, as well as from a variety of others, to have been the principal epoch in the prosperity of Ireland. The inland excise is a revenue so wretchedly administered, by the confession of the whole kingdom, that no conclusions whatever are to be drawn from it. The customs outwards have risen but little; and not at all in the last seven years; which is to be accounted for from some of the principal articles of the exports, such as linen, &c. being either duty-free, or having so small a custom as to be merely with design of ascertaining quantities; and also by the falling off in the export of the produce of pasturage, which I have shewed before, most of the articles of it having an ill-judged duty on them. But the customs inwards is not a bad one; for an increased import, though at first sight it seems to be against a nation, ought never to be taken in that light. No kingdom ever imports goods which it cannot pay for; and an increased consumption is the strongest proof of an increased ability to pay for it. I must however remark, that the increase in this column the last seven years is very trifling. There is in all the other columns, except hearth-money, a decline in this period, which very well deserves to be enquired into. That the kingdom has flourished in it I have little or no doubt; it may, therefore, probably be owing to the multiplication of abuses in the collection of the revenues, which, being so many cancers in the body politick, ought to be remedied with the utmost assiduity.

The increase of the hearth-money is a matter of importance, for it proves an increase of population clearly; which indeed could not be doubted from the increased prosperity and wealth of the kingdom, and from the repeated information I received all over it to that purport.

The whole gross revenues offer a different appearance from these particular duties; the following account shews there has been an increase, but owing to an increase of taxes.

Two years ending Lady-day.	Hereditary revenue gross.	Old additional duties gross.	For receiving revenue, paying drawbacks and premiums on corn, &c.	Nett produce of the hereditary and old additional duties.
	£	£	£	£
In the year 1751	1,048,858	366,462	192,513	1,233,943
1753	1,047,062	349,557	185,766	1,210,853
1755	1,127,552	367,980	193,259	1,302,274
1757	954,668	322,568	191,357	1,085,880
1759	989,937	320,415	205,290	1,105,062
1761	1,053,939	346,649	234,077	1,166,511
1763	1,201,300	418,258	260,602	1,358,956
Average .	1,060,474	355,698	208,981	1,209,068
In the year 1765	1,298,165	452,375	273,010	1,477,529
1767	1,295,317	471,240	318,044	1,448,513
1769	1,309,828	481,998	347,943	1,443,882
1771	1,276,711	454,955	349,275	1,382,391
1773	1,288,094	439,615	398,380	1,329,330
1775	1,279,275	404,415	428,180	1,255,509
1777	1,388,044	419,748	464,672	1,343,120
Average .	1,305,062	446,335	368,786	1,382,896
In the year 1779	1,175,145	346,696		

These are for sessions, not years. Besides these duties there are others appropriated by Parliament to particular purposes; these are for paying the interest of loans, for the encouragement of the linen manufacture, of tillage, of Protestant schools, and the cambrick manufacture.

The whole revenue of the kingdom for twenty years, in two periods of ten each, with the averages, will shew the general increase, whether owing to new duties or an increase of old ones.

Total Revenue of Ireland.

In the year 1758	£650,763	In the year 1768	£945,520
1759	714,918	1769	977,372
1760	717,022	1770	954,045
1761	746,151	1771	900,913
1762	878,068	1772	897,396
1763	850,895	1773	955,074
1764	939,139	1774	[1]957,498
1765	948,251	1775	[2]930,228
1766	990,744	1776	1,040,055
1767	910,780	1777	1,093,881
Average of ten years	£834,673	Average of ten years	£965,198
		Ditto of the former period	£834,673
		Increase	£130,525

But this revenue, considerable as it is, has not been equal to the national expenditure. In the sessions of 1759 there was a surplus in the treasury of £65,774 yet in the following one a considerable debt was contracted, as will be seen by the progress of the incumbrance.

Year 1761	£223,438 National debt.
1763	521,161 ditto.
1765	508,874 ditto.
1767	581,964 ditto.
1769	628,883 ditto.
1771	789,569 ditto.
1773	[3]999,686 ditto.

[1] Additional duties laid.
[2] Stamps ditto.
[3] This does not agree with the statement in vol. 17 of the Journals, see the following year.

Year 1775	. . . .	£976,117 National debt.
1777	. . . .	[1]825,426 ditto.
1779	. . . .	1,062,597 ditto.

Suppose the revenue a million, it is about a sixth part of the land rents of the kingdom. If there are three million of souls in Ireland, they pay exactly 6*s.* 8*d.* a head. It appeared before that the export of linen, yarn, corn, woollen, pork, beef, &c. &c. amounted to £3,250,471; suppose all other exports would make it up three and a half millions, the revenue of the kingdom amounts not quite to a third.

It will not be improper here to compare the burthens of Ireland with those of Great Britain.

	£	*s.*	*d.*	
British revenue of 13 millions paid by 9 millions of people is	1	9	0	a head.
Irish revenue of 1 million paid by 3 millions of people is	0	6	8	a head.
British revenue of 13 millions paid by 72 millions[2] of acres is	0	3	6	each.
Irish revenue of 1 million paid by 25 millions of acres is	0	0	10	each.
British revenue of 13 millions paid by a rental[3] of 24 millions is	0	10	10	in the pound.
Irish revenue of 1 million paid by a rental of 6 millions is	0	3	4	in the pound.
British revenue of 13 millions paid by an export of[4] 16 millions is	0	16	3	in the pound.
Irish revenue of 1 million paid by an export of 3½ millions is	0	5	9	in the pound.
British revenue of 13 millions paid by a balance of trade of 5 millions is . . .	2	12	0	in the pound.
Irish revenue of 1 million paid by a balance of trade of 1 million is . . .	1	0	0	in the pound.

The inferiority of the taxes of Ireland to those of Great Britain, upon every one of these comparisons, is very great; the parallel is, however, certainly not complete: the specie

[1] Extracted from the national accounts laid before Parliament every sessions.

[2] The exact number at 640 to a mile is 71,979,848.

[3] £20 that of England, and £4 allowed for Scotland.

[4] The last custom-house account.

of Ireland is £1,600,000; but it is difficult to say what that of England is, the gold coinage proved our calculators to be so amazingly out in their reckoning; but in this article, including paper, lies, I apprehend, the greater ease in England of paying taxes; which are light or heavy, not perhaps so much in proportion to the income of a people, as to the ease of circulation; that in England is out of all comparison greater than in Ireland, which would make it impossible for the preceding proportions to be raised in that kingdom as high as they are in Britain. But, fair allowances being made for this article, still we may with great safety conclude that this national burthen is vastly lighter there than with us. If the advantages of such a situation are not continued, it will certainly be owing to complaints of poverty, occasioning closer scrutinies into facts than have hitherto happened.

We come next to the expence which absorbs this income.

Two years ending Lady day.	Civil list.	Military list.	Extraordinary charges, including parliamentary grants.	Totals.
	£	£	£	£
In the year 1751	146,134	766,151	126,356	1,038,643
1753	143,705	762,571	152,415	1,058,691
1755	144,602	795,182	169,276	1,109,061
1757	161,223	794,364	362,674	1,318,263
1759	181,964	820,383	298,173	1,300,521
1761	202,052	997,072	281,888	1,481,013
1763	221,365	1,124,743	332,934	1,679,043
1765	241,271	988,535	275,955	1,505,761
1767	257,988	971,007	337,646	1,566,642
1769	270,040	954,426	327,094	1,551,561
1771	272,678	976,917	373,997	1,623,593
1773	323,833	1,172,723	389,634	1,886,191
1775	366,838	1,223,326	342,377	1,932,541
1777	410,904	1,112,682	410,172	1,933,758
1779	336,475	937,679	432,474	1,706,628

Two years ending Lady day.	Salaries exclusive of hearth-money collectors.	Two years ending Lady day.	Salaries exclusive of hearth-money collectors.
	£		£
In the year 1751	110,622	In the year 1765	151,655
1753	111,478	1767	156,157
1755	113,721	1769	164,364
1757	115,552	1771	165,574
1759	116,344	1773	169,567
1761	130,274	1775	176,107
1763	144,316	1777	171,578

Some of the particular duties which go towards raising the above revenue will be seen among the following articles.

Goods exported. Year 1773.	Duty.
Beef	£10,759
Bulls and cows	29
Butter	6,809
Candles	109
Cheese	52
Horses	88
Bacon flitches	120
Hides	2,857
Tallow, cwt.	2,994
Tongues	75
Total	£23,892

Goods imported. Year 1773.	Duty.
Tobacco	£121,148
Rum	161,080
Gin	21,935
Brandy	34,906
Tea	16,406
Salt and salt petre	11,305
Silk	18,382
Wine	[1]104,701
	£489,163

To lay a duty of near £24,000 a year upon the export of the produce of pasturage is heavy and most unpolitick, and ought to be abolished. The other articles in this list are very proper ones to tax.

The decline in several branches of the revenue having united with an increased expence to run the nation in debt, as above mentioned, new taxes are of course in contemplation every sessions. A LAND TAX has been a matter of conversation in Ireland for some years: some increase must be made to the revenue, but in what mode is an

[1] Commons Journals, vol. 16, p. 268.

enquiry of the most interesting nature to that kingdom; I shall for this reason offer a few remarks on the state of the country relative to the taxes which would be most proper for it.

There are a variety of objections to land taxes in general, besides the particular ones which apply immediately to Ireland. Taxes ought all to be equal, but an *equal* land tax must be a *variable* one, which is at once a *tythe*, the most pernicious burthen to which any nation can submit; it is the *taille*, the equal land tax of France, which is so well known to be the ruin of the agriculture of that kingdom: hence therefore equality must not be thought of in a land tax: and if there were no other objections, this alone ought for ever to preclude them. But suppose a fixed unequal tax, as in England, yet there are great evils in it; a man's possessions are rarely to be taken as a proof of his capability to bear a tax; a landlord who receives a thousand pounds a year from his estate, and pays seven hundred interest of mortgages, is taxed at his whole rental; what enormity and ruin is this! that the ability to bear the burthen is to be of no consequence in laying the tax. When the amazing amount of mortgages on landed property is considered, the greatness of this oppression must be fully felt. But land taxes when they are unequal are unproductive; hence the oppressions under this name which crush the agriculture of France, Milan, and the states of Austria and Prussia; in most of which actual *valuations* of the land are made periodically, as if no man's improvement should escape taxation: hence also the designs of the English ministry, once remarkably manifested, of dropping the present land tax in order to obtain an equal one: these are universal objections to land taxes.

But in Ireland there are others which concern that country singly, and therefore the more deserve attention; a vast proportion of it is under lease for ever; other parts let for five hundred years; others for lives and a hundred years; others for lives and fifty and thirty years; in a word, under leases of every description. How could a land tax be laid in that kingdom consistently with the reigning principle of the English tax, that the landlord only shall pay it? Difficulties innumerable would arise at every step; no gordian knot but the sword of power can cut; but the question is whether all the principles that have directed a similar tax in England would not be cut with them: for the tax to be either equal or productive it must be laid on some classes of tenantry: it ought certainly to be laid on all who do not occupy; but from that moment there is an end of it as an English land tax; it is a *taille*, a tax on tenantry: break the limits the great line between the owner of the land and the tenant, and who will say how far the innovation will be carried? the most dangerous that can ever be made in a kingdom. Adieu to all improvements in agriculture wherever such an one takes place.

Evils of this sort rarely make their full appearance at first; a land tax in Ireland would probably come in under a very fair appearance; but the state of the country ought to tell its inhabitants that such a tax would be too unproductive to last; the successive alterations would do the fatal business, and produce the mischief in its full deformity.

Administrations have had experience in England of the loss, as it has been called, to the revenue from a fixed tax; if ever therefore they introduced it into Ireland, it would be in a form which admitted alterations in order to avoid the circumstance which has more than once raised a strong inclination to a new assessment. For these and other reasons, too numerous to give in detail here, I am convinced that Ireland can never experience a more pernicious tax than that on land.

But, as I observed before, government must go on, and must be supported at an increasing expence; new taxes must consequently be had recourse to; and I shall not hesitate a moment in recommending excises as the only ones which can be much extended without any national injury: an entire change in the administration of them should take place; the monstrous abuses in them remedied, and new ones laid. The cheapness of whisky, with which a man may get dead drunk for two pence, is an enormity too great to be borne. The morals, health, peace, industry, agriculture, manufactures, commerce, and wealth of the kingdom, are all materially injured by the cheapness of this vile beverage: there is not an object in Ireland which would yield a more productive revenue; at the same time that every shilling government got would be half a crown benefit to the publick: a judicious and well collected excise on this liquor would raise an immense revenue. All other spirits, wines and tobacco, are also very well able to bear much heavier taxes than they labour under at present. An excise on tea also might be applicable; but there is no want of objects; and if the legislature of the kingdom will not set themselves very steadily to the business, a land tax will be the consequence, and in it all the mischiefs that must attend the measure.

The proposition for a land tax on absentees was very wisely rejected; the execution of it would have smoothed some of the difficulties, or at least rendered them familiar, and certainly have facilitated a general tax of the same nature.

The mode pursued in Ireland of raising money by tontine, at an exceeding high interest, so high even as 7 per cent., is very mischievous to the kingdom. The great want of that country is *capital;* consequently any measure which tends to lessen capitals that are employed in any branch of industry, is pernicious: seven per cent. interest in national funds must be a severe blow to every branch of industry; for who will lend money on private security at six per cent. while the publick gives seven? And what man will undergo the trouble, and run the hazard of manufactures or commerce, while he can set by his fireside with seven per cent. in his pocket. In England, where the capital is so immense, and with all that of Holland at command, similar transactions are found exceedingly detrimental; insomuch that no industry can be carried on which will not yield very large profits; no money to be procured on bond; scarce any on mortgage; vast sums drawing out of the general industry for investment in the publick funds; and a general fall in the value of that great portion of landed property which is obliged to be sold. But the sums borrowed in this country may be too large to raise by taxes; I do not think it is the same in Ireland; and that kingdom had much better raise their supplies within the session, than lessen their little capital by tontines.

SECTION XXI.

COMMERCE—FISHERIES—EMBARGOES.

UNFORTUNATELY for Ireland, the general commerce of it is to be fully treated in a very small compass; and the facts which I have already had occasion to lay before the reader in the two preceding sections, go very far towards completing the whole that is necessary to explain its state. Being a dependent country, the British legislature has, upon all occasions, controuled its commerce, sometimes with a very high hand, but universally upon the principles of monopoly, as if the poverty of that country was to form the wealth of Britain. I have on every occasion endeavoured to shew the futility of such an idea, and to prove, from the evidence of invariable facts, that the wealth of Ireland has always been, and is, the wealth of England; that whatever she gets is expended in a very large proportion in the consumption of British fabricks and commodities. The increased prosperity of Ireland, which she has experienced in spite of our absurd restrictions on her commerce, has raised her to be one of the greatest and best markets this kingdom possesses in any part of the globe.

It is a remarkable fact, which was pointed out to me by that very able politician the Earl of Shelburne, that the narrowness of our prohibitory laws in England is of late date; from the old English Acts of Parliament it appears that before the Restoration the true system of commerce was much better understood than it has been of late days: if the transactions of the Commonwealth are examined, there will appear great liberality, and the soundest principles in Cromwell and the leading men of those times;

and that it was the clear determination of the Protector as well as of the Long Parliament, to make the trade of Ireland as free as possible; nay, the Act of Navigation itself, at the Restoration, included Ireland upon the same footing as England; it was not till twelve years afterwards that the exception crept in by a single clause in another Act, which probably was passed at the desire of some merchant, without any person's caring about it, which has been the case with many an American Act. The next prohibitory law, which declared the importation of Irish cattle a nuisance, was a contested job between the Duke of Ormond and the Duke of Lauderdale; afterwards it became the fashion to pass Acts against Ireland, which nobody had the knowledge or liberality to oppose. In the full perfection of this spirit it was, that a bill, which passed in Ireland in 1759, for restricting the importation of damaged flour, was thrown out in England at the instigation of a single miller at Chichester.

Whenever old prejudices wear out, it will certainly be found for the interest of England to give every freedom possible to the trade of Ireland. I am convinced if this extended to its being an absolute free port, no mischief would result from it; but as to a free export to all the world, not the shadow of a good argument ever yet appeared against it; for upon what principles of policy, or of common sense, can we found a conduct which restrains our own subjects from the free sale of their products and manufactures, when the returns of such sales must flow into our own coffers by that extension of demand, which has been inseparably connected with the wealth of Ireland, when the population and the power that rise upon such wealth are our own? A mercantile landlord at London might as well say to his tenant in Yorkshire, You shall not sell your corn to whom you please, you shall ship it to me; you shall not convert your wool to the best purposes, you shall sell it raw to me. This language might be that of his leases; but it would be that of folly. Would he not soon find that by leaving his tenants to make the best of their own commodities, they would afford to pay him a better rent; their wealth becomes his; if he keeps them poor he must be so himself. The case of Ireland is exactly parallel; the inhabitants of that island, in their publick revenue, in their military, by their absentees, and in their commercial balance, pay to this kingdom a direct rent for it, which vibrates in its amount to the variations of their national wealth. While it was a wilderness of savages, it paid the rent which desarts everywhere yield; as it improved, our receipt has been proportioned, until it has become a cultivated flourishing estate, and yields a rent which marks to an iota the extent of the cultivation, and the degree of that prosperity. Of what use is the experience of a century of facts, if we are not to open our eyes to the lessons they convey? Long experience has told us what the effects of Irish wealth are; we feel those effects flowing like vital warmth through the whole extent of our own territory; and shall we yet hesitate to encourage and extend a prosperity which is the source and foundation of our own?

I have taken the great line of leading principles; will the littleness of commercial jealousy reply in its true spirit, that this town will be hurt, that that manfacture will be lost, that Manchester will be alarmed, and that Norwich will have apprehensions: it is not a question for the weavers of one place, or the merchants of another to decide; it is THE EMPIRE that is concerned: the general interest demands the measure, and ought to absorb every pitiful consideration; but all experience speaks only one language even to these mistaken individuals: I observed it before, and gave instances of manufactures sinking in the possession of a monopoly, and thriving from a rivalry; of markets rising to increasing industry; of the welfare of one country rising from the prosperity of others: truths as universal as the world. And shall we deny the application to a sister but dependent kingdom, from whom we have so many ways of gaining all the advantages of her wealth? But arguments are little wanted where facts are so numerous; to those I have already inserted let me add the following state of our imports and exports in the Irish trade.

Trade of Great Britain with Ireland.

In the year	Imports.	Exports.	Imports excess.	Exports excess.
	£	£	£	£
1697	223,913	251,262		27,348
1698	333,968	293,813	40,154	
1699	417,475	269,475	147,999	
1700	233,853	261,115		27,262
1701	285,390	296,144		10,753
1702	258,121	215,112	43,008	
1703	324,289	266,324	57,965	
1704	321,847	215,949	105,897	
1705	279,992	244,057	35,934	
1706	266,269	198,176	68,092	
1707	306,423	263,412	43,010	
1708	274,689	251,974	22,715	
1709	276,423	251,519	24.904	
1710	310,846	285,424	25,421	
1711	297,238	261,426	35,811	
1712	291,669	274,845	16,823	
1713	295,926	306,964		11,038
1714	326,391	397,048		70,656
1715	389,437	420,062		30,625
1716	561,673	345,252	216,421	
1717	469,657	429,880	39,776	
1718	326,283	333,988		7,704
1719	380,130	387,460		7,329
1720	282,812	328,583		45,771
1721	332,882	378,838		37,956
1722	356,095	488,370		132,274
1723	360,526	553,945		193,418
1724	367,889	468,257		100,367
1725	333,870	474,836		140,965
1726	332,604	569,553		236,949
1727	307,038	436,012		128,973
1728	318,147	475,762		157,615
1729	287,648	517,198		229,549
1730	294,156	532,698		238,542
1731	308,936	618,684		309,745
1732	294,484	614,754		225,731
1733	386,105	595,251		351,822
1734	401,422	627,154		225,731
1735	417,421	769,244		351,822
1736	447,176	720,555		273,378
1737	346,476	739,910		384,433
1738	381,372	696,590		315,218
1739	411,924	673,621		261,697

Trade of Great Britain with Ireland. (Continued.)

In the year	Imports.	Exports.	Imports excess.	Exports excess.
	£	£	£	£
1740	390,565	628,288		237,723
1741	404,863	698,715		293,851
1742	346,814	775,650		428,835
1743	816,797	860,178		43,380
1744	390,874	703,227		312,353
1745	1,441,498	910,920	530,578	
1746	532,686	796,157		263,471
1747	541,393	748,677		207,284
1748	464,489	906,424		441,935
1749	567,776	1,006,045		438,268
1750	612,808	1,316,600		703,792
1751	664,484	1,174,493		510,008
1752	563,959	1,140,608		576,648
1753	561,489	1,149,552		588,063
1754	610,466	1,173,829		563,362
1755	643,165	1,070,063		426,897
1756	827,811	1,111,801		283,990
1757	687,471	960,843		273,371
1758	1,050,331	926,886	123,446	
1759	832,127	931,358		99,231
1760	904,180	1,050,401		146,220
1761	853,804	1,476,114		622,310
1762	889,368	1,528,696		639,328
1763	769,379	1,640,713		871,333
1764	777,412	1,634,382		856,969
1765	1,070,533	1,767,020		696,486
1766	1,154,982	1,920,015		765,033
1767	1,103,285	1,880,486		777,201
1768	1,226,094	2,248,315		1,022,221
1769	1,265,107	1,964,742		699,634
1770	1,214,398	2,125,466		911,068
1771	1,380,737	1,983,818		603,081
1772	1,242,305	1,963,787		721,481
1773[1]	1,252,817	1,918,802		665,985

[1] Extracted from the accounts laid before the British Parliament.

It is a circumstance very much to be regretted that these accounts no longer see the light; they have not been laid before Parliament since 1773; why should a practice that had continued for above a century

The reader will recollect that it was the general tenour of the information received in the journey, that the year 1748 was the epoch of the modern prosperity of Ireland; all agree that after that peace Ireland advanced greatly; her rise of rental will mark this clearly. The following is a review of the minutes:

Rise of Rents.

Lord Longford more than doubled in thirty years—Earl of Inniskilling quadrupled in ditto—Mr. Cooper almost trebled since 1748.—Mayo trebled in forty years.—King's county two thirds since 1750—Tipperary doubled in twenty years.—Barony of Owna and Ara doubled in ditto.—Rich lands of Limerick risen a fourth in twenty years, and two thirds since 1748.

In the preceding enquiries the truth of this is confirmed by every proof which authentic records can shew; as the table now before us marks the commercial connection between Great Britain and Ireland, it is necessary to divide it into periods, in order to see the average of each. The table contains twenty-five years since 1748, during which period

	Imports.	Exports.
	£	£
The averages are	965,050	1,482,513
Ditto in the twenty-five preceding years	438,665	657,972
Latter period superior by	526,385	824,541

Here is an account that is worth a dozen arguments! It is from hence evident that our exports to Ireland have in the last twenty-five years considerably more than doubled, almost trebled; and this great rise has been exactly in the period of the internal prosperity of that island. If I did not know persons of very respectable characters in Parliament, who think very differently upon this great question of the freedom of Irish trade, I should be ashamed of dwelling a moment on the subject. How would it have

cease just then? If there were any trades, like the *American*, which did not offer a pleasing spectacle, there were others like those of Ireland, Russia, &c. to make amends.

been possible for that country to support such an increased importation, unless she had increased in wealth? And having proved that such advances in national prosperity have been attended by this increased demand for manufactures and products of England, are we not perfectly founded in concluding that future advantages to Ireland will also be attended by similar effects? The influx of wealth into that country brings a taste for the elegant luxuries with which we abound, and the capability of purchasing them ensures the purchase. An Englishman cannot go into a single house in Dublin, or see a person dressed, of either sex, without having this truth staring him in the face. But there is a circumstance in this account which deserves particular attention, and that is our import trade not having increased so much as the export one; from which this plain conclusion is to be drawn; that, let Ireland get her wealth from where she will, it comes infallibly to England. The fourth column of the table which shews the balance she pays us, and which amounts of late years from six hundred thousand to a million a year, could not possibly be supported with the absentee drain, unless she made by her trade elsewhere.

	Imports.	Exports.
	£	£
Average of the last seven years . . .	1,240,677	2,012,2[illegible]
Ditto of the preceding seven years . .	917,088	1,573,934
Increase	323,569	438,268

From this comparison we find that the rapid increase of our exports to Ireland is in late years; the stronger reason therefore to expect that, whatever increase of wealth she experiences, it will be England that will receive the full tribute of it. By means of the prosperity of Ireland, the trade we carry on with that kingdom is grown to be one of the most important which we possess; and, in the last year of this table, nearly equalled the export to the whole continent of North America.

Exports from England to the continent of North America, from Christmas, 1772, to 1773 . . .	£1,981,544
Ditto to Ireland	1,918,802

Freight, insurance and profit on both, twelve per cent. Hence therefore this nation has no demand of policy so strong on her at present, as to encourage Ireland to the utmost of her power, in order to increase her own trade to that island, that American losses may be the less sensibly felt; but this can only be done by embracing a system totally new. And here it is a tribute fairly due to genius long since departed, to observe that the relative interests of England and Ireland were better understood by Mr. Houghton, in 1682, than by any later writer, whose productions have come to my knowledge; and, as I have mentioned him on this occasion, I must remark that he seems to me to have had juster ideas of trade, manufactures, prices of provisions, enclosures, &c. than nine tenths of the authors who have treated of those subjects: "The richer Ireland grows, the more wealth will the land-"lords have, and the more will they that live here spend. "I am told by an inquisitive and understanding knight, "that hath a great estate there, and very well understands "the Irish affairs, that what their gentry spend here, with "the pensions and the rent that are paid from thence "to the city of London, amounts to about three hundred "thousand pounds per annum; and I see no reason why "this expence should not increase according to their "thriving."—"Even in the woollen manufacture I question "whether they could in *cloth* do more than the Dutch; and, "for other manufactures, why might it not *put both nations "at strife to find out some new consumptions, and so increase "the trades of both?* If there must be but a set quantity "consumed, seeing England bears up against, and in "cloathing outdoth *terra firma, why may we not,* IF IRE-"LAND BE JOINED TO US, *spoil the trade on the other side, "and so be both enriched?*"[1] Here is the interest of England, relative to that country, explained upon the most enlarged and most liberal principles of freedom and of commerce. This penetrating genius, who saw deeper into the true English interests than half our modern politicians, was sensible of no mischiefs from a free Irish woollen trade: the prevalence of commercial jealousy had not then arisen

[1] Collection of Husbandry and Trade, vol. 4, p. 48.

to the heights we have since seen it. Without any hesitation, Ireland ought to have an absolutely free trade of export and import to all our American colonies and African settlements; also a very considerable freedom in her exports to Europe: but when this subject was in conversation in the House of Commons, I heard the minister mention one circumstance, which seemed to stand in the way of doing justice to Ireland, that is to ourselves: taxes there being so much lower, that their manufactures, not being equally under the burthen of excises, would have an unfair start of ours.[1] With great submission, I think this will not be found sound doctrine either in fact or reason. I might here go into the question of a *poor* and *cheap* country robbing a rich one of her manufactures; for the assertion comes directly to this; but Dr. Tucker has treated it in so masterly a manner, and has so clearly proved the absurdity of the idea, that what he has said ought to be considered as conclusive. But why give in linen what you deny in other fabricks? Irish linen has all the advantages of a freedom from a great variety of excises, which the manufacturers of English linen labour under; and yet we not only support the competition but thrive under it, from there being a difference in the fabricks; and as great a difference would be in all other fabricks. Their broad cloth, also, is made under the same advantages; and compare it in both price and quality with that of England; I bought it at seventeen shillings and sixpence a yard at the Dublin Society's warehouse, without the master-manufacturer's profit and expences; and I will venture to assert, from wearing both, twenty-three shillings for English cloth to be cheaper. The same fact runs through a variety of their fabricks. The fixed trade, capital and skill of England will for ever bid defiance to the no-excises of Ireland. But something was forced to be given—had woollens been put down and linens not permitted, the oppressed and ruined people would have sought redress with arms in their hands. The monopolizing spirit of commercial jealousy gave as little as possible, and would not have given that little could she have helped it. But

[1] Written in June, 1779.

the argument says, that Ireland having few excises will get much trade and wealth: and is it not your design that she should? Ought not this, in common sense, to be your wish and aim? For whom does she grow rich? If I have not proved that point, there is no proof in fact, nor truth in figures. Why cannot she rival France, Holland and Germany, as well as England? But we have ample experience to tell us that she may rival without impoverishing us; that she may grow rich, and we great by her wealth; that she may advance, and we be prosperous. To assert, because there are not as many excises in one part of our dominions as another, that therefore their trade shall be cramped, is exactly like saying, that labour is cheap there, and for that reason shall never be dear; making the poverty of the kingdom the motive for keeping it poor.

Taxes flow from trade and consumption; give them the wealth to consume, and never fear but taxes will follow.

FISHERIES.

There is scarcely a part of Ireland but what is well situated for some fishery of consequence; her coasts and innumerable creeks and rivers' mouths are the resort of vast shoals of herring, cod, hake, mackarel, &c. which might, with proper attention, be converted into funds of wealth; but capital is such a universal want in Ireland that very little is done. The minutes of the journey contain some valuable information on this head; but the general picture is rather an exhibition of what ought to be done, than any thing that actually is executed; nor have the measures of the Legislature been attended with any considerable effect; some of them seem to have done mischief, of which the following is an instance.

By the 3 G. 3. c. 24.—Twenty shillings per ton on English or Irish-built vessels decked, after the commencement of this Act, not under twenty tons, nor to be paid for more than one hundred, to proceed from some port in Ireland.

Bounty of two shillings a barrel on export of white herrings.

Bounty of two shillings and sixpence on mackarel.
Ditto of five shillings for six score of ling.
Ditto of three shillings for hake, haddock, glassing, and conger eel.
Ditto of four shillings and three-pence halfpenny for every tierce of 41 gallons of wet fish exported.
Ditto of three pounds per ton for whale oil, manufactured in Ireland.
Ditto of thirty shillings per ton for other oil of fish, manufactured in Ireland.
Ditto of four pounds per cwt. for whalebone, manufactured in Ireland.

The following has been the effect of this measure.

Barrels of Herrings imported into Ireland for eighteen years.

	From G. Britain.	From E. Country.	Total.
	Barrels.	Barrels.	Barrels.
In the year . . 1756	28,999	1,277	30,276
1757	28,955	2,080	31,035
1758	29,960	1,370	31,330
1759	23,611	113	23,724
1760	17,038¾	¼	17,039
1761	20,411½	142	20,554
1762	21,388	844	22,232
1763	23,519	2,156	25,675
1764	14,932	8,661	23,593
Average of 9 years before the bounty	23,201	1,847	25,048
In the year . . 1765	14,587	17,030	31,617
1766	35,552	24,555	60,107
1767	12,094	12,618	24,712
1768	16,640	23,252	39,892
1769	11,286	25,847	37,133
1770	22,891	23,655	46,546
1771	12,952	26,555	39,507
1772	10,445	34,241	44,686
1773	13,471	40,539	54,010
Average of 9 years after the bounty	16,657	25,365	42,022

	£	s.	d.
Import of herrings in the nine years since the bounty exceed the preceding period in 155,156 barrels. Value at fifteen shillings per barrel .	116,367	11	3
Export less by 16,357 barrels, at twenty shillings per barrel	16,357	15	0
Loss also on the export and import of dry cod, 1,298 cwt. at 14s. per cwt.	973	10	0
Ditto on barrelled cod	364	17	6
	134,063	13	9
Hake 9,566 cwt. at fifteen shillings per cwt. . .	7,115	1	3
Salmon 1,108 tons, at twelve pounds per ton .	14,200	0	0
Mackarel, 2,666 barrels, at twenty shillings per barrel	2,666	0	0
Increased import since the bounty	[1] 158,604	15	0

Imported herrings for home consumption are from Scotland, for foreign use from Sweden. The former twenty shillings a barrel. The latter from fourteen to sixteen shillings. And their own from sixteen to twenty shillings.

Prices of other sorts of fish. Dry ling from eighteen to twenty shillings per cwt. Salmon from twelve to thirteen pounds per ton. Hake from fourteen to sixteen shillings per cwt. Dry cod from fourteen to sixteen shillings per cwt. Wet cod from fourteen to eighteen shillings per barrel.[2]

[1] Manuscript report of the Fish Committee, 1778, communicated by the Right Hon. William Burton.

[2] Manuscript report, communicated by the Right Hon. William Burton.

State of the Fishing Trade of Ireland, for Nine Years, since the commencement of the Bounty, compared with the Nine preceding Years.

	Import in 9 years to the 25th of March, 1773.	Import in 9 years to the 25th of March, 1784.	Increase in last 9 years.	Decrease in last 9 years.	Total loss in last 9 years.	Total gain in last 9 years.
Herrings, barrels.	379,631	224,475	155,156		171,514	
Codd, cwt. . . .	4,575	3,235	1,340		1,298	
Codd, barrels . .	1,103	236	867		486	
Ling, cwt. . . .	963	1,415		452		391
Salmon, tons . .	149	166		17		
Hake, cwt. . .		57		57		
Mackarel, barrels		128		128		
	Export in last 9 years.	Export in first 9 years.				
Herrings, barrels.	34,986	51,344		16,357		
Salmon, ton . .	2,759	4,084		1,125	1,108	
Hake, cwt. . . .	8,617	18,241		9,623	9,566	
Ling, cwt. . . .	411	472		61		
Mackarel, barrels	2,249	5,043		2,794	2,666	
Codd, cwt. . . .	2	42		42		
Codd, barrels . .	472	91$\frac{3}{8}$	381			

	£	s.	d.
Amount of premiums paid to fishing busses in last nine years	47,062	6	5
Ditto to exported fish	1,265	4	7
	[1] 48,328	4	7

Before I quit this article of Irish fisheries, I shall observe that, next to the cultivation of land, there is no object in their national economy of so much importance. No manufactures, no trade can be of half the consequence to Ireland that many of her fisheries might prove, if encouraged with judgment. There is no undertaking

[1] Manuscript report, communicated by the Right Hon. William Burton.

whatever in which a small capital goes so far; nor any in which the largest will pay such ample profits. Scotland has the herrings somewhat earlier; but they come in good time to Ireland for the Mediterranean trade, and in a plenty that ought to make their capture a favourite object. The bounties hitherto given have been so far from answering, that they have in some respects done mischief. I was present more than once at the meetings of the Fishery Committee of the Irish House of Commons, and I found them making anxious enquiries how to avoid great frauds; from which I found that notorious ones had been committed; this is the great misfortune of bounties, when they are not given with great judgement and care. Relative to the fisheries, the profit is so great that all acquainted with them will engage as far as their capital will admit; whatever bounties are given, therefore, should not be with a view to instigate men possessed of capital, for they do not exist, but to put capitals into the hands of those who will certainly make use of them. It appeared in the minutes of the Loch Swilly fishery that one boat and the nets sufficient cost £20; the best bounty would be to give boats and nets to men used to the fishery, because few are able to buy or build them. To give a premium on the export of the herrings or upon the tonnage of the boats will not answer; for it supposes them actually taken, and built, that is, it supposes the very difficulty got over which want of money makes perpetual. Before the boat is in the fishery it must be built, and before the fish are exported they must be taken; those who have money to do either will go to work without any bounty, the profit alone being sufficient. In countries so very poor, the first steps in such undertakings are the most difficult; and to assist in overcoming the early difficulties is what the Legislature should aim at. Giving boats and nets to men that would certainly use them does this, and would be productive of great national good; always supposing that frauds and jobbing are guarded against; if they are permitted to creep in, as in giving spinning-wheels, the mischief would be far more than the benefit. £20,000 per annum thus expended would give 1,000 boats, which would soon accumulate to a vast number; and if the effect was so great as to find the herrings regorge in the home market, then would be the time to drive them out by a bounty on the export, if their own cheapness did not bring the effect without it. I am far from from recommending a new system of bounties upon an object that had not received them before; they have been long given or jobbed; all I mean is, that if the publick is burthened with such payments, care should be taken that they are given in the mode that promises to be most advantageous.

EMBARGOES.

Of all the restrictions which England has at different times most impolitickly laid upon the trade of Ireland, there is none more obnoxious than the embargoes on their provision trade. The prohibitions on the export of woollens and various other articles, have this pretence at least in their favour, that they are advantageous to similar manufactures in England; and Ireland has long been trained to the sacrifice of her national advantage as a dependant country; but in respect to embargoes even this shallow pretence is wanting; a whole kingdom is sacrificed and plundered, not to enrich England, but three or four London contractors! a species of men of an odious cast, as thriving only on the ruin and desolation of their country. It is well known that all the embargoes that have ever been laid have been for the profit of these fellows, and that the Government has not profited a shilling by them. Whenever the affairs of Ireland come thoroughly to be considered in England, a new system in this respect must be embraced. It may not be proper for the Crown directly to give up the prerogative of laying them; but it ought never to be exerted in the cases and with the views with which we have seen it used. The single circumstance of sacrificing the interests of a whole people to a few monopolizing individuals in another country, is to make a nation the beasts of burthen to another people. But this is not the only point; the interest of England and of Government is equally sacrificed; for their object is to have beef plentiful and cheap. But to reduce it so low by embargoes as to discourage the grazier is to lessen the quantity; he increases his sheep, or ploughs more, or is ruined by his business; which necessarily renders the commodity too dear, from the very circumstance of having been too cheap. A steady regular good price from an active demand encourages the grazier so much, that he will produce a quantity sufficient to keep the price from ever rising unreasonably high; and Government would be better supplied. Another consideration is the loss to the kingdom by not taking French money, and sending them to other markets; if it could be proved, or indeed if the fact was possible, that you could keep their fleets in port for want of Irish beef, there would be an argument for an embargoe, perhaps, twice in half a century; but when all experience tells us that, if they have not beef from Ireland, they will get it from Holstein, from Denmark and elsewhere, is it not folly in the extreme to refuse their money, and send them to other markets. The Dutch were ridiculed in Louis XIV.'s reign for selling the French, before a campaign, the powder and ball which were afterwards used against themselves: but they were wise in so doing; they had not the universal monopoly of iron and gunpowder, as of spices; and, if they did not supply the enemy, others would; for no army ever yet staid at home in the heart of commercial countries for want of powder and ball: nor will a French fleet ever be confined to Brest for want of beef to feed the sailors. Embargoes therefore cannot be laid with any serious views of that sort; but when contracts are made, the contractors, gaping for monopoly, raise a clamour, and pretend that no beef can be had, if France is served, directly or indirectly; and, in order to make their bargains so much the more profitable, Government gives them an embargoe on the trade of a kingdom (like a lottery-ticket to a fund-subscriber) by way of *douceur*. This conduct is equally injurious to the true interest of England, of Ireland and of Government.

Before I conclude this section, I must observe one circumstance, which, though not important enough to stop the progress of commercial improvement in Ireland, yet must very much retard it; and that is the contempt in which trade is held by those who call themselves gentlemen. I heard a language common in Ireland, which, if it was to become universal, would effectually prevent her ever attaining greatness. I have remarked the houses of country gentlemen being full of brothers, cousins, &c. idlers, whose best employment is to follow a hare or a fox; *why are they not brought up to trade or manufacture?* TRADE! (the answer has been) THEY ARE GENTLEMEN;—to be poor till doomsday: a tradesman has not a right to the point of honour—you may refuse his challenge. Trinity College at Dublin swarms with lads who ought to be educated to the loom and the counting house. Many ill effects flow from these wretched prejudices; one consequence, manifest over the whole kingdom, is commercial people quitting trade or manufactures, when they have made from five to ten thousand pounds, to *become gentlemen;* where trade is dishonourable it will not flourish; this is taking people from industry at the very moment they are the best able to command success. Many Quakers who are, (take them for all in all) the most sensible class of people in that kingdom, are exceptions to this folly: and mark the consequence, they are the only wealthy traders in the island. The Irish are ready enough to imitate the vices and follies of England; let them imitate her virtues, her respect for commercial industry, which has carried her splendour and her power to the remotest corners of the earth.

SECTION XXII.

GOVERNMENT—UNION.

THERE never was a juster idea than that which I had occasion in another section to quote, that the Revolution did not extend to Ireland; the case of the hereditary revenue was a remarkable instance, but the whole government of that island is one collective proof of it. The Revolution was a moment in which all the *forms* of government were broken through, in order to assert the *spirit* of liberty; but Ireland lost that opportunity; meeting security against the Roman Catholicks in the victorious arms of King William, she rested satisfied with a government which secured her against the immediate enemy. It is certainly more a government of prerogative than that of England; and the law of the Empire, the common law of the land, is in favour of that prerogative; hence the absurdity of proving the rights of Ireland in the details of common law, as Fitzgibbon and Mc.—— have done. Ireland, from distance and backwardness, lost those fortuitous opportunities which proved so important to the liberty of England; she could not claim the letter of the Revolution, but she could have claimed the spirit of it.

The contribution of that territory to the general wants of the Empire is in two shapes. 1. By the pension list. 2. By the military establishment. The great liberal line for that kingdom to pursue is to examine, not only the present amount of these articles, but what might be a fair estimate for the future. To come openly to the English Government with an offer of an equal revenue applicable to whatever purposes Government should find most beneficial for the interest of the whole Empire; with this necessary condition, that the military should be absolutely in the power of the Crown, to remove and employ wherever it pleased. To think of tying down Government to keeping troops in any spot is an absurdity. Government can alone be the judge where troops are most wanting; it has an unlimited power in this respect in England, and it ought to have the same in Ireland; the good of the Empire demands it. It is the fleet of England that has proved, and must prove, the real defence of Ireland; and that island should take its chance of defence in common with England. At the same time, any apprehensions that they would be left without troops would be absurd; since it would be the King's interest to keep a great body of forces there for several reasons; among others, the cheapness of provisions, which would render their subsistence comparatively easy; also, barracks being built all over the kingdom: another point which would induce him is the assistance their circulation would be of to the kingdom, whereas in England they would be a burthen. But the point might as well be given up chearfully, as to have it carried by a majority in Parliament. Pensions have been always on the increase, and will be so; and as to the troops, Government carries its point at present, and ought to do so; why not therefore give up the point chearfully for a valuable consideration? As these things are managed now, Government is forced to buy, at a great expence, the concurrence of an Irish Parliament to what is really necessary; would it not be more for the publick interest to have a fixed permanent plan, than the present illiberal and injurious system? The military list of Ireland, on an average of the last seven years, has amounted to £528,544; to which add £80,000 pensions, and the total makes £608,544. Would it not be wise in Ireland to say to the British Government—"I will pay you a neat seven or eight hundred thousand pounds[1] a year, applicable to your annual supplies, or paying off your debt, and leave the defence of the kingdom entirely to your own discretion, on condition that I shall never have any military charge or

[1] I have mentioned seven hundred thousand pounds; but the sum would depend of course on the liberality of the return; a free trade would be worth purchasing at a much higher rate.

pensions laid on me; the remainder of the revenue to be at the application of my own Parliament, for the uses of interior government only, and for the encouragement of the trade, manufactures and agriculture of the Kingdom. That you shall give me a specified freedom of commerce, and come to a liberal explanation of the powers of your Attorney General, the Privy Council, and Poyning's Act." It would be the best bargain that Ireland ever made.

If the Government was once placed on such a footing, the office of Lord Lieutenant would be that of a liberal representative of Majesty, without any of those disagreeable consequences which flow from difficulties essentially necessary for him to overcome; and the Government of England, having in Ireland no views but the prosperity of that Kingdom, would necessarily be revered by all ranks of people. The Parliament of the Kingdom would still retain both importance and business; for all that at present comes before it would then be within its province, except the military, and complaints of pension lists and restricted commerce. Perhaps the advantages of a Union would be enjoyed without its inconveniences; for the Parliament would remain for the civil protection of the kingdom, and the British Legislature would not be deluged by an addition of Irish peers and commoners; one reason, among others, which made the late Earl of Chatham repeatedly declare himself against such a measure.[1]

The great object of a Union is a free trade, which appears to be of as much importance to England as to Ireland; if this was gained, the uses of an entire coalition would not be numerous to Ireland; and to England, the certain revenue, without the necessity of buying majorities in Parliament, would be a great object. But as to the objections to a Union common in Ireland, I cannot see their propriety; I have heard but three that have even the appearance of weight; these are: 1. The increase of absentees. 2. The want of a Parliament for protection against the officers of the Crown. 3. The increase of taxation. To the first and last, supposing they followed, and were admitted evils, the

[1] The Earl of Shelburne has assured me of this fact; nor let me omit to add, that to that nobleman I am indebted for the outline of the preceding plan.

question is, whether a free trade would not more than balance them; they imply the impoverishment of the Kingdom, and were objected in Scotland against that Union which has taken place; but the fact has been directly otherwise, and Scotland has been continually on the increase of wealth ever since; nay, Edinburgh itself, which was naturally expected most to suffer, seems to have gained as much as any other part of the kingdom. Nor can I upon any principles think a nation is losing, who exchanges the residence of a set of idle country gentlemen for a numerous race of industrious farmers, manufacturers, merchants, and sailors. But the fact in the first objection does not seem well founded. I cannot see any inevitable necessity for absentees increasing; a family might reside the winter at London without becoming absentees; and frequent journies to England, where every branch of industry and useful knowledge are in such perfection, could not fail to enlarge the views and cure the prejudices which obstruct the improvement of Ireland. As to taxation, it ought to be considered as a circumstance that always did, and always will follow prosperity and wealth. Savages pay no taxes, but those who are hourly increasing in the conveniences, luxuries, and enjoyments of life, do not by any means find taxes such a burthen as to make them wish for poverty and barbarity, in order to avoid taxation. In respect to the second objection, it seems to bear nearly as strong in the case of Scotland; and yet the evil has had no existence; the Four-Courts at Dublin would of course remain, nor do I see at present any great protection resulting to individuals from a Parliament which the law of the land does not give; it seems therefore to be an apprehension not very well founded. So much in answer to objections; not by way of proving that an entire Union is absolutely necessary; as without such a measure Ireland might certainly have great commercial freedom, and pay for it to the satisfaction of England.

SECTION XXIII.

GENERAL STATE OF IRELAND.

IT may not be disadvantageous to a clear idea of the subject at large, to draw into one view the material facts dispersed in the preceding enquiry, which throw a light on the general state of the Kingdom; and to add one or two others, which did not properly come in under any of the former heads; that we may be able to have a distinct notion of that degree of prosperity which appears to have been, of late years, the inheritance of her rising industry.

Buildings.

These, improving, or falling into decay, are unerring signs of a nation's increasing grandeur or declension: the minutes of the journey, as well as observations already made, shew that Ireland has been absolutely new-built within these twenty years, and in a manner far superior to any thing that was seen in it before; it is a fact universal over the whole Kingdom; cities, towns, and country seats; but the present is the æra for this improvement, there being now far more elegant seats rising than ever were known before.

Roads.

The roads of Ireland may be said all to have originated from Mr. French's Presentment Bill, and are now in a state that do honour to the kingdom; there has been probably expended, in consequence of that Bill, considerably above a million sterling.

Towns.

The towns of Ireland have very much increased in the last twenty years; all publick registers prove this, and it is a strong mark of rising prosperity. Towns are markets which enrich and cultivate the country, and can therefore never depopulate it, as some visionary theorists have pretended. The country is always the most populous within the sphere of great cities, if I may use the expression; and the increased cultivation of the remotest corners shew that this sphere extends, like the circulating undulations of water, until they reach the most distant shores. Besides, towns can only increase from an increase of manufactures, commerce and luxury; all three are other words for riches and employment, and these again for a general increase of people.

Rise of Rents.

The minutes of the journey shew that the rents of land have at least doubled in twenty-five years, which is a most unerring proof of a great prosperity. The rise of rents proves a variety of circumstances all favourable; that there is more capital to cultivate land; that there is a greater demand for the products of the earth, and consequently a higher price; that towns thrive, and are therefore able to pay higher prices; that manufactures and foreign commerce increase. The variations of the rent of land, from the boundless and fertile plains of the Mississipi, where it yields none, to the province of Holland, where every foot is valuable, shew the gradations of wealth, power and importance between the one territory and the other. The present rental of Ireland appeared to be £5,293,312; and, for reasons before given, probably not less than six millions.

Manufactures.

Linens, the great fabrick of the kingdom for exportation, have increased rapidly;

The export from 1750 to 1756, in value of cloth and yarn was	£904,479
Ditto from 1757 to 1763	1,166,136
Increase	£261,657

From 1764 to 1770	£1,379,512	
Increase		£213,376
From 1771 to 1777	1,615,654	
Increase		236,142
From 1771 to 1777	1,615,654	
From 1750 to 1756	904,479	
Increase		711,175
Thirty years since 1748 greater than thirty years before, by		810,548

Commerce.

Trade in Ireland, in all its branches, has increased greatly in twenty-five years; this has been a natural effect from the other articles of prosperity already enumerated.

The Irish exports to Great Britain, on an average of twenty-five years before 1748, were	£438,665
Ditto on twenty-five years since	965,050
Increase	526,385

This greatest article of her trade has therefore more than doubled.

Export to Great Britain per annum for the last seven years	£1,240,677
The preceding seven years	917,088
	323,569

The greatest exports of Ireland, on an average of the last seven years, are:

Linen	£1,615,654
The product of oxen and cows	1,218,902
Ditto of sheep	200,413
Ditto of hogs	150,631
Ditto of corn	64,871
	3,250,471

Her total exports are probably three millions and a half. The balance of trade in her favour must be above a million.[1]

Consumption.

A people always consume in proportion to their wealth; hence an increase in the one marks clearly that of the other. The following table will shew several of the principal articles of Irish consumption.

Years.	Beer, ale and porter barrels at 32 gallons.	Brandy, gallons.	Rum, gallons.	Sugar, Muscov.	Tea, lbs.	Tobacco, lbs.	Wine, tuns.
1750			439,302		179,641[2]		
1751			700,905		130,306		
1752			513,266		191,556		
1753			784,945		140,465		
1754			987,122		166,558	3,574,037[3]	
1755			507,864		199,938	4,154,203[3]	
1756	13,572		815,887		163,693	3,424,359[2]	
			678,470		167,451		

[1] Mr. Gordon, Surveyor General of Munster, favoured me with an account of the trade, which made the total exports in 1772 to amount to

	£	s.	d.
	5,167,159	2	0
The imports	2,147,079	3	2
Balance .	3,020,079	18	10

But the above table clearly proves that this is exaggerated; for the exports not included in my account can never amount to two millions.

If her balance, however, was not above a million, it would be impossible for her to pay £800,000 in absentees and pensions, besides offices, interest of money, &c. &c.; to do that, and yet increase as she has done in wealth, it should be near £1,200,000.

[2] Commons' Journals, vol. 10, p. 318.

[3] Ibid, vol. 11, p. 169.

Years.	Beer, ale and porter barrels at 32 gallons.	Brandy, gallons.	Rum, gallons.	Sugar, Muscov.	Tea, lbs.	Tobacco, lbs.	Wine, tuns.
1757	10,949		511,682[1]		104,926[2]	4,769,975[3]	
1758	15,222		534,692		117,111[4]	4,958,721[3]	
1759	16,517		820,915		129,673[5]	3,662,246[3]	
1760	13,500		249,197				
1761	18,837		341,975				
1762	18,007		656,531				
1763	22,099		691,027				
	16,447		543,717				
1764	28,935	657,037	913,120	167,011	204,891	5,725,777	4,685
1765	27,787	757,105	1,230,840	129,331	236,908	4,431,801	6,416
1766	32,440	651,943	1,480,697	133,249	297,988	6,049,270	5,938
1767	29,487	770,319	1,667,540	133,829	183,267	4,083,379	5,683
1768	40,542	685,661	1,873,273	181,924	239,800	4,346,769	5,786
1769	45,452	420,584	2,100,419	183,337	1,007,693	4,842,197	5,870
1770	38,439	437,437	1,640,791	183,245	1,130,486	5,445,942	5,129
Average	34,726	625,726	1,558,097	158,846	471,576	4,988,162	5,643
1771	44,104	408,011	2,035,388	176,924	913,296	5,012,979	4,948
1772	47,735	374,144	1,973,731	188,260	741,762	5,525,849	4,634
1773	58,675	310,025	1,704,557	201,109	839,218	5,231,714	5,425
1774	51,995	395,740	1,503,086	171,347	1,207,764	5,434,924	5,709
1775	53,906	556,133	1,322,506	205,858	1,041,517	3,949,740	4,698
1776	65,922[6]	403,706	1,888,068	238,746	680,526	5,379,405	4,521
1777	70,382[6]	479,996	1,680,233	193,258	704,221	3,916,409	4,646
Average	56,102	289,679	1,729,652	196,500	875,472	4,921,572	4,941

[1] The following years differ in another account, Com. Jour. vol. 14, p. 141.

		gallons.			gallons.
In the year 1757	Rum	513,193	In the year 1760	Rum	275,732
1758	,,	618,945	1761	,,	370,011
1759	,,	903,809			

[2] Commons Journals, vol. 10, p. 318.
[3] Commons Journal, vol. 11, page 179.
[4] Ibid, page 169.
[5] Ibid, page 180.
[6] These two years are only of beer.

The articles of beer, rum, and sugar, are greatly increased; tea quadrupled; wine having lessened is certainly owing to the increased sobriety of the kingdom, which must have made a difference in the import. The imports of silks and woollen goods, given on a former occasion, spoke the same language of increased consumption.

Specie.

The specie of Ireland, gold and silver, is calculated by the Dublin bankers at £1,600,000.

Population.

This article, which in so many treatises is reckoned to be the only object worth attention, I put the last of all, not as being unimportant, but depending totally on the preceding articles. It is perfectly needless to speak of population, after shewing that agriculture is improved, manufactures and commerce increased, and the general appearance of the kingdom carrying the face of a rising prosperity; it follows inevitably from all this that the people must have increased; and, accordingly, the information, from one end of the island to the other, confirmed it: but no country should wish for population in the first instance; let it flow from an increase of industry and employment, and it will be valuable; but population that arises, supposing it possible, without it, such a cause would, instead of being valuable, prove useless, probably pernicious: population, therefore, singly taken, ought never to be an enquiry at all; there is not even any strength resulting from numbers without wealth, to arm, support, pay and discipline them. The hearth-tax in 1778 produced £61,646, which cannot indicate a less population, exceptions included, than three millions. The minutes of souls, per cabbin, at Castle Caldwell, Drumoland, and Kilfane, gave 6 and 6½.

Upon the whole, we may safely determine that, judging by those appearances and circumstances, which have been generally agreed to mark the prosperity or declension of a country, Ireland has since the year 1748 made as great advances as could possibly be expected, perhaps greater than any other country in Europe.

Since that period her linen exports have just TREBLED.

Her general exports to Great-Britain more than DOUBLED.

The rental of the kingdom DOUBLED.

And, I may add, her linen and general exports have increased proportionably to this in the last seven years, consequently her wealth is at present on a like increase.

SECTION XXIV.

STATE OF IRELAND, BROUGHT DOWN TO THE END OF THE YEAR, 1779—DISTRESSES—FREE TRADE—OBSERVATIONS—ARMED ASSOCIATIONS.

THE preceding sections have been written near a twelvemonth; events have since happened, which are of an importance that will not permit me to pass them by in silence, much as I wish to do it. The moment of national expectation and heat is seldom that of cool discussion. When the minds of men are in a ferment, questions originally simple become complex from forced combinations. To publish opinions, however candidly formed, at such times, is a most unpleasant business; for it is almost impossible to avoid censure; but, as a dead silence upon events of such importance would look either like ignorance or affectation, I shall lay before the reader the result of my own researches.

Upon the meeting of the Irish Parliament in October last, the great topic, which seemed to engross all their attention, was the distress of the kingdom, and the remedy demanded—*A free trade.* In the preceding papers Ireland exhibits the picture of a country, perhaps the most rising in prosperity of any in Europe, the data upon which that idea was formed were brought down to Lady-day 1778. I must therefore naturally enquire into the circumstances of a situation which seems to have changed so suddenly, and to so great a degree. I have taken every measure to gain whatever proofs I could of the real declension in Ireland during this period, and I find the circumstance of the revenue producing so much less than usual particularly insisted on; the following is the state of it.

The greatest declension is in these articles:

In the years.	1776.	1777.	1778.	1779.
	£	£	£	£
Customs inwards .	248,491	251,055	198,550	165,802
Customs outwards .	42,488	35,883	36,027	31,717
Import excise . .	152,238	153,727	131,284	106,070
Wine, *first* . . .	15,825	16,124	13,497	8,933

The totals are as follow, including the hereditary revenue, old and new additional duties, stamps, and appropriated duties.

In the years.	1776.	1777.	1778.	1779.
	£	£	£	£
Totals . . .	1,040,055	1,093,881	968,683	862,823

The total decline in the last year amounts to about one hundred thousand pounds; and from the particulars it appears to lie on the import account; for, as to the fall of five thousand pounds on the export customs, it is very trivial; those distresses which have, by associations or naturally, so immediate an effect in cutting off the expences of importation, while exports remain nearly as they were, have a wonderful tendency to produce a cure the moment the disease is known; for that balance of wealth, arising from such an account, must animate every branch of industry in a country, whose greatest evil is the want of capital and circulation.

Generally speaking, a declining revenue is a proof of declining wealth; but the present case is so strong an exception, that the very contrary is the fact; the Irish were very free and liberal consumers of foreign commodities; they have greatly curtailed that consumption, not from poverty, for their exports have many of them increased, and none declined comparably with their imports, circumstances marked by the course of exchange being much in their favour, as well as by these and other accounts; this liberal consumption being lessened from other motives, they are necessarily accumulating a considerable superlucration of wealth, which in spite of fate will revive their revenues, while it increases every exertion of their national industry.

In the years	1776.	1777.	1778.	1779.
	£	£	£	£
In the above account customs inwards, import excise, and wine duty, added together, amount to these sums, being	416,554	420,906	343,331	280,802
Customs outwards	42,488	35,883	36,027	31,717

From 1777 to 1778, the customs on their exports increased, but their customs on imports declined above £77,000. From 1778 to 1779 the former fell £4,310, or more than a ninth, at the same time the import duty fell £63,000 or a fifth; this difference in these articles is very great, and, if all the heads of the revenue were included, it would be more still.

It is not surprizing that the national debt should increase while the revenue declines. At Lady-day 1779, it amounted to £1,062,597, which is more than in 1777 by £237,171.

But the decline of the revenue has by no means been general, as will be seen by the following table of articles, which have been upon the rise.

In the years	1776.	1777.	1778.	1779.
	£	£	£	£
Ale licences	7,272	7,182	7,363	7,511
Wine and strong water ditto	19,563	19,984	20,823	20,298
Hearth-money	60,966	60,580	61,646	60,617
Tea duty residues	4,404	4,590	7,300	5,747
Tobacco	58,046	51,453	47,698	52,558
Strong waters, third . . .	5,659	18,586	18,782	18,233
Stamps	19,725	20,784	21,174	21,316
Hops	2,141	3,984	2,427	4,012

All of which, except the article of stamps, are laid upon the great consumption of the common people; whatever distress, therefore, is marked by a falling revenue, the lower classes do not seem, fortunately, to have suffered proportionably with the higher ones. But let us farther enquire how far the declension of revenue is owing to an increase of poverty; and how far to a forced artificial measure, that of associations for non-import. These have been very general in Ireland during 1779, and must have had a considerable effect. In order to understand the question, the facts themselves must be seen; the following tables will explain them. The revenue of Ireland is raised chiefly on the import of spirits, tea, wine, tobacco, and sugar.

In the year	Coals.	Muscovado sugar.	Brandy.	Geneva.	Rum.
	Tons.	Cwt.	Gallons.	Gallons.	Gallons.
1776	217,938	238,746	403,706	153,430	1,888,068
1777	240,893	193,258	479,996	137,474	1,680,233
1778	237,101	139,816	226,434	144,438	1,234,502
1779	219,992	145,540	180,705	87,423	1,183,865

In the year	Tea, Bohea.	Tea, Green.	Wines of all sorts.	Tobacco.
	lb.	lb.	Tuns.	lb.
1776	308,558	371,968	5,075	5,379,405
1777	359,475	344,726	5,129	3,916,409
1778	336,470	479,115	4,319	3,629,056
1779	402,594	375,269	2,806	4,038,479

The great decline is in spirits and wine. Tea has not fallen upon the whole; and tobacco in 1779 is superior to 1778. Sugar since 1776 is much fallen, but from 1778 to 1779 there is a rise. Coals are tolerably equal. The strongest circumstance is that of wine, which has fallen very greatly indeed. The principal cause of the decline of the revenue is to be found in these imports. The remark I made before seems to be strongly confirmed, that the distress of Ireland seems more to have affected the higher than the lower classes; wine, green tea and brandy, are fallen off considerably, but tobacco, bohea tea, and muscovado sugar, are increased from 1778 to 1779. This is strongly confirmed by the import of loaf sugar having fallen while muscovado has risen: the loaf in 1776 is 8,907 cwt., in 1777 it is 15,928 cwt., in 1778 it is 12,365 cwt., but in 1779 it is only 5,931 cwt. Other instances may be produced: imported millinery, a mere article of luxury for people of fashion, has fallen greatly: English beer, consumed by the better ranks, declines much; but hops for Irish beer, which is drank by the lower ones, has risen exceedingly.

	Hops.	Millinery Ware.	Beer.
	Cwt.	Value.	Barrels.
In the year 1776	9,694	£13,758	65,922
1777	18,067	16,881	70,382
1778	10,974	15,667	68,960
1779	18,191	8,317	47,437

From this circumstance I draw a very strong conclusion, that rents are not paid as well as they ought, and that tenants and agents make a pretence of bad times to an extent far beyond the fact. The common expression of *bad times* does some mischief of this kind in England; but in Ireland it is much more effective, especially in excuses sent to absentees instead of remittances.

The great decline of the import of British manufactures and goods, which is remarkable, must be attributed to the non-import associations bearing particularly against them; they have dropped so much, that we may hope the Irish manufactures they have interfered with may have risen in consequence.

In the year	New drapery.	Old drapery.	Muslin.	Silk manufac.
	Yds.	Yds.	Yds.	lb.
1776	676,485	290,215	116,552	17,326
1777	731,819	381,330	162,663	24,187
1778	741,426	378,077	121,934	27,223
1779	270,839	176,196	44,507	15,794

In most of these articles we find such a decline of import, that there is no wonder the revenue should have suffered. If it is said that this decreased import is to be attributed to a preceding poverty; it will only throw back the period of enquiry into the years discussed in a preceding section, and from which no national decline can by any means be deduced.

Some articles of import, however, contain such a decline, as induces me to think there must be more distress than appears from others. The following are the objects I fix on.

	Flax-seed.	Hemp-seed.	Clover-seed.	Raw silk.	Cotton wool.	Mohair yarn.
	Hhds.	Hhds.	Cwt.	lb.	Cwt.	lb.
Year 1776	24,077	150	4,648	41,594	3,860	29,345
1777	32,613	159	5,988	54,043	4,569	27,424
1778	37,211	106	5,664	51,873	4,565	18,327
1779	20,419	69	3,852	29,633	1,345	4,552

These are demanded by the agriculture or the manufactures of the kingdom, and are the last that ought to fall.

The declension in the trade of Ireland is not, however, in imports only; there is a great decline in many export articles, enough to convince any one that all is not right in that country; the following particulars will shew this.

In the year	Beef.	Hides.	Tallow.	Butter.	Pork.	Hog's lard.	Candles.
	barrels.	No.	Cwt.	Cwt.	barrels.	Cwt.	Cwt.
1776	203,685	108,574	50,549	272,411	72,714	3,216	3,155
1777	168,578	84,391	48,502	264,181	72,931	2,981	1,764
1778	190,695	79,531	38,450	258,144	77,612	3,428	938
1779	138,918	55,823	41,384	227,829	70,066	3,527	1,827

It is some consolation that hogs have not experienced the declension which has attended oxen and cows. The article beef puzzles me. I have been informed that for these two years all Government contracts for beef, &c. have not been entered on the custom-house books, by an order of Mr. Gordon, the Surveyor General; if this is the fact, it accounts for the heaviest articles in this declension.[1] The circumstance that the export of ox-horns has scarcely declined at all, that the export of ox-guts has greatly increased, and that glew has risen, would justify one in supposing that something of this sort must have affected the accounts of beef, &c.

	Ox-horns.	Ox-guts.	Glew.
	Cwt.	Barrels.	Cwt.
In the year 1776	577	141	1,025
1777	338	243	1,215
1778	928	171	1,127
1779	896	350	1,154[2]

I need not observe that the greatest export of provisions from Ireland by far is to great Britain, especially in time of war: now the accounts which have been laid on the table of our House of Commons do not admit the same conclusions as the Irish accounts, owing probably to some circumstances with which we are not fully aquainted, if not to the

[1] See above, p. 90, the author's note to the account of the export of the products of pasturage.

[2] The preceding tables in this section are taken from a MS. account of export and import communicated by William Eden, Esq.

identical one I have mentioned. The following particulars are extracted from the accounts brought in by Lord North.

Imports from Ireland.

	Value of beef.	Value of butter.	Value of tallow.	Value of pork.
	£	£	£	£
In the year 1768	55,802	173,259	52,557	28,609
1769	55,107	260,357	45,635	18,544
1770	51,695	149,464	44,928	22,240
1771	64,072	236,403	43,274	25,504
1772	48,434	204,810	17,419	22,401
1773	45,364	229,528	43,230	30,198
1774	46,064	211,152	38,247	21,836
1775	50,299	245,624	46,398	40,358
1776	95,194	237,926	48,072	42,737
1777	106,915	274,535	41,695	29,575
1778	106,202	210,986	39,209	37,981

As far as this account comes, for the year 1779 is not in it, here is almost every appearance of increase; or at least the decline, where there is any, is much too inconsiderable to found any conclusions on. Let us examine manufactured exports from the same account.

In the year.	Linen.		Linen yarn raw.		Bay yarn.	
	Yards.	Value.	lb.	Value.	Cwt.	Value.
1768	15,249,248	500,778	4,794,926	209,778	21,043	47,426
1769	16,496,271	549,875	4,107,478	179,702	19,332	43,580
1770	18,195,087	606,502	5,240,687	229,280	19,903	44,864
1771	20,622,217	687,407	4,035,756	176,564	18,588	41,894
1772	19,171,771	639,059	3,608,424	157,649	14,828	33,421
1773	17,876,617	595,887	3,082,274	134,869	11,073	24,964
1774	21,447,198	714,906	4,660,833	203,911	12,549	28,289
1775	21,916,171	730,539	4,363,582	190,906	13,882	31,294
1776	20,943,847	698,128	3,914,351	171,252	18,091	40,778
1777	21,132,548	704,418	3,198,437	139,931	17,897	40,269
1778	18,869,447	628,981	3,788,603	165,751	15,053	33,870

From hence we find that these articles have not fallen off so much as might for many reasons have been expected. Linen yarn has risen from 1777 to 1778 considerably. Cloth has fallen, but not enough to give any alarm. From 1770 to 1771 in linen yarn was almost as great a fall, without any ill effects ensuing. The following table contains the total export from Ireland.

Export of Yarn, Linen, &c.

	Linen cloth.	Linen yarn.	Worsted yarn.
	Yards.	Cwt.	Stones.
In the year 1776	20,502,587	36,152	86,527
1777	19,714,638	29,698	114,703
1778	21,945,729	28,108	122,755
1779	18,836,042	35,673	100,939

Which does not mark any such decline as happened upon the bankruptcy of Mr. Fordyce. It is remarkable from these two accounts, how great a proportion of the exported linen of Ireland is taken off by England; in the year 1776 it absorbed the whole. Indeed it appears to have more than done it; which apparent error arises from the Irish accounts ending at Lady day, and the English ones the 31st of December. But, in order to explain this business as much as possible, I shall in the next place insert the English account of all the exports and imports to and from Ireland.

	Exports to Ireland of English manufacture, foreign goods and merchandize, in and out of time, and exported from Scotland.	Goods and merchandize imported from Ireland to England.	Balance against Ireland.
	£	£	£
In the year 1768	2,248,314	1,226,094	1,022,220
1769	2,347,801	1,542,253	805,548
1770	2,544,737	1,358,899	1,185,838
1771	2,436,853	1,547,237	889,616
1772	2,396,152	1,416,285	979,867
1773	2,123,705	1,392,759	730,946
1774	2,414,666	1,573,345	841,321
1775	2,401,686	1,641,069	760,617
1776	2,461,290	1,654,226	807,064
1777	2,211,689	1,639,871	571,818
1778	1,731,808	1,510,881	220,927

In the year 1768, the export and import between Scotland and Ireland is not included, but in the rest it is. This table is drawn from the accounts laid before Parliament at the close of the sessions of 177$\frac{8}{9}$; relative to the valuation, here followed, of the custom-house, I should remark it has been supposed, that the *real* balance is in favour of Ireland, notwithstanding the valuation speaks the contrary; and Lord North, in December last, gave this as his information to the House of Commons. But, taking the account as it stands here, it must evidently appear that the distresses which have come upon Ireland within the last year or two do not in the smallest degree originate in her commercial connections with England; for during the last nine or ten years her balance has grown less and less. From 1776 to 77 it sunk £230,000; and from 77 to 78 it fell £350,000. If therefore Ireland was prosperous while she paid us a balance of 7, 8, and £900,000 a year, surely she ought not to be more distressed under less than a fourth of it? That kingdom must upon the face of this account have had a superlucration of wealth, arising of late years upon this trade, to a very great amount. But this account does not include the pear 1779, of which, upon the general payments between the two kingdoms, I have no other authority than to mention the course of exchange. Mr. Eden observes (*Four letters to the Earl of Carlisle*) that during the year 1778 and 1779, the exchange of Dublin on London has varied from $5\frac{1}{4}$ to $7\frac{1}{3}$; par. is $8\frac{1}{3}$. October 27, 1779 it was at $6\frac{1}{4}$, which is remarkably low, and proves that Ireland must have been accumulating wealth through that period.

The reader will naturally remark that these are all external authorities: some of them seem to mark a distress in Ireland, but others speak very strongly a direct contrary language; it remains to be observed, that the interior authorities have been much insisted on. It has been asserted, and by very respectable persons, that rents have fallen, lands untenanted, prices low,[1] people unemployed, and

[1] January 24th, 1780. I have this minute received from my very obliging friend Mr. Bolton (member for Waterford) the following note: "Butter has been here (Waterford) all this winter at 42*s.* per cwt. Pork at the beginning of the winter 23*s.* to 23*s.* 9*d.*; from that it rose by degrees, and is now 26*s.* 6*d.* per cwt." The butter is very low, lower

poverty universal. The misfortune of these circumstances, when produced as argument, is that they admit no proof. I ask for figures, and you give me anecdote: my Lord this is ruined—the Duke of t'other cannot afford to live at Dublin, the Earl of A. has no remittances, Mr. C. has £18,000 arrears. This is a repetition of the complaints which the English House of Commons heard so much of in 1773. I am very far from denying them, but only desire that *assertions* may not be accepted as *proofs*. They are national complaints when a new system of policy is called for; the palpable consequence of which is, that they are exaggerated—such complaints always were, and always will exceed the truth.

Let it not however be imagined that I contend Ireland suffers none, or very little distress: while we see very great distress in England, we need not wonder that Ireland should, though in a less degree, suffer likewise. We see the funds have in a few years fallen 27 per cent. The years' purchase of land reduced from 33 to 23. The prices of all products fallen from 30 to 100 per cent. Wheat from 7*s.* to 3*s.* a bushel; other grain in proportion. Wool from 18*s.* to 12*s.*; all greatly owing to the scarcity of money arising from the high interest paid for the publick loans: I can hardly conceive those operations to have drawn money from the channels of industry in every part of this island, without likewise affecting our neighbour, much of whose national industry was, if not *supported*, at least much assisted by English capitals. Therefore, from reasoning, I should suppose they must have been somewhat distressed; but the preceding facts will not permit me to imagine that distress to be anything like what is represented; at the same time that they shew it is in many articles wearing out even while the complaints are loudest.

Admitting some distress, and connecting it with the general state of the Kingdom rather than peculiarly to the present moment, I may be asked *to what is it owing?* The

than for ten years; but pork keeps up its price. At Limerick the minutes shew that 29*s.* 3*d.* is a very high price, and that 12*s.* was the price only eleven years ago." I am yet in hope, from an expression in Mr. Bolton's letter, to receive the price of other commodities before the work is entirely finished at press.—[*Author's note.*]

preceding sections have been an answer to that question; but to bring their result into a very short compass I should here observe, that the causes which have impeded the progress of Irish prosperity are,

I. The oppression of the Catholicks, which, by loading the industry of two millions of subjects has done more to retard the progress of the kingdom than all other causes put together.

II. The bounty on the inland carriage of corn to Dublin, which, by changing a beneficial pasturage to an execrable tillage at a heavy expence to the publick, has done much mischief to the kingdom, besides involving it in debt.

III. The perpetual interference of Parliament in every branch of domestic industry, either for laying restrictions or giving bounties, but always doing mischief.

IV. The mode of conducting the linen manufacture, which, by spreading over all the north, has annihilated agriculture throughout a fourth part of the kingdom, and taken from a great and flourishing manufacture the usual effect of being an *encouragement* to every branch of husbandry.

V. The stoppage of emigration for five years, which has accumulated a surplus of population, and thereby distressed those who are rivalled by their staying at home.[1]

[1] This single circumstance is sufficient to account for any distress that may be found in the north. Men who emigrate are, from the nature of the circumstance, the most active, hardy, daring, bold, and resolute spirits, and probably the most mischievous also. The intelligence in the minutes speaks that language; it was every year the loose, disorderly, worthless fellows that emigrated; upon an average of twenty years the number was four or five thousand; but, from the great increasing population of the country, the number in the four or five years last past would have been greater. At any rate, there must be from twenty-five to forty thousand of the most disorderly worthless spirits accumulated, much against their wills, at home, and are fully sufficient to account for violence and riots, much more for clamour and complaint.—[*Author's note.*]

VI. The ill-judged restrictions laid by Great Britain on the commerce of Ireland, which have prevented the general industry of the country from being animated proportionably with that of others.

VII. The great drain of the rents of absentees' estates being remitted to England, which has an effect, I believe, not quite so mischievous as commonly supposed.

Is it upon the whole to be concluded, relative to the present moment, that the freedom of trade now giving to Ireland, is a wrong measure? I by no means either think or assert such an opinion. In the preceding sections I have repeatedly endeavoured to shew that no policy was ever more absurd than the restricting system of England, which has been as prejudicial to herself as to Ireland; but, because a measure is wise and prudent, is it proper to admit for truths facts which do not appear to be founded? the question of political prudence is a question only of the moment; but to admit circumstances to speak a national declension, which prove no such thing, is laying the foundation of future deception; it is bringing false principles into the political science, in a point than which none can be more important, ascertaining the circumstances relative to all future cases as well as the present, which prove the prosperity or declension of a kingdom. And here the reader will, I hope, pardon a digression on the conduct of one set of men in the present noise of distress; it is a circumstance in the state of Ireland, that should make more impression upon the country gentlemen of that kingdom than it does: they have united with merchants and manufacturers in the violent cry for a free trade, and they have regularly in Parliament promoted all those visionary and expensive projects set on foot by interested people, for giving premiums and bounties, to the amount of above an hundred thousand pounds a year; and which alone accounts for the whole of that national debt, and declining revenue, which will make many new taxes necessary. The Irish are a grateful and a loyal people, and will not receive this free trade without making a return for it; that can only be in taxation; nay, they already speak in Parliament of a return. Thus have the country gentlemen of that kingdom been such dupes, as to agree to measures for running themselves in debt, and have joined in the cry for a favour, which, I have shewn, cannot be of any considerable use perhaps for half a century, but for which they are immediately to pay a solid return; and if that return takes the shape of a land tax, they have nobody to thank but themselves. What I would conclude from this is, and would urge it as a lesson for the future, that it is always for the benefit of the landed interest TO BE QUIET. Let merchants and manufacturers complain, riot, associate, and do whatever they please; but never unite with them; restrain, but never inflame them. The whole tenour of the preceding minutes proves that Ireland has flourished for these last thirty years to an uncommon degree, I believe more than any country in Europe. Was not this enough? Was not this a reason for being silent and still? Why not submit to a temporary distress, rather than by loud complaints, bring the state and situation of your country into question at all? Why demand useless favours in order to pay solid returns? During the whole flow of your prosperity what have been the additional burthens laid on you in taxation? Every country in Europe has added to those burthens considerably, England immensely, but you not at all, or to so trifling an amount as to be the same thing. Could your most sanguine hopes picture a more happy situation? And yet to yourselves are you indebted for bounties on the carriage of corn, for premiums on corn-stands, for ideal navigations through bogs to convey turf to Whitehaven, for collieries where there is no coal, for bridges where there are no rivers, navigable cuts where there is no water, harbours where there are no ships, and churches where there are no congregations.[1]

Party may have dictated such measures, in order to render Government poor and dependent; but, rely on it, such a conduct was for their own, not your advantage; as the absolute necessity of new taxes will most feelingly con-

[1] The assertion is not founded on the following charge in the national accounts, 1779, though one might presume something upon it:

To the Board of First-fruits, for building new churches, and rebuilding old churches, in such parishes as no divine public service has been performed for twenty years past . £6,000

vince you. Thus have you been duped by one set into measures, which have impoverished the public and burthened you with a debt; and because another description of men suffer a distress, in its very nature temporary, you join in their cry to buy that, which if any good arose from it, would be theirs,[1] while you only are to pay the piper. Henceforward, therefore, execrate, silence, confound, and abash the men, who raise clamours at distresses, whether real or imaginary; you know from the progressive prosperity of your country, that such cannot be radical; weighty experience has told you also, that you may have to pay for relief that goes but imaginarily to others, in giving up your solid gold for their ideal profits. Reflect that the great period of your increasing wealth was a time of quiet and silence, and that you did not complain of poverty until you were proved to be a golden object of taxation. Ponder well on these facts, and be in future silent. That the measure of giving freedom to the Irish commerce is a wise one, I have not a doubt; but I must own, I regret its not having been done upon principles of sound policy, rather than at a time when it can bear the construction, true or false, of being extorted; and this leads me to one or two observations on the armed associations, which have made too much noise in England.

If ill-founded apprehensions have led the Legislature of Britain to do now what it ought to have done long ago, the effect is beneficial to both countries; but I cannot admit that it is merely giving charity to a sturdy beggar, who frightens us by the brandishing and size of his crutch. To suppose that Great Britain is at the mercy of Ireland, and that an Irish Congress may arise, supported by forty thousand bayonets, is mere idle declamation; we have the strongest reason entirely to reject such ideas, because it could not possibly end in anything but the ruin of Ireland; the very conflict would arrest all that prosperity which has

[1] I am well aware of what may be here said upon the advantage of landlords being in proportion to the prosperity of manufactures and commerce: in general it certainly is so, and always when things are left to take their natural course; but when they rise above the tenour of that smooth quiet current, the conclusion may not be just; all the measures condemned in the text are forced and artificial.—[*Author's note.*]

been gradually flowing in upon her for these thirty years past, and leave her exposed, a divided,[1] weakened people, open to the attack of every potent neighbour. What a senseless, military mob, led by men who have nothing to lose, would wish or attempt, may be doubted; but that military associations, officered and commanded by men of the first property, who have not named a grievance without redress following, and who have experienced more favour from three sessions of the British Parliament than from three centuries before:—to suppose that such men, having everything to lose by public confusion, but nothing to gain, would so entirely turn their back to the most powerful pleadings of their own interest and that of their country, is to suppose a case which never did nor ever will happen. Apprehensions of any extremities are idle; but there is this misfortune in a series of concessions, not given to reason, but to clamour, that they rather invite new demands than satisfy old ones; and from this circumstance results the great superiority of coming at once to a universal explanation, and agreeing either to a Union, or to such a modification of one, as I stated in section xxii. In the next place let me inquire what degree of relief (supposing the distresses of that kingdom to be as they may) will result from the freedom lately given to the Irish in respect to their woollen and American trades, which will naturally lead me to the question, whether any prejudice is likely to result to England.

Whatever the distress may be in Ireland, it appears that these freedoms will not strike immediately at the evil, nor bring any considerable remedy; they are general favours, and not applicable to the distress of the time; this ought to be well understood in Ireland, because false hopes lead only to disappointment. It was highly proper to repeal those restrictions; but it is every day in the power of the Irish to render to themselves much more important services. In order to convert their new situation to immediate advantage, they must establish woollen fabrics for the new

[1] Those who are so wild as for a moment to conceive an idea of this sort, must surely have forgot the Roman catholics in that kingdom. It would be easy to enlarge on this point, but for every reason improper. —[*Author's note.*]

markets opened to them; those already in the kingdom I cannot suppose to be exported for this plain reason—they are rivalled in their own markets by similar manufactures from England, I mean particularly fine broad cloths and ratteens; if the Irish fabrics cannot stand the competition of ours in the market of Dublin, while they have a heavy land carriage in England, freight, commission, and duties on landing, and while the Irish cloth has a great bounty by the Dublin Society to encourage it, they certainly will not be able to oppose us in foreign markets, where we meet on equal terms; this removes the expected advantage to *new* fabrics, which, let me observe, require new capitals, new establishments, new exertions, and new difficulties to be overcome; and all this in a country where the old-established and flourishing fabric could scarcely be supported without English credit. It may farther be observed that the reason why that credit and support have been given to the linen of Ireland, is its being a fabric not interfering with those of Britain; it is a different manufacture, demanded for different purposes. Had it been otherwise, the superiority of English capitals, and the advantage of long-established skill and industry, would have crushed the competition of the Irish linen; as in future they *will* crush any competition in woollens if of the same kinds we manufacture ourselves. When the capital of Ireland becomes much larger, when new habits of industry are introduced, and when time has established new funds of skill, then new fabrics may be undertaken with advantage, but it must be a work of time, and can no more operate as a remedy to present evils, than any scheme of the most visionary nature. Their West India trade, I believe, will be of as little service; everything in commerce depends on capital; in order to send ships freighted with Irish commodities to those colonies, reloaded with West-India goods, capital and credit are necessary; they have it not for new trades; the progressive prosperity of the kingdom has increased all the old branches of their commerce, but they all exhibit a proof that they are still cramped for want of greater exertions, which time is bringing. If new speculations change the current of old capitals, the advantage may be very problematical; if this is not done, new trades will demand new capitals; and I believe it will be difficult to point out three men in the kingdom with an unemployed wealth applicable to new undertakings.

But it is said that English capitals will be employed; an argument equally used to prove the gain of Ireland and the loss of England; but in fact proving neither one nor the other. If the wealth of England is employed there, it will be for the benefit of England. Before the present troubles three-fourths of the trade, industry, and even agriculture of North America were put in motion by English capitals, but assuredly for our own benefit; the profit was remitted to England; and, whenever the fund itself was withdrawn, it was to the same country. Is it for the benefit of Portugal that English factors reside at Oporto?

Supposing the fact should happen, that English manufacturers or merchants should establish factors or partners at Corke or Waterford, to carry on woollen fabrics, I see not a shadow of objection; the profit of those undertakings would center most assuredly in England; and, if in doing it the Irish were benefited also, who can repine? Were not the Americans benefited in the same manner? That England would suffer no loss, if this was to happen, is to me clear; but I believe Ireland has very little reason to expect it for many years. I have shewn already that such a plan could never be thought of for such fabrics as are in Ireland rivalled by English goods of the same sort; if it was to happen, it must be in new fabrics; but let me ask a sensible manufacturer, whether it would not be easier for him to establish such amidst the long-established skill and ingenuity of England, rather than go into a country where the whole must be a creation; where cheapness of provisions, and the habit of subsisting on potatoes, at so small an expence, would baffle his endeavours for half an age, to make the people industrious, and where, under that disadvantage, the price of his labour would be as high as in England? I have a right to conclude this, seeing the fact in the linen manufacture, throughout the North of Ireland, where the weavers earn on average 1*s.* 5*d.* a day, and where also the cheapness of provisions proves very often detrimental to the fabric.

As a general question, there is nothing more mistaken

than dearness and cheapness of labour. Artizans and manufacturers of all sorts are as well paid by the day as in England; but the *quantity* of work they give for it, and in many cases the *quality*, differ exceedingly. Husbandry labour is very low priced, but by no means cheap; I have in a preceding section shown this, and asserted on experience that two shillings a day in Suffolk is cheaper than sixpence in Corke. If a Huron would dig for twopence, I have little doubt but it might be dearer than the Irishman's sixpence.

If an English manufacturer could not attempt an Irish fabric for cheapness of labour, what other motive could influence him? Not the price of the raw material, for wool is on an average forty-seven per cent. dearer than in England, which alone is a most heavy burthen. Other reasons, were the above not sufficient, would induce me to believe, on the one hand, that the Irish will not immediately reap any benefit from English capitals employed in their woollen fabrics, and, on the other, that if it was to happen, England would sustain no loss. What time may effect is another question; Ireland has been so fast increasing in prosperity, that she will gradually form a capital of her own for new trades, and I doubt not will flourish in them without the least prejudice to Britain. Those who are apt to think the contrary, cannot consider with too much attention that case in point: North Britain, which, by means of cheap labour and provisions, has not been able to rival, with any dangerous success, one single English fabric, yet has she raised many to a great degree of prosperity; but she has flourished in them without injury to us; and her greatest manufactures, such as stockings, linen, &c., &c., have grown with the unrivalled prosperity of similar fabrics in England. If English capitals have been assistant, have we, upon review, a single reason to regret it? The plenty of coals in Scotland is an advantage that Ireland does not enjoy, where fuel is dearer than in England.

But let me suppose for a moment, that the contrary of all this was fact, that English capitals would go, that Ireland would gain, and that England would lose. Is it imagined that the account would stop there? By no means. Why would English capitals go? Because they could be employed to more advantage; and will anyone convince us, that it is not for the general benefit of the Empire, that capitals should be employed where they would be most productive? Is it even for the advantage of England, that a thousand pounds should here be employed in a fabric at twelve per cent. profit, if the same could make twenty in Ireland? This is not at all clear; but no position is plainer than another, because it is founded on uniform facts, that the wealth of Ireland is the wealth of England, and that the consumption in Ireland of English manufactures thrives exactly in proportion to that wealth. While the great profit of the linen manufacture centers at last in England, and while English capitals, and English factors, and partners, have gone to the North of Ireland to advance that fabric, so much to the benefit of England, what shadow of an apprehension can arise, that other branches of Irish prosperity may arise by the same means, and with the same effect? Take into one general idea the consumption of British goods in that kingdom; the interest they pay us for money; and the remittances from absentee estates; and then let any one judge, if they can possibly increase in wealth without a vast proportion of every shilling of that wealth at last centering here. It is for this reason that I think myself the warmest friend to Britain, by urging the importance of Irish prosperity; we can never thrive to the extent of our capacity till local prejudices are done away; and they are not done away until we believe the advantage the same, whether wealth arises in Roscommon or in Berkshire.

Upon the whole it appears, that the Irish have no reason to look for relief from this new and liberal system, to any distress peculiar to the present moment; the silent progress of time is doing that for them, which they are much too apt to look for in statutes, regulations and repeals. Their distress will most assuredly be only temporary. The increase of wealth, which has for some time been flowing into that kingdom, will animate their industry; to put it in the future is improper, it must be doing it at this moment; and he is no friend to Britain that does not wish it may continue in the most rapid progression. In this idea I shall not hesitate to declare, that the freedoms granted to Ireland, whenever they shall take effect to the benefit of that kingdom, will prove the wisest measures for enriching this; and that all apprehensions of ills arising from them are equally contrary to the dictates of experience, and to the conclusions of the soundest theory.

MODES OF AGRICULTURE

RECOMMENDED TO THE

GENTLEMEN OF IRELAND.

HAVING been repeatedly requested, by gentlemen in all parts of the kingdom, to name such courses of crops as I thought would be advantageous; I very readily complied to the best of my judgment with the desire; but, as it is necessary to be more diffuse in explanations than possible on the leaf of a pocket-book, I promised many to be more particular in my intended publication; I shall, therefore, venture to recommend such modes of cultivation as I think, after viewing the greatest part of the kingdom, will be found most advantageous.

Turnep Course.[1]

1. Turneps.
2. Barley.
3. Clover.
4. Wheat.

Directions.

Plough the field once in October into flat lands; give the second ploughing the beginning of March; a third in April; a fourth in May; upon this spread the manure, whatever it may be, if any is designed for the crop; dung is the best. About midsummer plough for the last time. You must be attentive in all these ploughings thoroughly

[1] For dry and light soils.

to extirpate all root weeds, particularly couch (*triticum repens*) and water-grass; the former is the white root, which is under ground, the latter, that which knots on the surface, and is, if possible, more mischievous than the former. Children, with baskets, should follow the plough in every furrow, to pick it all up and burn it; and as fast as it is done, sow and harrow in the turnep seed. The best way of sowing is to provide a trough, from twelve to sixteen feet long, three inches wide and four deep, made of slit deal half an inch thick; let it have partitions twelve inches asunder, and a bottom of pierced tin to every other division; the holes in the tin should be just large enough for a seed to fall through with ease, three of them to each tin; in the middle of the trough two circular handles of iron; the seed is to be put, a small quantity at a time, into the bottomed divisions; and a man, taking the trough in his hands, walks with a steady pace over the land, shaking it sideways as he goes: if he guides himself by the centers and furrows of the beds, he will be sure not to miss any land; cover the seed with a light pair of harrows. A pint and half of seed the proper quantity for a plantation-acre; the large globular white Norfolk sort, which grows above ground, yields the greatest produce.

As soon as the crop comes up, watch them well to see if attacked by the fly; and, if very large spaces are quite eaten up, instantly plough again, and sow and harrow as before. When the plant gets the third or rough leaf, they are safe from the fly; and as soon as they spread a diameter of three or four inches is the time to begin to hand-hoe them, an operation so indispensably necessary, that to cultivate turneps without it, is much worse management than not to cultivate them at all. Procure hand-hoes from England, eleven inches wide, and, taking them into the field, make the men set out the turneps to the distance of from twelve to eighteen inches asunder, according to the richness of the soil; the richer the greater the distance, cutting up all weeds and turneps which grow within those spaces, and not leaving two or three plants together in knots. Make them do a piece of land perfectly well while you are with them, and leave it as a sample. They will be slow and awkward at first, but will improve quickly. Do not apprehend the expence; that will lessen as the men become handy. On no account permit them to do the work with their fingers, unless to separate two turneps close together; for they will then never understand the work, and the expence will always be great. Employ hands enough to finish the field in three weeks As soon as they have done it, they are to begin again and hoe a second time, to correct the deficiencies of the first; and for a few years, until the men become skilful in the business, attend in the same manner to remedy the omissions of the second. And if afterwards, when the turneps are closed, and exclude all hoeing, any weeds should rise and shew themselves above the crop, children and women should be sent in to pull them by hand.

In order to feed the crop where they grow, which is an essential article, herdles must be procured; as a part therefore of the system, plant two or three acres of the strait timber sally, in the same manner as for a twig garden, only the plants not quite so close; these at two years growth will make very good sheep herdles; they should be 6 or 7 feet long and 3 feet high, the bottoms of the upright stakes sharpened, and projecting from the wattlework 6 inches; they are fixed down by means of stakes, one stake to each herdle, and a band of year-old sally goes over the two end stakes of the herdle and the moveable stake they are fixed with: the herdles are very easily made, but the best way would be to send over an Irish labourer to England to become a master of it, which he would do in a couple of months.

Being thus provided with herdles, and making some other shift till the sallies are grown, you must feed your crop (if you would apply them to the best advantage) with fat wethers, beginning the middle of November, or first week in December; and, herdling off a piece proportioned to the number of your sheep, let them live there, night and day; when they have nearly eaten the piece up, give them another, and so on while your crops last: when you come to have plenty of herdles, there should be a double row, in order to let your lean sheep follow the fat ones, and eat up their leavings; by which means none will be lost. The great profit of this practice in Ireland is being able to sell your fat sheep in the spring, when mutton almost doubles its price. If you fat oxen with turneps, they must be given in sheds, well littered, and kept clean; and the beasts should have good hay. Take care never to attempt to fatten either beasts or wethers with them that are lean at putting them to turneps; the application is profitable only for animals that are not less than half fat.

Upon the crop being eaten, there is a variation of conduct founded on circumstances not easy fully to describe; which is, ploughing once, twice, or thrice for barley; the soil must be dry, loose, and friable for that grain; and, as clover is always to be sown on it, it must be fine; but, if the first ploughing is hit in proper time and weather, the land will be in finer order on many soils than after successive ploughings. The farmer in his field must be the judge of this: suffice it to say, that the right moment to send the ploughs into a field is one of the most difficult points to be learned in tillage, and which no instructions can teach. It is practice alone that can do it. As to the time of sowing the barley in Ireland, I should miss no season after the middle of February if I had my land in order. Sow three quarters of a barrel, or a barrel and quarter of barley, to the plantation acre, according to the richness of the land; if it had a moderate manuring for turneps, and fed with fat sheep, three quarters or a whole one would be sufficient; but if you doubt your land being in heart, sow one and a quarter. Plough first, (whether once, twice or thrice) and then sow and cover with harrows of middling weight, finishing with a light harrow. When the barley is three inches high, sow not less than 20lb. of red clover to each plantation-acre; if the seed is not very good, do not sow less than 25lb., and immediately run a light roller once over it; but take care that this is in a dry day, and when the earth does not stick at all to the roller. When the barley is cut, and carried from the field, feed the clover before winter, but not very bare, and do not let any cattle be on it in the winter. Early in the spring, before it shoots, pick up the stones, clean off where you intend mowing it for hay; but, if you feed it, this is unnecessary. As to the application of the crop for hay or food, it must be directed by the occasions of the farmer; I shall however remark, that it may be made exceedingly conducive to increase the number of hogs in Ireland, as it will singly support all quarter, half, and full-grown pigs. If mown, it should be cut as soon as the field looks reddish from the blossoms: it will yield two full crops of hay.

Within the month of October let it be well ploughed, with an even regular furrow, and from half to three quarters of a barrel of wheat seed sown, according to the richness of the land, and harrowed well in. When this crop is reaped and cleared, the course ends, and you begin again for turneps as before.

This system is very well adapted to sheep, as the clover fattens them in summer, and the turneps in winter.—Excellent as it is for dry soils, it is not adapted to wet ones; the following is preferable.

Bean Course.[1]

1. Beans.
2. Oats.
3. Clover.
4. Wheat.

Directions.

Whatever the preceding crop, whether corn or old grass, (for the first, manure is properly applied, but unnecessary on the latter), plough but once for planting beans, which should be performed from the middle of December to the middle of February, the earlier the better,[2] and chuse either the mazagan or the horse-bean according to your market; the single ploughing given must be performed so as to arch the land up, and leave deep furrows to serve as open drains. Harrow the land after ploughing. Provide slit planed deal poles, ten feet long, an inch thick, and two inches broad; bore holes through them exactly at sixteen

[1] For strong and wet soils.

[2] In England it is proper to wait till the heavy Christmas frost breaks up; but, as such are rare in Ireland, the same precaution is not necessary.—[*Author's note.*]

inches asunder, pass pack-threads through these holes to the length of the lands you are about to plant, and there should be a pole at every fifty yards; four stakes at the corners of the extreme poles, fasten them to the ground; the intention is to keep the lines everywhere at equal distances and strait, which are great points to the bean husbandry to facilitate horse-hoeing. This being ready, women take some beans in their aprons, and with a dibber pointed with iron make the holes along the strings with their right hand, and put the bean in with their left; while they are doing one set of lines, another should be prepared and fixed ready for them. Near London they are paid 3*s.* and 3*s.* 6*d.* a bushel for this work of planting; but where they are not accustomed to it they do it by the day. The beans are put three inches asunder, and two or three inches deep. A barrel will plant a plantation-acre. A light pair of harrows are used to cover the seed in the holes, stuck with a few bushes. By the time the cold easterly winds come in the spring they will be high enough to hand-hoe, if they were early planted; and it is of consequence on strong soils to catch every dry season for such operations. The hoes should be eight inches wide, and the whole surface of the space between the rows carefully cut, and every weed eradicated. This hoeing costs, near London, from 5*s.* to 7*s.* 6*d.* per English acre; but, with unskilful hands in Ireland, I should suppose it would cost from 12*s.* to 14*s.* per plantation-acre, according to the laziness in working I have remarked there. When the beans are about six inches high, they should be horse-hoed with a shim, the cutting part ten or eleven inches wide. A plate of this tool is to be seen in my *Eastern Tour.* It is cheap, simple, and not apt to be out of order; one horse draws it, which should be led by a careful person; another should hold the shim, and guide it carefully in the center between the rows. It cuts up all weeds effectually, and loosens the earth two or three inches deep; in a little time after this operation the hand-hoe should be sent in again to cut any slips which the shim might have passed, and to extract the weeds that grew too near the plants for that tool to take them. This is but a slight hoeing. If the weather is dry enough, a second horse-hoeing with the shim should follow when the beans are nine or ten inches high; but if the weather is wet it must be omitted; the hand-hoe however must be kept at work enough to keep the beans perfectly free from weeds. Reap the crop as soon as a few of the pods turn darkish, and while many of them are green; you had much better cut too soon than too late. You may get them off in the month of August, (in England the mazagans are reaped in July) which leaves a sufficient season for half a fallow. Plough the ground directly, if the weather is dry; and if dry seasons permit (but you must be guided entirely by the state of the weather, taking care on this soil never to go on it when wet) give it two ploughings more before winter, leaving the lands rounded up so as to shoot off all water, with deep and well cleansed furrows for the winter. It is of particular consequence for an early spring sowing, that not a drop of water rest on the land through winter.

The first season dry enough after the middle of February, plough and sow the oats, harrowing them in, from three fourths of a barrel, to a barrel and a quarter, according to the richness of the land. As the sowing must be on this one ploughing, you must be attentive to timing it right, and by no means to lose a dry season; cleanse the furrows, and leave the lands in such a round neat shape that no water can lodge; and when the oats are three or four inches high, as in the case before mentioned of barley, roll in the clover seed as before, taking care to do it in a dry season. I need not carry the direction farther, as those for the turnep course are to be applied to the clover and wheat.

The great object on these strong and wet soils is to be very careful never to let your horses go on them in wet weather; and, in the forming your lands, always to keep them the segment of a circle, that water may no where rest, with cuts for conveying it away. Another course for this land is:

1. Beans.
2. Wheat.

In which, the beans being managed exactly as before directed, three ploughings are given to the land, the third of which covers the wheat seed: this is a very profitable course.

Potatoe Course.[1]

1. Potatoes.
2. Wheat.
3. Turneps.
4. Barley.
5. Clover.
6. Wheat.

Directions.

I will suppose the land to be a stubble, upon which spread the dung or compost equally over the whole field, in quantity not less than 60 cubical yards to a plantation. If the land be quite dry, lay it flat; if inclinable to wetness, arch it gently; in this first ploughing, which should be given the latter end of February or the beginning of March, the potatoes are to be planted. Women are to lay the sets in every other furrow, at the distance of 12 inches from set to set, close to the unploughed land, in order that the horses may tread the less on them. There should be women enough to plant one furrow in the time the ploughman is turning another; the furrows should be not more than 5 inches deep, nor broader than 9 inches; because, when the potatoes come up, they should be in rows 18 inches asunder. The furrows should also be straight, that the rows may be so for horse-hoeing. Having finished the field, harrow it well to lay the surface smooth, and break all the clods; and, if the weather be quite dry, any time in a fortnight after planting run a light roller over it followed by a light harrow. About a fortnight before the potatoes appear, shim over the whole surface of the field with one whose cutting edge is 2 feet long, going not more than 2 inches deep; this loosens the surface mould, and cuts off all the young weeds that may be just coming up. When

[1] For light and dry soils; potatoes never answer on clays or strong wet soils.—[*Author's note.*]

the potatoes are three inches high, horse-hoe them with a shim, as directed for beans, that cuts 12 inches wide, and go 3 inches deep, and immediately after hand-hoe the rows, cutting the surface well between plant and plant, and also the space missed by the shim. Repeat both these operations when the plants are six or seven inches high; and in about three weeks after give a hand-hoeing, directing the men gently to earth up the plants, but not to lay the mould higher to their stems than three inches. After this nothing more is to be done than sending women in to draw out any weeds that may appear by hand. Take them up the beginning of October, first carrying away all the stalks to the farm yard to make dung; then plough them up *across* the field; making these new lands very wide, that is 4, 5, or 6 perch over, in order to leave as few furrows that way as possible. Provide to every plough from ten to fifteen men with three pronged forks, and a boy or girl with a basket to every man, and dispose eight or ten cars along the land to receive the crop; I used three wheeled carts, as they do not require a horse while they are idle. Have your wheat seed ready brined, and limed, and the seedsman with his basket in the field; as soon as the ploughman turns a furrow, the seedsman follows him close, spraining the seed, not into the furrow just opened, but into the land thrown over by the plough, the fork-men then divide themselves at equal distances along it, and, shaking the mould which the ploughman turned over with their forks, the boys pick up the potatoes. In using their forks they must attend to leaving the land regular and handsome, without holes or inequalities, as there is to be no other tillage for the wheat. They are also always to stand and move on the part unploughed, and never to tread on the other; they are also to break all the land in pieces which the ploughman turns over, not only for getting all the potatoes, but also for covering the wheat. And thus they are to go on till the field is finished. If your men are lazy, and do not work hard enough to keep the plough constantly going, you must get more; for they should never stand still. The treatment of this wheat wants no directions, and the succeeding crops of the course are to be managed exactly as before directed; only you need not manure for the turneps, if the potatoes had in that respect justice done them.

Flax Course.

1. Turneps.
2. Flax.
3. Clover.
4. Wheat.

Directions.

This for flax on light and dry soils, the turneps to be managed exactly as before directed, and the remarks on the tillage of the turnep land for barley are all applicable to flax, which requires the land to be very fine and friable; I would roll in the clover seed in the same manner; and the weeding and pulling the flax will assist its growth. Let the flax be saved and stacked like corn, threshed in the spring, and the process of watering and dressing gone through the same as in the common way. This husbandry is exceedingly profitable.

1. Beans.
2. Flax.
3. Clover.
4. Wheat.

This for strong soils. The bean land to be prepared for the flax exactly in the same manner as before directed for oats.

1. Potatoes.
2. Flax.
3. Clover.
4. Wheat.

For any soils except the very strong ones. The potatoes to be managed exactly as before directed; only, upon taking them up, the land to be left till spring; but, if wet, no water to be suffered on it in the winter. In the spring, to apply more or fewer ploughings as will best ensure a fine friable surface to sow the flax in.

General Observations.

In very stoney soils, the implement called a shim cannot be used to any advantage; in which case the operations directed for it must be effected by extra hand-hoeings. By *land* I mean those beds formed in ploughing by the finishing open furrows: the space from furrow to furrow is the *land*.

In ploughing wet soils be attentive to get these lands gradually into a right shape, which is a direct segment of a circle. A large segment of a small circle raises the centers too high, and makes the sides too steep; but a small segment of a large circle is the proper form—for instance:—

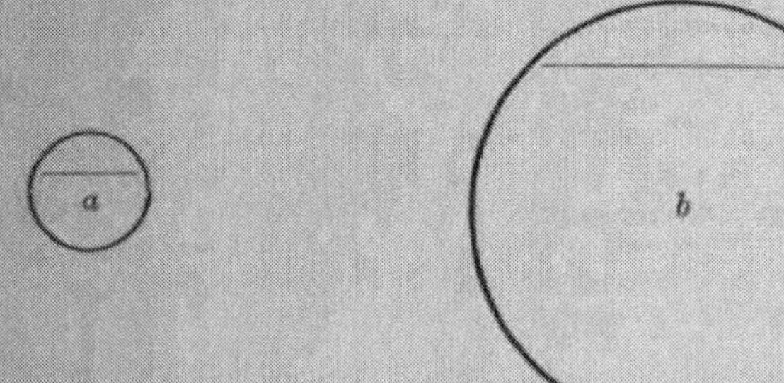

The segment of *a* appears at once to be an improper shape for a broad land; but that of *b* is the right form; keeping wet soils in that shape very much corrects the natural disadvantages. Permitting the teams to go on to wet soils in wet weather is a most mischievous practice; but it is much worse in the spring than in the autumn. In all these courses, it is proper to remark that, keeping the fallow crops, that is, the turneps, beans and potatoes, absolutely free from all weeds, and in a loose friable order, is essential to success. It is not necessary only for those crops, but the successive ones depend entirely on this conduct. It is the principle of this husbandry to banish fallows, which are equally expensive and useless; but then it is absolutely necessary to be assiduous to the last degree in keeping these crops in the utmost perfection of management; not a shilling can be laid out on them that will not pay amply.

There are in the preceding courses several refinements and practices, which I not only approve, but have practised; but omitted here, as I do not think them likely to meet with the necessary attention in Ireland.

Laying Land to Grass.

There is no part of husbandry in Ireland less understood than this branch; and yet, where land is to be laid down, none is more important.

Begin, according to the soil, with either turneps, beans or potatoes, and manage them as prescribed in the preceding instructions. If the land has been long under a bad system, by which it has been exhausted and filled with noxious weeds, take a second crop, managed exactly like the first, but one only to be manured. After this sow either barley, oats, or flax, according to the tenor of the preceding directions; but, instead of clover seed rolled in, harrow in the following seeds, with those spring crops: quantities for a plantation-acre,

15lb. perennial red clover, called cow grass, (*trifolium alpestre*).
12lb. of white clover, (*trifolium repens*).
15lb. of narrow leaved plantation, called rib grass, (*plantago lanceolata*).
10lb. of yellow trefoil.

Which, if bought at the best hand, will not usually exceed above twenty-five shillings. All the ploughings given for this end must tend to reduce the surface to an exact level; but then a very correct attention must be used to dig open furrows, in order to convey away all water.

AUTHOR'S APPENDIX.

THE FOLLOWING PARTICULARS WERE OMITTED UNDER THEIR RESPECTIVE HEADS.

Derry.

THE shipping of this place in 1760 consisted of sixty-seven sail, from thirty to three hundred and fifty tons.

7	of and above	300 tons,	18 to 20	men and boys.
21	„ „	200 „	14 „ 16 „	„
18	„ „	100 „	12 „ 14 „	„
21	under	100 „	5 . „	„
	Total, 10,820 tons.			

In 1776, about two thirds of the above; the decline owing to that of the passenger trade, and in the import of flax-seed; for eighteen to twenty years back, two thousand four hundred persons went annually; not more in 1772 and 1773 than usual.

Corke.

I was informed that there was no foundation for Dr. Campbell's assertion, that this city suffers remarkably in time of war.[1]

Extent.

Dr. Grew calculated what the real contents of England and Wales were, not at the rate of the geographic mile, but real statute square, one containing 640 acres, and

[1] "Political Survey of Britain," vol. i. p. 243.

makes it 46,080,000 acres,[1] instead of the geographick content of 31,648,000. Ireland, measured in the same manner, contains about twenty-five millions of English acres, or fifteen millions and a half Irish; which, at nine shillings and sevenpence an acre, make the rental £7,427,083. Those who consider this attentively will not think I am above the truth at six millions; as all uncultivated bog, mountain and lake, are included in the valuation.

Rental.

The rental of England is stated at page 16 of the second part to be thirteen shillings; but it is not accurate to compare that with the 9*s*. 7*d*. Irish rent. The latter is the gross rent of all the island, including every thing, *let or not*, deductions being made for the portions of lake, bog, river, &c. But that of England, at 13*s*., is only what is occupied by the farmers or landlords, and does not include large rivers, lakes, royal forests, or common pastures (mountains, bogs, marshes and moors not to be excluded, as they are parts of the lands let, from which the calculation was made). Upon a very large allowance, if these are estimated at an eighth part of the whole, the account will be 7-8ths of England at 13*s*. and 1-8th at nothing, average 11*s*. 4*d*. per acre, instead of 13*s*. The comparison with Ireland then will be,

	s.	*d.*
Ireland, rent and roads	9	10
England, rent	11	4
Rates	1	2½
	12	6½
Irish acre and money	9	10
Which for an English acre and English money is	5	7

Instead of which it is 12*s*. 6½*d*.; consequently the proportion between the rent of land in England and Ireland is nearly as five to eleven; in other words, that space of land,

[1] "Phil. Trans." No. 330, p. 266.

which in Ireland lets for 5*s*., would in England produce 11*s*.

Deaneries of Ireland.

Raphoe	£1,600	Elphin	£250
Derry	1,600	Ross	20
Ardfert	60	Killala	150
Connor	200	Cloyne	220
Clonmacnoise	50	Kilfenora	210
Corke	400	Dromore	400
St. Patrick's	800	Clonfert	20
Down	1,700	Leighlin	80
Kildare	120	Armagh	150
Achonry	100	Waterford	400
Killaloe	140	Christ Church	2,000
Ossory	600	Limerick	600
Kilmacdaugh	120	Cashel	200
Lismore	306	Clogher	800
Ardagh	200	Tuam	300
Emly	100	Ferns	300
Kilmore	600	Archdeaconry of Kells	1,200

Idleness.

La sociedad economica de Dublin ha levantado enteramente de nuevo las lencerias de Irlanda; *cuyos habitantes estaban poseidos de gran indolencia.* Han extendido su agricultura, en lugar que antes vivian de ganados y pastos, como los tartaros. See the "Appendice a la Educacion Popular." Parte Quarta. p. 35. Madrid 1777, by Campomanes.

Fall in the Price of the Products of Land.

Having in the preceding sheets mentioned much distress being felt in England from the great fall in the price of all products, I think I may be pardoned one or two observations in defence of opinions I have formerly held, and which then subjected me to much censure from the pens of a variety of pamphleteers.

From the conclusion of the last peace, in 1762, to 1775 inclusive, the prices of all the products of the earth were at so high a price, that complaints were innumerable. I have a shelf in my study almost full of publications on the subject; and Parliament itself was employed more than once in enquiring into the causes. The suppositions of the publick were endless, there was scarcely an object in the kingdom, which was not mentioned as a cause; jobbers, regrators, forestallers, sample selling, export bounty, post horses, stage coaches, hounds, &c. &c.; but some respectable complainants fixed on great farms and inclosures. During that period I more than once endeavoured to persuade the publick, that the complaint itself was not well founded, that prices were not comparatively so high as had been asserted; that the rise was not owing to any one of the causes mentioned, and that a considerable increase of national wealth was fully sufficient to account for it.

In the years 1776, 1777, and 1778, prices fell considerably; and in 1779 so low, that very general complaints have been heard of ruined farmers and distressed landlords; and at the time I am now writing the fact holds, that there is a very considerable fall in all products, and great numbers of farmers ruined. I have the prices of wool now for forty years before me; and that which from 1758 to 1767 was from 18*s.* to 21*s.* a tod, is for 1779 only 12*s.* and was in 1778 but 14*s.* We must go back to 1754 to find a year so low as the last. Wheat and all sorts of grain are greatly fallen.[1]

In addition to these facts, let me observe that great farms and enclosures are now as prevalent as ever. If they were the occasion of high prices before, how come they not to have the same effect now? But it is quite unnecessary to dwell upon a fact, which at the first blush brings with it the most complete conviction.

[1] The comparison in general must stand thus:

Wheat, 3*s.* to 3*s.* 6*d.*	which five years ago was	6*s.* to 7*s.*
Barley, 2*s.*	ditto	3*s.* 6*d.*
Oats, 2*s.*	ditto	2*s.* 6*d.*
Beans, 2*s.* 10*d.* to 3*s.*	ditto	3*s.* 6*d.*
Wool, 12*d.* to 15*s.*	ditto	16*s.* to 21*s.*
Lambs, 6*s.*	ditto	12*s.*
2 year old wethers, 10*s.* . .	which were	20*s.*
Cows, £5 to £6	,,	£7 to £9.
Hogs, 20*s.*	,,	26*s.*
4 year old steers, £3 10*s.* to £5	,,	£7 to £10.
Oak timber, £3 to £4 . . .	,,	£3 10*s.* to £4 10*s.*
Ash ditto, £2 to £2 5*s.* . .	,,	£2 10*s.* to £3.

—[*Author's note.*]

After the peace of 1762, there was a very great influx of wealth into this kingdom, which had the effect of nominally raising all prices, not of corn and cattle only, but of land itself; prices have declined in 1776, 1777 and 1778, but greatly in 1779. I am very apt to believe, that as the former *dearness*, as we called it, was owing to PLENTY of money, the present *cheapness* is owing to SCARCITY; not to a scarcity, generally speaking, because there is a proof that the specie of the kingdom was never greater than at present, but to a scarcity in these innumerable channels, which like the smaller veins and ramifications of the human body, carry the blood to the least of the extremities. There is no scarcity of money in London, as I am informed by several very considerable bankers and merchants. But why is it so plentiful there? In order to be applied at seven or eight per cent. interest in publick loans. This circumstance it is which collects it from every part of the country, from every branch of national industry, and which occasions the effect now so generally complained of, a fall in all prices. The reason why the farmers are ruined, which is really the case with numbers, is their having taken tenures of their lands at a rent proportioned to high prices; nor is this the only circumstance; labour ought to fall with other commodities; but Government, having four hundred thousand men in pay, and consequently to be recruited, bids high in the market against the farmer. Poor-rates also ought to fall; but there is so much folly, knavery, and infatuation, in every part of that abominable administration, that I am not at all surprised at seeing them rise, which is the fact. These three circumstances easily account for the distress of the farmer.

We may in future, I apprehend, expect to see more accurate ideas of what has been called *dear* and *cheap* rates of products, and never more to hear of great farms, engrossers of farms, commanding and monopolizing markets, or enclosures, condemned for doing that which we now find them so utterly incapable of doing, that the farmers are ruined and in gaol for want of the power to effect matters, for which they were before so execrated. We at least gain something, if the present experience gives the lie direct to all that folly, nonsense and absurdity, with which the publick was so repeatedly pestered. And there is the more reason for this, because, if such a peace succeeds the present war, as leaves us a wealthy and prosperous people, prices will assuredly rise; when that folly might again be met with, if not at present displayed in the true colours.

I know there are persons, who attribute both the former high, and the present low prices, to difference of crops, speaking much of plentiful and scarce years; I have been uniformly of opinion, that the difference of product, upon an average of all soils, to be extremely small, so small as not to operate upon price; and even upon particular spots the difference is not nearly so great, as to account for any considerable rise or fall. If this was a proper place, I could offer many reasons and facts for this opinion; but, if we accept the idea, then there is at once an end to great farms and enclosures as the cause of the rise, which are the two circumstances the most insisted on.

"I have lately received an account of a large common "field in Leicestershire, which used to produce annually 800 "qrs. of corn, besides maintaining 200 cattle, but which "now, in consequence of *being inclosed and getting into few* "*hands*, produces little or no corn; and maintains no more "cattle than before, though the rents are considerably "advanced."—DR. PRICE'S *Supp. to Obs. on Rev. Pay.* p. 388. "In Northamptonshire and Leicestershire, enclosing has "greatly prevailed, and most of the new enclosed lordships "are turned into pasturage, in consequence of which many "lordships have not now 50 acres ploughed yearly, in which "1,500, or at least 1,000 were ploughed formerly; and "scarce an ear of corn is now to be seen in some that bore "hundreds of qrs.; and so severely are the effects of this "felt, that more wheat had been lately sold in these "counties, on an average, at 7*s.* and 7*s.* 6*d.* the Winchester "bushel, than used to be sold at 3*s.* 6*d.*" REV. MR. ADDINGTON'S *Reasons against Enclosing Open Fields.* As enclosures have since proceeded as rapidly as ever—pray, why is wheat down at 3*s.* 6*d.* again, if it was enclosing that raised it to 7*s.* 6*d.*?

APPENDIX.

ARTHUR YOUNG'S CONTRIBUTIONS ON IRELAND TO THE "ANNALS OF AGRICULTURE."

Observations on the Commercial Arrangement with Ireland.

"Annals," Vol. III. (1785), p. 257.

If a proposal for breaking down some of the innumerable bars and obstacles to freedom of trade, had been made in the last century, we know the reception it would have met with in an age busily employed in multiplying restrictions and prohibitions; but that such a proposition should be seriously opposed towards the close of the eighteenth century, may make one conclude, that the science of politics is yet in its infancy; and that traders will never cease their arduous endeavours to deceive, while indolence and ignorance are found to believe them. It should always be had in recollection, by any person who examines this or any similar question, that monopoly is the trader's god. Their first object is to get a market; and their second, to keep off all competitors; in proportion as they can do this, they buy cheap and sell dear, and a small capital makes as great returns as a large one would do under different circumstances. The desire is exceedingly natural; and I am far from reprobating men for pursuing, with eagerness, what they conceive to be strongly their own interest. But when, in order to promote that interest, they bring all sorts of evidence and allegations to the bar of a House of Parliament, should they deceive the members of a Legislature too indolent to take the trouble of thoroughly examining a question seemingly complex—such a Legislature may sacrifice the interests of a silent many, to those of the clamorous few; in which case they would merit the reproaches of an oppressed people.

The monopolizing spirit has filled our statute-books with restrictions and prohibitions of almost every species of foreign manufacture, in order to give our own the unrivalled command of our markets. There is not a doubt but the effect has been in several instances to vitiate our fabrics; since nothing tends more powerfully to protect them, than a brisk competition, which keeps invention and exertion on the stretch. But, to secure the monopoly of our home-market to ourselves, has been thought essential to the national interests, and yet if the idea became universal, all trade and intercourse between nations would cease; being in truth a false and mean principle, as injurious to the society at large, as it seems beneficial to those who furnish the supply.

In fact, it is only by the competition arising from a free or equal trade, that a nation can discover what are those great and leading objects which ought to employ her capital, and command the attention of her industry. Fabrics that suit so little the climate, products, taste, and genius of the people, as to stand in need of a monopolizing encouragement, are of so sickly a growth, that they are rather national evils—a deviation of capital from more favourable pursuits, than beneficial enough to demand such pernicious means of support. A foreign competition in our own markets, which turned aside such ill-employed capitals into more productive channels, in which were enjoyed superior advantages, would be very far from a national evil, however hard it might bear on certain individuals.

In every discussion of this sort, we should remember there are two very distinct interests in the kingdom, the commercial, and the consuming. It is the interest of the former to sell as dear as they can; it is the interest of the latter to buy as cheap as they can. The Legislature that conducts itself on principles which mark a greater attention to the first than to the latter of these classes, proceeds very blindly indeed.

We must not be told, that the commercial part of the society forms a third or a half of the total, and, therefore, merits a proportional attention: this would be entirely fallacious, for the manufacturing classes rank in both situations. The individual selling the product of his own manufacture, is in the commercial class; but buying for his use the product of other manufactures, he is clearly among the consumers. A cotton manufacturer is interested in his fabric meeting with no competition; but the greater the rivalship in all others which he consumes the better. Thus every manufacturer in England, except the Manchester ones, are interested that cotton goods should be cheap: all the fabrics in Britain, except the woollen, that cloth should be cheap; and the whole commercial interest of the kingdom, except Birmingham, Sheffield, &c. that hardware should be no monopoly. Thus the circle revolves, and arranges with the consuming class, a very considerable deduction from the commercial one.

To apply these principles; let us suppose a proposal from the Court of Versailles, pursuant to the article in the last treaty, for settling the commerce of the two kingdoms upon a reciprocal footing, that all the manufactures of each shall be received in the other, paying equal duties; should such a proposal be accepted? The Chamber of Manufactures might blow their horn for objections from Axminster to Glasgow. One place would find out, that provisions are cheaper in France than in England: another, that nominal labour is as three to five: a third, that French flax is better than English: a fourth, that France produces raw silk: a fifth, that Sèvres porcelaine would rival Worcester and Derby; and a hundred others would come, each with his objection. The scheme thus violently opposed, what ought the Legislature to do? Certainly to set aside minute objections, and look only to the great outline; the national advantage upon the whole. That always calls for freedom: for ever demands the annihilation of restriction and prohibition: two neighbouring, great, populous, industrious, and wealthy nations are formed to be reciprocal markets to each other: commercial jealousy, listened to in barbarous ages, and by ignorant legislators, propagated the idea, that the poverty of one nation formed the wealth of another; till seasons of peace brought no pacification in industry. Political friendship existed with commercial enmity: the war of the sword might cease, but that of duties and prohibitions was endless. There is no friendship in trade.

But it may be said, ought we not to calculate on which

side the advantage will lay? The less the better. Such calculations are very congenial with the warehouse and the counter; but ought to have little weight with an enlightened Legislature. A thousand instances have told us how fallacious and short-sighted they are always found. Provisions 7 per cent.; raw material 2 per cent.; fuel 4 per cent.; taxes 10 per cent.; navigation 1½ per cent. It is all against us. We shall be undone! Such has been the language a thousand times; and yet events have rarely failed of giving the lie to it. To encourage freedom; to break down the mounds that have been raised against mutual traffic; to animate industry by competition, and to check the jealousy of the commercial spirit; to do all this, is to proceed on sound and efficient principles that are worth a thousand calculations.

But, if you *will* calculate, do it on grounds which long experience has proved to be the true foundation. Enquire which country has the greatest commercial capital; the most improved and animated industry; the best workmen and the best tools; in a word, which has, in general manufacture, made the largest strides: rest assured that these are the circumstances that will decide the future competition, and laugh at the little minds that calculate the minutiæ of the balance on paper, yet forget the animating soul of established prosperity, that inspirits, invigorates, and extends every effort of national industry: that finds, in present possession, the means of future increase; that looks with pleasure on the wealth, not the poverty, of neighbours, secure in the superiority of skill and application for converting their prosperity into the means of her own aggrandizement.

But the question is with Ireland!—It is of no consequence with what country. The principle I have touched upon, Freedom of Commerce, applies to all; to France, to Spain, to Germany. It would be starting a paradox, indeed, to assert, that that rule of national conduct, which is right with all the world, with foes as well as friends, can be wrong with Ireland.

But here I shall be told of manufacturers examined at the bar of the House of Commons, who have asserted directly the contrary of all this; who have drawn parallels between Britain and Ireland, tending to show that the latter has so many advantages that she will run away with our manufactures and commerce, and that we shall be ruined by the proposed approximation to a free trade.

Before I enter into the details necessary to this question, permit me a word or two upon the credit to be given to these sort of examinations of men who conceive themselves to be very deeply interested in enquiries, in which party is but too apt to mingle. My observations do not go to any particular evidence, but generally to all; and upon other questions as well as this of Irish commerce.

Those who have read, or recollect the evidence which merchants and manufacturers have given upon various subjects at the bar of the House of Commons, when they have had some favourite measure to carry, will be convinced that all such examinations are to be listened to with great caution and allowances. I was an auditor in the gallery of one that lasted a part of two sessions in 1773 and 1774, when the whole linen trade of England, Scotland, and Ireland, appeared at the bar to implore for what would now be called protecting duties, that is, higher customs on foreign linens, pleading the utter declension and threatened ruin of their fabrics. Their facts, in the great outline, were all false, and their apprehensions visionary, as experience began to prove, even before the examination ended; and, if the authentic registers of that trade, such as the import from Ireland, export with bounty, and yards stamped for sale, be now looked into, the reader that takes the trouble will be amazed at the hardiness that could raise such a spirit of complaint, when there was so little reason for it; the evil being, in truth, nothing more than a very temporary stagnation, owing to the check which every branch of industry sustained on the failures of Mr. Fordyce, &c.

Another examination which I heard, and which made a great noise in its time, was upon the bill for cutting off the commercial intercourse between Newfoundland, the West Indies, and the revolted Colonies; the utter ruin of those trades, if the bill passed, was the object to be proved at the bar; and more desperate destruction never appeared there: but the bill passed, and every iota of what had been so clearly proved, was found to be speculative and imaginary. In the great declension and ruin, as it was called, of the woollen fabrics, when petitions for severer punishments on running (*owling* it was then called) of raw wool, and stricter prohibitions on every species of foreign goods, imported or smuggled, were called for; Parliament was teazed with examinations, committees sat, and the press swarmed with croaking publications. At that very period, when the custom-house came to be examined, the export of our woollen manufacture was found to be greater than it had ever been before; and men were with good reason astonished at the commercial impudence which had instigated the whole trade to complain of ruin, because wool happened to be a little dearer than common.

A yet more remarkable instance was the number of petitions which flowed into Parliament against the bill that permitted the import of woollen yarn free of duty. The cheapness of spinning in Ireland is so much greater than in England, that it was apprehended such a measure would totally ruin our own spinning trade. The opposition to the measure failed; and time has now so completely convinced our manufacturers of that egregious folly, that should a duty now be proposed on the import, they would, and much more justly, be in a flame.

To instance every case would fill a volume; our traders have generally been successful, and worried Parliament into measures pernicious to the kingdom. To this have been owing the prohibitions and high duties on foreign linens, laces, cambrics, and a thousand of other articles, which have induced other powers to copy our policy, and prohibit our hardware and woollens; we have listened to the interested manufacturers of petty articles, and by it, injured in almost every other country our great and essential fabrics. To this has been entirely owing the horrible restrictions and oppressions on the colony commerce, which caused three wars, a debt of 200 millions, and at last the loss (if it be a loss) of all America. To this spirit we are solely obliged for having the present question before us; for had not Ireland been governed, or rather oppressed, by the same prohibitions, in order for her market to be made a monopoly, she had not been in the predicament of this day. The loss of America, and the independency of Ireland, are obviously to be carried to our commercial account.

Such are the fatal consequences that have flowed, and

will ever flow from conducting the politics of trade, by the interested advice of merchants and manufacturers!

But the spirit still continues; and we are now in the midst of more examinations, the great object of which is still monopoly. Keep our markets to ourselves; and do not let the Irish come in competition; if this is not done, Ireland will run away with the supply; the gain will be all hers, the loss alone ours. Our great manufacturers will emigrate with their capitals to Ireland, for carrying on their business to more advantage.

This wretched stuff, which it is a folly to hear, and a disgrace to answer, refutes itself, and has been refuted a thousand times by experience. There never was a single examination at the bar for these hundred years past, in which this identical assertion has not been made. The emigration of great stocks, great skill, and a great manufacture from a rich country to a poor one! I will venture to assert that the whole world cannot give an instance of it. We may defy the men that talk this language to quote one. But they say they will do it themselves.—It is now doing. Springes to catch woodcocks. If it was never done before, it will not be done now. Will you not believe a man's positive assertion? Why should I believe A. more than B.? Positive record tells me that B. C. D. E. &c. appeared at the bar upon interested questions, and gave an evidence calculated only to deceive. Is it a manufacturer at your bar that asks for a monopoly?—Yes. Why then he shall have no credit from me: whether he comes from North, South, East, or West; whatever his fabric, I am now smarting in common with my fellow subjects, under a heavy category of taxes, owing merely to such evidences being listened to and believed; and common sense unites with experience to dictate my rejecting the whole.

But, let us reason a moment upon the assertion that considerable manufacturers will emigrate. I am not willing to repeat what has been written already; but Dr. Tucker has fully proved the impracticability of this imaginary transfer of stocks, capital, buildings, implements, and all the complex system upon which a great fabric depends. I shall, however, add that, granting a master-manufacturer ready to emigrate with his capital, that he will, supposing the cheapness of labour contended for in Ireland,[1] find his workmen of a very different opinion; the emigration from high wages to low; from 8*s.* to 4*s*; from beef to potatoes, from porter to butter-milk, is perfectly incomprehensible in their ideas. These men, therefore, who assert that manufacturing labour in Ireland is 100 per cent. cheaper than in England, and yet that our fabrics will move, start a manifest contradiction. The emigration of a manufacture, is the emigration of the workmen, not the master: and though the latter must be a great friend to low wages in theory, he will not be so in practice; for such lowness is merely nominal: it is the cheapness of barbarity, backwardness, and ignorance:[2] it is a cheapness that keeps men poor and wretched, without making the masters rich. Corn, in Ireland, sells higher than in England, and the price of husbandry labour but one third of what it is with us. What a fine thing for their farmers, who must all be rich! Just the contrary, they are beggars, and for that reason. In truth, manufacturers never emigrate but for higher wages than such as they have been accustomed to: they may be, and certainly are, tempted abroad, to carry their skill into other countries. But is it by potatoes and milk? is it by the inducement of low wages? Ridiculous contradiction to common sense! Yet has this been swallowed at the bar of a House of Parliament. Upon the article, however, of low wages, I lay little stress; for the fact is not so relative to the master-manufacturer, though there is some truth in it relative to the men: cheap labour to the master, and the benefit of his fabric, is not to be discovered by the pay per diem; for skill, goodness of work, &c. come into the question, and form a material part of it. To compare the price of labour of two countries, can only be done by taking a piece of linen, woollen, or cotton goods, and enquiring at what

[1] It is asserted to be 100 per cent. cheaper!

[2] "The lowness of labour is a nugatory argument; for, until the instant that the price of labour is equal, the superiority of manufacture will remain with the English. The price of labour rises with the growth of manufacture, and is highest when the manufacture is best. The experience of every day tells us, that where the price of labour is highest, the manufacturer is able to sell his commodity at the lowest price." Mr. Burke's speech in 1778, on the Irish Bill. Parl. Deb., vol. ix., p. 179.

average price it can be equally well made in both. In this mode of enquiry, 10*s*. per week will generally be found to be cheaper wages than 8*s*.

It has been asserted at the bar of the House of Commons, that the price of weaving-labour is 4*s*. a week in Ireland, and 8*s*. in England; meaning, I suppose, on an average. This is an instance, and a remarkable one, how little reliance is to be placed on such examinations, commenced after some favourite measure is to be carried, or apprehended evil deprecated. At a time when no public question was in agitation, when party and commerce were not in any union, and there was no temptation, because no motive, to deceive, I went from one end of Ireland to the other, and made innumerable inquiries into the state of all their manufactures, and particularly the price of labour. I had my intelligence at the fountain-head; for the principal master-manufacturers gave it me, and it was confirmed by the men. I found the average of linen-weaving was, in fine goods, 8*s*. 6*d*. per week, and in coarse ones 6*s*. 3*d*.: I did not meet with a single instance where it was so low as 4*s*. This was not the price in any particular period, but general when the men had employment: nor was it the price in any temporary stagnation of the trade, which threw numbers out of employment, and in which, of course, earnings would be lower.

If it is said, that some years have elapsed since those enquiries, the reply is plain, no change has taken place since in the rates of labour, but what have been temporary, and owing to stagnations that have nothing permanent in them; my private intelligence long since received assures me of this, and it is confirmed by a variety of authority.

As this point of manufacturing-labour has had a great stress laid on it, in my opinion very absurdly, I shall add another circumstance or two. I found in the woollen fabrics, in the county of Cork, at Kilbrac, that combers earned 10*s*. per week, and weavers the same, losing one day in 18. At Castlemartyr, combers 8*s*., and in other woollen fabrics in that country combers from 8*s*. to 10*s*., and weavers 7*s*. These combing prices are not quite so high as in England, but they are high enough to banish every idea of Ireland rivalling us from lowness of labour. I found some years ago in similar inquiries in England, that upon an average of nine[1] places, men earned 8*s.* 5*d.* a week: in sixteen[2] others, men 9*s.* 6*d.* women 4*s.* 7*d.* and children 2*s.* 8*d.* A weaver, at Norwich, with his boy included, did not earn more than 7*s.* a week on an average; but with industry could make more. Darlington, linen weavers 7*s.* to 8*s.* but some so low as 3*s.*[3]

Upon the whole, these prices will not allow us to conjecture, that the real value of labour is lower in Ireland than it is in England; and, if we take into the account the greater cheapness of provisions, the sure encourager of idleness, and consequently of bad work, we shall be convinced, that the article labour is more in favour of the English manufacturer than his Irish rival: but let it ever be remembered, that this comparison depends on skill, and habitual and steady exertion, which certainly render labour, in that view, uniformly cheapest in the dearest countries. I have, on another occasion, taken notice of the nominal cheapness of husbandry-labour in Ireland: it is 6½*d.* a day; and I aver that pay (nor do I speak ignorantly, having had above 40 labourers in my employ there) is really dearer, though so much nominally cheaper, than 2*s.* would be in Suffolk. It would be very difficult to convince me, that something of this sort is not likewise found in manufactures. If it is not, what are the principles that govern a well-known fact, that we can undersell the Irish, and have always done it, in their own markets, in a variety of goods, in spite of nominal labour-taxes, freight, insurance, &c.? We actually do it in some branches, even of their favourite manufacture, linen.

While the information of the day is subject to so much error and deception, particulars gained and declared previous to this public agitation are valuable, and far more decisive than any to be had at present. Mr. Arbuthnot, inspector of the linen manufacture in Ireland, was employed in 1782 to examine the fabrics of the kingdom, and report their state and situation. In his first report in that year,

[1] Lavenham, Sudbury, Hedingham, Braintree, Witney, Wilton, Salisbury, Rumsey, Gloucester.

[2] Bedford, Rotherham, Sheffield, Wakefield, Leeds, Ayton, Darlington, Newcastle, Carlisle, Kendal, Warrington, Liverpool, Manchester, Burslem, Newcastle, Worcester.

[3] Report of the Linen Committee, 1773.

he describes the great undertaking in the cotton branch, at the new town of Prosperous. These are the prices of labour he minutes. A sheeting-weaver, who earns only 10*s.* or 11*s.* a week, will in the cotton earn 13*s.* to 15*s.* A lad of 13, who had served but a year, earned 8*s.* or 9*s.* Active lads at the spinning-jenny 11*s.* to 15*s.* Girls from 9*s.* to 11*s.*, who at flax spinning could get no more than 2*s.* or 3*s.* Such are the low rates of labour, which we are now told are to overturn the fixed established stocks, skill, and industry of our Manchester fabrics, as if they were the fabrics of a vision! The same unimpeached authority was informed in Limerick, by the manufacturers, that the prices of woollen-weavers were then higher than in England. And by Messrs. Lane, near Cork, that the Irish weavers will not work so much in the day as the English.[1] Does not this tally exactly with the result of all my enquiries in Ireland; and confirm the suspicion I just now hinted, that the nominal rates of labour deceive; and that the real superiority is with England? And does any reason remain for surprise, that England actually undersells Ireland in cloth made of Irish yarn? The clearest proof in the world that the dear and wealthy country will, in almost every competition, get the better of the cheap and poor one.

It has, in the same manner, been apprehended, that they would navigate so much cheaper, as to rival us in the carrying, and even coasting trades: but there never was the shadow of an authority for this idea. I found, at Waterford, that ship-building was £10 per ton; that is 20*s.* dearer than in the Thames, where it is dearer than in any other part of the kingdom.[2]

At Belfast, Waterford, and Cork, seamen in peace were paid 28*s.* to 30*s.* a month, but in war from 40*s.* to 60*s.* The peace price in England is 25*s.* to 30*s.*[3] Add to all this, that the freight and insurance from Cork to the West Indies, is the same as from London.[4] But, it is further contended, that should the cheapness of Irish labour not have the dreaded event, the lowness of their taxes compared

[1] Third Report.
[2] £9 a ton. At Hull, Whitby, &c., £7 10*s.* In the South and West, £8.—Lord Sheffield.
[3] Ibid. [4] Commercial Arrangement with Ireland explained p. 57.

with ours would ensure the evil. This is another vulgar error, thrown out to catch uninformed people, that have not taken the trouble to make themselves masters of the combinations that regulate this question. To assert that taxes cannot ruin a manufacture would be preposterous; but experience has given us no instances of it in this kingdom, where it is a fact known to all the world, that notwithstanding our vast increase of taxation, many of our fabrics, perhaps the most important of them, have sunk in their price; not because the taxes increased, but in spite of them; and because large capitals, extensive correspondence and credit, improved skill and active industry, will secure the superiority, when they come in competition with the no taxes of poorer countries. For, let it be remembered, that taxes follow wealth; and are in every country of the world paid easiest where they are highest: their height being little more than a proof of the wealth that is able to support and even thrive under them. The reader sees, of course, that I speak in reference only to the industrious classes. If this observation was not completely true, all the export of British manufactures would have perished long ago. But the fact is, that this immensely taxed country undersells every neighbour she has in the world, much more than she is undersold, and none so decidedly as the poor countries that pay scarcely any taxes. Ireland is a pregnant instance of this fact. If we have any rivals, we must not look for them in poor countries, where the public burthens are low, we must go to Holland and Flanders, among the richest and highest taxed territories of Europe: and to some great wealthy French cities, where provisions are dearer, and taxes higher, than in any other towns of the monarchy. Irish land pays no land-tax, no poor-rates, and is wrought by men at 6*d*. a day: according to that mode of reasoning which I am combating, the corn of that land should be much more than cent. per cent. cheaper than that of England. The contrary, however, is the fact; and it is uniformly dearer.[1] Why? I have examined the agri-

[1] It is no reply to say, that cattle being the product of Ireland, corn must be dear; for the soil is proper for both, and there is a free vibration between different products; cattle are cheap, and corn dear, which ought to encourage the latter; the real cause is, that feeding cattle demands

culture of both kingdoms, more, I may without vanity assert, than any other man ever did, and I can reply in three words—Capital, Skill, and Industry are less. With such a prodigious superiority in the eye of the theorist, why do not British capitals go over to improve the lands of Ireland? Because nothing is so difficult as the transfer of capital from one country to another; a bill of exchange will convey the cash, but the owner of it is not so easily transported: habit, custom, engagements, fixed property, and a thousand other circumstances impede his removal.

I have stated, that the price of corn is higher in Ireland than in England; it is so; but provisions in general are certainly cheaper,[1] and this is brought as a fact that threatens us in the future manufacturing competition between the two kingdoms. But, in the opinion of the best writers,[2] this is not to the advantage of Ireland. It is an evil in the ideas of all their own master-manufacturers, as they assured me themselves; and the notion was general amongst the best informed people there. The minutes of my Irish Tour will shew this in various instances.[3]

no skill, but the culture of corn is a business that requires unremitted attention, and the people are too backward to do it to advantage. Land, in Suffolk, pays 3s. in the pound land-tax, 3s. more poor-rates, and is wrought by men who have 16*d*. and 18*d*. a day; yet the corn of this county, under the expenses of land-carriage, freight, lading, unlading, insurance, commission, and port-charges, undersells Irish corn in the markets of Ireland.

[1] The price of meat in Ireland to the price in England, as 11 to 14.

[2] To advance trade in Ireland provisions must be rendered dear.—Sir William Temple.

Trade can never be extended where the necessaries of life are very cheap.—Sir W. Petty, and Sir Jos. Child.

Provisions cheap in North America, and labour therefore dear.—Dr. Franklin.

High taxes make provisions dear, and thereby promote industry.—De Witte.

Dutch industry, from high prices of provisions, bought our rape, made oil, and with it undersold us in our own markets.—Mr. Locke.

[3] Cullen: The linen-manufacture never flourishes when oatmeal is cheap. The greatest exports when it is dearest.

Lurgan: When provisions are cheap, the weavers live at whisky-houses.

Warrenstown: When provisions are dear, the more linen comes to market.

Lisburne: Meal and cloth never cheap together—the men work no more than to live, &c. &c.

I am not surprised that, in this general alarm at the imaginary superiority of Ireland, the article fuel should have been named: but surely never anything was more unfortunately brought in; for in this respect there is no comparison between the two countries. Ireland has coals, but her collieries are worked in so incomplete a manner, for want of capital, that she cannot with the assistance of a parliamentary bounty supply even her own capital. It is a fact, that the colliers employed in some of her impracticable coal-mines, actually burnt peat as the cheaper fuel in their own cottages. But the import of English and Scotch coals will shew, in a moment, what is to be expected from Irish collieries.

	Tons.
Average per ann. of 7 years, from 1764 to 1770 .	180.113
Seven do. from 1771 to 1777	204,566
The year 1782	241,331
Value at 15*s*. . . £180,998.	

As to peat, it is the dearest of all fires.

When fuel is, upon an average, so much dearer than in England, what must we think of apprehensions, lest Birmingham, Sheffield, Wolverhampton, and Rotherham should be undersold by Irish hardware. Much reasoning on such questions as these should be avoided when we can bring experience to decide them. Seven years ago Lord North brought into the House of Commons his five trade bills; the object of which was partially to lay open the colony and African trade to the Irish; and to permit the import, into Great Britain, of cotton, yarn, cordage, and sail-cloth, from Ireland, duty free. While the resolutions to this purpose stood on the Journals of the House, the whole manufacturing interest of the kingdom took the alarm, and the table was covered with petitions against the measure, as utterly ruinous and destructive.

The petitions from the following now lie before me:—

Preston—Linen, &c.
Bridport—Sail-cloth.
Stourbridge and Dudley—Glass and nails.
Glasgow—Traders and manufacturers.
Walsall—Brass and iron.
Worcester—Gloves.

Bristol—Merchants and manufacturers, hemp, iron, steel, glass, and soap.
Yeovil, &c.—Sail-cloth.
Aberbrothock.
Wolverhampton—Iron.
Lancaster—Sail-cloth and soap.
Newton.
Warrington—Sail-cloth, &c.
Liverpool—Tallow, soap, glass, and merchants.
County of Chester.
Stockport—Checks, &c.
Prescot, &c.—Sail-cloth.
Blackburn—Calico-printers.
Manchester—Linen and cotton.
London—Tallow-chandlers, sugar-refiners, and glass.
Exeter—Woollens.

The number of petitions was 62, the tenour of them nearly similar: there was not one concession made to Ireland, in the resolutions at which they were alarmed, that they did not expressly declare would be utterly ruinous to the respective manufacturers of England and Scotland. They urged, that the low taxes, cheap provisions and labour, and local advantages of Ireland, would raise a competition against them, which it would be impossible to withstand; that themselves and workmen must emigrate, that the poor would be without employment, poor rates prodigiously increased, general poverty and distress the general consequence, and that land-rents must necessarily sink. In one word, they raised a clamour nearly though not quite so great as exists at present.

A circumstance happened in the progress of those petitions truly curious, and which shewed the grounds lighter than air on which our manufacturers could bring their apprehensions before the Legislature: the permission for importing sail-cloth duty free from Ireland, had been in being many years before; but Mr. Burke, without knowing that such a law existed, brought in the bill then before the House. The English sail-cloth manufacturers, especially those of Somersetshire, took the alarm, and stated the manifold injuries that would befall them should such a measure take place. May 4, 1778, Mr. Burke remarks to the House, that if the bill was to be productive of the consequences stated in the petitions, it was a little extraordinary the petitioners forgot to complain when they were hurt; and now feel so strongly when there is not even a possibility of sustaining any injury. From this he inferred, that the jealousy entertained of the other Irish bills was equally ill founded, and only originated in gross prejudice, or the selfish views of interested individuals.[1]

In the years 1778, 1779, and 1780, all that these petitions apprehended was enacted; and a great deal more by the acknowledged legislative independence of 1782. So that, owing to the liberal spirit of Lord North and Mr. Fox, that was done, which, according to the tenour of these petitions, must necessarily entail distress and ruin on so many branches of trade and fabric.

Now let us enquire into the event, which from five to seven years' experience enables us clearly to ascertain; let us examine whether the horrible apprehensions breathed by the petitions, were founded in truth and propriety, or whether they were no more than the chimeras of monopoly—the agitations of distempered imaginations.

If the effects which terrified our traders and manufacturers took place, we must find them either in a decline of our own manufactures and commerce, or in the alarming increase of those of Ireland.

Linen stamped for sale in Scotland.

	Yards.
The highest year previous to 1773, was that of 1771, when there were	13,466,274
In 1782	15,348,741
In 1783	17,074,774

While British linen has thus thriven, our import of Irish has not increased.

1775	21,976,822 yards.
1776	20,989,371 „
1777	21,151,063 „
1782	24,692,072 „
1783	15,212,968 „

The registered broad and narrow woollen cloths of Yorkshire have increased.

	Broads. Yards.	Narrows. Yards.
In 1778 being the greatest of any preceding year	3,795,990	2,746,712
In 1782	4,563,376	3,292,002

[1] Parl. Reg. vol. ix., p. 162—1778.

The import into Ireland of English woollens, manufactured silks, and British linen, cotton, and silk, to March, 1784, has increased considerably, as a late ingenious writer has shown by custom-house registers;[1] that is to say, they have increased at the very time the manufacturers of them ought to have been, according to their petitions, in utter ruin. Lord Sheffield, in his excellent work on Irish commerce, not only makes a similar remark, but foretells the utter improbability of Ireland ever being able to rival England in the woollen manufacture.[2]

Import of Stockings.

	Woollen pairs.		Worsted pairs.
Average 1772 and 1773. . .	191	...	5,102
„ 1782 „ 1783. . .	1,467	...	9,280

The cotton manufacture is quite a new branch in Ireland, but it is said to have thriven wonderfully in four or five years; a circumstance, however, in it that deserves attention, is its being set on foot and established by captains, colonels, and the relations of great families. The greatest undertaking is that of Prosperous, by Captain Brook. Gentlemen being thus employed, is the most decisive proof in the world, and worth a thousand arguments, of the want of capital in that country: we see no instances of the sort in England, and for a very plain reason—because we do not want them. Whatever is done in Ireland, is either by such artificial means, or by force of public money. Where are the English capitals that were to emigrate? Is it not very extraordinary, that in this new undertaking, in which the petitioners had such apprehensions of their property and workmen shifting to Ireland, not one establishment is affected by such means, nor is a single instance to be produced of it in the whole kingdom?

But, with all the progress it has made, we may easily judge in what degree it has rivalled the British fabrics, by the import of manufactures, and mixtures of cotton into Ireland.

[1] "Arrangements with Ireland considered." 2 edit., p. 37, 38, 39.
[2] P. 162.

	Value.
Average of three years ending March 1773 . . .	£18,278 16 2
Ditto „ „ „ 1783 . . .	103,119 8 5½

	Pairs.
Imported of cotton stockings into Ireland, average of 3 years ending 1773	10,406
Ditto ending 1783	20,524

Yet, their imports of muslins, in the same period, is decreased; but most assuredly not to the prejudice of our manufacture; since we find, on the same authority,[1] that five cotton mills are newly erected in Scotland; and, in the city of Glasgow alone, above 1,000 looms have been set up, last year, in the muslin branch, which is an almost incredible progress.

The silk manufacture will exhibit just the same result. The general import I have already mentioned.

Manufactured Silk.

	Ribbands. lb.	Silk. lb.	Stockings. Pairs.
Average of 3 years ending March 1773	557	15,786	373
Ditto ditto 1783	1,864	22,626	611

Our brewers and maltsters being at present alarmed, let us examine what the Irish have done in their way towards that immense improvement dreaded by our petitioners.

	Import barrels.	Export barrels.
Average of 3 years ending 1773 .	45,585	3,550
Ditto ditto 1783 .	54,546	959

The petitions from our hardware-manufacture were particularly strenuous in their assertion that Ireland would run away with their export trade. The Irish export of hardware arose from £16 in 1781, to £213 in 1783. And that of ironmonger's-ware fell from £253 to £85; but their import of the same manufactures from England increased.

But, while the advantages which Ireland has derived from the freedom given her, are not to be found by

[1] Lord Sheffield on the Irish Trade, p. 199, 207.

referring to these particular branches of commerce, the general account between the two kingdoms offers a fact that well deserves our attention, and shews, that if Ireland has gained upon the whole, that it has not been without a corresponding advantage to Britain.

	Value.
Average import from Britain into Ireland of 3 years ending 1780	£1,765,955[1]
Ditto 3 years ending 1783	2,343,606
Superiority	£577,651

To pursue these facts through every article of the national commerce would be tedious. The leading ones, and such as bear immediately upon the prayer of those petitions which expressed such apprehensions of the future rise and prosperity of Ireland, I have laid before the reader. They are very striking, and speak a language too clear to be misrepresented or misunderstood. It appears evidently from them, on large and ample experience, that the fears of our manufacturers were vain, mistaken, and frivolous. That they suffered themselves to be led away and deceived by narrow and contracted views; and that the ardent desire of monopolies would not permit them to see the liberation of Irish commerce in any other light than that of jealousy and rivalship. To take off commercial restrictions must necessarily be beneficial to any country; but it is surprising to many, to see how little Ireland has yet been benefited by so liberal a system. Five years ago, however, I foretold[2] this event very exactly, and asserted that it would be probably half a century before any very material effects showed from the new system. I founded the idea on the general backwardness of that kingdom; on the remarkable deficiency of capital, which in every country accumulates slowly—on the want of industry and animation, owing to cheap provisions, cheap labour, and low taxes; that is, owing to the very causes which are now, and have been so long apprehended as the sure foundations of her prosperity. I viewed the whole kingdom with attention, my opinion was directly

[1] Three years ending 1773 are still lower.
[2] See the conclusion of my Irish Tour.

contrary to that of more than threescore of our greatest manufacturing towns; the event, as far as seven years' experience stands, is before the world; let the reader judge, whether it confirms my prophesy or their complaints.

If then the apprehensions of our manufacturers in 1778, upon this very subject of Irish commercial freedom, urged upon the same principles, supported by the same assertions, and expressed almost in the same words as the present opposition, has been proved by the undoubted evidence of facts, to have been utterly void of foundation, is not this a most powerful argument for suspecting the assertions which are at present brought forward, and for rejecting petitions, the prayer of which so manifestly tends to sacrifice public to private interests?

I do not enter into the question, whether the present proposition conveys a positive and most accurate equality between the two countries. It is said that in the articles of iron and silk, the duties ought to be a little varied, more to the disadvantage of Ireland: but the contrary is contended for in that kingdom. This is a theoretical question not easily settled to pence or shillings; but certain I am that the practical advantages will be on the side of England, and that the hardware manufacturers of this kingdom will retain so prodigious a superiority as to set at defiance the competition of our neighbours. Kingdoms cannot deal upon the huckstering higgling principles of chapmen and pedlars. Propositions are made upon great and simple principles; they must be accepted or rejected. To fritter them down by finding out minute objections, and to think it possible, that such great affairs, when national prejudices mingle in them, can be brought to an exact balance of profit and loss, like the pages of a merchant's ledger, is to expect what the nature of the business denies, and must for ever deny. A century of examinations would be insufficient to conduct the business to a conclusion on such principles.

As warm a friend as I must declare myself to the general principle of a free trade between the two kingdoms, yet is there one part of the proposition which it would have been better to omit. The application of the future surplus of a deficient revenue, to the defence of the empire at the disposal of the Irish Parliament, was a resolution that had nothing at all to do with the commercial question. If any idea of recompense came into the measure, of a political nature, it ought certainly to have been an explanation of a future connection between the two kingdoms in case of a war. If it is possible that we can ever be in the predicament of war with France, but Ireland neutral, it is a subject much more proper for apprehension, and demands more attention than fifty surpluses of revenue.

The arrangement of trade can only stand on its own merits. If it is not found, after mature consideration, to be as much in favour of England as of Ireland, it ought not to take place. We are under no obligation to make presents or concessions to that country; and, if the measure now under consideration could be considered in that light, it ought not to pass without a very different equivalent than that I have just mentioned.[1] The contrary is, however, the case; for the more it is examined the more clearly will it appear, that the proposed freedom of trade is as advantageous to England, as it can be to Ireland; and, for the various reasons I have already given, more likely to bring with it advantages to ourselves than to that nation. Nor should it be forgotten, that if this measure does not receive the sanction of the British Legislature, our export trade to Ireland will be open in future to all that blindness, prejudice, and illiberality which constitute the commercial spirit of monopoly in that country as well as in this. We shall be at all times liable, upon every temporary stagnation of their manufactures, to the call for protecting duties and prohibitions. An incessant war of regulations and customs must necessarily arise between the two countries; and our manufacturers, when it is too late, will curse their own folly that prevented a measure taking place, which would have secured to them the Irish market upon equal terms, free from all further restrictions.

Party having mingled very much in this question, though

[1] It must be confessed, that the relative situation of the two kingdoms at present may not permit so great a political question to be mingled with the commercial one; and that the repeal in 1782, of the 6th of Geo. I., was a proper time to have settled such a point: on the other hand, the proposition now made, to give a naval recompense, actually does mix the political and commercial questions.

nothing ought to be more remote from it, I cannot conclude without assuring the reader, that it has not the smallest influence on my mind. Those who have read the register of my Irish tour, as well as various essays in this work, will recollect at once, that I have ventured few opinions at present which I have not on other occasions most strenuously defended. The advantages to England, of giving freedom to the Irish trade, I have before explained, and attempted to shew, that in proportion to such freedom will be the security of converting the rising wealth of that country into the increasing prosperity of this. It is conviction alone, an old conviction, that induces me to take up the pen at present; and by no means a partiality for any minister; a race of men for whom few have less reason than myself to be partial to. A race so generally in the habit of doing commercial mischief, that it is seldom they merit support. When, however, they are right, the public good calls on every friend of his country to promote the measure—a motive that has pierced the neglected shade of my retirement, and produced this fugitive, but public protest against the madness of manufacturing opposition.

Review of "Observations on the Manufactures, Trade, and Present State of Ireland"; by John Lord Sheffield. 8vo. *Debrett.* 5s.

"Annals," Vol. III. (1785), p. 336.

The career which this noble author has opened for himself upon commercial subjects, is likely to prove as beneficial to his country, as it is undoubtedly honourable to himself. In his work on American commerce, he laid the foundation for a growing reputation, and he has, by this new performance, bid fair to outstrip every competitor.

It treats of a great variety of topics, and enters fully into the effects which the proposed arrangement with Ireland is likely to have upon the agriculture, trade, and manufactures of both kingdoms. In general, he thinks, and gives reasons highly deserving attention, that the relaxation of the navigation laws may be mischievous; but that there is little or no danger of Ireland ever being able to rival the manufactures of Britain; contending, at the same time, that, in the articles of silk and iron, the proposed system will not include a sufficient equality of duties being too much in favour of Ireland. "Ireland might, at least, be satisfied, until she finds herself in the situation of being able to say to Britain, 'My ports shall be open to all your manufactures, free of all duties, on condition that your ports shall be open to mine in the like manner.' Ireland is hardly in the situation to agree to that proposal; and the generality of Englishmen would probably at first object; but there is nothing in it which should alarm them. Great Britain could undersell Ireland in most manufactures; such is the predominancy of superior skill, industry, and capital, over low-priced labour, and comparatively very few taxes." He concludes with a very animated and most interesting enquiry into the internal and political state of that kingdom; and offers many observations, highly deserving attention, upon the volunteer corps, the arming of the Roman Catholics, and the interference of France in future. Upon the whole, this work is essentially necessary to all who wish to be well-informed upon this eventful subject; displaying uncommon knowledge in the author, and great abilities in arranging it for the reader's use.

Extracts.

Abstract of wool sold at Ballinasloe Fair, July 1771, to July 1778:—

	Bags sold.	Bags unsold.	Total.
1771, July . .	1,492	15	1,507
1772 " . .	1,286	11	1,297
1773 " . .	1,550	33	1,583
1774 " . .	1,623	25	1,648
1775 " . .	1,574	61	1,635
1776 " . .	1,857	64	1,921
1777 " . .	2,004	70	2,074
1778 " . .	1,359	553	1,912
Total	12,745	833	13,577
Yearly average.	1,593	104	1,697

The failure in 1778, arose from the stagnation of credit, and a decrease of the demand for bay-yarn from England.

Sheep sold at the said fair :—

	Sold.	Unsold.	Total.
1771, October .	51,950	—	51,950
1772 " .	53,632	50	53,682
1773 " .	55,242	6,390	61,682
1774 " .	60,796	5,302	66,633
1775 " .	63,904	1,020	64,924
1776 " .	66,873	639	67,512
1777 " .	63,792	12,743	76,535
1778 " .	44,894	31,588	76,482

Bullocks sold at the said fair :—

	Sold.	Unsold.	Total.
1771, October .	10,876	—	10,876
1772 " .	12,346	257	12,603
1773 " .	9,764	469	10,233
1774 " .	9,328	263	9,591
1775 " .	10.201	113	10,314
1776 " .	9,635	4,475	14.110
1777 " .	9,646	1,815	11,461
1778 " .	7,920	4,448	12,368

The noble author gives the following account of his flock :—"The writer of these observations can say, from experience, that the increased quantity of wool more than compensates for quality. His flock, consisting of above 1,000 sheep, was originally from the South Downs of Sussex. It was crossed ten years ago with one of Mr. Bakewell's rams, whose wool was by no means of the coarsest or longest kind. The fleeces of the flock were increased, from an average of 2½lb. which sold for 9*d.* per lb., to full 5lb. which sold for 8*d.* at the time wool was cheapest. The fleeces have returned towards their former weight; they average about 2¾lb. It sold in the year 1784, at 10*d.* per lb. only, although the price of fine wool is higher than it was a few years ago, and although some of the fleeces were so fine as to weigh only 1lb. 5ozs. It is clear then, than 5lb. of coarse wool at 8*d.* answers better than 2¾lb. at 10*d.* and in general what is most beneficial to the individual in matters of this kind, is best for the country."

Prices of wool in different parts of England.

1779.		per lb. *s.* *d.*
Norfolk at		0 6½
Sussex, South Down, weighs about 2½ lb. on an average		0 9
The finest sells some years at near 15*d.* per lb.		
Kent—West Kent South Down wool		0 7
West country horned-sheep brought into West Kent, weighs about 3½ lb. the fleece		0 6
East Kent South Down		0 5½
Romney Marsh (large)		0 5
West country		0 4½
Lincoln—Long 9½ lb. the fleece		0 6
Heath wool 5½		0 5
Nottingham—Fallow-field 4 lb.		0 5
Forest 2 lb.		0 7¾
	1778.	1779.
York—Long-combing	0 5½	0 3½
Hog and wether mixed	0 9¼	0 7
Superfine clothing	1 7	1 6
Second ditto	1 2	1 0½
Third ditto	0 8	0 6¼
Fourth ditto	0 6	0 4

Inclosures and artificial grasses have introduced large sheep, and have, in some parts of England, diminished the quantity of fine wool; this is the case in parts of Shropshire. The finest wool of that county is at Morf, near Bridgenorth, and at the Wrekin, the fleece is about 1½lb. This year, 1784, it sold at 24*s.* per stone of 14lb. sometimes it is as low as 18*s.* or a guinea, or 1*s.* 6*d.* a lb. is the average. It is said to be as good as any in England, except that of Ross in Herefordshire, which rises as high as 2*s.* 6*d.* per lb.

Size of Farms.

"The great farmer, of whom so many ignorantly complain in England, preserves us from scarcity, or extravagant prices in summer; his opulence answers the purpose of public granaries. A good system of agriculture, and intelligence and riches among farmers, are the best granaries on which a country can depend, and neither produce expence nor abuse. Such farmers are enabled to preserve part of their crop, and to wait the market of the ensuing summer. The little farmer, of very small capital, at the same time that he is the wretched sport of every irregularity of seasons, or of every trifling accident, is obliged to go to market with all his corn and all his produce at the time the price is lowest, and before the winter is finished. A more pitiable creature does not live, even when compared with the lowest labourer. He exists under an unremitting succession of struggles and anxieties, useless to himself, and hurtful to the public. For the soil in his hands is not sufficiently cultivated, or half stocked, nor half the produce derived from it, that might be in the occupation of a more opulent man. The expense of cattle, husbandry utensils, of attendance, &c. are proportionably greater than on one of a moderate size. The profit is consumed by the team or necessary cattle on a small farm, or the land is not tilled, at least in due time."—Nothing can be more true than these observations.

Comparative State of the Iron Manufactory in England and Ireland.

"Annals," Vol. III. (1785), p. 388.

Article VII. Most of the iron slit into rods used in Ireland has been imported from London, where it is brought from Russia, much cheaper than it can be carried to Dublin. It is frequently imported to London as ballast (with hemp in general) at 5*s.* per ton freight; the common freight is 15*s.* The Irish pay from 30*s.* to 35*s.* per ton,—the insurance there 50*s.*—to England 30*s.*

There are eight slitting and rolling mills in Ireland, which it is supposed slit and roll from 1700 to 2000 tons a year. In England, 16 mills slit from 800 to 1500 tons each per year, and some, it is said, a greater quantity. Some nails have been exported from Ireland to America; but the experiment is not likely to be repeated, as they were sold to a loss.

Much stress is laid on the cheapness of labour in Ireland; but the fact is, that nails are made, and nail-rods slit, much cheaper in England than in Ireland.

A considerable manufacturer in this country has asserted, that nail rods and hoops can be brought to market in Ireland, as cheap as the raw material can be had in the London market: the raw material in London has been at £14 to £14 10*s.* per ton; the price of rod-iron in Dublin is from £18 10*s.* to £19 per ton; and in England it is believed now to be about £18 per ton.

Answer VII. The assertion of this manufacturer is demonstrably true; nor can it be invalidated by this artful method of stating what the price of raw material has been in London, and what it now is in Dublin. The difference of duty being nearly 50*s.* in favour of Ireland, and the waste of metal, and charge of slitting, not exceeding 30*s.* is full proof of this, which is attempted by this writer to be answered by the difference of freight and insurance between London and Dublin.[1]

Article VIII. The state of the iron-founderies in Ireland is as follows:—The principal smelting-furnace is at Enniscorthy; its produce annually, when at work, may be about 300 tons, chiefly of castings, from 40 to 60 tons, of which 300 tons are pigs for the forge. There is another of the same sort at Mountrath, in the Queen's County; but, from the great scarcity of charcoal, it does not work above three or four months every third or fourth year; when this furnace is at work, that at Enniscorthy is idle. There are other founderies in Ireland, but not of the smelting kind; they work by recasting pig-iron; of these, there is one at Belfast, and another near to the town; one in Newry, and five in Dublin; it is believed there are no others in Ireland. The ore is English, and is raised in Lancashire.

The only iron ore, which, it is understood, has been raised

[1] If this argument were fair, a counter statement would have been given, and the present and late prices of both added; that not being done, the conclusion is evident.—A. Y.

in Ireland, is in the neighbourhood of Ballyporeen, but it cannot be worked to advantage without a large portion of iron ore from England; this work has been idle for many years past. The founderies in Ireland which work upon pig-iron, are supplied with it chiefly from Bristol and Chepstow, with some from Workington, some from Carron by Glasgow, and last year were supplied with about 150 tons from the south coast of Wales. The price is from £6 to £6 10*s.* per ton. The duty 10*s.* 6*d.* per ton.

With respect to the fuel used at the Irish founderies, smelting ones use charred wood. Some of the Dublin founderies, charred English pit-coal (only one of them it is believed continues to use Kilkenny coal); the fuel which is used in the founderies in the north cannot be spoke to with certainty. The general price of coal is from 16*s.* 6*d.* to 17*s.* 6*d.* per ton; and the best coal for this purpose, to be had in Dublin, is brought from Harrington, in the neighbourhood of Workington.

The average price of Kilkenny coal at the pit is 5*d.* per hundred. The price in Dublin varies with the season. In winter it has sold for 3*s.* 6*d.* per hundred. In summer from 1*s.* 8*d.* to 2*s.* 2*d.*

Kilkenny coal has been tried in the smelting of iron ore, but it will not answer—no raw fuel of any sort, in its natural state, can possibly be used with success in obtaining metal from its ore; its quality, whether it be pit coal or wood, must be changed by fire or heat, before it will smelt with success. Charring deprives both of its sulphur, which is an enemy to metals. Before the late dispute with America, Ireland sent there articles of cast iron for flour mills, such as spindles, forks, gudgeons for water-wheels, shafts, &c. but since that period none of the produce of her iron-founderies has been exported there or anywhere else. Great quantities of foundery goods have been imported from the northern coasts of England, though on pots there is a heavy duty; but, being entered for the use of the linen-manufacture, they are admitted under an easy one, if any at all is paid for them.

Answer VIII. Nothing conclusive can be drawn from the state of furnaces in Ireland, at the present time; it is well known that Ireland is possessed of the raw materials for iron, and labour is cheaper than in England; add to this, that she can import ore from Lancashire, on as good terms as the English furnaces at Chepstow, and other places, in South Wales. Nothing, therefore, can be wanting, but a perseverance in industrious and spirited exertions to improve these natural advantages.

Article IX. The price of coal at Birmingham is 6*s.* 8*d.* a ton; and in some places they are cheaper.

The prices of the different kinds of foundery-work both in England and Ireland, are various, arising from the goodness of the metal used in making the article, and the labour employed upon it after it is cast; as any of the most indifferent metal will make sash-weights, clock weights, scale weights, and all such articles that are used merely for their heaviness; these, therefore, fell from £12 to £14 per ton: pots, pans, and hollow ware in general, require the best and most expensive pig-iron, and also require more time in the moulding, as well as the hand of the best workman; the value consequently is greater, and the prices higher, from £16 to £18 and from that to £28 per ton; such articles as bear the latter price are increased in value by the work of the smith, and the addition of bar-iron.

	Per ton.
The customary price for bar-iron made in Ireland is .	£20 0 0
Cast hammers and anvils, imported into Ireland, cost .	14 11 8
The prices in Ireland	16 0 0

The duty ad valorem.

Bar-iron made in Ireland, and imported.

		Per ton.
Irish iron (very little made)		20 0 0
Stockholm iron at	£16 15 0 to	17 10 0
Russia ditto	15 10 0 „	16 0 0

Answer IX. Much weight is laid on the difference of the price of coal in the two countries; but this will be removed as soon as the Irish work their mines, and complete the canals, which they have already begun.[1] Coals, at Birmingham, cost 6*s.* 8*d.* at the wharf, but the carriage of them to

[1] Here is speculation given in answer to positive fact.

the works is to be added, which makes them 1*s.* 4*d.* dearer. Further, to shew how little weight is to be laid on this difference in price of coals, so much insisted on by this writer, it ought to be observed, that at London, and its neighbourhood, where most of the hoops made in the kingdom are cut, and a great proportion of other heavy work, such as anchors, ship-work, &c. is carried on, coals, &c., are at least thirty per cent. dearer than in Dublin.[1]

Article X:—

	Per ton.
Freight of bar-iron from London to Dublin	£0 10 0
Insurance at 1½ per cent.	
Duty 10*s.* 6*d.* per ton, charges 3*s.* 3*d.*	0 13 9
The Portage Act adds	0 0 9
Freight from Stockholm	1 11 6
Insurance at £1 10*s.* to £4 10*s.* per cent.	

Article XI:—

Freight from Petersburg	£1 13 6
Insurance at £1 10*s.* to £4 10*s.* per cent.	
Duty and charges as above.	
If a ship is very late in the year, insurance runs higher.	

[1] This is a very remarkable fact, and, as it comes from those who oppose the propositions, it deserves particular attention. That coals are dearer on the Thames than in Ireland I readily grant; but on comparing the prices generally between the two islands, there is a prodigious difference in favour of England; for the most considerable works in Ireland are carried on by means of English coal: but from this fact I must make one observation: it is contended, that cheap labour, cheap coals, and a small difference in duty, would be sufficient to enable the Irish to run away with the hoop and wire manufactures, the comparison being drawn between theirs and ours on the Thames; but is not this a most powerful argument full in the teeth of those who are enemies to the propositions; since it appears most manifestly, that cheap labour and cheap coals are of so little importance in this fabric, that our master-manufacturers find it more advantageous to keep their works on the Thames, with the dearest labour and coals of the whole kingdom, than remove them, as they might do, where labour is much lower, and coals 200 per cent. cheaper, than on that river? If such fabrics, owing to circumstances that certainly are well understood by such master-manufacturers, can not only hold up their heads in competition with other parts of the kingdom, but can, and do actually undersell the Irish in their own markets, how little apprehension ought we to have at that ideal superiority which is to arise among that people in some distant vague and unknown period, in predictions of which we have not the shadow of data on which to reason. Should such a competition arise, could not our fabrics, by partially removing from the Thames to our coal-pits, retain their superiority?—A. Y.

	Tons.
Ireland, imported in 1782 and 1783 from England . . .	7,305¼
And from the East country	10,136½
Of which, Dublin took from England	3,605
East country	5,237
	8,842

Is per year 4,421 tons; but on an average of seven years, is only 3,398½. What iron the Irish import from Russia, or Stockholm, must be paid for in bills on London, for which they are charged by their correspondence half per cent. for advance, and so much for commission.

Coals to the Irish slitter cost, on an average, .	£1 5 0	per ton.
„ to the English at . . . . 2*s.* 6*d.* to	0 2 8	„

How important the great difference in the price of coals is to the English manufacturer, need hardly be urged, when the addition of only three shillings a chaldron was last year stated as likely to be ruinous to their trade.

Observations on the Earl of Dundonald's Scheme for transferring the Tax on Salt to Hearths.

"Annals," Vol. III. (1785) p. 399.

This worthy nobleman, who has lately published a pamphlet, entitled "The Present State of the Manufacture of Salt explained," is at present well known to the public, by a patent for extracting tar from coals, the prolongation of which has been agitated in Parliament. I mention this circumstance, as it gives me an opportunity of adding the weak voice of my praise to that of many other persons, who justly commend the pursuits in which a noble person has spent his life and a considerable part of his fortune; a proof of the highest merit, and deserving that tribute of applause due from the public to those who labour for the common good. The process of freeing common salt from its impurities and rendering it by that means more proper for curing fish, meat, butter, &c. must depend for its establishment on various experiments. It does not come within the sphere of this work; but his lordship, having, in the same performance, proposed a great political measure, which would essentially affect the interests of every order of men connected with agriculture, it is incumbent on me to explain what would be its consequences, that my readers may in future (should this plan ever find its way into Parliament) be prepared to give it the examination it demands.

The scheme is no other than taking off all the present duties on salt, and laying them by commutation on hearths. As I think this is most ruinous to the whole landed interest, and beneficial only to certain classes of the commercial, I must necessarily condemn it *in toto*—in doing this, however, let it be not be imagined that I am insensible to the merit of the noble author. His discovery of purifying salt is, I dare-say, highly valuable, and his researches into the evils of the salt-tax judicious and useful; but when he contends, because of those evils, not for a remedy, but for so total a change, it is incumbent on the classes that are intimately concerned, to sift into the political part of the proposition; and with the greater attention, as report has given a similar scheme to a right honourable gentleman high in office,[1] who is in a situation to support the opinion he imbibes.

The noble earl states, from proper documents, that the gross receipts of the salt duties amounted, in 1776, to £895,489. That there is deducted for drawbacks, bounties, and discount, £622,866, and for charges of management £26,410, consequently that the nett produce of the revenue is no more than £246,213; but in 1784, owing to new duties, this nett produce was £332,735. He also shews, that there are great frauds and abuses in this revenue, and much encouragement to smuggling salt from Ireland. To obviate which, he would revive the tax of 2*s.* on every hearth, abolished at the Revolution. This is the outline of his plan; the subordinate parts do not demand particular attention. It is a branch of a general scheme, formed at large by Sir Matthew Decker, of abolishing customs and excises, and laying the whole amount upon houses. A part was carried into execution by Mr. Pitt's tea commutation tax, which

[1] Mr. Dundass.

has spawned the present proposition; and, if this is listened to, will soon produce other copies, till the commercial classes have thrown their whole share of taxation on the landed interest. The subject necessarily forms itself into two questions by the double operation proposed: first, the merit of taxes on consumption; and second, that of taxes on property, on the worst species of property, that of houses; for a tax upon hearths, windows, chimneys, doors, &c. is *ipso facto* a tax upon houses.

Taxes upon consumption, such as an excise upon salt, are the very best, and most unexceptionable of all others; this is admitted by the greatest and most enlightened authors; and indeed their operation in common life is such as ought for ever to recommend them. The ease and well-being of the subject who pays the tax, ought surely to be considered as well as the interest of the exchequer that receives it; and that method of levying by which the subject can with least difficulty pay the most, ought always to be preferred. Now taxes upon consumption, being blended with the price of the commodity, are paid without being known or felt; he who wishes to consume a bottle of wine, or a pound of salt, knows the price; and if that price, including the tax, is too high for him, he can avoid the whole by desisting from the consumption. This prevents such taxes from ever being really burthensome upon the individual. They cannot by extension be made so, because, when raised so high as to check consumption, two and two no longer make four, as Swift observed, but only three; and Government would find, that an increase of the tax would be a decrease of the revenue. Another admirable circumstance attending taxes on consumption, is their being strictly proportionable: every man pays exactly according to his expenditure; if I consume 1000 bushels of salt, I pay the tax on that quantity; if I consume none, I pay no tax. This equitable equality is fair, just, and prevents the tax ever being cruel, or even burthensome. These are circumstances attending all taxes on consumption, which, falling equally on every class of the people, are hurtful to none.

Reverse the medal, and examine a tax that is laid, not upon real property, but its appearance, such as an estate or a house, and we shall find it essentially failing in every one of these particulars. I will not dwell on the former, though the case is nearly as strong as in that of a house, for the real property is in the mortgagee or annuitant who escape taxation, not in the ostensible possessor. But in what manner, or by what rule, is a house or the number of windows or hearths, an index to either the property, consumption or ability to pay a tax in the person inhabiting such house? The wit of man could hardly suggest a more vague or false estimate. A man of small fortune has many hearths, a man of immense property may have very few. Examine the houses of country gentlemen of £2,000 a year, does any person imagine they have twice the number of hearths of others with half the estate? But the disproportion in every rank of people is so great, that a worse rule of ascertaining a man's income, it is obvious could not be thought of.

But this mode of taxation does not only totally fail in equality of burthen, but in the capability of payment when the tax is demanded. You come to a man for his tax at a time when he is utterly unable to pay it without distress; for his having so many hearths in his house is no proof whatever that he has so much money in his pocket; but his going to a shop for a bushel of salt, is a proof that he can pay for it with either money or credit, and no distress or hardship can arise from the tax. It was just so with tea; and the change to a window-tax was to the last degree cruel, if it was possible to have converted the custom into an excise upon the consumption, in such manner as to have subjected smuggled tea to the tax equally with that fairly imported. This salt scheme is open also to another objection in common with the tea commutation. Cottages pay nothing to that window-tax; yet their inhabitants are very great consumers of tea; and there is not in the range of taxation any objects more proper than the luxurious consumption of the poor. Why was not the window-tax extended to them? because they neither would or could pay it. Ask a poor labourer for a hearth-tax of a penny, he will not, perhaps cannot pay it. But excise his tea, ale, or salt, and he pays you without his knowing it. No minister in this country will ever dare to lay any taxes on the poor, except those of consumption—disgust, discontent, riots, and perhaps something worse would be the consequence of levying them strictly; for this reason, all commutations which take off taxes on consumption, and lay them on apparent property, such as land, houses, windows, hearths, &c. are bad in principle, tending to exempt the great mass of the people, whose consumption always yields the most productive levies, to add to the burthens of those who are already oppressed by the disproportionate manner in which they contribute to the necessities of the public.

The noble author of this scheme would copy the old hearth-tax, which exempted all houses that did not pay to church and poor—that is, he falls into this great error, by the necessity of the case, knowing how impossible it would be to levy a tax on the hearths of cottages.

The origin of this scheme deserves some attention, for it may perhaps be a guide to us how readily we ought to agree to it. I shall not lay any stress on the noble earl possessing considerable salt works himself, because there is reason to believe, from his known liberality, that such a circumstance would not influence him; but every man knows the enquiry which has been instituted into the state of the Scotch fisheries, of which Mr. Dempster was at the head. I understand that one great means of promoting those fisheries, strongly recommended, and doubtless very ably, has been this business of freeing salt from the duty. I am too well convinced of the importance of encouraging fisheries to offer one syllable against giving them all possible assistance, providing it is done upon fair and equitable terms; but I see no shadow of reason for giving a bounty to fisheries in the western isles, by laying a commutation tax on my hearths in Suffolk. It is not that local taxes should be laid for local purposes—I call for no such measure; if the encouragement of those fisheries is a national object (of which no one can doubt) let bounties be given in an effective manner by the national revenue: but do not take off a fair and equal tax on consumption, which falls lightly on an infinite number of points, to commute it for another tax which would fall with scarcely any weight on those who are the greatest consumers of salt, but most heavily on others who consume very little. This is not a commutation but a trick—Not the change of one tax for another; but taking an old tax off one part of the kingdom, and laying a new one upon another part: which is a sort of commutation which I trust will not very readily be agreed to.

In order to show what degree of fairness there would be in the execution of this project, let me take an instance in which I can be perfectly correct, and therefore reason from safely—myself. I find, that in the year 1784, my family, ten in number, consumed 125lb. of salt,[1] or 2¼ bushels,[2] the duty on which, at 5*s.* a bushel, amounts to 11*s.* 3*d.*; suppose there is added to this 12 per cent. on advancing the tax, it will not amount to quite 1*s.* 6*d.*, call it 12*s.* 9*d.* for my salt tax. Now turn to the precious project of the hearth account. There are 16 in this house, which at 2*s.* are £1 12*s.* instead of 12*s.* 9*d.*[3] That is to say, an advance of exactly 150 per cent! And the noble author gives facts to show that less than 2*s.* would not probably answer the purpose.

Connect the idea of laying an addition of 150 per cent. tax on Suffolk, in order to encourage fisheries in Argyle, and you have a proposal, to the modesty of which I am ready to give full credit. I do not lay much stress on the difficult circumstance of excisemen having a power to enter all the apartments, however private, of every house: the real necessities of the State cannot demand this: to mention it,

[1] This is correct, for it was bought of the grocer, and his bill lies before me, from which I have extracted it.

[2] Lord Dundonald, from Mons. Necker, calculates the consumption of salt in France at 19¼ lb. per head of the whole people per annum, and supposes, because salt is cheaper, that the average in England is 25 lb., equal to 23 French pounds; I am apt to believe that this is an error in political arithmetic, and that the consumption is not nearly so large. That of my family, including butter, bread, and salted pork, is only 12 lb. per head. I have made enquiries among the poor, such as labourers, weavers, combers, &c., and I find that on an average of various families, their consumption, inclusive of bread, is only half a stone per family.

In France the use of salt for cattle and sheep is almost everywhere common and considerable; we have no traces of such a practice in England. Another circumstance is the arbitrariness of the tax, in which every family is supposed to consume a certain quantity, and taxed accordingly: these points make the analogy between the French and English consumption a very vague mode of calculating.

[3] A gentleman, a neighbour of mine, 20 in family, consumes 5½ bushels in a year, his tax £1 7*s.* 6*d.*, but he has 25 hearths, the tax on which would be £2 10*s.*

is sufficient to shew, that there is no parallel between such a power, and that of passing through a house to view an inner court. There is little occasion to be solicitous against such exertions, in order to lay bad taxes, while the great prosperity of the kingdom offers so many objects for good ones.

The noble author of the scheme himself starts one objection, which is very strong, and by no means removed by a baker's licence. He is sensible that bakers, who are great consumers of salt, would not sink the price of bread proportioned to the advantage they gained by taking off the salt-tax; he calculates that the quantity they consume ought to pay at present above £200,000. It is by no means a trifling objection to a plan of commutation, when there are such obvious means of turning that to a private advantage which ought to be solely a public one. And this extends to a variety of trades besides bakers; all of whom are to be greatly favoured at the expence of the landed interest, who would most materially suffer by a hearth-tax.

But I return with pleasure to that part of the scheme to which every one must readily agree; that some method should be found to prevent the abuses that attend the present salt-tax. There is sufficient reason to think, that these take place more in drawbacks than in any other part of the business. A due investigation by the employment of proper persons to examine that matter on the spot, and in detail, would probably suggest effective means of correcting such abuses, and leaving so eligible a revenue open to few or no objections.

Much stress is laid in this business on a point which will probably come again and again before the public—the prevention of smuggling. Reasons are not wanting to imagine, that this matter in relation to salt is much exaggerated, and that the quantity smuggled from Ireland, is not very considerable; but if it was as great as the noble author imagines; and if similar and greater abuses should exist in other branches of the revenue, they cannot amount to any sound argument for changing the mode of our taxation from positive consumption to apparent property. That doctrine, if adopted, goes the full length which Sir Matthew Decker contended for; and calls for the abolition of all customs and all excises which are partly borne by the commercial classes, in order to throw a most enormous proportion of the burthen on the owners of land and houses. A doctrine that will always have its advocates, while private interest is found in commerce and manufacture.

The Minister, in his late budget, has proposed a small extension of the salt-tax, by a regulation of allowance; we may, from hence, conclude, that the present project is not in his contemplation. It is to be hoped that he will be too enlightened to admit the principle on which it is founded; and too prudent to hazard the practice which the experiment would necessarily involve.

I cannot conclude this paper, without noticing the progress made in the ideas of our mercantile classes, in relation to taking taxes from their own shoulders and throwing them upon those of others. Sir Matthew Decker's scheme is above forty years old, and has beeu refuted repeatedly in the most clear and satisfactory manner; but since the tea commutation tax has given an example, the spirits of our manufacturers are quite animated with the expectation of seeing the plan pursued. I have not often met with a more barefaced repetition of these commercial extravagances, than in a pamphlet lately published, entitled "Manufactures improper subjects of Taxation," the author of which, in the true commercial spirit, finds fault with every tax that but touches a manufacturer, and raises an outcry against even the receipt-tax (one of the best ever laid) because it is troublesome: he proposes to take off all taxes that are troublesome to trade, and lay the lumping amount on the rents of lands and houses, with which he is so perfectly ignorant as to assert, that 1*s.* in the pound fairly levied would produce two millions, which is just an error of a half; and he employs much time to shew that this would be a very good thing for landlords, because the farmers would draw back the tax by raising the prices of their products: in which again he is utterly wrong, and ignorant of all the principles of taxation; because he might have known that a land-tax cannot be drawn back, and consequently that his scheme would be completely ruinous to the greatest and most considerable class of people in the State. Such wretched folly would be unworthy of all attention, if similar doctrines had not been broached from much more respectable quarters. The landed interest in Parliament ought to see clearly, that these plans, which creep in this manner from speculation to project, and from project to practice, should be rejected in the first instance with the scorn and contempt they deserve. By agreeing to the tea commutation tax[1] they have opened the door to endless schemes equally mischievous: a stand must be made somewhere, and the sooner it is made the better.

A. Y.

BRADFIELD HALL, *May 10th*, 1785.

"*Reflections on the present matters in dispute between Great Britain and Ireland.*" *By J. Tucker, D.D., Dean of Gloucester.* 8vo. 1*s*. *Cadell.*

"Annals," Vol. III. (1785), p. 417.

Whatever comes from the pen of the celebrated projector, who, previous to the American War, gave a well-known article of advice to his country, which, had it been followed, would have saved this kingdom above one hundred millions sterling—must deserve no common attention. It will perhaps be found, that in his present performance he is not by any means equally happy, though always able, and in a great measure original.

The ideas started in this pamphlet are peculiar: the author thinks that the freedom of trade given by the first resolutions to Ireland (not as amended by the Minister in the debate) will be attended with the following effects:

1. To lay open the monopoly of the East India Company, by Ireland's free trade thither, which would ensure that of England.
2. To lay open the monopoly of the trade to Egypt, the Levant, &c.
3. A free importation of sugar from wherever it is to be had cheapest.

[1] The idea might be necessary; but laying the whole burthen on windows was oppressive; 5 per cent. addition on the revenue in general, with exception of various articles, would have answered the same purpose.

4. The entire abolition of the Navigation Act, which he considers as a monopoly.
5. A free import and export of grain.

A recital of these advantages will make the reader be ready to imagine, that the Dean has written the whole ironically, and that he means to condemn the system for having these effects: but it is very sober and serious. The Minister's emendation of the resolutions will, if they are accepted, overturn most of the benefits which our reverend politician has deduced from them: effectually those of the East and West Indies. But this mode of attaining a right system of British trade, by beginning with giving it to Ireland, in order afterwards to receive it ourselves, is refining almost to a degree of paradox.

As to the free export and import of corn, the part of the subject which connects the pamphlet with this work, the author's ideas are such as it is impossible to approve. He considers corn as the raw material of a manufacture, "consequently every encouragement ought to be given to the growth of it at home, and the importation of it from abroad."

The idea of classing corn as a raw material of manufacture, is totally erroneous, and, if accepted, would lead immediately to absurd conclusions. Upon this principle the cheaper corn is the better: but the contrary is fact; a very great cheapness of corn is ruinous to all manufactures, being a sure cause of idleness and profligacy among workmen. No sooner does a writer set out upon such an unlucky axiom, than it is sure to follow him through the whole texture of his enquiry; and accordingly the Dean treats the whole question of corn upon that principle only. A free import and export, could it be attained under our government, would be, for reasons exceedingly different from those given by this author, the very best policy of that commodity: but every one who reflects upon our corn trade, and upon the effect which clamour is sure to have when the popularity of a minister comes in competition with the public good, must necessarily see, that this pretended free trade, would be freedom of import without a freedom of export. The Dean himself would restrain exportation "when crops have failed in other countries"—

which shews what sort of a free trade it would be: whenever prices had risen much, we should soon hear of failing crops, and famines; and we should see a London mob, or a London Corporation petitioning (as it once did) for bounties upon import. Hence there is nothing that can be offered on the subject so inapplicable and frivolous, as propositions for a freedom of trade in this article, which every man of common sense knows (however desirable it certainly is) can never take place under our government. The landed interest ought strenuously to resist so fallacious a plan; and not be tricked (for it would be no better than a trick) out of a measure essential to their well-being—a regulation of import, as they are morally certain there never will be permitted an unregulated export. The Dean's observations on the bill now depending for making the prices of London regulate the export and import of the whole kingdom, are just and pointed. It is, in truth, one of the most barefaced impositions on the public that perhaps was ever laid before them. But his idea, that the western parts of Ireland are more likely to become an emporium of imported corn (not much for the advantage of her agriculture if she was) will probably be thought to have little foundation.

The author annexes an appendix, containing subjects for dissertations and premiums to be offered to the graduate students of the universities of England and Scotland. The first on the comparison or compactability of the military spirit and commercial pursuits. The second on the proper military defence of a commercial people. The third and fourth on the employment of slaves in the West Indies, &c. The fifth on the revocation of all monopolies. He proposes that £200 a year be given in premiums for dissertations on these subjects; and very generously offers £20 himself, and £20 more from his friends; also that he will continue his own subscription for life. This is very noble; and it is with great pleasure that I see steps gradually taking, which seem not only to evince a conviction of the deficient education of our universities, but to propose the means of remedying it.

An "Essay on the Population of Ireland." 8vo. 1*s*. *Richardson. By the Rev. J. Howlett.*

"Annals," Vol. V. (1786), p. 486.

This gentleman, who is so well known by his indefatigable researches into the population of England, has turned his attention to the neighbouring kingdom, and has, with the assistance of the Right Hon. Mr. Beresford, First Commissioner of the Revenue in that kingdom, given the theory of Dr. Price, in what he lays down concerning Ireland, as complete an overthrow as he had before effected with relation to English population.

The number of houses returned for the whole kingdom in the year ending at Lady-day 1781, were:—

With one hearth	400,783
With from 2 to 5 hearths inclusive	43,980
With more than five	15,098
Excused on account of poverty	17,741
	477,602

Mr. Beresford remarks, that deficient returns, barracks, houses of revenue offices, &c., &c. will make the number 500,000; which, at five to a house, makes 2,500,000 souls; but more probably, he says, at five and a half it is 2,750,000.

From "Memoirs of the last Thirty Years of the Editor's Farming Life, with notes."

"Annals," Vol. XV. (1791), p. 152.

My journies to Ireland, the register of which I published, occupied the years 1776, 1777, 1778, and 1779.[1] Of that work, I have not much apprehension, though the success in relation to profit (even with the assistance of a subscription),

[1] Including a residence in the county of Corke, of something more than a year, employed in arranging and letting part of the estate of Lord Viscount Kingsborough.

was nothing; yet it will stand its ground, and I trust merit, in some small degree, the most flattering encomiums it has received in many parts of Europe.

I cannot, on such an occasion, name Ireland without remarking, that though the Irish are certainly a generous people, and liberal sometimes almost to excess, yet I have to complain, that not a ray of that spirit was by any public body shed on my labours. Without my seeking it, after I had left the kingdom, and published the Tour in England, I received the following letter, written by order of the Dublin Society:—

"Sir,

"With great pleasure I take up the pen in obedience to the commands of the Dublin Society, to communicate to you their thanks for the late publication of your Tour in Ireland; a treatise which, in doing justice to this country, puts us in a most respectable view; for which reason we consider you to have great merit. But what particularly gained the attention of the Society, were your just and excellent observations and reasoning, in the second part of that work, relative to the agriculture, manufactures, trades, and police of the kingdom. And gentlemen thought the publication of that part, particularly so as to fall into the hands of the generality of the people of this country, might be of great benefit and use; and we wish you would let us know your sentiments relative to the preparing of a publication of that kind, and in what mode you would think it most proper, and would answer best, and what you would think a reasonable amends for all this trouble, that we may lay the same before the Society at our next meeting, the beginning of November.

"I am, Sir,
"Your most obedient humble servant,
"Red. Morres."

"Dublin, *Sept.* 16, 1780."

"P.S.—There are a great many useful observations and hints, interspersed in many parts of your Tour, which may be of great use to throw into the hands of the public."

"At a meeting of the Dublin Society, at their house in Grafton Street, Thursday, August 31, 1780,

"The Rev. Dean WOODWARD, V.P., in the chair.

"Resolved, That this Society do highly approve of the work lately published by Arthur Young, Esq., an Honorary Member of the Society, entitled 'A Tour in Ireland'; and that the Secretary be directed to communicate the thanks of the Society to Mr. Young for the said work.

"Resolved, That Mr. Young be requested to prepare the second part, or Appendix, of his Tour in Ireland, in such manner that the same may be published separately; and that Sir Lucius O'Brien and Redmond Morres, Esq., be requested to write to Mr. Young on this subject.

"Signed, by Order of the Society,

"THOMAS LYSTER, Assistant Secretary."

In answer to this letter I returned sincere thanks for the honour of the vote; and assured them, that I should be ready either to publish any part of the work separately, or to make an abridgement of the whole; reduced in such a manner as to be diffused at a small expense over all the kingdom.

In a few posts I received, under the Dublin post-mark, an envelope, enclosing an anonymous essay, cut out of a newspaper; which referred to the transactions of the Society relative to me, and condemning pretty heavily my whole publication: and in this unhandsome manner the business ended. I heard no more of them. In a Society which disposes of £10,000 a year of public money, granted by Parliament chiefly with a view, as the Act expresses, to encourage agriculture, but which patronizes manufactures far more, there will necessarily be an agricultural party and a manufacturing one. According as one or the other happens to prevail, such contradictions will arise. All that is to be said of my case now is, that it was not so bad as that of poor Whyn Baker, who settled in Ireland as their experimenter in agriculture—lived there in poverty ten or twelve years—and broke his heart on account of the treatment which he met with.

But, while their Societies acted thus, the Parliament of the kingdom paid my book a far greater compliment than any Society could do; for they passed more than one Act almost directly, which received the royal assent, to alter and vary in a good measure the police of corn, &c. which I had proved was vicious; but which, till then, had been universally esteemed as the chief pillar of their national prosperity: and I had thus the satisfaction of seeing the Legislature of the kingdom improving the policy of it, from the known and confessed suggestions of a work that, in other respects, had proved to the author a mere barren blank. But I have since learned from the conversation of many most respectable gentlemen of Ireland, as well as from the correspondence of others, that the book is now esteemed of some value to Ireland; and that the agriculture of the kingdom has been advanced in consequence of it. But it is time to dismiss a subject upon which I have dilated too much, and spoken perhaps with unguarded vanity and self-love, which would ill become me. I have but one word to say: to Ireland I am not in debt.[1]

State of Ireland in 1748 *and* 1792 *compared.*

"Annals," Vol. XX. (1793), p. 215.

	1748.		1792.
Land about Cork, English acre	12*s.* to 22*s.*	...	£2 to £6.
About Dublin, Irish acre	£2 to £4	...	£5 to £12.
Wool, per stone	6*s.* to 8*s.*	...	16*s.* to 17*s.*
Sheep, from	4*s.* to 14*s.*	...	12*s.* to 40*s.*
Oxen, fat	£4 to £6	...	£8 to £16.
Milch cows	£1 15*s.* to £2 5*s.* 6*d.*	...	£5 to £10.

1748.	1792.
Corn was occasionally very low and very high; but so unequal was the country to feed itself, that Dublin alone paid to foreign parts, for wheat and flour, above £100,000 annually.	There is not only now an ample supply, but Ireland has, upon an average, exported, latterly, 300,000 barrels of wheat and 500,000 barrels of oats.

1 The reader will see that I speak nationally, and not of individuals; for I have had many hospitable acquaintances there, and some friends; among the latter let me be proud to name Cornelius Bolton, Esq., of Faithlegg, near Waterford; and these "Annals" have testified the singular attention of Henry Arthur Herbert, Esq., of Muckruss.

Bounty on the Inland Carriage of Corn in Ireland.

"Annals," Vol. xxix. (1797) p. 157.

IRISH HOUSE OF LORDS, *Friday, March* 31.

On the second reading of the Corn Bounty Repeal Bill, the Earl of Farnham opposed it as injurious to the agriculture of the country, and unjust to a numerous class of men, the millers, who had expended large sums in the erection of extensive mills, relying on the continuance of the bounty. His lordship said, that there had been between two and three hundred bolting mills erected in this country, and that it would be impossible to make compensation to the proprietors for the loss of the bounty. He admitted, that at first great profits had been obtained by the millers, because then there was no competition; but latterly competition had lessened the profits; the miller was only the medium of the bounty, which ultimately centred in the farmer: consequently the farmer would be the sufferer, and agriculture would necessarily decline. I will, said his lordship, suppose a case, that there had been held out by Parliament an encouragement to build a bridge, for which the builder was to be repaid by tolls, that the tolls turned out to be profitable, and that the Legislature should say the builder had got money enough, we will now appropriate the profits. In such a situation would the millers be left if their profits had been taken away. Their corn had been already purchased or agreed for without the knowledge of this bill being passed; what loss must they not sustain by the discontinuance of the bounty? His lordship said he was not fond of making experiments, particularly on a subject of such importance as the removal of a bounty which had existed upwards of forty years, and which had been attended with the best effects; at any time such an experiment would be hazardous; but, when such an encouragement, as there was this day held out to pasturage existed, it was in his opinion highly dangerous. His lordship concluded by declaring it as his opinion that such a bill ought not to pass.

The Lord Chancellor said, that the bill was not intended as a bill of supply; on such grounds he certainly would not have supported it; on the contrary he would have conceived it an unwise and impolitic measure. The city of Dublin paid £100,000 a year bounty for inland carriage; and he was bold to say there was no town in Europe the markets of which were worse supplied. Since the year 1784 (when the import of foreign corn was restricted) to the present day, the market of Dublin has been infinitely worse supplied than when it principally depended on a foreign supply: there had been an export bounty in England, which enabled the English exporter to come to our market with advantage over the Irish farmer. A regulation had been adopted by the Legislature of Ireland, in favour of the Irish farmer, which prohibited importation till the price of corn rose to a certain height; and the market had been ever since more scanty than before—What a State solecism (said his lordship) it is, in a country abounding with navigable rivers, to pay £100,000 a year for inland carriage! You stop export from the city of Dublin, though the best situated of any other port in the kingdom for it, and from which so great a number of vessels daily sail in ballast, in order to fill your market; and the consequence is diametrically opposite to the intention. Your markets are scantily supplied, because there is no export for the redundance.—The inland bounties operate not only against the supply of the metropolis, but against the agriculture of the kingdom. It will astonish your lordships to hear, that within two or three months it occurred, that not one day's provision of corn was in the market of Dublin; and that the Lord Lieutenant deemed it necessary to have vessels in Liverpool freighted with corn, to prevent a famine in Dublin! Allow the export of corn, and the banks of your canals will be covered with granaries: let the port of Dublin be added to the other exporting towns of the kingdom, and her markets will be equally well supplied, because the redundancy can be disposed of to advantage abroad, if not at home. I have no doubt, my lords, but Dublin will then become a great export town, and that its own consumption will be more abundantly supplied than it has been heretofore. It is a well-known fact that flour is now dealt out to the inhabitants of Dublin, in such quantities as do not afford a plenty, much less a redundancy; and under the present restraining laws that power will continue in the same hands, and be exercised in the same way. The principal millers in the neighbourhood of Clonmell, a part of the kingdom from which there is a considerable influx of corn to the city, do not complain of the bill; on the contrary, many have declared that they will not suffer any loss from it. I conceive, said his lordship, the bounty to be an idle expense; the cause for which it was granted is removed—Ireland has become what she was not when it was given, a corn country, not only of ample supply for herself, but capable of exporting a considerable redundancy for her advantage; and under this impression I declare myself an advocate for the bill: but, I repeat, not as a bill of supply, for in that point of view I would be adverse to it, but as a bill calculated to promote the agriculture of the kingdom, and to provide for the consumption of the metropolis.

Lord Desart premised that he did not mean to oppose government; he conceived it the duty of every man in the present day to give all possible support to government; but his opinion was that by granting the export trade now to Dublin, it would be impossible to control it hereafter, and that it must ultimately be carried to an extent too great. When the inland bounty was first granted, Ireland had no agriculture; the country was laid out in farms of one, two or three thousand acres each, with a few herdsmen tending cattle. From the encouragement afforded by the the bounty, these large uncultivated tracts of land had been divided into small farms, at present covered with crops, and inhabited by thousands. His lordship contended that by opening the port of Dublin to export, the exporting trade of the country towns would be stopped, and consequently the farmer, wanting a market for his provisions, would be discouraged from agricultural improvement. His lordship could not think of supporting the bill, when he considered that the flourishing state of our agriculture has been owing to the bounty.

The Earl of Portarlington supported the bill on the ground that England had materially profited by encouraging an export trade.

Lord Sheffield said, the great increase of Irish tillage

must not be attributed to the carriage bounty on corn; that an examination of the import and export of corn for the last fifty years, and of the circumstances which had taken place during that period, would demonstrate what he asserted. He observed that the quantity of corn imported and exported on an average of fourteen years, following the date of those bounties, namely 1758, (when compared to the great increase of export, and decrease of import, which took place in consequence of other laws) did not differ much from the average of fourteen years preceding the granting of those bounties, and that the export did not exceed the import till other circumstances began to have effect, namely, the new arrangement of the English corn-laws in 1772, by which corn from Ireland was admitted at a considerably lower price than had been allowed near a hundred preceding years, namely, wheat *5s. 4d.* per quarter lower. In 1774, the Parliament in Ireland added a bounty on the export, and then, on an average of the next period, previous to passing the corn-laws in Ireland, in 1783, we find a great decrease of import and increase of export; but after the establishment of the corn-laws, which protected at the same time that they encouraged Irish tillage, then, and not till then, we saw, on an average of eight years preceding the present war, a most extraordinary increase of export, and the importation sunk almost to nothing. Here his lordship stated the average import and export of corn at different periods during the last fifty years. His lordship observed, it had been argued, that the Legislature, having by bounties encouraged an improvement, would do a great injury if those bounties were not continued: he said bounties were not justifiable, except as regulations on foreign trade, or to encourage undertakings in the beginning, and for a limited time. The case in question was of the latter description, and surely had been most amply encouraged, and for a great length of time, near forty years; and when an undertaking has been established, if it cannot go on by itself, it is contrary to all policy to force it, by extravagant premiums of £80,000 yearly, on an average; and especially at this time, it would be a shameful waste of public treasure. He then observed that the professed object of the inland carriage bounty was the supply of Dublin with Irish instead of English corn. The late corn-law secured that supply, and the opening the port of Dublin for exportation will secure a more steady supply for that city, than had hitherto been the case, by giving a market for a surplus; and Dublin, from its situation, is likely to have a steady and permanent export of corn to the north western parts of Great Britain, which do not raise nearly sufficient for its numerous inhabitants, and which have hitherto been supplied from the southern, and even very largely from the eastern coast of England: and this trade is farther secured to Ireland, by the ports of Great Britain being not long since open to corn from hence, at lower prices than corn coming from foreign countries. He said, all the other parts of the bill had been so ably treated by the learned lord on the woolsack, that it was unnecessary, and it would be presumption, to attempt to add anything. That he seemed to himself to endeavour to prove a self-evident proposition, which he argued in favour of the bill, and that he should apologize for having trespassed on their lordships with so little pretensions. He was happy in the opportunity of adding, that although he had not the honour of residing long in the country, no man could more ardently wish to promote the prosperity of Ireland than he did.

The bill was then read a second time, and committed for to-morrow.[1]

A. Y.

[1] In the year 1779, I explained fully, from very detailed calculations, the mischievous tendency of the inland bounty, so much to the satisfaction of the leading men in that kingdom, that the very next ensuing sessions of Parliament (as appears by Sir Henry Cavendish's "State of the Public Revenue") it was reduced half, to the saving of £40,000 per annum to Ireland. At last the whole measure is repealed. It is not every individual that has the opportunity, in so obscure a situation as myself, to make savings for the public. I should not mention it here, if it was not a matter of public record. I have upon another occasion mentioned the return which a public body in Ireland at that time made me.—A. Y.

BIBLIOGRAPHY OF ARTHUR YOUNG.

BY JOHN P. ANDERSON, OF THE BRITISH MUSEUM.

1891.

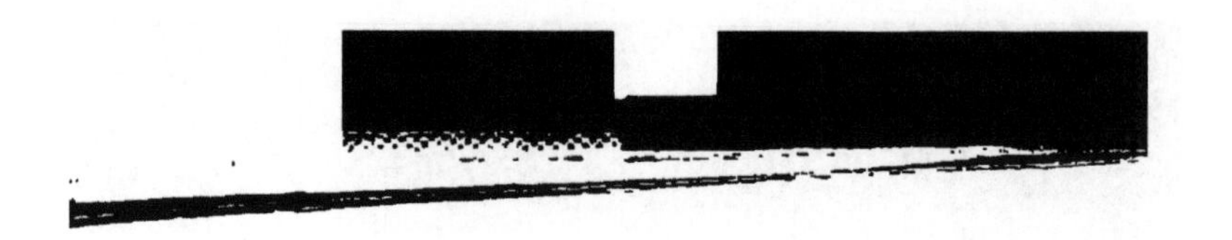

BIBLIOGRAPHY OF ARTHUR YOUNG.

I.

WORKS.

The Theatre of the Present War in North America. By A. Y * * * *. London, 1758, 8vo.

Reflections on the Present State of Affairs at Home and Abroad. London, 1759, 8vo.

[According to the "Biographie Universelle" (vol. xlv., p. 273), A. Y. began in 1759 a periodical called "The Universal Museum," which he discontinued after six numbers, by the advice of Dr. Johnson. In 1760 he contributed (according to the same authority) to the "Museum Rusticum." In any case these dates must be wrong, as the former magazine only began to appear in 1762 and the latter in 1766.]

The Farmer's Letters to the People of England; containing the sentiments of a practical husbandman, &c. London, 1767, 8vo.

—— Second Edition. London, 1768, 8vo.

—— Third Edition, enlarged, 2 vols. London, 1771, 8vo.

A Six Weeks' Tour through the Southern Counties of England and Wales, &c. London, 1768, 8vo.

Reprinted in Dublin. 1768, 12vo.

—— Second Edition. London, 1769, 8vo.

—— Third Edition. London, 1772, 8vo.

Letters concerning the Present State of the French Nation, &c. London, 1769, 8vo.

An Essay on the Management of Hogs; including experiments on rearing and fattening them, &c. London, 1769, 8vo.

—— Essays on the Management of Hogs and the Culture of Cole-seed. Second edition, with additions, 2 pts. London, 1770, 12mo.

The Expediency of a Free Exportation of Corn at this time, &c. London, 1769, 8vo.

—— Second Edition. London, 1770, 8vo.

A Six Months' Tour through the North of England; containing an account of the Present State of Agriculture, Manufactures, and Population in several Counties of this Kingdom, interspersed with descriptions of the Seats of the Nobility and Gentry, &c. 4 vols. London, 1770, 8vo.

—— Second Edition. 4 vols. London, 1771, 8vo.

Extracts from Mr. Young's Six Months' Tour through the North of England, &c. London, 1774, 8vo.

The Farmer's Guide in Hiring and Stocking Farms; with plans of Farmyards and sections of the necessary Buildings, &c. 2 vols. London, 1770, 8vo.

Rural Œconomy: or, Essays on the practical parts of Husbandry; to which is added The Rural Socrates, being memoirs of a [Swiss] Country Philosopher [M. Hirzel]. London, 1770, 8vo.

—— Reprinted in Dublin. 1770, 8vo.

—— Second Edition, 1773; and reprinted at Philadelphia. 1775, 8vo.

A Course of Experimental Agriculture; containing an exact register of all the business transacted during five years on near three hundred acres of various soils; including a variety of experiments on the cultivation of all sorts of grain and pulse, both in the old and new methods, &c. 2 vols. London, 1770, 4to.

The Farmer's Tour through the East of England; being the register of a journey through various Counties of this Kingdom, to enquire into the state of Agriculture, &c. 4 vols. London, 1771, 8vo.

The Farmer's Calendar; containing the business necessary to be performed on various kinds of Farms, during every month of the year. London, 1771, 8vo.

[There are numerous editions of this work.]

Proposals to the Legislature for Numbering the People; containing some observations on the population of Great Britain, &c. London, 1771, 8vo.

Letter from Arthur Young, dated North Mimms, March 28, 1772, in answer to Dr. Price's observations on the decrease of population.

[In "London Magazine" for 1772, pp. 162-165.]

Political Essays concerning the Present State of the British Empire, &c. London, 1772, 4to.

[Not mentioned by Lowndes or Watts. Given here on the authority of Dr. Paris in his memoir of A. Young, in the "Quarterly Journal of Science," vol. ix.]

Observations on the Present State of the Waste Lands of Great Britain, &c. London, 1773, 8vo.

Political Arithmetic; containing observations on the Present State of Great Britain and the principles of her policy in the encouragement of Agriculture, &c. London, 1774, 8vo.

Political Arithmetic. Part II. Containing considerations

on the means of raising the supplies within the year. Occasioned by Mr. Pulteney's pamphlet on that subject.
London, 1779, 8vo.

A Tour in Ireland, with general observations on the Present State of that Kingdom, made in the years 1776, 1777, and 1778, and brought down to the end of 1779. 2 pts.
London, 1780, 4to.

—— Reprinted in 2 vols. Dublin, 1780, 8vo.

—— Reprinted in *Pinkerton's* "General Collection of Voyages," &c. Vol. iii. 1808, 4to.

—— Also, in part, in *Mavor's* "British Tourists," vol. iii.
1798, 12mo.

—— And again in vol ii., 1809.

—— Another Edition [containing only a few extracts]. A Tour in Ireland, 1776-1779. London, 1887, 16mo.

[Vol. lxxvi. of "Cassell's National Library."]

An Inquiry into the Legality and Expediency of increasing the Royal Navy by subscriptions for building County Ships. Being the correspondence on that subject between Arthur Young and Capel Lofft, Esqs. London, 1783, 8vo.

Annals of Agriculture and other useful Arts; collected and published by A. Young. 46 vols. London, 1784-1815, 8vo.

—— Vol. xlvi. consists of No. 270, "An Inquiry into the progressive value of Money," &c., dated 1812; and No. 271, "An Inquiry into the Rise of Prices in Europe," &c., dated 1815.

[For A. Y.'s contributions to the "Annals," see below.]

The Question of Wool truly stated. In which the facts are examined for and against the Bill now depending in Parliament.
London, 1788, 8vo.

A Speech on the Wool Bill that might have been spoken in the House of Commons, May the 1st, 1788, on the Question of adjourning the consideration to that day three months.
London, 1788, 8vo.

Travels during the years 1787, 1788, and 1789; undertaken more particularly with a view of ascertaining the cultivation, wealth, resources, and national prosperity of the Kingdom of France. 2 vols. Bury St. Edmunds, 1792, 4to.

—— Second Edition. London, 1794, 4to.

—— Reprinted in *Pinkerton's* "General Collection of Voyages," vol. iv. 1808, 4to.

—— Another Edition. Travels in France during the years 1787, 1788, 1789, with an introduction, biographical sketch, and notes by M. Betham-Edwards.

—— Second Edition. London, 1889, 8vo.

[Part of "Bohn's Standard Library." N.B. This Edition omits the Spanish and Italian portions of the Travels, as also the statistical portions of vol. ii.]

Address proposing a Loyal Association to the inhabitants of the hundreds of Thedwastry and Thingoe.
[Bury St Edmunds ?] 1792, s. sh. fol.

A Letter on Tithes to Arthur Young [by J. S.], with his remarks on it; and a second letter to those remarks.
London, 1792, 8vo.

The Example of France, a warning to Britain. (Appendix).
London, 1793, 8vo.

—— Second Edition. Bury St. Edmunds, 1793, 8vo.

—— Third Edition. Bury St. Edmunds, 1793, 8vo.

—— Fourth Edition. London, 1794, 8vo.

—— An Abstract of the Example of France, a warning to Britain. London, 1793, 8vo.

General View of the Agriculture of the County of Sussex. Drawn up for the consideration of the Board of Agriculture, &c.
London, 1793, 4to.

—— Another Edition. London, 1808, 8vo.

Postscript to the Survey of Hampshire. [By A. and W. Driver.] London, 1794, 4to.

General View of the Agriculture of the County of Suffolk, with observations on the means of its improvement.
London, 1794, 4to.

—— Another Edition. London, 1797, 8vo.

An Idea of the Present State of France, and of the consequences of the events passing in that Kingdom. Second Edition.
London, 1795, 8vo.

The Constitution Safe without Reform; containing some remarks on a book entitled "The Commonwealth in Danger," by J. Cartwright. Bury St. Edmunds, 1795, 8vo.

A Farming Tour in the South and West of England. See "Annals of Agriculture," vols. xxviii., &c., 1796, &c.

National Danger, and the means of Safety. [Being Letters to the Yeomanry, &c., subscribed by A. Y.] London, 1797, 8vo.

An Enquiry into the State of the Public Mind amongst the Lower Classes; and on the means of turning it to the welfare of the State: in a letter to William Wilberforce. London, 1798, 8vo.

General View of the Agriculture of the County of Lincoln. Drawn up for the consideration of the Board of Agriculture and Internal Improvement. London, 1799, 8vo.

The Question of Scarcity plainly stated, and Remedies considered; with observations on permanent measures to keep wheat at a more regular price. London, 1800, 8vo.

An Inquiry into the Propriety of applying Wastes to the better maintenance and support of the Poor, &c.
London, 1801, 8vo.

On the Size of Farms. (An Essay in "Georgical Essays," by A. Hunter, vol. iv., pp. 555-570). York, 1803, 8vo.

Letters from George Washington to Arthur Young, &c. [Letters on Agriculture. Edited by Arthur Young.] Alexandria, 1803, 8vo.

Essay on Manures. London, 1804, 8vo.

An Essay on Manures. (Art. x. of the Bath Society Papers, vol. x. pp. 95-198). Bath, 1805, 8vo.

General View of the Agriculture of Hertfordshire. Drawn up for the consideration of the Board of Agriculture and Internal Improvement. London, 1804, 8vo.

General View of the Agriculture of the County of Norfolk. Drawn up for the consideration of the Board of Agriculture and Internal Improvement. London, 1804, 8vo.

On Hogs and their Management.—On Carrots.—On Beans. (Essays in "Georgical Essays," by A. Hunter, vol. v. pp. 64-93, 418-440, 488-490). York. 1804, 8vo.

On Summer Fallowing. (An Essay in "Georgical Essays," by A. Hunter, vol. vi. pp. 128-144). York, 1804, 8vo.

General View of the Agriculture of the County of Essex. Drawn up for the consideration of the Board of Agriculture and Internal Improvement. 2 vols. London, 1807, 8vo.

General Report on Inclosures. London, 1807, 8vo.

On the Advantages which have resulted from the Establishment of the Board of Agriculture: being the substance of a lecture read to that Institution, May 26th, 1809. London, 1809, 8vo.

View of the Agriculture of Oxfordshire. Drawn up for the Board of Agriculture and Internal Improvement. London, 1809, 8vo.

On the Husbandry of the three celebrated Farmers, Messrs. Bakewell, Arbuthnot, and Ducket: being a lecture read to the Board of Agriculture, June 6, 1811. London, 1812, 8vo.

An Inquiry into the progressive value of Money, as marked by the Price of Agricultural Products. London, 1812, 8vo.

[No. 270 of vol. xlvi. of the "Annals of Agriculture."]

An Inquiry into the Rise of Prices in Europe during the last twenty-five years, compared with that which has taken place in England, &c. London, 1815, 8vo.

[Printed also in the "Pamphleteer," vol. vi., 1815. Forms No. 271 of vol. xlvi. of the "Annals of Agriculture."]

Baxteriana: containing a Selection from the Works of Baxter. Collected by Arthur Young. London, 1815, 12mo.

Oweniana: or, Select Passages from the Works of Owen. Arranged by A. Young. London, 1817, 12mo.

II.

TRANSLATIONS INTO FOREIGN LANGUAGES.

Le Cultivateur Anglois, ou œuvres choisies d'Agriculture, et d'économie rurale et politique, d'Arthur Young, traduit de l'anglois par CC. Lamarre, Benoist et Billecocq; avec des notes par le citoyen Delalauze. Avec des planches. 18 tom. Paris, 1800-1801, 8vo.

Voyage agronomique, precédé du parfait fermier, conténant l'état général de la culture anglaise, traduit par de Fréville. 2 vols. Paris, 1774, 8vo.

Arithmétique politique, adressée aux sociétés économiques établies en Europe, traduit par M. Fréville; 2 tom. La Haye, 1775, 8vo.

Recueil d'ouvrages d'économie politique et rurale, traduit de l'anglais. 2 vols. Paris, 1780, 8vo.

Le Guide du Fermier, ou Instructions pour élever, nourrir, acheter et vendre les bêtes à cornes, les brebis, &c. 2 parts. Paris, 1782, 12mo.

Filature, commerce et prix des laines en Angleterre, ou Correspondence sur ses matières. Paris, 1790, 8vo.

Voyage en France, pendant les années 1787-90; traduit de l'Anglais par F. S. Soulés, avec notes et observations par Cazeaux. 3 vols. Paris, 1793, 8vo.

—— Seconde édition. 3 vols. Paris, 1794, 8vo.

—— Nouvelle traduction par M. Lesage. 2 vols. Paris, 1860, 12mo.

L'Exemple de la France, avis aux Anglais et aux autres nations, &c. Bruxelles, 1793, 8vo.

Voyage en Italie, pendant les années 1787-90, traduit par F. Soulés. Paris [1796], 8vo.

Voyage en Italie et en Espagne pendant les années 1787 et 1789. Traduction de M. Lesage. Paris, 1860, 12mo.

Voyage en Irlande, traduit par Ch. Millon, avec des recherches sur l'Irlande par le traducteur. 2 vols. Paris, 1799, 8vo.

Essai sur la nature des engrais, traduit par M. M * * *.
Paris, 1808, 12mo.

Mémoires sur l'education, les maladies, l'engrais, et l'emploi du porc. Paris, 1823, 8vo.

—— Seconde édition, corrigée et augmentée, &c.
Paris, 1835, 8vo.

Annalen des Ackerbaues und die Künste; aus dem Englischen von Hahnemann, mit Anmerkungen von Riem.
3 Thle. Leipzig, 1790-1802, 8vo.

Politische Arithmetik; aus dem Englischen (von C. J. Kraus). Königsberg, 1779, 8vo.

Reisen durch England, in Absicht auf die Oekonomie, Mannfacturen, etc. 4 Thle. Leipzig, 1772-75, 8vo.

Reisen durch Frankreich und einen Theil von Italien in dem Jahren 1787 bis 1790. Aus dem Englischen von E. A. W. Zimmermann. 3 Bde. Berlin, 1793-95, 8vo.

Reise durch Irland; aus dem Englischen.
2 Bde. Leipzig, 1780-82, 8vo.

Ueber Grossbritanniens Staatswirthschaft, Polizei und Handlung; aus dem Englischen von F. A. Klockenbring.
Gotha, 1793, 8vo.

[According to the "Biographie Universelle," the three English Tours ("Six Weeks' Tour through the Southern Counties," "Six Months' Tour through the North of England," and "The Farmer's Tour through the East of England,") were translated into Russian by order of Catherine II. The "Six Weeks' Tour" was certainly so translated. See "Annals of Agriculture," vol. ii., p. 232.]

III.

APPENDIX.

BIOGRAPHY, CRITICISM, ETC.

Annuaire Necrologique. Mahul.
Paris, 1821, 8vo.
Arthur Young, pp. 384-390.

Baudrillart, Henri. Publicistes modernes. Paris, 1863, 8vo.
—— Second Edition, 1873.
Arthur Young et la France de 1789, pp. 22-63.

Biographie universelle, ancienne et moderne.
Paris, 1828, 8vo.
Arthur Young, tom. li., pp. 502-509.
Also the last edition, Paris and Leipzig. n. d.
Vol. xlv., pp. 273-277; article by Després.

Nouvelle biographie générale (Hoefer). Paris, 1866.
Vol. xlvi., pp. 902-905.

Biographie universelle et portative des Contemporains, &c.
Paris, 1834, 8vo.
Arthur Young, vol. iv., pp. 1615-1617.

Cartwright, John. The Commonwealth in Danger; with an introduction, containing remarks on some late Writings of Arthur Young. London, 1795, 8vo.

Day, Thomas. A Letter to Arthur Young, Esq., on the Bill now depending in Parliament to prevent the Exportation of Wool. London, 1788, 8vo.

Dictionnaire d'économie politique (Coquelin et Guillaumin).
Paris, 1873.
Arthur Young, vol. ii., p. 870.

Donaldson, John. Agricultural Biography; containing a notice of the Life and Writings of the British Authors on Agriculture, &c. London, 1854, 8vo.
Arthur Young, pp. 55-57.

Egremont, John. Observations on the Mildew, suggested by the Queries of Mr. Arthur Young. London, 1806, 8vo.

The Encyclopædia Britannica, Ninth Edition.
Edinburgh, 1888, 8vo.
Arthur Young, vol. xxiv., pp. 755-756.

[By J. K. Ingram. There is also a brief notice in the 8th edition.]

Knight, Charles. The English Cyclopædia.
London, 1857, 4to.
Arthur Young, vol. vi., pp. 878-884.

Pell, Albert. Arthur Young. Published for the Farmer's Club. London, 1882, 8vo.

Public Characters of 1801-1802. London, 1801, 8vo.
Arthur Young, pp. 559-594.

Sinclair, Sir John. The Correspondence of Sir John Sinclair, Bart. 2 vols. London, 1831, 8vo.
Arthur Young, vol i., pp. 406-408.

Somerville, J., *Lord*. A Letter to . . . Lord Somerville . . . with a review of the pamphlet of Arthur Young and William Brooke upon the present high price of provisions.
London, 1800, 8vo.

Stuart, Daniel. Peace and Reform against War and Corruption. In answer to a pamphlet, by Arthur Young, entitled "The Example of France, a warning to Britain." By D. Stuart.
London, 1794, 8vo.

Upcott, William. A Biographical Dictionary of the Living Authors of Great Britain and Ireland, &c. London, 1816, 8vo.
Arthur Young, pp. 403-405.

Wakefield, Edward. An Account of Ireland. 2 vols.
London, 1812, 4to.
Arthur Young, vol. i., p. viii., &c.

Wright, Rev. T. The Formation and Management of Floated Meadows; with corrections of Errors found in the treatises of Messrs. Davis, Marshall, Boswell, Young, and Smith.
Northampton, 1808, 8vo.

[There is a notice of Arthur Young in vol. xci., pp. 106-111 of Davy's Suffolk Collections, in the MS. Dept. British Museum.]

A. Y. gives some autobiographical notes in his Annals of Agriculture:—

Vol. iii., 1785, pp. 56-58 and 481 [unimportant].
Vol. xiii., 1790, pp. 154-158 [on his return from France].
Vol. xv., 1791, pp. 152-182 [interesting and important].
Vol. xxix., 1797, pp. 167 and 473-490 [on the Irish corn bounty, and on the official translation of A. Y.'s works into French].

[For a full list of A. Y.'s contributions to the "Annals of Agriculture," see below.]

MAGAZINE ARTICLES.

Young, Arthur.—

—— Account of. European Magazine (with a portrait), vol. xxviii., 1795, pp. 363-365; also vol. lxxvii., 1820, giving details about his death.

—— Agriculture of the County of Essex. Monthly Review, vol. lv., 1808, pp. 153-161.

—— Agriculture of Hertfordshire. Monthly Review, vol. xlv., 1804, pp. 151-157.

—— Agriculture of the County of Lincoln. Monthly Review, vol. xxx., 1799, pp. 55-60, vol. xxxiv., 1801, pp. 367-374.

—— Agriculture of the County of Suffolk. Monthly Review, vol. xxviii., 1799, pp. 69-79.

—— Agriculture of the County of Sussex. Monthly Review, vol. lx., 1809, pp. 137-147.

—— Annals of Agriculture. Monthly Review, vol. lxxvi., 1787, pp. 39-42.

—— Biography of. The Annual Biography and Obituary for the year 1821. London, 1821, 8vo. Arthur Young, vol. v., pp. 121-137.

—— Example of France to Britain. Critical Review, vol. vii., 1793, pp. 277-282.

—— Farmer's Calendar. Monthly Review, vol. xlviii., 1805, pp. 283-286.

—— Inquiry into Waste Lands. Monthly Review, vol. xxxix., 1802, pp. 415-420.

—— Memoir of. Quarterly Journal of Science, by J. A. Paris, vol. ix., 1820, pp. 279-309; same article in German in Zeitgenossen, Bd. vi., 1821.—Congregational Magazine, vol. iii., 1820, pp. 465-471.—Gentleman's Magazine, vol. xc. pt. 1, 1820, pp. 469-470.

—— Political Arithmetic. Monthly Review, vol. li., 1774. pp. 470-473.

—— Present State of France. Monthly Review, vol. xvi., 1795, pp. 287-295.

—— Les Réformateurs agricoles du xviiie siècle en Angleterre. Revue britannique (from the "Quarterly Journal of Agriculture"), 1839, pp. 57-79.

—— Tour in Ireland. Monthly Review, vol. lxiii., 1780, pp. 38-45, 97-104, 161-171.

—— Travels in France. Monthly Review, vol. x., 1793, pp. 1-13, 152-168, 279-290; vol. xviii., 1795, pp. 203-212.—Critical Review, vol. xviii., 1796, pp. 264-273.

—— Works of. Quarterly Journal of Agriculture, by C. W. Johnson, vol. xiii., 1842, pp. 129-152.

IV.

CHRONOLOGICAL LIST OF WORKS.

The Theatre of the Present War in North America. 1758.

Reflections on the Present State of Affairs at Home and Abroad. 1759.

The Farmer's Letters to the People of England. 1767.

Six Weeks' Tour through the Southern Counties of England and Wales. 1768.

Letters Concerning the Present State of the French Nation, &c. 1769.

Essay on the Management of Hogs. 1769.

The Expediency of a Free Exportation of Corn at this time. 1769.

Six Month's Tour through the North of England. 1770.

The Farmer's Guide in Hiring and Stocking Farms. 1770.

Rural Œconomy. 1770.

Course of Experimental Agriculture. 1770.

Farmer's Tour through the East of England. 1771.

The Farmer's Calendar. 1771.

Proposals to the Legislature for Numbering the People. 1771.

Political Essays concerning the Present State of the British Empire. 1772.

Observations on the Present State of the Waste Lands of Great Britain. 1773.

Political Arithmetic. 1774.

Political Arithmetic, part ii. 1779.

Tour in Ireland. 1780.

Annals of Agriculture. 1784-1815.

The Question of Wool truly stated. 1788.

Travels in France during the years 1787, 1788, and 1789. 1792.

The Example of France a Warning to Britain. 1793.

General View of the Agriculture of the County of Sussex. 1793.

General View of the Agriculture of the County of Suffolk. 1794

The Constitution Safe without Reform. 1795

An Idea of the Present State of France. 1795

National Danger and the Means of Safety. 1797

Enquiry into the State of the Public Mind amongst the Lowe[r] Classes. 1798

General View of the Agriculture of the County of Lincoln. 1799

The Question of Scarcity plainly stated. 1800

Inquiry into the propriety of applying Wastes to the bette[r] maintenance and support of the Poor. 1801

Essay on Manures. 1804

General View of the Agriculture of Hertfordshire. 1804

General View of the Agriculture of Norfolk. 1804

General View of the Agriculture of the County of Essex. 1807

General Report on Inclosures. 1807

On the Advantages which have resulted from the Establish ment of the Board of Agriculture. 1809

View of the Agriculture of Oxfordshire. 1809

On the Husbandry of the three celebrated Farmers, Bakewell Arbuthnot, and Ducket. 1811

Inquiry into the Progressive Value of Money. 1812

Inquiry into the Rise of Prices in Europe. 1815

Baxteriana. 1815

Oweniana. 1817

V.

ARTHUR YOUNG'S CONTRIBUTIONS TO THE "ANNALS OF AGRICULTURE."

Vol. I., 1784.

An enquiry into the situation of the kingdom on the conclusion to the late treaty, and into the surest means of adding to the national resources by a proper application of the arts of peace, 9-87.
A *coup d'œil* on the present state of the nation, 119-126.
Experiments to ascertain how far and in what form phlogiston is the food of plants, 139-189.
On the price of land at present in England, 203-206.
Advertisement in Italian, French, and Latin for the coöperation of Italian, French, and German writers on agriculture, between pp. 220 and 221.
Experiments on the food of plants, 254-272.
Experiments on fattening hogs, 333-353.
Review of vols. iii.-vi. of Robert Wight's "Present State of Husbandry in Scotland," 357-369.
Review of Lord Sheffield's "Commerce of the American States," 369-388.
Considerations on the connection between the agriculture of England and the commercial policy of her Sugar-islands, particularly respecting a free trade with N. America, 437-447.
Review of M. d'Auberton's "Instruction pour les Bergers," 447-461.
Appeal for more subscribers to the Annals, 461-467.

Vol. II., 1784.

Observations on the petition for an Act to restrain the export of rabbit's-wool, 12-17.
Experiments on manures, 17-32.
A Fortnight's Tour in Kent and Essex, 33-104.
A Five Days' Tour to Woodbridge, &c., 105-168.

Observations on the means of promoting Russian husbandry; a Memoir inscribed to the Free Œconomical Society of Petersburg, 238-253.
Observations on the window-tax as a commutation for the duty on tea, 301-313.
An observation on the brick and tile tax, 314-315.
Reviews of new publications relating to agriculture, 316-342.
A minute of the husbandry at Helkham of Thomas Wm. Coke, Esq., 353-383.
The course of exchange and the price of bullion, 402-412.
On the pleasures of agriculture, 456-487.

VOL. III., 1785.

On housing cows, 58-62.
Experiments on manures, 63-81.
Continuation of the experiments on the food of plants, 103-127.
On emigrations to America for practising agriculture with advantage, 169-182.
On anonymous correspondence, 223-230.
Price of provisions at Paris in January, 1785, 253-255.
Observations on the commercial arrangement with Ireland, 257-291.
Review of Lord Sheffield's "Observations on the Manufactures, Trade, and Present State of Ireland, 336-342.
Observations on the late Count Bentinck's proposed embankment against the sea, 353-359.
Comparative state of the iron manufactory in England and Ireland, 388-411.
Observations on the Earl of Dundonald's scheme for transferring the tax on salt to hearths, 399-411.
Review of Dr. Tucker's "Reflections on the Present Matters in Dispute between England and Ireland," 417-421.
On the growth of trees, 429-432.
Thoughts on establishing a Chamber of Manufacturers, 452-455.
Considerations on the means of ascertaining the prices of corn for the regulation of export and import, 456-468.
Queries concerning phlogiston as the food of animals, 476-481.
Review of Necker's "Administration des finances de la France," 504-525.

VOL. IV., 1785.

How far a new arrangement of trade between Great Britain and France may affect the agriculture of either kingdom, 16-28.
Review of the 3rd vol. of Necker's "Administration des finances de la France," 53-56.
French Edict in consequence of the scarcity in France, with observations, 63-71.
On the French Edict prohibiting British manufactures, 116-120.

On the expences of keeping horses, 124-132.
On a sort of wheat called "velvit," 132-135.
Queries on sowing wheat, 135-137.
A Tour to Shropshire, 138-190.
Publishing account of Vols. I., II., and III. of the "Annals of Agriculture," 249-252.
Price of bullion, 286-287.
Memoirs of corn for the last fourteen years, 361-410.
An idea of an experimental farm, 455-466.
Review of French official publications on agriculture, 522-527.

VOL. V., 1786.

On the conduct of experiments in agriculture, 17-46.
Minutes in rural œconomy taken at Rainham, the seat of the Lord Viscount Townshend, in Jan., 1785; 119-137.
State of the manufactures at Lyons and Carcassonne, 150-155.
Influence of liberty on the prosperity of nations, in reply to M. de Lazowski, 164-180.
Minutes relating to the dairy farms of High Suffolk, taken at Aspal, the seat of the Rev. Mr. Chevallier, in Jan., 1786; 193-224.
Review of French official publications on agriculture and of French pamphlets printed in London; 299-306.
Review of Senebier's "Recherches sur l'influence de la lumière," &c.; 306-317.
Resources of the kingdom.—Inclosure of the Royal Forests; 386-410.
Observations on spinning, 419-422.
Farming news from abroad, 430-432.
Review of the Memoirs of the Literary and Philosophical Society of Manchester, 478-485.
Review of J. Howlett's "Essay on the Population of Ireland," 485-486.
Review of J. Howlett's "Enquiry upon the Influence of Enclosures," 486-489.
Review of French publications on agriculture, 489-496.
Review of James Anderson's "Present State of the Hebrides," 496-509.
Experiments on the food of plants, 1785; 515-535.

VOL. VI., 1786.

A Tour to the West of England, 116-151.
Farming news, Bohemia, France, Germany, and England, 169-173.
Additional notes to the Tour in Suffolk, 217-230.
On the air expelled from the earth, &c.; 265-323.

Abstract of an Act appointing Commissioners to enquire into the Crown Lands, with observations; 396-405.
Experiments on the food of plants, 1786; 442-452.
A ten day's Tour to Mr. Bakewell's, 452-502.
Observations on the Bill for restraining the growers, &c., of wool, 506-528.

VOL. VII., 1786.

Observations on the Duke of Grafton's sheep-farming, 16-20.
On the price of provisions, 42-58.
On the Wool Bill, 94-96 and 134-175.
Review of Dr. Hunter's edition of Evelyn's "Silva and Terra," 192-199.
Experiment on the culture of beans, 204-210.
Experiments on expelling air from soils, 217-248.
On the commercial treaty with France, 265-276.
On the Wool Bill, 288-291.
Review of Marshall's "Rural Œconomy of Norfolk," 342-354.
Review of a "Commercio-Political Essay on the balance of foreign trade," 354-362.
Review of Baron Reisbeck's "Travels through Germany," 362-368.
Review of "Observations on the Corn Bill," 368-378.
To anonymous correspondents, 380-381.
The philosophical system of the anti-phlogistonites, 397-404.
Reply to the Manufacturer's defence of the Wool Bill, 405-428.
Of the population of different periods, 429-457.
Review of "Collection des Memoires presentés à l'Assemblée des Notables," 469-473.
Sale of Crown lands, 478-480.
Review of Gilbert's "Considerations on the Bills for the better Relief of the Poor," 480-482.
On the necessity of avoiding all public regulations relative to the size of farms, 510-526.
Review of M. Herrenschwand's works on "Political Economy," 530-556.
A journey to Dover (*en route* for France), 561-574.

VOL. VIII., 1787.

Experiments on expelling air from calcareous earths, 14-28.
A Tour in Wales (in 1776 and 1778), 31-88.
Some particulars relative to the late John Whyn Baker, Esq.; 125-133.
On the chemical analysis of soils, translated from the Italian of Fabbroni; 173-181.
Tour in Catalonia, 193-275. (Reprinted in an abridged form in the "Travels in France.")

A *coup d'œil* on the present situation of Europe, 276-284.
On a method of fattening oxen in Limosin, in France, 325-332.
Farming news; Italy, France, and Lorraine; 343-345.
Review of French publications on agriculture, 351-370.
Experiment on the smut in wheat, 409-413.
Account of the net produce of all the taxes, with observations; 414-427.
Review of the Rev. J. Howlett "On Enclosures," 427-439.
Reviews of two pamphlets on the laws relating to the woollen manufactory, 439-467 [misprinted].
On the export of wool and the bill now in Parliament, 467-490.

VOL. IX., 1788.

Review of the "Mémoires d'Agriculture de la Société Royal d'Agriculture de Paris," 1786; 32-40.
Act for encouraging the growth of hemp and flax, with observations; 73-81.
On the abolition of slavery in the West Indies, 88-96.
Experiment on the comparison of different preparations for barley, 129-164.
Review of the Chevalier Lamerville's "Observations pratiques sur les bêtes à laine," 174-178.
Notice of pamphlets concerning the poor, 178-179.
On the profit of a farm, 235-244.
Effect of the monopoly of rabbit-wool, 244-247.
Review of "Whilst we live let us live," 248-252.
On the prices of wool and state of spinning at present in England, 266-376.
Review of John Hustler's "Observations on the Wool Bill," 458-465.
Bounty on the growth of hemp and flax, 473-477.
Experiments on manures for potatoes, 651-654.
On the Hay Bill, 655-657.
To the wool-growers of Great Britain, 657.

VOL. X., 1788.

The Wool Act, 1-126, 139-185, 521-524, 545-559, and 577-589.
A day at Mr. Ducket's, 186-198.
Royal Society of Agriculture at Paris, 214-216.
Note concerning succory, 216-217.
Experiment on the smut in wheat, 231-232.
On the police of wool and the neglect of the farming interest in this country, 235-282.
West Indian agriculture, 335-362.
Observations on Mr. Moses Grant's "Letter on Tithes," 399-402.
On the necessity of County Associations of the landed interest, 402-418.

Review of M. de Fresne's "Traité d'Agriculture," 517-519.
Sheep controversy between Messieurs Chaplin and Bakewell, 560-579.
Conclusion of the first ten volumes of this work, 589-594.

VOL. XI., 1789.

Review of Adam Dickson's "Husbandry of the Ancients," 66-74.
Russian farming news, 143-145.
Extracts (with notes) from the Count de Mirabeau's "De la monarchie prussienne," 146-169.
A Tour in Sussex, 170-304.
Communications relating to the late severe frost, 321-342 and 617-662.
Observations on wool, 371-373.
Review of Sir John Dalrymple "On the Foreign Policy of England," 373-376.
Review of the Rev. T. Wright "On Watering Meadows," 376-377.
Review of Dr. Priestley's "Lectures on History and General Policy," 377-380.
On the Hessian fly, 386-390 and 406-613.

VOL. XII., 1789.

Course of the exchange for the year 1788, 38-39.
Some minutes taken at Houghton, the seat of the Earl of Oxford; 40-52.
Further extracts (with notes) from the Count de Mirabeau's "De la monarchie prussienne," 111-132, and 465-477, 280-303.
On the winter and spring provision for sheep and cattle, 221-238.
Remarks on Mr. Morley's tare and buckwheat husbandry, 303-309.
Experiments on expelling air from soils, 392-413.

VOL. XIII., 1790.

Observations on the prohibition of the export of corn, 152-154, 163-182.
The Editor's return to England, 154-163.
Circular Letter on the Corn Laws, 185-187.
On the Corn Bill, 456-460.

VOL. XIV., 1790.

Observations on the present season, July, 1790; 64-74.
Review of intelligence on corn, 75-79.
Experiments in weighing fatting cattle alive, 140-163.
On the effect of electricity upon plants, 221-226.
Observations on a project for the cultivation of commonable lands, 312-314.
Circular letter on sheep, wool, and corn; 405-407.

VOL. XV., 1791.

Memoirs of the last thirty years of the Editor's farming life, with notes, 152-197.
Experiment in the introduction of South Down sheep into Suffolk, 286-334.
Average prices of corn, 1787 and 1788, with observations, 372-378.
Review of Lord Sheffield's "Observations on the Corn Bill," 386-394.
An account of experiments with chickory, 395-400.
A few notes taken in Sussex, 427-434.
Review of Townsend's "Journey through Spain in 1786 and 1787," 459-481.
English settlements in the Crimea, 547-552.

VOL. XVI., 1791.

Miscellaneous notes, minuted at Houghton in April, 1791, 41-48.
Account of grazing twelve bullocks, 1790-91, 64-80.
On the taxes paid by landed property in England, 108-112.
On the present season, 1791, 121-123.
Plan for a barn, and the buildings necessary for cattle, 149-155.
Upon the irrigation in Cambridgeshire made by Pallavicino, 177-182.
Observations on tythes, 278-283.
Observations on Russian agriculture, 331.
Miscellaneous notes, 351-365.
Experiment on dibbling barley, 382-384.
Enquiry how far the common practice of a country is to be considered experimental, 412-420.
Notes on the cultivation and advance of value of burnt fen in the county of Suffolk, 462-476.
A Month's Tour to Northamptonshire, Leicestershire, &c., 480-607.

VOL. XVII., 1792.

Gleanings in an excursion to Lewes Fair, 1791, 127-178.
Circular on a proposed premium for ascertaining the merits of the different breeds of sheep, 209-212.
Sheep, *Table raisonné* of the contents of Vols. I.-XVII. of the Annals concerning, 602-627.

VOL. XVIII., 1792.

Some experiments in a winter's support of cattle and sheep, 84-124.
Notes on a report of the Committee of Twelve in the French National Assembly, 144-147.
The Farmer's cart, 178-192.
A few notes on an excursion to Bedfordshire, 220-228.

Review of "Wool encouraged without Exportation," by "A Wiltshire Clothier," 321-330.
A week in Essex, 391-444.
French events applicable to British agriculture, 486-495, and 582-596.

Vol. XIX., 1793.

French events applicable to British agriculture, 36-51.
Experiment of meadow land, 211-216.
On the variety of teams used in different countries, 419-422.
A week in Norfolk, 441-499.

Vol. XX., 1793.

Circular letter on the spinning of wool, 178, 179.
Experiments on chickory, 188-203.
Plan for establishing a Board of Agriculture, 204-213.
State of Ireland in 1748 and 1792 compared, 215.
Some farming notes in Essex, Kent, and Sussex, 220-297, and 499-512.
Experiments in laying down arable land to grass, 512-529.
General index to Vols. I.-XX. of the Annals.

Vol. XXI., 1793.

Experiments on the foot-rot in sheep, 58-69.
Agriculture as capable of being made a pursuit for the education of children, &c., 229-279.
Arrangement of the Agricultural Surveys, 346-354.
Writers on Husbandry, 450-465, and 574-601.
Experiments on chicory and the summer support of sheep, 601-620. Also, Vol. xxiv., 23-29, and Vol. xxvi., 489-494.

Vol. XXII., 1794.

Of the drill husbandry before the late improvements, 72-90.
A Tour through Sussex, 1793, by the Rev. Arthur Young, 171-334, and 494-631.

Vol. XXIII., 1795.

A fortnight's Tour in East Suffolk, 18-52.
On some watered meadows in Hampshire, 264-268.
An idea of the present agricultural state of France, &c., 274-311.
Of the rent of land, 336-340.
On planting, 393-403.
On keeping grass a year before feeding, 406-410.
Some notes at Riddlesworth, 437-444.
Experiment on some courses of crops, 471-507.

Vol. XXIV., 1795.

Estimate of Waste Lands in Great Britain, with sketch of an Act for a General Enclosure of Commons, 10-17.

Circular on the scarcity of provisions, 42, 43.
Consequences of rioting on account of the high price of provisions, 536-545.
Substitutes for wheat flour, 576-578.

VOL. XXV., 1796.

Queries concerning the food of horses, 25, 26.
The Constitution Safe without Reform, 246-293.
Tax of Corn in kind levied in France, 294-297.
Political remarks on the high price of corn, 449-472.
A good method of assisting the poor, 530, 531.
Rice bread, 535-537.

VOL. XXVI., 1796.

Sermon on the scarcity of corn, 197-208.
A farmer's letter to the yeomanry of Suffolk, 516-521.

VOL. XXVII., 1796.

A farmer's letter to the yeomanry of England, 49-54.
Excursion to Yorkshire, 287-312.
Experiments on some grasses, 372-407.
Serradilla, a Portuguese grass, 503-510.
A farmer's second letter to the yeomanry of England, 528-538.
Song by "a Suffolk Yeoman"—"Hear ye not the din from far?" 539.
Notes on the experimental husbandry of Mr. Parkinson, of Doncaster, 555-557, and 561-564.

VOL. XXVIII., 1797.

A farming Tour in the south and west of England, 61-109, 113-129, 225-240, 353-379, 460-483, 620-640.
A farmer's third letter to the yeomanry of Britain, 177-187.
Experiments upon the winter and summer support of sheep, 258-268.
Queries on horses, 405-407.
A word in season (Letter iv.) at a critical moment, to landlords, yeomen, and farmers, 426-443.

VOL. XXIX., 1797.

Potatoes, 38-62.
A farming Tour in the south and West of England, 89-98, 195-208, 309-318, 427-439, 557-587.
Note on the repeal of the bounty on the inland carriage of corn in Ireland, 167, 168.
Some notes on the Earl of Exeter's husbandry, 379-385.
French translation of the Editor's works, 473-482.
Petworth Prize Meeting, Nov. 20, 1797, 505-520.
Mr. Bentham's pauper tables, 556-557.

VOL. XXX., 1798.

A farming Tour in the south and west of England, 72-88, 185-201, 299-319, 330-357.

On certain principles of taxation, 177-184.

General index to Vols. i.-xxx.

VOL. XXXI., 1798.

A farming Tour in the south and west of England, 79-94.

Holderness, Beverley, Hull, some notes in 1797, 118-164.

Some notes at Newark, 201-203.

Experiments on the winter and summer support of sheep, 204-224.

Notes on inclosures, 529-554.

VOL. XXXII., 1799.

Queries relating to tithes, &c., 275-278.

Some notes on the Earl of Winchilsea's husbandry, 351-382.

On the conduct of Workhouses, 382-388.

VOL. XXXIII., 1799.

On waste lands, 12-59.

Experiments on the winter and summer support of sheep, 180-190.

Warping in Lincolnshire, 383-399.

Remarks on the late severe winter and backward spring, 400-404.

Circular stack and threshing yard, 488-498.

On the price of corn and the situation of the poor in the ensuing winter, 621-629.

VOL. XXXIV., 1800.

Experiments in planting, 54-68.

Price of provisions and state of the poor, 100-107.

On the state of the poor, 186-192.

Experiments on the winter and summer support of sheep, 414-425.

VOL. XXXV., 1800.

Note on the examination of the woollen manufacturers before the House of Commons on occasion of the Union with Ireland, 473-474.

Observations on the price of corn in September, 1800, 569-582.

VOL. XXXVI., 1801.

Circular letter on the state of the poor, 113, 114.

Observations on the King's Proclamation concerning the present scarcity, 196-198.

General Enclosure, 210-214.
Inquiry into the propriety of applying wastes to the maintenance of the poor, 497-547.

Vol. XXXVII., 1801.

Experiments on the winter and summer support of sheep, 273-276.
Sermon to a country congregation, 614-633.

Vol. XXXVIII., 1802.

Experiment in making hay, 1, 2.
On premiums offered by Agricultural Societies, 322-324.

Vol. XXXIX., 1803.

A day at Buxhall, 73-83.
A year's observations on hogs, 371-382.
The husbandry of His Grace the late Duke of Bedford, 385-458.
Doubts concerning the season of making farm-yard manure, 602-606.

Vol. XL., 1803.

Reflections on the political economy that ought to be pursued in peace, 79-92.
Experiment in manuring the soil of Bagshot Heath, 97-104.
On Sainfoin, 142-150.
Lucerne and Guinea grass in Bengal, 164-166.
On some circumstances to be attended to in the establishment of a new colony, 437-440.
General index to vols. xxxi.-xl.

Vol. XLI., 1804.

Circular letter to Agricultural Societies, 25-27.
On the new Malt Tax, 39-52.
Of the English Poor-laws, 52-71.
Experiments on some courses of crops, 97-158.
A day at Ardleigh, 497-505.

Vol. XLII., 1804.

Useful horse-shoe, 84.
Idea of a cottage, cheap to build and warm to inhabit, 284-286.
On the effects of the modern agricultural system, 299-318.
Mole-plough drawn by the force of women applied mechanically, 413-422.
Parliamentary enclosures in the county of Cambridge, 471-502. Also vol. xliii. 42-59 and 111-118.
Some notes at Cricklade, 517-526.

Vol. XLIII., 1805.

Price of corn, land, and labour, 35-42.

Notes on a fallowed farm, 101-110.
New information on paring and burning, 133-152, 198-231, 300-321, and 539-573.
On the crop of 1804, 244-253.
Experiments on manures, 433-455. Also vol. xliv. 344-359, and vol. xlv. 105-109, and 330-339.
A farmery, 473-478.

VOL. XLIV., 1806.

Minutes on enclosures, 39-62, 174-201, 288-307, and 426-432.
A day at Noddishall, 257-272.
An ass-car, 366.
The example of Europe a warning to Britain, 386-410.
Monument to the memory of Luther, 506.

VOL. XLV., 1808.

By what rule ought tithes to be rated? 193-208.
The abolition of the slave trade, 211, 212.
The fen paring-plough, 230-231.
The Isle of Thanet shim, 240-241.
Account of a flock of Southdown sheep, 298-316.
On hemp, 321-330.
Circular on stopping the malt-distillery, 513-515.
Evidence before the House of Commons' Committee on the grand distillery question, 573-604.
Plain facts on the grand distillery question, 605-608.

VOL. XLVI., 1809.

On chalk as manure, 62.

⁂ The publication of the Annals was discontinued after page 64 of this number (270). But the following tracts, published in 1812 and 1815 respectively, and paged continuously, were marked as Nos. 270 and 271 of vol. xlvi. :—

An enquiry into the progressive value of money in England, pp. viii. and 137.
An enquiry into the rise of prices in Europe during the last twenty-five years, 141-219.
List of publications for and against the Corn Bill, 1814-15, 220.

INDEX.

Subjects have been as far as possible, classified under the following general headings, *e.g.* :—

Labouring Poor—Land—Landlord and Tenant—Manufacture—Religion—Revenue and Taxes.

THE END.

CHISWICK PRESS:—C. WHITTINGHAM AND CO., TOOKS COURT, CHANCERY LANE.

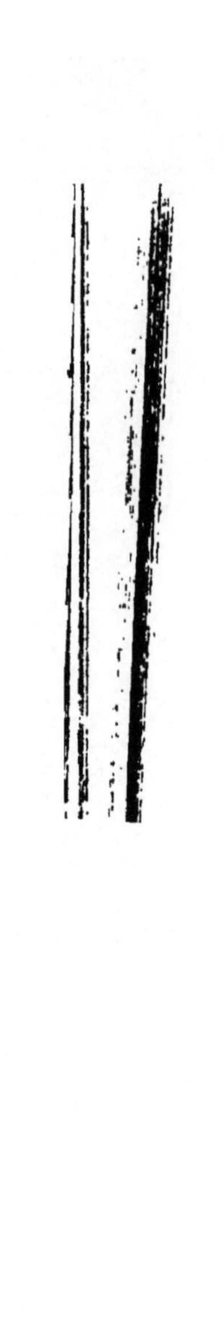

CATALOGUE OF

BOHN'S LIBRARIES.

740 *Volumes,* £158 14*s.*

The Publishers are now issuing the Libraries in a NEW AND MORE ATTRACTIVE STYLE OF BINDING. The original bindings endeared to many book-lovers by association will still be kept in stock, but henceforth all orders will be executed in the New binding, unless the contrary is expressly stated.

New Volumes of Standard Works in the various branches of Literature are constantly being added to this Series, which is already unsurpassed in respect to the number, variety, and cheapness of the Works contained in it. The Publishers beg to announce the following Volumes as recently issued or now in preparation:—

Goethe's Faust. Part I. The Original Text, with Hayward's Translation and Notes, carefully revised, with an Introduction and Bibliography, by C. A. Buchheim, Ph.D., Professor of German Language and Literature at King's College, London. [*Immediately.*

Arthur Young's Tour in Ireland. Edited by A. W. Hutton, Librarian, National Liberal Club. 2 vols. [*Preparing.*

Euripides. A New Literal Translation in Prose. y E. P. Coleridge. 2 vols. 5*s.* each.

Vol. I.—Rhesus—Medea—Hippolytus—Alcestis—Heraclidæ—Supplices—Troades—Ion—Helena.

II.—Andromache—Electra—Bacchae—Hecuba—Hercules Furens—Phœnissæ—Orestes—Iphigenia in Tauris—Iphigenia in Aulis—Cyclops. [*See p.* 15.

Voltaire's Tales. Translated by R. B. Boswell. Vol. I. 3*s.* 6*d.* [*See p.* 8.

Count Grammont's Memoirs of the Court of Charles II. With the Boscobel Tracts, &c. New Edition. 5*s.* [*See p.* 9.

Gray's Letters. New Edition. Edited by the Rev. D. C. Tovey, M.A. [*In the press.*

Schools and Masters of Fence. By C. Egerton Castle. New Edition. With numerous Illustrations. [*In the press.*

Montaigne's Essays. Cotton's Translation, revised by W. C. Hazlitt. New Edition. 3 Vols. [*In the press.*

Hartley Coleridge's Essays and Marginalia. Edited by the Lord Chief Justice. [*Preparing.*

Hoffmann's Works. Translated by Lieut.-Colonel Ewing. Vol. II. [*In the press.*

Bohn's Handbooks of Games. New enlarged edition. In 2 vols. *See p.* 21.

Vol. I.—Table Games, by Major-General Drayson, R.A., R. F. Green, and 'Berkeley.'
II.—Card Games, by Dr. W. Pole, F.R.S., R. F. Green, 'Berkeley, and Baxter-Wray.

Bohn's Handbooks of Athletic Sports. 8 Vols. [*See p.* 21.

For BOHN'S SELECT LIBRARY, see p. 23.

CELLINI (Benvenuto). Memoirs of, by himself. With Notes of G. P. Carpani. Trans. by T. Roscoe. Portrait.

CERVANTES' Galatea. A Pastoral Romance. Trans. by G. W. J. Gyll.

— **Exemplary Novels.** Trans. by W. K. Kelly.

— **Don Quixote de la Mancha.** Motteux's Translation revised. With Lockhart's Life and Notes. 2 vols.

CHAUCER'S Poetical Works. With Poems formerly attributed to him. With a Memoir, Introduction, Notes, and a Glossary, by R. Bell. Improved edition, with Preliminary Essay by Rev. W. W. Skeat, M.A. Portrait. 4 vols.

CLASSIC TALES, containing Rasselas, Vicar of Wakefield, Gulliver's Travels, and The Sentimental Journey.

COLERIDGE'S (S. T.) Friend. A Series of Essays on Morals, Politics, and Religion. Portrait.

— **Aids to Reflection. Confessions** of an Inquiring Spirit; and Essays on Faith and the Common Prayer-book. New Edition, revised.

— **Table-Talk and Omniana.** By T. Ashe, B.A.

— **Lectures on Shakespeare and** other Poets. Edit. by T. Ashe, B.A.

Containing the lectures taken down in 1811-12 by J. P. Collier, and those delivered at Bristol in 1813.

— **Biographia Literaria; or, Biographical** Sketches of my Literary Life and Opinions; with Two Lay Sermons.

— **Miscellanies, Æsthetic and** Literary; to which is added, THE THEORY OF LIFE. Collected and arranged by T. Ashe, B.A.

COMMINES.—*See Philip.*

CONDÉ'S History of the Dominion of the Arabs in Spain. Trans. by Mrs. Foster. Portrait of Abderahmen ben Moavia. 3 vols.

COWPER'S Complete Works, Poems, Correspondence, and Translations. Edit. with Memoir by R. Southey. 45 Engravings. 8 vols.

COXE'S Memoirs of the Duke of Marlborough. With his original Correspondence, from family records at Blenheim. Revised edition. Portraits. 3 vols.

*** An Atlas of the plans of Marlborough's campaigns, 4to. 10s. 6d.

COXE'S History of the House of Austria. From the Foundation of the Monarchy by Rhodolph of Hapsburgh to the Death of Leopold II., 1218-1792. By Archdn. Coxe. With Continuation from the Accession of Francis I. to the Revolution of 1848. 4 Portraits. 4 vols.

CUNNINGHAM'S Lives of the most Eminent British Painters. With Notes and 16 fresh Lives by Mrs. Heaton. 3 vols.

DEFOE'S Novels and Miscellaneous Works. With Prefaces and Notes, including those attributed to Sir W. Scott. Portrait. 7 vols.

DE LOLME'S Constitution of England, in which it is compared both with the Republican form of Government and the other Monarchies of Europe. Edit., with Life and Notes, by J. Macgregor.

DUNLOP'S History of Fiction. New Edition, revised. By Henry Wilson. 2 vols., 5s. each.

EDGEWORTH'S Stories for Children. With 8 Illustrations by L. Speed.

ELZE'S Shakespeare.—*See Shakespeare.*

EMERSON'S Works. 3 vols.

Vol. I.—Essays, Lectures, and Poems.

Vol. II.—English Traits, Nature, and Conduct of Life.

Vol. III.—Society and Solitude—Letters and Social Aims—Miscellaneous Papers (hitherto uncollected)—May-Day, &c.

FOSTER'S (John) Life and Correspondence. Edit. by J. E. Ryland. Portrait. 2 vols.

— **Lectures at Broadmead Chapel.** Edit. by J. E. Ryland. 2 vols.

— **Critical Essays contributed to** the 'Eclectic Review.' Edit. by J. E. Ryland. 2 vols.

— **Essays: On Decision of Character;** on a Man's writing Memoirs of Himself; on the epithet Romantic; on the aversion of Men of Taste to Evangelical Religion.

— **Essays on the Evils of Popular** Ignorance, and a Discourse on the Propagation of Christianity in India.

— **Essay on the Improvement of** Time, with Notes of Sermons and other Pieces.

— **Fosteriana:** selected from periodical papers, edit. by H. G. Bohn.

FOX (Rt. Hon. C. J.)—*See Carrel.*

GIBBON'S Decline and Fall of the Roman Empire. Complete and unabridged, with variorum Notes; including those of Guizot, Wenck, Niebuhr, Hugo, Neander, and others. 7 vols. 2 Maps and Portrait.

GOETHE'S Works. Trans. into English by E. A. Bowring, C.B., Anna Swanwick, Sir Walter Scott, &c. &c. 14 vols.

Vols. I. and II.—Autobiography and Annals. Portrait.

Vol. III.—Faust. Complete.

Vol. IV.—Novels and Tales; containing Elective Affinities, Sorrows of Werther, The German Emigrants, The Good Women, and a Nouvelette.

Vol. V.—Wilhelm Meister's Apprenticeship.

Vol. VI.—Conversations with Eckerman and Soret.

Vol. VII.—Poems and Ballads in the original Metres, including Hermann and Dorothea.

Vol. VIII.—Goetzvon Berlichingen, Torquato Tasso, Egmont, Iphigenia, Clavigo, Wayward Lover, and Fellow Culprits.

Vol. IX.—Wilhelm Meister's Travels. Complete Edition.

Vol. X.—Tour in Italy. Two Parts. And Second Residence in Rome.

Vol. XI.—Miscellaneous Travels, Letters from Switzerland, Campaign in France, Siege of Mainz, and Rhine Tour.

Vol. XII.—Early and Miscellaneous Letters, including Letters to his Mother, with Biography and Notes.

Vol. XIII.—Correspondence with Zelter.

Vol. XIV.—Reineke Fox, West-Eastern Divan and Achilleid. Translated in original metres by A. Rogers.

—— Correspondence with Schiller. 2 vols.—*See Schiller.*

—— Faust.—*See Collegiate Series.*

GOLDSMITH'S Works. 5 vols.

Vol. I.—Life, Vicar of Wakefield, Essays, and Letters.

Vol. II.—Poems, Plays, Bee, Cock Lane Ghost.

Vol. III.—The Citizen of the World, Polite Learning in Europe.

Vol. IV.—Biographies, Criticisms, Later Essays.

Vol. V.—Prefaces, Natural History, Letters, Goody Two-Shoes, Index.

GREENE, MARLOWE, and BEN JONSON (Poems of). With Notes and Memoirs by R. Bell.

GREGORY'S (Dr.) The Evidences, Doctrines, and Duties of the Christian Religion.

GRIMM'S Household Tales. With the Original Notes. Trans. by Mrs. A. Hunt. Introduction by Andrew Lang, M.A. 2 vols.

GUIZOT'S History of Representative Government in Europe. Trans. by A. R. Scoble.

—— English Revolution of 1640. From the Accession of Charles I. to his Death. Trans. by W. Hazlitt. Portrait.

—— History of Civilisation. From the Roman Empire to the French Revolution. Trans. by W. Hazlitt. Portraits. 3 vols.

HALL'S (Rev. Robert) Works and Remains. Memoir by Dr. Gregory and Essay by J. Foster. Portrait.

HAUFF'S Tales. The Caravan—The Sheikh of Alexandria—The Inn in the Spessart. Translated by Prof. S. Mendel.

HAWTHORNE'S Tales. 3 vols.

Vol. I.—Twice-told Tales, and the Snow Image.

Vol. II.—Scarlet Letter, and the House with Seven Gables.

Vol. III.—Transformation, and Blithedale Romance.

HAZLITT'S (W.) Works. 7 vols.

—— Table-Talk.

—— The Literature of the Age of Elizabeth and Characters of Shakespeare's Plays.

—— English Poets and English Comic Writers.

—— The Plain Speaker. Opinions on Books, Men, and Things.

—— Round Table. Conversations of James Northcote, R.A.; Characteristics.

—— Sketches and Essays, and Winterslow.

—— Spirit of the Age; or, Contemporary Portraits. New Edition, by W. Carew Hazlitt.

HEINE'S Poems. Translated in the original Metres, with Life by E. A. Bowring, C.B.

—— Travel-Pictures. The Tour in the Harz, Norderney, and Book of Ideas, together with the Romantic School. Trans. by F. Storr. With Maps and Appendices.

HOFFMANN'S Works. The Serapion Brethren. Vol. I. Trans. by Lt.-Col. Ewing. [*Vol. II. in the press.*

HOOPER'S (G.) Waterloo: The Downfall of the First Napoleon: a History of the Campaign of 1815. By George Hooper. With Maps and Plans. New Edition, revised

HUGO'S (Victor) Dramatic Works. Hernani—Ruy Blas—The King's Diversion. Translated by Mrs. Newton Crosland and F. L. Slous.

— **Poems,** chiefly Lyrical. Collected by H. L. Williams.

HUNGARY: its History and Revolution, with Memoir of Kossuth. Portrait.

HUTCHINSON (Colonel). Memoirs of. By his Widow, with her Autobiography, and the Siege of Lathom House. Portrait.

IRVING'S (Washington) Complete Works. 15 vols.

— **Life and Letters.** By his Nephew, Pierre E. Irving. With Index and a Portrait. 2 vols.

JAMES'S (G. P. R.) Life of Richard Cœur de Lion. Portraits of Richard and Philip Augustus. 2 vols.

— **Louis XIV.** Portraits. 2 vols.

JAMESON (Mrs.) Shakespeare's Heroines. Characteristics of Women. By Mrs. Jameson.

JEAN PAUL.—*See Richter.*

JOHNSON'S Lives of the Poets. Edited, with Notes, by Mrs. Alexander Napier. And an Introduction by Professor J. W. Hales, M.A. 3 vols.

JONSON (Ben). Poems of.—*See Greene.*

JOSEPHUS (Flavius), The Works of. Whiston's Translation. Revised by Rev. A. R. Shilleto, M.A. With Topographical and Geographical Notes by Colonel Sir C. W. Wilson, K.C.B. 5 vols.

JUNIUS'S Letters. With Woodfall's Notes. An Essay on the Authorship. Facsimiles of Handwriting. 2 vols.

LA FONTAINE'S Fables. In English Verse, with Essay on the Fabulists. By Elizur Wright.

LAMARTINE'S The Girondists, or Personal Memoirs of the Patriots of the French Revolution. Trans. by H. T. Ryde. Portraits of Robespierre, Madame Roland, and Charlotte Corday. 3 vols.

— **The Restoration of Monarchy** in France (a Sequel to The Girondists). 5 Portraits. 4 vols.

— **The French Revolution of 1848.** Portraits.

LAMB'S (Charles) Elia and Eliana. Complete Edition. Portrait.

LAMB'S (Charles) Specimens of English Dramatic Poets of the time of Elizabeth. With Notes and the Extracts from the Garrick Plays.

— **Talfourd's Letters of Charles** Lamb. New Edition, by W. Carew Hazlitt. 2 vols.

LANZI'S History of Painting in Italy, from the Period of the Revival of the Fine Arts to the End of the 18th Century. With Memoir and Portraits. Trans. by T. Roscoe. 3 vols.

LAPPENBERG'S England under the Anglo-Saxon Kings. Trans. by B. Thorpe, F.S.A. 2 vols.

LESSING'S Dramatic Works. Complete. By E. Bell, M.A. With Memoir by H. Zimmern. Portrait. 2 vols.

— **Laokoon, Dramatic Notes, and** Representation of Death by the Ancients. Trans. by E. C. Beasley and Helen Zimmern. Frontispiece.

LOCKE'S Philosophical Works, containing Human Understanding, Controversy with Bishop of Worcester, Malebranche's Opinions, Natural Philosophy, Reading and Study. With Introduction, Analysis, and Notes, by J. A. St. John. Portrait. 2 vols.

— **Life and Letters,** with Extracts from his Common-place Books. By Lord King.

LOCKHART (J. G.)—*See Burns.*

LUTHER'S Table-Talk. Trans. by W. Hazlitt. With Life by A. Chalmers, and LUTHER'S CATECHISM. Portrait after Cranach.

— **Autobiography.**—*See Michelet.*

MACHIAVELLI'S History of Florence, THE PRINCE, Savonarola, Historical Tracts, and Memoir. Portrait.

MARLOWE. Poems of.—*See Greene.*

MARTINEAU'S (Harriet) History of England (including History of the Peace) from 1800-1846. 5 vols.

MENZEL'S History of Germany, from the Earliest Period to 1842. Portraits. 3 vols.

MICHELET'S Autobiography of Luther. Trans. by W. Hazlitt. With Notes.

— **The French Revolution** to the Flight of the King in 1791. Frontispiece.

MIGNET'S The French Revolution, from 1789 to 1814. Portrait of Napoleon.

MILTON'S Prose Works. With Preface, Preliminary Remarks by J. A. St. John, and Index. 5 vols. Portraits.

— **Poetical Works.** With 120 Wood Engravings. 2 vols.

MITFORD'S (Miss) Our Village. Sketches of Rural Character and Scenery. 2 Engravings. 2 vols.

MOLIÈRE'S Dramatic Works. In English Prose, by C. H. Wall. With a Life and a Portrait. 3 vols.

'It is not too much to say that we have here probably as good a translation of Molière as can be given.'—*Academy.*

MONTAGU. Letters and Works of Lady Mary Wortley Montagu. Lord Wharncliffe's Third Edition. Edited by W. Moy Thomas. New and revised edition. With steel plates. 2 vols. 5s. each.

MONTESQUIEU'S Spirit of Laws. Revised Edition, with D'Alembert's Analysis, Notes, and Memoir. 2 vols.

NEANDER (Dr. A.) History of the Christian Religion and Church. Trans. by J. Torrey. With Short Memoir. 10 vols.

— **Life of Jesus Christ, in its Historical** Connexion and Development.

— **The Planting and Training of** the Christian Church by the Apostles. With the Antignosticus, or Spirit of Tertullian. Trans. by J. E. Ryland. 2 vols.

— **Lectures on the History of** Christian Dogmas. Trans. by J. E. Ryland. 2 vols.

— **Memorials of Christian Life in** the Early and Middle Ages; including Light in Dark Places. Trans. by J. E. Ryland

NORTH'S Lives of the Right Hon. Francis North, Baron Guildford, the Hon. Sir Dudley North, and the Hon. and Rev. Dr. John North. By the Hon. Roger North. Edited by A. Jessopp, D.D. With 3 Portraits. 3 vols. 3s. 6d. each.

'Lovers of good literature will rejoice at the appearance of a new, handy, and complete edition of so justly famous a book, and will congratulate themselves that it has found so competent and skilful an editor as Dr. Jessopp.'—*Times.*

OCKLEY (S.) History of the Saracens and their Conquests in Syria, Persia, and Egypt. Comprising the Lives of Mohammed and his Successors to the Death of Abdalmelik, the Eleventh Caliph. By Simon Ockley, B.D., Portrait of Mohammed.

PASCAL'S Thoughts. Translated from the Text of M. Auguste Molinier by C. Kegan Paul. 3rd edition.

PERCY'S Reliques of Ancient English Poetry, consisting of Ballads, Songs, and other Pieces of our earlier Poets, with some few of later date. With Essay on Ancient Minstrels, and Glossary. 2 vols.

PHILIP DE COMMINES. Memoirs of. Containing the Histories of Louis XI. and Charles VIII., and Charles the Bold, Duke of Burgundy. With the History of Louis XI., by Jean de Troyes. Translated, with a Life and Notes, by A. R. Scoble. Portraits. 2 vols.

PLUTARCH'S LIVES. Translated, with Notes and Life, by A. Stewart, M.A., late Fellow of Trinity College, Cambridge, and G. Long, M.A. 4 vols.

POETRY OF AMERICA. Selections from One Hundred Poets, from 1776 to 1876. With Introductory Review, and Specimens of Negro Melody, by W. J. Linton. Portrait of W. Whitman.

RACINE'S (Jean) Dramatic Works. A metrical English version, with Biographical notice. By R. Bruce Boswell, M.A. Oxon. 2 vols.

RANKE (L.) History of the Popes, their Church and State, and their Conflicts with Protestantism in the 16th and 17th Centuries. Trans. by E. Foster. Portraits 3 vols.

— **History of Servia.** Trans. by Mrs. Kerr. To which is added, The Slave Provinces of Turkey, by Cyprien Robert.

— **History of the Latin and Teutonic** Nations. 1494-1514. Trans. by P. A. Ashworth, translator of Dr. Gneist's 'History of the English Constitution.'

REUMONT (Alfred de).—*See Carafas.*

REYNOLDS' (Sir J.) Literary Works. With Memoir and Remarks by H. W. Beechy. 2 vols.

RICHTER (Jean Paul). Levana, a Treatise on Education; together with the Autobiography, and a short Memoir.

— **Flower, Fruit, and Thorn Pieces,** or the Wedded Life, Death, and Marriage of Siebenkaes. Translated by Alex. Ewing. The only complete English translation.

ROSCOE'S (W.) Life of Leo X., with Notes, Historical Documents, and Dissertation on Lucretia Borgia. 3 Portraits. 2 vols.

— **Lorenzo de' Medici,** called 'The Magnificent,' with Copyright Notes, Poems, Letters, &c. With Memoir of Roscoe and Portrait of Lorenzo.

RUSSIA, History of, from the earliest Period to the Crimean War. By W. K. Kelly. 3 Portraits. 2 vols.

SCHILLER'S Works. 7 vols.

Vol. I.—History of the Thirty Years' War. Rev. A. J. W. Morrison, M.A. Portrait.

Vol. II.—History of the Revolt in the Netherlands, the Trials of Counts Egmont and Horn, the Siege of Antwerp, and the Disturbance of France preceding the Reign of Henry IV. Translated by Rev. A. J. W. Morrison and L. Dora Schmitz.

Vol. III.—Don Carlos. R. D. Boylan—Mary Stuart. Mellish—Maid of Orleans. Anna Swanwick—Bride of Messina. A. Lodge, M.A. Together with the Use of the Chorus in Tragedy (a short Essay). Engravings.

These Dramas are all translated in metre.

Vol. IV.—Robbers—Fiesco—Love and Intrigue—Demetrius—Ghost Seer—Sport of Divinity.

The Dramas in this volume are in prose.

Vol. V.—Poems. E. A. Bowring, C.B.

Vol. VI.—Essays, Æsthetical and Philosophical, including the Dissertation on the Connexion between the Animal and Spiritual in Man.

Vol. VII.—Wallenstein's Camp. J. Churchill.—Piccolomini and Death of Wallenstein. S. T. Coleridge.—William Tell. Sir Theodore Martin, K.C.B., LL.D.

SCHILLER and GOETHE. Correspondence between, from A.D. 1794-1805. Trans. by L. Dora Schmitz. 2 vols.

SCHLEGEL (F.) Lectures on the Philosophy of Life and the Philosophy of Language. Trans. by A. J. W. Morrison.

—— **The History of Literature,** Ancient and Modern.

—— **The Philosophy of History.** With Memoir and Portrait. Trans. by J. B. Robertson.

—— **Modern History,** with the Lectures entitled Cæsar and Alexander, and The Beginning of our History. Translated by L. Purcell and R. H. Whitelock.

—— **Æsthetic and Miscellaneous** Works, containing Letters on Christian Art, Essay on Gothic Architecture, Remarks on the Romance Poetry of the Middle Ages, on Shakspeare, the Limits of the Beautiful, and on the Language and Wisdom of the Indians. By E. J. Millington.

SCHLEGEL (A. W.) Dramatic Art and Literature. By J. Black. With Memoir by Rev. A. J. W. Morrison. Portrait.

SCHUMANN (Robert), His Life and Works. By A. Reissmann. Trans. by A. L. Alger.

—— **Early Letters.** Translated by May Herbert. With Preface by Sir G. Grove.

SHAKESPEARE'S Dramatic Art. The History and Character of Shakspeare's Plays. By Dr. H. Ulrici. Trans. by L. Dora Schmitz. 2 vols.

SHAKESPEARE (William). A Literary Biography by Karl Elze, Ph.D., LL.D. Translated by L. Dora Schmitz. 5s.

SHERIDAN'S Dramatic Works. With Memoir. Portrait (after Reynolds).

SISMONDI'S History of the Literature of the South of Europe. Trans. by T. Roscoe. Portraits. 2 vols.

SMITH'S (Adam) Theory of Moral Sentiments; with Essay on the First Formation of Languages, and Critical Memoir by Dugald Stewart.

—— *See Economic Library.*

SMYTH'S (Professor) Lectures on Modern History; from the Irruption of the Northern Nations to the close of the American Revolution. 2 vols.

—— **Lectures on the French Revolution.** With Index. 2 vols.

SOUTHEY.—*See Cowper, Wesley, and (Illustrated Library) Nelson.*

STURM'S Morning Communings with God, or Devotional Meditations for Every Day. Trans. by W. Johnstone, M.A.

SULLY. Memoirs of the Duke of, Prime Minister to Henry the Great. With Notes and Historical Introduction. 4 Portraits. 4 vols.

TAYLOR'S (Bishop Jeremy) Holy Living and Dying, with Prayers, containing the Whole Duty of a Christian and the parts of Devotion fitted to all Occasions. Portrait.

TEN BRINK.—*See Brink.*

THIERRY'S Conquest of England by the Normans; its Causes, and its Consequences in England and the Continent. By W. Hazlitt. With short Memoir. 2 Portraits. 2 vols.

ULRICI (Dr.)—*See Shakespeare.*

VASARI. Lives of the most Eminent Painters, Sculptors, and Architects. By Mrs. J. Foster, with selected Notes. Portrait. 6 vols., Vol. VI. being an additional Volume of Notes by Dr. J. P. Richter.

VOLTAIRE'S Tales. Translated by R. B. Boswell. Vol. I., containing 'Bababec,' Memnon, Candide, L'Ingénu, and other Tales.

WERNER'S Templars in Cyprus. Trans. by E. A. M. Lewis.

WESLEY, the Life of, and the Rise and Progress of Methodism. By Robert Southey. Portrait. 5s.

WHEATLEY. A Rational Illustration of the Book of Common Prayer.

YOUNG (Arthur) Travels in France. Edited by Miss Betham Edwards. With a Portrait.

HISTORICAL LIBRARY.

23 *Volumes at 5s. each.* (5*l.* 15*s. per set.*)

EVELYN'S Diary and Correspondence, with the Private Correspondence of Charles I. and Sir Edward Nicholas, and between Sir Edward Hyde (Earl of Clarendon) and Sir Richard Browne. Edited from the Original MSS. by W. Bray, F.A.S. 4 vols. 45 Engravings (after Vandyke, Lely, Kneller, and Jamieson, &c.).

N.B.—This edition contains 130 letters from Evelyn and his wife, printed by permission, and contained in no other edition.

JESSE'S Memoirs of the Court of England under the Stuarts, including the Protectorate. 3 vols. With Index and 42 Portraits (after Vandyke, Lely, &c.).

— Memoirs of the Pretenders and their Adherents. 6 Portraits.

GRAMMONT (Count). Memoirs of the Court of Charles II. Edited by Sir Walter Scott. Together with the 'Boscobel Tracts,' including two not before published, &c. New Edition, thoroughly revised. With Portrait of Nell Gwynne.

PEPYS' Diary and Correspondence. With Life and Notes, by Lord Braybrooke. With Appendix containing additional Letters and Index. 4 vols., with 31 Engravings (after Vandyke, Sir P. Lely, Holbein, Kneller, &c.).

N.B.—This is a reprint of Lord Braybrooke's fourth and last edition, containing all his latest notes and corrections, the copyright of the publishers.

NUGENT'S (Lord) Memorials of Hampden, his Party and Times. With Memoir. 12 Portraits (after Vandyke and others).

STRICKLAND'S (Agnes) Lives of the Queens of England from the Norman Conquest. From authentic Documents, public and private. 6 Portraits. 6 vols.

— Life of Mary Queen of Scots. 2 Portraits. 2 vols.

— Lives of the Tudor and Stuart Princesses. With 2 Portraits.

PHILOSOPHICAL LIBRARY.

17 *Vols. at 5s. each, excepting those marked otherwise.* (3*l.* 19*s. per set.*)

BACON'S Novum Organum and Advancement of Learning. With Notes by J. Devey, M.A.

BAX. A Handbook of the History of Philosophy, for the use of Students. By E. Belfort Bax, Editor of Kant's 'Prolegomena.'

COMTE'S Philosophy of the Sciences. An Exposition of the Principles of the *Cours de Philosophie Positive*. By G. H. Lewes, Author of 'The Life of Goethe.'

DRAPER (Dr. J. W.) A History of the Intellectual Development of Europe. 2 vols.

HEGEL'S Philosophy of History. By J. Sibree, M.A.

KANT'S Critique of Pure Reason. By J. M. D. Meiklejohn.

— Prolegomena and Metaphysical Foundations of Natural Science, with Biography and Memoir by E. Belfort Bax. Portrait.

LOGIC, or the Science of Inference. A Popular Manual. By J. Devey.

MILLER (Professor). History Philosophically Illustrated, from the Fall of the Roman Empire to the French Revolution. With Memoir. 4 vols. 3*s.* 6*d.* each.

SCHOPENHAUER on the Fourfold Root of the Principle of Sufficient Reason, and on the Will in Nature. Trans. from the German.

— Essays. Selected and Translated by E. Belfort Bax.

SPINOZA'S Chief Works. Trans. with Introduction by R. H. M. Elwes. 2 vols.

Vol. I.—Tractatus Theologico-Politicus —Political Treatise.

Vol. II.—Improvement of the Understanding—Ethics—Letters.

THEOLOGICAL LIBRARY.

15 *Vols. at* 5*s. each* (*except Chillingworth,* 3*s.* 6*d.*). (3*l.* 13*s.* 6*d. per set.*)

BLEEK. Introduction to the Old Testament. By Friedrich Bleek. Trans. under the supervision of Rev. E. Venables, Residentiary Canon of Lincoln. 2 vols.

CHILLINGWORTH'S Religion of Protestants. 3*s.* 6*d.*

EUSEBIUS. Ecclesiastical History of Eusebius Pamphilus, Bishop of Cæsarea. Trans. by Rev. C. F. Cruse, M.A. With Notes, Life, and Chronological Tables.

EVAGRIUS. History of the Church. —*See Theodoret.*

HARDWICK. History of the Articles of Religion; to which is added a Series of Documents from A.D. 1536 to A.D. 1615. Ed. by Rev. F. Proctor.

HENRY'S (Matthew) Exposition of the Book of Psalms. Numerous Woodcuts.

PEARSON (John, D.D.) Exposition of the Creed. Edit. by E. Walford, M.A. With Notes, Analysis, and Indexes.

PHILO-JUDÆUS, Works of. The Contemporary of Josephus. Trans. by C. D. Yonge. 4 vols.

PHILOSTORGIUS. Ecclesiastical History of.—*See Sozomen.*

SOCRATES' Ecclesiastical History. Comprising a History of the Church from Constantine, A.D. 305, to the 38th year of Theodosius II. With Short Account of the Author, and selected Notes.

SOZOMEN'S Ecclesiastical History. A.D. 324-440. With Notes, Prefatory Remarks by Valesius, and Short Memoir. Together with the ECCLESIASTICAL HISTORY OF PHILOSTORGIUS, as epitomised by Photius. Trans. by Rev. E. Walford, M.A. With Notes and brief Life.

THEODORET and EVAGRIUS. Histories of the Church from A.D. 332 to the Death of Theodore of Mopsuestia, A.D. 427; and from A.D. 431 to A.D. 544. With Memoirs.

WIESELER'S (Karl) Chronological Synopsis of the Four Gospels. Trans. by Rev. Canon Venables.

ANTIQUARIAN LIBRARY.

35 *Vols. at* 5*s. each.* (8*l.* 15*s. per set.*)

ANGLO-SAXON CHRONICLE. —*See Bede.*

ASSER'S Life of Alfred.—*See Six O. E. Chronicles.*

BEDE'S (Venerable) Ecclesiastical History of England. Together with the ANGLO-SAXON CHRONICLE. With Notes, Short Life, Analysis, and Map. Edit. by J. A. Giles, D.C.L.

BOETHIUS'S Consolation of Philosophy. King Alfred's Anglo-Saxon Version of. With an English Translation on opposite pages, Notes, Introduction, and Glossary, by Rev. S. Fox, M.A. To which is added the Anglo-Saxon Version of the METRES OF BOETHIUS, with a free Translation by Martin F. Tupper, D.C.L.

BRAND'S Popular Antiquities of England, Scotland, and Ireland. Illustrating the Origin of our Vulgar and Provincial Customs, Ceremonies, and Superstitions. By Sir Henry Ellis, K.H., F.R.S. Frontispiece. 3 vols.

CHRONICLES of the CRUSADES. Contemporary Narratives of Richard Cœur de Lion, by Richard of Devizes and Geoffrey de Vinsauf; and of the Crusade at Saint Louis, by Lord John de Joinville. With Short Notes. Illuminated Frontispiece from an old MS.

DYER'S (T. F. T.) British Popular Customs, Present and Past. An Account of the various Games and Customs associated with different Days of the Year in the British Isles, arranged according to the Calendar. By the Rev. T. F. Thiselton Dyer, M.A.

EARLY TRAVELS IN PALESTINE. Comprising the Narratives of Arculf, Willibald, Bernard, Sæwulf, Sigurd, Benjamin of Tudela, Sir John Maundeville, De la Brocquière, and Maundrell; all unabridged. With Introduction and Notes by Thomas Wright. Map of Jerusalem.

ELLIS (G.) Specimens of Early English Metrical Romances, relating to Arthur, Merlin, Guy of Warwick, Richard Cœur de Lion, Charlemagne, Roland, &c. &c. With Historical Introduction by J. O. Halliwell, F.R.S. Illuminated Frontispiece from an old MS.

ETHELWERD. Chronicle of.—*See Six O. E. Chronicles.*

FLORENCE OF WORCESTER'S Chronicle, with the Two Continuations: comprising Annals of English History from the Departure of the Romans to the Reign of Edward I. Trans., with Notes, by Thomas Forester, M.A.

GEOFFREY OF MONMOUTH. Chronicle of.—*See Six O. E. Chronicles.*

GESTA ROMANORUM, or Entertaining Moral Stories invented by the Monks. Trans. with Notes by the Rev. Charles Swan. Edit. by W. Hooper, M.A.

GILDAS. Chronicle of.—*See Six O. E. Chronicles.*

GIRALDUS CAMBRENSIS' Historical Works. Containing Topography of Ireland, and History of the Conquest of Ireland, by Th. Forester, M.A. Itinerary through Wales, and Description of Wales, by Sir R. Colt Hoare.

HENRY OF HUNTINGDON'S History of the English, from the Roman Invasion to the Accession of Henry II.; with the Acts of King Stephen, and the Letter to Walter. By T. Forester, M.A. Frontispiece from an old MS.

INGULPH'S Chronicles of the Abbey of Croyland, with the CONTINUATION by Peter of Blois and others. Trans. with Notes by H. T. Riley, B.A.

KEIGHTLEY'S (Thomas) Fairy Mythology, illustrative of the Romance and Superstition of Various Countries. Frontispiece by Cruikshank.

LEPSIUS'S Letters from Egypt, Ethiopia, and the Peninsula of Sinai; to which are added, Extracts from his Chronology of the Egyptians, with reference to the Exodus of the Israelites. By L. and J. B. Horner. Maps and Coloured View of Mount Barkal.

MALLET'S Northern Antiquities, or an Historical Account of the Manners, Customs, Religions, and Literature of the Ancient Scandinavians. Trans. by Bishop Percy. With Translation of the PROSE EDDA, and Notes by J. A. Blackwell. Also an Abstract of the 'Eyrbyggia Saga' by Sir Walter Scott. With Glossary and Coloured Frontispiece.

MARCO POLO'S Travels; with Notes and Introduction. Edit. by T. Wright.

MATTHEW PARIS'S English History, from 1235 to 1273. By Rev. J. A. Giles, D.C.L. With Frontispiece. 3 vols.—*See also Roger of Wendover.*

MATTHEW OF WESTMINSTER'S Flowers of History, especially such as relate to the affairs of Britain, from the beginning of the World to A.D. 1307. By C. D. Yonge. 2 vols.

NENNIUS. Chronicle of.—*See Six O. E. Chronicles.*

ORDERICUS VITALIS' Ecclesiastical History of England and Normandy. With Notes, Introduction of Guizot, and the Critical Notice of M. Delille, by T. Forester, M.A. To which is added the CHRONICLE OF ST. EVROULT. With General and Chronological Indexes. 4 vols.

PAULI'S (Dr. R.) Life of Alfred the Great. To which is appended Alfred's ANGLO-SAXON VERSION OF OROSIUS. With literal Translation interpaged, Notes, and an ANGLO-SAXON GRAMMAR and Glossary, by B. Thorpe. Frontispiece.

RICHARD OF CIRENCESTER. Chronicle of.—*See Six O. E. Chronicles.*

ROGER DE HOVEDEN'S Annals of English History, comprising the History of England and of other Countries of Europe from A.D. 732 to A.D. 1201. With Notes by H. T. Riley, B.A. 2 vols.

ROGER OF WENDOVER'S Flowers of History, comprising the History of England from the Descent of the Saxons to A.D. 1235, formerly ascribed to Matthew Paris. With Notes and Index by J. A. Giles, D.C.L. 2 vols.

SIX OLD ENGLISH CHRONICLES: viz., Asser's Life of Alfred and the Chronicles of Ethelwerd, Gildas, Nennius, Geoffrey of Monmouth, and Richard of Cirencester. Edit., with Notes, by J. A. Giles, D.C.L. Portrait of Alfred.

WILLIAM OF MALMESBURY'S Chronicle of the Kings of England, from the Earliest Period to King Stephen. By Rev. J. Sharpe. With Notes by J. A. Giles, D.C.L. Frontispiece.

YULE-TIDE STORIES. A Collection of Scandinavian and North-German Popular Tales and Traditions, from the Swedish, Danish, and German. Edit. by B. Thorpe.

ILLUSTRATED LIBRARY.

78 Vols. at 5s. each, excepting those marked otherwise. (19*l.* 7*s.* 6*d.* *per set.*)

ALLEN'S (Joseph, R.N.) Battles of the British Navy. Revised edition, with Indexes of Names and Events, and 57 Portraits and Plans. 2 vols.

ANDERSEN'S Danish Fairy Tales. By Caroline Peachey. With Short Life and 120 Wood Engravings.

ARIOSTO'S Orlando Furioso. In English Verse by W. S. Rose. With Notes and Short Memoir. Portrait after Titian, and 24 Steel Engravings. 2 vols.

BECHSTEIN'S Cage and Chamber Birds; their Natural History, Habits, &c. Together with SWEET'S BRITISH WARBLERS. 43 Coloured Plates and Woodcuts.

BONOMI'S Nineveh and its Palaces. The Discoveries of Botta and Layard applied to the Elucidation of Holy Writ. 7 Plates and 294 Woodcuts.

BUTLER'S Hudibras, with Variorum Notes and Biography. Portrait and 28 Illustrations.

CATTERMOLE'S Evenings at Haddon Hall. Romantic Tales of the Olden Times. With 24 Steel Engravings after Cattermole.

CHINA, Pictorial, Descriptive, and Historical, with some account of Ava and the Burmese, Siam, and Anam. Map, and nearly 100 Illustrations.

CRAIK'S (G. L.) Pursuit of Knowledge under Difficulties. Illustrated by Anecdotes and Memoirs. Numerous Woodcut Portraits.

CRUIKSHANK'S Three Courses and a Dessert; comprising three Sets of Tales, West Country, Irish, and Legal; and a Mélange. With 50 Illustrations by Cruikshank.

—— **Punch and Judy.** The Dialogue of the Puppet Show; an Account of its Origin, &c. 24 Illustrations and Coloured Plates by Cruikshank.

DANTE, in English Verse, by I. C. Wright, M.A. With Introduction and Memoir. Portrait and 34 Steel Engravings after Flaxman.

DIDRON'S Christian Iconography; a History of Christian Art in the Middle Ages. By the late A. N. Didron. Trans. by E. J. Millington, and completed, with Additions and Appendices, by Margaret Stokes. 2 vols. With numerous Illustrations.

Vol. I. The History of the Nimbus, the Aureole, and the Glory; Representations of the Persons of the Trinity.

Vol. II. The Trinity; Angels; Devils; The Soul; The Christian Scheme. Appendices.

DYER (Dr. T. H.) Pompeii: its Buildings and Antiquities. An Account of the City, with full Description of the Remains and Recent Excavations, and an Itinerary for Visitors. By T. H. Dyer, LL.D. Nearly 300 Wood Engravings, Map, and Plan. 7*s.* 6*d.*

—— **Rome:** History of the City, with Introduction on recent Excavations. 8 Engravings, Frontispiece, and 2 Maps.

GIL BLAS. The Adventures of. From the French of Lesage by Smollett. 24 Engravings after Smirke, and 10 Etchings by Cruikshank. 612 pages. 6*s.*

GRIMM'S Gammer Grethel; or, German Fairy Tales and Popular Stories, containing 42 Fairy Tales. By Edgar Taylor. Numerous Woodcuts after Cruikshank and Ludwig Grimm. 3*s.* 6*d.*

HOLBEIN'S Dance of Death and Bible Cuts. Upwards of 150 Subjects, engraved in facsimile, with Introduction and Descriptions by the late Francis Douce and Dr. Dibdin.

INDIA, Pictorial, Descriptive, and Historical, from the Earliest Times. 100 Engravings on Wood and Map.

JESSE'S Anecdotes of Dogs. With 40 Woodcuts after Harvey, Bewick, and others; and 34 Steel Engravings after Cooper and Landseer.

KING'S (C. W.) Natural History of Precious Stones and Metals. Illustrations. 6*s.*

LODGE'S Portraits of Illustrious Personages of Great Britain, with Biographical and Historical Memoirs. 240 Portraits engraved on Steel, with the respective Biographies unabridged. Complete in 8 vols.

LONGFELLOW'S Poetical Works, including his Translations and Notes. 24 full-page Woodcuts by Birket Foster and others, and a Portrait.

—— Without the Illustrations, 3*s*. 6*d*.

—— **Prose Works.** With 16 full-page Woodcuts by Birket Foster and others.

LOUDON'S (Mrs.) Entertaining Naturalist. Popular Descriptions, Tales, and Anecdotes, of more than 500 Animals. Numerous Woodcuts.

MARRYAT'S (Capt., R.N.) Masterman Ready; or, the Wreck of the *Pacific*. (Written for Young People.) With 93 Woodcuts. 3*s*. 6*d*.

—— **Mission; or, Scenes in Africa.** (Written for Young People.) Illustrated by Gilbert and Dalziel. 3*s*. 6*d*.

—— **Pirate and Three Cutters.** (Written for Young People.) With a Memoir. 8 Steel Engravings after Clarkson Stanfield, R.A. 3*s*. 6*d*.

—— **Privateersman.** Adventures by Sea and Land One Hundred Years Ago. (Written for Young People.) 8 Steel Engravings. 3*s*. 6*d*.

—— **Settlers in Canada.** (Written for Young People.) 10 Engravings by Gilbert and Dalziel. 3*s*. 6*d*.

—— **Poor Jack.** (Written for Young People.) With 16 Illustrations after Clarkson Stanfield, R.A. 3*s*. 6*d*.

—— **Midshipman Easy.** With 8 full-page Illustrations. Small post 8vo. 3*s*. 6*d*.

—— **Peter Simple.** With 8 full-page Illustrations. Small post 8vo. 3*s*. 6*d*.

MAXWELL'S Victories of Wellington and the British Armies. Frontispiece and 4 Portraits.

MICHAEL ANGELO and RAPHAEL, Their Lives and Works. By Duppa and Quatremère de Quincy. Portraits and Engravings, including the Last Judgment, and Cartoons.

MUDIE'S History of British Birds. Revised by W. C. L. Martin. 52 Figures of Birds and 7 coloured Plates of Eggs. 2 vols.

NAVAL and MILITARY HEROES of Great Britain; a Record of British Valour on every Day in the year, from William the Conqueror to the Battle of Inkermann. By Major Johns, R.M., and Lieut. P. H. Nicolas, R.M. Indexes. 24 Portraits after Holbein, Reynolds, &c. 6*s*.

NICOLINI'S History of the Jesuits: their Origin, Progress, Doctrines, and Designs. 8 Portraits.

PETRARCH'S Sonnets, Triumphs, and other Poems, in English Verse. With Life by Thomas Campbell. Portrait and 15 Steel Engravings.

PICKERING'S History of the Races of Man, and their Geographical Distribution; with AN ANALYTICAL SYNOPSIS OF THE NATURAL HISTORY OF MAN. By Dr. Hall. Map of the World and 12 coloured Plates.

POPE'S Poetical Works, including Translations. Edit., with Notes, by R. Carruthers. 2 vols. With numerous Illustrations.

—— **Homer's Iliad,** with Introduction and Notes by Rev. J. S. Watson, M.A. With Flaxman's Designs.

—— **Homer's Odyssey,** with the BATTLE OF FROGS AND MICE, Hymns, &c., by other translators including Chapman. Introduction and Notes by J. S. Watson, M.A. With Flaxman's Designs.

—— **Life,** including many of his Letters. By R. Carruthers. Numerous Illustrations.

POTTERY AND PORCELAIN, and other objects of Vertu. Comprising an Illustrated Catalogue of the Bernal Collection, with the prices and names of the Possessors. Also an Introductory Lecture on Pottery and Porcelain, and an Engraved List of all Marks and Monograms. By H. G. Bohn. Numerous Woodcuts.

—— With coloured Illustrations, 10*s*. 6*d*.

PROUT'S (Father) Reliques. Edited by Rev. F. Mahony. Copyright edition, with the Author's last corrections and additions. 21 Etchings by D. Maclise, R.A. Nearly 600 pages.

RECREATIONS IN SHOOTING. With some Account of the Game found in the British Isles, and Directions for the Management of Dog and Gun. By 'Craven.' 62 Woodcuts and 9 Steel Engravings after A. Cooper, R.A.

RENNIE. Insect Architecture. Revised by Rev. J. G. Wood, M.A. 186 Woodcuts.

ROBINSON CRUSOE. With Memoir of Defoe, 12 Steel Engravings and 74 Woodcuts after Stothard and Harvey.

—— Without the Engravings, 3*s.* 6*d.*

ROME IN THE NINETEENTH CENTURY. An Account in 1817 of the Ruins of the Ancient City, and Monuments of Modern Times. By C. A. Eaton. 34 Steel Engravings. 2 vols.

SHARPE (S.) The History of Egypt, from the Earliest Times till the Conquest by the Arabs, A.D. 640. 2 Maps and upwards of 400 Woodcuts. 2 vols.

SOUTHEY'S Life of Nelson. With Additional Notes, Facsimiles of Nelson's Writing, Portraits, Plans, and 50 Engravings, after Birket Foster, &c.

STARLING'S (Miss) Noble Deeds of Women; or, Examples of Female Courage, Fortitude, and Virtue. With 14 Steel Portraits.

STUART and REVETT'S Antiquities of Athens, and other Monuments of Greece; with Glossary of Terms used in Grecian Architecture. 71 Steel Plates and numerous Woodcuts.

SWEET'S British Warblers. 5*s.*—*See Bechstein.*

TALES OF THE GENII; or, the Delightful Lessons of Horam, the Son of Asmar. Trans. by Sir C. Morrell. Numerous Woodcuts.

TASSO'S Jerusalem Delivered. In English Spenserian Verse, with Life, by J. H. Wiffen. With 8 Engravings and 24 Woodcuts.

WALKER'S Manly Exercises; containing Skating, Riding, Driving, Hunting, Shooting, Sailing, Rowing, Swimming, &c. 44 Engravings and numerous Woodcuts.

WALTON'S Complete Angler, or the Contemplative Man's Recreation, by Izaak Walton and Charles Cotton. With Memoirs and Notes by E. Jesse. Also an Account of Fishing Stations, Tackle, &c., by H. G. Bohn. Portrait and 203 Woodcuts, and 26 Engravings on Steel.

—— **Lives of Donne, Wotton, Hooker,** &c., with Notes. A New Edition, revised by A. H. Bullen, with a Memoir of Izaak Walton by William Dowling. 6 Portraits, 6 Autograph Signatures, &c.

WELLINGTON, Life of. From the Materials of Maxwell. 18 Steel Engravings.

—— **Victories of.**—*See Maxwell.*

WESTROPP (H. M.) A Handbook of Archæology, Egyptian, Greek, Etruscan, Roman. By H. M. Westropp. Numerous Illustrations.

WHITE'S Natural History of Selborne, with Observations on various Parts of Nature, and the Naturalists' Calendar. Sir W. Jardine. Edit., with Notes and Memoir, by E. Jesse. 40 Portraits and coloured Plates.

CLASSICAL LIBRARY.

TRANSLATIONS FROM THE GREEK AND LATIN.

105 *Vols. at* 5*s. each, excepting those marked otherwise.* (25*l.* 13*s. per set.*)

ACHILLES TATIUS.—*See Greek Romances.*

ÆSCHYLUS, The Dramas of. In English Verse by Anna Swanwick. 4th edition.

—— **The Tragedies of.** In Prose, with Notes and Introduction, by T. A. Buckley, B.A. Portrait. 3*s.* 6*d.*

AMMIANUS MARCELLINUS. History of Rome during the Reigns of Constantius, Julian, Jovianus, Valentinian, and Valens, by C. D. Yonge, B.A. Double volume. 7*s.* 6*d.*

ANTONINUS (M. Aurelius), The Thoughts of. Translated, with Notes, Biographical Sketch, and Essay on the Philosophy, by George Long, M.A. 3*s.* 6*d.* Fine Paper edition on hand-made paper. 6*s.*

APOLLONIUS RHODIUS. 'The Argonautica.' Translated by E. P. Coleridge.

APULEIUS, The Works of. Comprising the Golden Ass, God of Socrates, Florida, and Discourse of Magic. &c. Frontispiece.

ARISTOPHANES' Comedies. Trans., with Notes and Extracts from Frere's and other Metrical Versions, by W. J. Hickie. Portrait. 2 vols.

ARISTOTLE'S Nicomachean Ethics. Trans., with Notes, Analytical Introduction, and Questions for Students, by Ven. Archdn. Browne.

— **Politics and Economics.** Trans., with Notes, Analyses, and Index, by E. Walford, M.A., and an Essay and Life by Dr. Gillies.

— **Metaphysics.** Trans., with Notes, Analysis, and Examination Questions, by Rev. John H. M'Mahon, M.A.

— **History of Animals.** In Ten Books. Trans., with Notes and Index, by R. Cresswell, M.A.

— **Organon**; or, Logical Treatises, and the Introduction of Porphyry. With Notes, Analysis, and Introduction, by Rev. O. F. Owen, M.A. 2 vols. 3s. 6d. each.

— **Rhetoric and Poetics.** Trans., with Hobbes' Analysis, Exam. Questions, and Notes, by T. Buckley, B.A. Portrait.

ATHENÆUS. The Deipnosophists. Trans. by C. D. Yonge, B.A. With an Appendix of Poetical Fragments. 3 vols.

ATLAS of Classical Geography. 22 large Coloured Maps. With a complete Index. Imp. 8vo. 7s. 6d.

BION.—*See Theocritus.*

CÆSAR. Commentaries on the Gallic and Civil Wars, with the Supplementary Books attributed to Hirtius, including the complete Alexandrian, African, and Spanish Wars. Portrait.

CATULLUS, Tibullus, and the Vigil of Venus. Trans. with Notes and Biographical Introduction. To which are added, Metrical Versions by Lamb, Grainger, and others. Frontispiece.

CICERO'S Orations. Trans. by C. D. Yonge, B.A. 4 vols.

— **On Oratory and Orators.** With Letters to Quintus and Brutus. Trans., with Notes, by Rev. J. S. Watson, M.A.

— **On the Nature of the Gods,** Divination, Fate, Laws, a Republic, Consulship. Trans. by C. D. Yonge, B.A.

— **Academics,** De Finibus, and Tusculan Questions. By C. D. Yonge, B.A. With Sketch of the Greek Philosophers mentioned by Cicero.

CICERO'S Offices; or, Moral Duties. Cato Major, an Essay on Old Age; Lælius, an Essay on Friendship; Scipio's Dream; Paradoxes; Letter to Quintus on Magistrates. Trans., with Notes, by C. R. Edmonds. Portrait. 3s. 6d.

DEMOSTHENES' Orations. Trans., with Notes, Arguments, a Chronological Abstract, and Appendices, by C. Rann Kennedy. 5 vols. (One, 3s. 6d.; four, 5s.)

DICTIONARY of LATIN and GREEK Quotations; including Proverbs, Maxims, Mottoes, Law Terms and Phrases. With the Quantities marked, and English Translations. With Index Verborum (622 pages).

DIOGENES LAERTIUS. Lives and Opinions of the Ancient Philosophers. Trans., with Notes, by C. D. Yonge, B.A.

EPICTETUS. The Discourses of. With the Encheiridion and Fragments. With Notes, Life, and View of his Philosophy, by George Long, M.A.

EURIPIDES. A New Literal Translation in Prose. By E. P. Coleridge. 2 vols.

EURIPIDES. Trans. by T. A. Buckley, B.A. Portrait. 2 vols.

GREEK ANTHOLOGY. In English Prose by G. Burges, M.A. With Metrical Versions by Bland, Merivale, and others.

GREEK ROMANCES of Heliodorus, Longus, and Achilles Tatius; viz., The Adventures of Theagenes and Chariclea; Amours of Daphnis and Chloe; and Loves of Clitopho and Leucippe. Trans., with Notes, by Rev R. Smith, M.A.

HELIODORUS.—*See Greek Romances.*

HERODOTUS. Literally trans. by Rev. Henry Cary, M.A. Portrait. 3s. 6d.

HESIOD, CALLIMACHUS, and Theognis. In Prose, with Notes and Biographical Notices by Rev. J. Banks, M.A. Together with the Metrical Versions of Hesiod, by Elton; Callimachus, by Tytler; and Theognis, by Frere.

HOMER'S Iliad. In English Prose, with Notes by T. A. Buckley, B.A. Portrait.

— **Odyssey,** Hymns, Epigrams, and Battle of the Frogs and Mice. In English Prose, with Notes and Memoir by T. A. Buckley, B.A.

HORACE. In Prose by Smart, with Notes selected by T. A. Buckley, B.A. Portrait. 3s. 6d.

JULIAN THE EMPEROR. Containing Gregory Nazianzen's Two Invectives and Libanus' Monody, with Julian's Theosophical Works. By the Rev. C. W. King, M.A.

JUSTIN, CORNELIUS NEPOS, and Eutropius. Trans., with Notes, by Rev. J. S. Watson, M.A.

JUVENAL, PERSIUS, SULPICIA, and Lucilius. In Prose, with Notes, Chronological Tables, Arguments, by L. Evans, M.A. To which is added the Metrical Version of Juvenal and Persius by Gifford. Frontispiece.

LIVY. The History of Rome. Trans. by Dr. Spillan and others. 4 vols. Portrait.

LONGUS. Daphnis and Chloe.—*See Greek Romances.*

LUCAN'S Pharsalia. In Prose, with Notes by H. T. Riley.

LUCIAN'S Dialogues of the Gods, of the Sea Gods, and of the Dead. Trans. by Howard Williams, M.A.

LUCRETIUS. In Prose, with Notes and Biographical Introduction by Rev. J. S. Watson, M.A. To which is added the Metrical Version by J. M. Good.

MARTIAL'S Epigrams, complete. In Prose, with Verse Translations selected from English Poets, and other sources. Dble. vol. (670 pages). 7*s.* 6*d.*

MOSCHUS.—*See Theocritus.*

OVID'S Works, complete. In Prose, with Notes and Introduction. 3 vols.

PAUSANIAS' Description of Greece. Trans., with Notes and Index, by Rev. A. R. Shilleto, M.A., sometime Scholar of Trinity College, Cambridge. 2 vols.

PHALARIS. Bentley's Dissertations upon the Epistles of Phalaris, Themistocles, Socrates, Euripides, and the Fables of Æsop. With Introduction and Notes by Prof. W. Wagner, Ph.D.

PINDAR. In Prose, with Introduction and Notes by Dawson W. Turner. Together with the Metrical Version by Abraham Moore. Portrait.

PLATO'S Works. Trans. by Rev. H. Cary, H. Davis, and G. Burges. 6 vols.

—— **Dialogues.** A Summary and Analysis of. With Analytical Index to the Greek text of modern editions and to the above translations, by A. Day, LL.D.

PLAUTUS'S Comedies. In Prose, with Notes by H. T. Riley, B.A. 2 vols.

PLINY'S Natural History. Trans., with Notes, by J. Bostock, M.D., F.R.S., and H. T. Riley, B.A. 6 vols.

PLINY. The Letters of Pliny the Younger. Melmoth's Translation, revised, with Notes and short Life, by Rev. F. C. T. Bosanquet, M.A.

PLUTARCH'S Morals. Theosophical Essays. Trans. by Rev. C. W. King, M.A.

—— **Ethical Essays.** Trans. by Rev. A. R. Shilleto, M.A.

—— **Lives.** *See page 7.*

PROPERTIUS, The Elegies of. With Notes, translated by Rev. P. J. F. Gantillon, M.A., with metrical versions of Select Elegies by Nott and Elton. 3*s.* 6*d.*

QUINTILIAN'S Institutes of Oratory. Trans., by Rev. J. S. Watson, M.A. 2 vols.

SALLUST, FLORUS, and VELLEIUS Paterculus. Trans., with Notes and Biographical Notices, by J. S. Watson, M.A.

SENECA DE BENEFICIIS. Translated by Aubrey Stewart, M.A. 3*s.* 6*d.*

SENECA'S Minor Essays. Translated by A. Stewart, M.A.

SOPHOCLES. The Tragedies of. In Prose, with Notes, Arguments, and Introduction. Portrait.

STRABO'S Geography. Trans., with Notes, by W. Falconer, M.A., and H. C. Hamilton. Copious Index, giving Ancient and Modern Names. 3 vols.

SUETONIUS' Lives of the Twelve Cæsars and Lives of the Grammarians. The Translation of Thomson, revised, with Notes, by T. Forester.

TACITUS. The Works of. Trans., with Notes. 2 vols.

TERENCE and PHÆDRUS. In English Prose, with Notes and Arguments, by H. T. Riley, B.A. To which is added Smart's Metrical Version of Phædrus. With Frontispiece.

THEOCRITUS, BION, MOSCHUS, and Tyrtæus. In Prose, with Notes and Arguments, by Rev. J. Banks, M.A. To which are appended the METRICAL VERSIONS of Chapman. Portrait of Theocritus.

THUCYDIDES. The Peloponnesian War. Trans., with Notes, by Rev. H. Dale. Portrait. 2 vols. 3*s.* 6*d.* each.

TYRTÆUS.—*See Theocritus.*

VIRGIL. The Works of. In Prose, with Notes by Davidson. Revised, with additional Notes and Biographical Notice, by T. A. Buckley, B.A. Portrait. 3*s.* 6*d.*

XENOPHON'S Works. Trans., with Notes, by J. S. Watson, M.A., and Rev. H. Dale. Portrait. In 3 vols.

COLLEGIATE SERIES.

11 *Vols. at 5s. each.* (*2l. 15s. per set.*)

DANTE. The Inferno. Prose Trans., with the Text of the Original on the same page, and Explanatory Notes, by John A. Carlyle, M.D. Portrait.

— **The Purgatorio.** Prose Trans., with the Original on the same page, and Explanatory Notes, by W. S. Dugdale.

DOBREE'S Adversaria. (Notes on the Greek and Latin Classics.) Edited by the late Prof. Wagner. 2 vols.

DONALDSON (Dr.) The Theatre of the Greeks. With Supplementary Treatise on the Language, Metres, and Prosody of the Greek Dramatists. Numerous Illustrations and 3 Plans. By J. W. Donaldson, D.D.

GOETHE'S Faust. Part I. German Text, with Hayward's Prose Translation and Notes. Revised, with Introduction and Bibliography, by Dr. C. A. Buchheim. 5s.

KEIGHTLEY'S (Thomas) Mythology of Ancient Greece and Italy. Revised by Dr. Leonhard Schmitz. 12 Plates.

HERODOTUS, Notes on. Original and Selected from the best Commentators. By D. W. Turner, M.A. Coloured Map.

— **Analysis and Summary of,** with a Synchronistical Table of Events—Tables of Weights, Measures, Money, and Distances—an Outline of the History and Geography—and the Dates completed from Gaisford, Baehr, &c. By J. T. Wheeler.

NEW TESTAMENT (The) in Greek. Griesbach's Text, with the Readings of Mill and Scholz, and Parallel References. Also a Critical Introduction and Chronological Tables. Two Fac-similes of Greek Manuscripts. 650 pages. 3s. 6d.

— or bound up with a Greek and English Lexicon to the New Testament (250 pages additional, making in all 900). 5s.

The Lexicon separately, 2s.

THUCYDIDES. An Analysis and Summary of. With Chronological Table of Events, &c., by J. T. Wheeler.

SCIENTIFIC LIBRARY.

48 *Vols. at 5s. each, excepting those marked otherwise.* (*12l. 19s. per set.*)

AGASSIZ and GOULD. Outline of Comparative Physiology. Enlarged by Dr. Wright. With Index and 300 Illustrative Woodcuts.

BOLLEY'S Manual of Technical Analysis; a Guide for the Testing and Valuation of the various Natural and Artificial Substances employed in the Arts and Domestic Economy, founded on the work of Dr. Bolley. Edit. by Dr. Paul. 100 Woodcuts.

BRIDGEWATER TREATISES.

— **Bell (Sir Charles) on the Hand;** its Mechanism and Vital Endowments, as evincing Design. Preceded by an Account of the Author's Discoveries in the Nervous System by A. Shaw. Numerous Woodcuts.

— **Kirby on the History, Habits,** and Instincts of Animals. With Notes by T. Rymer Jones. 100 Woodcuts. 2 vols.

— **Buckland's Geology and Mineralogy.** With Additions by Prof. Owen, Prof. Phillips, and R. Brown. Memoir of Buckland. Portrait. 2 vols. 15s. Vol. I. Text. Vol. II. 90 large plates with letterpress.

BRIDGEWATER TREATISES. *Continued.*

— **Chalmers on the Adaptation of** External Nature to the Moral and Intellectual Constitution of Man. With Memoir by Rev. Dr. Cumming. Portrait.

— **Prout's Treatise on Chemistry,** Meteorology, and the Function of Digestion, with reference to Natural Theology. Edit. by Dr. J. W. Griffith. 2 Maps.

— **Roget's Animal and Vegetable** Physiology. 463 Woodcuts. 2 vols. 6s. each.

— **Kidd on the Adaptation of External Nature to the Physical Condition of Man.** 3s. 6d.

CARPENTER'S (Dr. W. B.) Zoology. A Systematic View of the Structure, Habits, Instincts, and Uses of the principal Families of the Animal Kingdom, and of the chief Forms of Fossil Remains. Revised by W. S. Dallas, F.L.S. Numerous Woodcuts. 2 vols. 6s. each.

— **Mechanical Philosophy, Astronomy, and Horology.** A Popular Exposition. 181 Woodcuts.

CARPENTER'S Works.—*Continued.*

— **Vegetable Physiology and Systematic Botany.** A complete Introduction to the Knowledge of Plants. Revised by E. Lankester, M.D., &c. Numerous Woodcuts. 6*s*.

— **Animal Physiology.** Revised Edition. 300 Woodcuts. 6*s*.

CHEVREUL on Colour. Containing the Principles of Harmony and Contrast of Colours, and their Application to the Arts; including Painting, Decoration, Tapestries, Carpets, Mosaics, Glazing, Staining, Calico Printing, Letterpress Printing, Map Colouring, Dress, Landscape and Flower Gardening, &c. Trans. by C. Martel. Several Plates.

— With an additional series of 16 Plates in Colours, 7*s*. 6*d*.

ENNEMOSER'S History of Magic. Trans. by W. Howitt. With an Appendix of the most remarkable and best authenticated Stories of Apparitions, Dreams, Second Sight, Table-Turning, and Spirit-Rapping, &c. 2 vols.

HOGG'S (Jabez) Elements of Experimental and Natural Philosophy. Being an Easy Introduction to the Study of Mechanics, Pneumatics, Hydrostatics, Hydraulics, Acoustics, Optics, Caloric, Electricity, Voltaism, and Magnetism. 400 Woodcuts.

HUMBOLDT'S Cosmos; or, Sketch of a Physical Description of the Universe. Trans. by E. C. Otté, B. H. Paul, and W. S. Dallas, F.L.S. Portrait. 5 vols. 3*s*. 6*d*. each, excepting vol. v., 5*s*.

— **Personal Narrative of his Travels** in America during the years 1799-1804. Trans., with Notes, by T. Ross. 3 vols.

— **Views of Nature; or, Contemplations** of the Sublime Phenomena of Creation, with Scientific Illustrations. Trans. by E. C. Otté.

HUNT'S (Robert) Poetry of Science; or, Studies of the Physical Phenomena of Nature. By Robert Hunt, Professor at the School of Mines.

JOYCE'S Scientific Dialogues. A Familiar Introduction to the Arts and Sciences. For Schools and Young People. Numerous Woodcuts.

JUKES-BROWNE'S Student's Handbook of Physical Geology. By A. J. Jukes-Browne, of the Geological Survey of England. With numerous Diagrams and Illustrations, 6*s*.

JUKES-BROWNE'S Works.—*Cont.*

— **The Student's Handbook of Historical Geology.** By A. J. Jukes-Brown, B.A., F.G.S., of the Geological Survey of England and Wales. With numerous Diagrams and Illustrations. 6*s*.

— **The Building of the British Islands.** A Study in Geographical Evolution. By A. J. Jukes-Browne, F.G.S. 7*s*. 6*d*.

KNIGHT'S (Charles) Knowledge is Power. A Popular Manual of Political Economy.

LILLY. Introduction to Astrology. With a Grammar of Astrology and Tables for calculating Nativities, by Zadkiel.

MANTELL'S (Dr.) Geological Excursions through the Isle of Wight and along the Dorset Coast. Numerous Woodcuts and Geological Map.

— **Petrifactions and their Teachings.** Handbook to the Organic Remains in the British Museum. Numerous Woodcuts. 6*s*.

— **Wonders of Geology; or, a** Familiar Exposition of Geological Phenomena. A coloured Geological Map of England, Plates, and 200 Woodcuts. 2 vols. 7*s*. 6*d*. each.

SCHOUW'S Earth, Plants, and Man. Popular Pictures of Nature. And Kobell's Sketches from the Mineral Kingdom. Trans. by A. Henfrey, F.R.S. Coloured Map of the Geography of Plants.

SMITH'S (Pye) Geology and Scripture; or, the Relation between the Scriptures and Geological Science. With Memoir.

STANLEY'S Classified Synopsis of the Principal Painters of the Dutch and Flemish Schools, including an Account of some of the early German Masters. By George Stanley.

STAUNTON'S Chess Works. — *See page 21.*

STÖCKHARDT'S Experimental Chemistry. A Handbook for the Study of the Science by simple Experiments. Edit. by C. W. Heaton, F.C.S. Numerous Woodcuts.

URE'S (Dr. A.) Cotton Manufacture of Great Britain, systematically investigated; with an Introductory View of its Comparative State in Foreign Countries. Revised by P. L. Simmonds. 150 Illustrations. 2 vols.

— **Philosophy of Manufactures,** or an Exposition of the Scientific, Moral, and Commercial Economy of the Factory System of Great Britain. Revised by P. L. Simmonds. Numerous Figures. 800 pages. 7*s*. 6*d*.

ECONOMICS AND FINANCE.

5 *Volumes.* (1*l.* 2*s.* *per set.*)

GILBART'S History, Principles, and Practice of Banking. Revised to 1881 by A. S. Michie, of the Royal Bank of Scotland. Portrait of Gilbart. 2 vols. 10*s.*

RICARDO on the Principles of Political Economy and Taxation. Edited by E. C. K. Gonner, M.A., Lecturer, University College, Liverpool. 5*s.*

SMITH (Adam). The Wealth of Nations. An Inquiry into the Nature and Causes of. Edited by E. Belfort Bax. 2 vols. 7*s.*

REFERENCE LIBRARY.

32 *Volumes at Various Prices.* (8*l.* 3*s.* *per set.*)

BLAIR'S Chronological Tables. Comprehending the Chronology and History of the World, from the Earliest Times to the Russian Treaty of Peace, April 1856. By J. W. Rosse. 800 pages. 10*s.*

— Index of Dates. Comprehending the principal Facts in the Chronology and History of the World, from the Earliest to the Present, alphabetically arranged; being a complete Index to the foregoing. By J. W. Rosse. 2 vols. 5*s.* each.

BOHN'S Dictionary of Quotations from the English Poets. 4th and cheaper Edition. 6*s.*

BOND'S Handy-book of Rules and Tables for Verifying Dates with the Christian Era. 4th Edition. 5*s.*

BUCHANAN'S Dictionary of Science and Technical Terms used in Philosophy, Literature, Professions, Commerce, Arts, and Trades. By W. H. Buchanan, with Supplement. Edited by Jas. A. Smith. 6*s.*

CHRONICLES OF THE TOMBS. A Select Collection of Epitaphs, with Essay on Epitaphs and Observations on Sepulchral Antiquities. By T. J. Pettigrew, F.R.S., F.S.A. 5*s.*

CLARK'S (Hugh) Introduction to Heraldry. Revised by J. R. Planché. 5*s.* 950 Illustrations.

— *With the Illustrations coloured*, 15*s.*

COINS, Manual of.—*See Humphreys.*

COOPER'S Biographical Dictionary, Containing concise notices of upwards of 15,000 eminent persons of all ages and countries. 2 vols. 5*s.* each.

DATES, Index of.—*See Blair.*

DICTIONARY of Obsolete and Provincial English. Containing Words from English Writers previous to the 19th Century. By Thomas Wright, M.A., F.S.A., &c. 2 vols. 5*s.* each.

EPIGRAMMATISTS (The). A Selection from the Epigrammatic Literature of Ancient, Mediæval, and Modern Times. With Introduction, Notes, Observations, Illustrations, an Appendix on Works connected with Epigrammatic Literature, by Rev. H. Dodd, M.A. 6*s.*

GAMES, Handbook of. Edited by Henry G. Bohn. Numerous Diagrams. 5*s.* (*See also page* 21.)

HENFREY'S Guide to English Coins. Revised Edition, by C. F. Keary, M.A., F.S.A. With an Historical Introduction. 6*s.*

HUMPHREYS' Coin Collectors' Manual. An Historical Account of the Progress of Coinage from the Earliest Time, by H. N. Humphreys. 140 Illustrations. 2 vols. 5*s.* each.

LOWNDES' Bibliographer's Manual of English Literature. Containing an Account of Rare and Curious Books published in or relating to Great Britain and Ireland, from the Invention of Printing, with Biographical Notices and Prices, by W. T. Lowndes. Revised Edition by H. G. Bohn. 6 vols. cloth, 5*s.* each, or in 4 vols., half morocco, 2*l.* 2*s.*

MEDICINE, Handbook of Domestic, Popularly Arranged. By Dr. H. Davies. 700 pages. 5*s.*

NOTED NAMES OF FICTION. Dictionary of. Including also Familiar Pseudonyms, Surnames bestowed on Eminent Men, &c. By W. A. Wheeler, M.A. 5*s.*

POLITICAL CYCLOPÆDIA. A Dictionary of Political, Constitutional, Statistical, and Forensic Knowledge; forming a Work of Reference on subjects of Civil Administration, Political Economy, Finance, Commerce, Laws, and Social Relations. 4 vols. 3*s.* 6*d.* each.

PROVERBS, Handbook of. Containing an entire Republication of Ray's Collection, with Additions from Foreign Languages and Sayings, Sentences, Maxims, and Phrases. 5*s.*

—— **A Polyglot of Foreign.** Comprising French, Italian, German, Dutch, Spanish, Portuguese, and Danish. With English Translations. 5*s.*

SYNONYMS and ANTONYMS; or, Kindred Words and their Opposites, Collected and Contrasted by Ven. C. J. Smith, M.A. 5*s.*

WRIGHT (Th.)—*See Dictionary.*

NOVELISTS' LIBRARY.

13 *Volumes at* 3*s.* 6*d. each, excepting those marked otherwise.* (2*l.* 8*s.* 6*d. per set.*)

BJÖRNSON'S Arne and the Fisher Lassie. Translated from the Norse with an Introduction by W. H. Low, M.A.

BURNEY'S Evelina; or, a Young Lady's Entrance into the World. By F. Burney (Mme. D'Arblay). With Introduction and Notes by A. R. Ellis, Author of 'Sylvestra,' &c.

—— **Cecilia.** With Introduction and Notes by A. R. Ellis. 2 vols.

DE STAËL. Corinne or Italy. By Madame de Staël. Translated by Emily Baldwin and Paulina Driver.

EBERS' Egyptian Princess. Trans. by Emma Buchheim.

FIELDING'S Joseph Andrews and his Friend Mr. Abraham Adams. With Roscoe's Biography. *Cruikshank's Illustrations.*

—— **Amelia.** Roscoe's Edition, revised. *Cruikshank's Illustrations.* 5*s.*

—— **History of Tom Jones, a Foundling.** Roscoe's Edition. *Cruikshank's Illustrations.* 2 vols.

GROSSI'S Marco Visconti. Trans. by A. F. D.

MANZONI. The Betrothed: being a Translation of 'I Promessi Sposi.' Numerous Woodcuts. 1 vol. 5*s.*

STOWE (Mrs. H. B.) Uncle Tom's Cabin; or, Life among the Lowly. 8 full-page Illustrations.

ARTISTS' LIBRARY.

9 *Volumes at Various Prices.* (2*l.* 8*s.* 6*d. per set.*)

BELL (Sir Charles). The Anatomy and Philosophy of Expression, as Connected with the Fine Arts. 5*s.* Illustrated.

DEMMIN. History of Arms and Armour from the Earliest Period. By Auguste Demmin. Trans. by C. C. Black, M.A., Assistant Keeper, S. K. Museum. 1900 Illustrations. 7*s.* 6*d.*

FAIRHOLT'S Costume in England. Third Edition. Enlarged and Revised by the Hon. H. A. Dillon, F.S.A. With more than 700 Engravings. 2 vols. 5*s.* each.

Vol. I. History. Vol. II. Glossary.

FLAXMAN. Lectures on Sculpture. With Three Addresses to the R.A. by Sir R. Westmacott, R.A., and Memoir of Flaxman. Portrait and 53 Plates. 6*s.*

HEATON'S Concise History of Painting. New Edition, revised by W. Cosmo Monkhouse. 5*s.*

LECTURES ON PAINTING by the Royal Academicians, Barry, Opie, Fuseli. With Introductory Essay and Notes by R. Wornum. Portrait of Fuseli. 5*s.*

LEONARDO DA VINCI'S Treatise on Painting. Trans. by J. F. Rigaud, R.A. With a Life and an Account of his Works by J. W. Brown. Numerous Plates. 5*s.*

PLANCHÉ'S History of British Costume, from the Earliest Time to the 19th Century. By J. R. Planché. 400 Illustrations. 5*s.*

LIBRARY OF SPORTS AND GAMES.

14 Volumes at 3s. 6d. and 5s. each. (2l. 18s. per set.)

BOHN'S Handbooks of Athletic Sports. With numerous Illustrations. In 8 vols. 3s. 6d. each.

Vol. I.—Cricket, by Hon. and Rev. E. Lyttelton; Lawn Tennis, by H. W. W. Wilberforce; Tennis, Rackets, and Fives, by Julian Marshall, Major Spens, and J. A. Tait; Golf, by W. T. Linskill; Hockey, by F. S. Creswell.

Vol. II.—Rowing and Sculling, by W. B. Woodgate; Sailing, by E. F. Knight; Swimming, by M. and J. R. Cobbett.

Vol. III.—Boxing, by R. G. Allanson-Winn; Broad-sword and Single Stick, &c., by R. G. Allanson-Winn and C. Phillipps-Wolley; Wrestling, by Walter Armstrong; Fencing, by H. A. Colmore Dunn.

Vol. IV.—Rugby Football, by Harry Vassall; Association Football, by C. W. Alcock; Baseball, by Newton Crane; Rounders, Field Ball, Baseball-Rounders, Bowls, Quoits, Curling, Skittles, &c., by J. M. Walker, M.A., and C. C. Mott.

Vol. V.—Cycling and Athletics, by H. H. Griffin; Skating, by Douglas Adams.

Vol. VI.—Practical Horsemanship, including Riding for Ladies. By W. A. Kerr, V.C.

Vol. VII.—Driving, and Stable Management. By W. A. Kerr, V.C. [*Preparing.*

Vol. VIII.—Gymnastics, by A. F. Jenkin; Clubs and Dumb-bells, by G. T. B. Cobbett and A. F. Jenkin. [*In the press.*

BOHN'S Handbooks of Games. New Edition, entirely rewritten. 2 volumes. 3s. 6d. each.

Vol. I. TABLE GAMES.

Contents:—Billiards, with Pool, Pyramids, and Snooker, by Major-Gen. A. W. Drayson, F.R.A.S., with a preface by W. J. Peall—Bagatelle, by 'Berkeley'—Chess, by R. F. Green—Draughts, Backgammon, Dominoes, Solitaire, Reversi, Go Bang, Rouge et noir, Roulette, E.O., Hazard, Faro, by 'Berkeley.'

Vol. II. CARD GAMES.

Contents:—Whist, by Dr. William Pole, F.R.S., Author of 'The Philosophy of Whist, &c.'—Solo Whist, and Poker, by R. F. Green; Piquet, Ecarté, Euchre, Bézique, and Cribbage, by 'Berkeley;' Loo, Vingt-et-un, Napoleon, Newmarket, Rouge et Noir, Pope Joan, Speculation, &c. &c., by Baxter-Wray.

CHESS CONGRESS of 1862. A collection of the games played. Edited by J. Löwenthal. New edition, 5s.

MORPHY'S Games of Chess, being the Matches and best Games played by the American Champion, with explanatory and analytical Notes by J. Löwenthal. With short Memoir and Portrait of Morphy. 5s.

STAUNTON'S Chess-Player's Handbook. A Popular and Scientific Introduction to the Game, with numerous Diagrams. 5s.

— **Chess Praxis.** A Supplement to the Chess-player's Handbook. Containing the most important modern Improvements in the Openings; Code of Chess Laws; and a Selection of Morphy's Games. Annotated. 636 pages. Diagrams. 5s.

— **Chess-Player's Companion.** Comprising a Treatise on Odds, Collection of Match Games, including the French Match with M. St. Amant, and a Selection of Original Problems. Diagrams and Coloured Frontispiece. 5s.

— **Chess Tournament of 1851.** A Collection of Games played at this celebrated assemblage. With Introduction and Notes. Numerous Diagrams. 5s.

BOHN'S CHEAP SERIES.

Price 1s. each.

A Series of Complete Stories or Essays, mostly reprinted from Vols. in Bohn's Libraries, and neatly bound in stiff paper cover, with cut edges, suitable for Railway Reading.

ASCHAM (Roger). Scholemaster. By Professor Mayor.

CARPENTER (Dr. W. B.). Physiology of Temperance and Total Abstinence.

EMERSON. England and English Characteristics. Lectures on the Race, Ability, Manners, Truth, Character, Wealth, Religion. &c. &c.

— **Nature:** An Essay. To which are added Orations, Lectures, and Addresses.

— **Representative Men:** Seven Lectures on PLATO, SWEDENBORG, MONTAIGNE, SHAKESPEARE, NAPOLEON, and GOETHE.

— **Twenty Essays on Various Subjects.**

— **The Conduct of Life.**

FRANKLIN (Benjamin). Autobiography. Edited by J. Sparks.

HAWTHORNE (Nathaniel). Twice-told Tales. Two Vols.

— **Snow Image,** and Other Tales.

— **Scarlet Letter.**

— **House with the Seven Gables.**

— **Transformation;** or the Marble Fawn. Two Parts.

HAZLITT (W.). Table-talk: Essays on Men and Manners. Three Parts.

— **Plain Speaker:** Opinions on Books, Men, and Things. Three Parts.

— **Lectures on the English Comic Writers.**

— **Lectures on the English Poets.**

— **Lectures on the Characters of** Shakespeare's Plays.

— **Lectures on the Literature of** the Age Elizabeth, chiefly Dramatic.

IRVING (Washington). Lives of Successors of Mohammed.

— **Life of Goldsmith.**

— **Sketch-book.**

— **Tales of a Traveller**

— **Tour on the Prairies**

— **Conquests of Granada and** Spain. Two Parts.

— **Life and Voyages of Columbus.** Two Parts.

— **Companions of Columbus:** Their Voyages and Discoveries.

— **Adventures of Captain Bonne**ville in the Rocky Mountains and the West.

— **Knickerbocker's History of New** York, from the beginning of the World to the End of the Dutch Dynasty.

— **Tales of the Alhambra.**

— **Conquest of Florida under Her**nando de Soto.

— **Abbotsford & Newstead Abbey.**

— **Salmagundi;** or, The Whim-Whams and Opinions of LAUNCELOT LANGSTAFF, Esq.

— **Bracebridge Hall; or, The Hu**mourists.

— **Astoria;** or, Anecdotes of an Enterprise beyond the Rocky Mountains.

— **Wolfert's Roost,** and other Tales.

LAMB (Charles). Essays of Elia. With a Portrait.

— **Last Essays of Elia.**

— **Eliana.** With Memoir.

MARRYAT (Captain). Pirate and the Three Cutters. With a Memoir of the Author.

Bohn's Select Library of Standard Works.

Price 1*s.* in paper covers, and 1*s.* 6*d.* in cloth.

1. BACON'S ESSAYS. With Introduction and Notes.
2. LESSING'S LAOKOON. Beasley's Translation, revised, with Introduction, Notes, &c., by Edward Bell, M.A. With Frontispiece.
3. DANTE'S INFERNO. Translated, with Notes, by Rev. H. F. Cary.
4. GOETHE'S FAUST. Part I. Translated, with Introduction, by Anna Swanwick.
5. GOETHE'S BOYHOOD. Being Part I. of the Autobiography Translated by J. Oxenford.
6. SCHILLER'S MARY STUART and THE MAID OF ORLEANS. Translated by J. Mellish and Anna Swanwick.
7. THE QUEEN'S ENGLISH. By the late Dean Alford.
8. LIFE AND LABOURS OF THE LATE THOMAS BRASSEY. By Sir A. Helps, K.C.B.
9. PLATO'S DIALOGUES: The Apology—Crito—Phaedo—Protagoras. With Introductions.
10. MOLIÈRE'S PLAYS: The Miser—Tartuffe—The Shopkeeper turned Gentleman. Translated by C. H. Walt, M.A. With brief Memoir.
11. GOETHE'S REINEKE FOX, in English Hexameters. By A. Rogers.
12. OLIVER GOLDSMITH'S PLAYS.
13. LESSING'S PLAYS: Nathan the Wise—Minna von Barnhelm.
14. PLAUTUS'S COMEDIES: Trinummus — Menaechmi — Aulularia — Captivi.
15. WATERLOO DAYS. By C. A. Eaton. With Preface and Notes by Edward Bell.
16. DEMOSTHENES—ON THE CROWN. Translated by C. Rann Kennedy.
17. THE VICAR OF WAKEFIELD.
18. OLIVER CROMWELL. By Dr. Reinhold Pauli.
19. THE PERFECT LIFE. By Dr. Channing. Edited by his nephew, Rev. W. H. Channing.
20. LADIES IN PARLIAMENT, HORACE AT ATHENS, and other pieces, by Sir George Otto Trevelyan, Bart.
21. DEFOE'S THE PLAGUE IN LONDON.
22. IRVING'S LIFE OF MAHOMET.
23. HORACE'S ODES, by various hands. [*Out of Print.*
24. BURKE'S ESSAY ON 'THE SUBLIME AND BEAUTIFUL.' With Short Memoir.
25. HAUFF'S CARAVAN.
26. SHERIDAN'S PLAYS.
27. DANTE'S PURGATORIO. Translated by Cary.
28. HARVEY'S TREATISE ON THE CIRCULATION OF THE BLOOD
29. CICERO'S FRIENDSHIP AND OLD AGE.
30. DANTE'S PARADISO. Translated by Cary.
31. CHRONICLE OF HENRY VIII. Translated by Major M. A. S. Hume.

Lightning Source UK Ltd.
Milton Keynes UK
UKHW022259080223
416651UK00001B/448